SITTING WITH JESUS

SITTING WITH JESUS

a yearlong faith journey

TERA ELNESS

REGNERY
FAITH

Regnery Faith books may be purchased in bulk at special discounts for sales promotion, corporate gifts, fund-raising, or educational purposes. Special editions can also be created to specifications. For details, contact the Special Sales Department, Regnery Faith, 307 West 36th Street, 11th Floor, New York, NY 10018 or info@skyhorsepublishing.com.

Unless otherwise noted, all Scripture quotations come from the New Revised Standard Version Bible, copyright © 1989 National Council of the Churches of Christ in the United States of America. Used by permission. All rights reserved worldwide.

Scriptures marked KJV are taken from the King James Version, public domain.

Scriptures marked CEV are taken from the Contemporary English Version. Copyright © 1995 by the American Bible Society. Used by permission.

Published in association with Mary DeMuth Literary, mary@marydemuthliterary.com.

Regnery Faith™ is an imprint of Skyhorse Publishing, Inc.®, a Delaware corporation. Visit our website at www.regnery.com.

Please follow our publisher Tony Lyons on Instagram @tonylyonsisuncertain.

10 9 8 7 6 5 4 3 2 1

Library of Congress Cataloging-in-Publication Data is available on file.

Cover design by David Ter-Avanesyan
Cover photo credit by Krystal Sieban

Print ISBN: 978-1-5107-8230-3
Ebook ISBN: 978-1-5107-8232-7

Printed in the United States of America

To all those who don't stop believin' . . .

CONTENTS

INTRODUCTION

Years ago, God asked me, "If I never take you beyond this chair, will you still do what I've called you to do?"

I remember thinking, "Of course, God, because I can't *not* write, and I can't *not* talk, and I can't *not* do this—I wouldn't know how."

And over the course of the last several years, God *has*, in fact, taken me places without ever leaving this chair.

He's brought me into your heartaches and into your hospital rooms, into your waiting rooms and into your living rooms, into your pain and into your prayers, and also into your desperate pleas for relief. He's brought me into your struggles and fears and even into your weaknesses as you wrestle with God through the doubts . . . and the droughts . . . and the seasons you thought would never end.

He's brought me into your cars and your conference rooms, your treatment centers and your group texts. He's brought me into your safe, secret places where the tears freely flow and into the shame you've been carrying around for years. The shame—that needs to go.

He's brought me to you each day, Beloved, without ever leaving this chair, and I pray that through the pages of this book, this day-by-day devotional, He still will.

I love you.

Tera

AUTHOR'S NOTE

Beloved, I am not a pastor, a theologian, or a seminarian; I'm just a small-town girl who, along her journey, has come to know her great big God. As you read through this daily devotional, there will be days that include specific Scripture references and those that do not. This is because, more often than not, my writings are fueled and inspired by a multitude of verses, passages, or stories that I have gleaned over the past decade-plus while sitting with Jesus each morning—in addition, of course, to my very own journey on Earth thus far.

Should you come across a name from Scripture you want to know more about, or a theme I mention that you'd love to explore deeper, I encourage you to make a quick internet search with just a few key words. I have no doubt you'll find what you're looking for. God's Word is indeed a great treasure chest to be discovered, filled with glorious riches.

Happy seeking!

ASK HIM AGAIN

Ask Him again.

I know, I know—you've already asked Him a million times. I see those eyes rolling. But today, ask Him a million and one. Yes. Ask Him *again*. Ask Him again for that child to come home. That marriage to be healed. That mountain to move. Ask Him again for that friendship to mend. That work to begin. That end-of-tunnel light to appear. Ask Him again for the one who needs rescue, the one who needs healing, the one who needs new direction, new guidance, new focus. Yes. Even if that "one" is you. Ask Him again for what you need. For what you want. For joy in the sorrow. Help in the struggle. A sip of living water in the heat of your schedule . . . and the time to just sit at the well, amen? Ask Him again. Ask Him again to provide springs in your land; and while you're at it, give thanks for that land, no matter how dry it is now, knowing He's given it to you with good purpose.

Yes. Ask Him again. Ask Him again to dig up the soil and plant the seeds. Ask Him again to stir up and settle, make and remake, pour out His peace that passes all understanding, because frankly, you could use a hefty dose about now. Yes. And amen. Ask Him again for all that seems lost and all that seems nowhere even near the vicinity of possible . . . and ask Him, believing He can. Yes.

Ask Him again. Not because you don't think He heard you the first million times, but because you are realizing the longer you (truly) live, that persistence is a pretty strong faith-builder—not to mention how close it keeps you to Him, for whom all things are possible and nothing is too hard, and because faith-based strength to persevere and closeness with your Creator is what you *really* need. Whew. Yes. Absolutely.

Ask Him again. With fresh eyes and a renewed spirit and a passionate resolve that He can, and if it's His Will . . . He will. And if it's not, you will keep on asking. You will keep on seeking. You will keep on believing, just like Steve Perry says. Because persistent faith is where it's at. It fastens its gaze on hope. The hope that is always three steps (Father, Son, Holy Spirit) ahead, providing the perfect focal point. Yes. And it never disappoints. Amen.

So today—bow low, look up, and ask Him *again*.

MAYBE THIS IS MY YEAR

Maybe it's your year too.

Your year to take courage. Maybe.

Maybe you've remained hidden, and that time was no doubt well spent. But maybe now it's your time to take courage based on Who you know God to be, armed with the knowledge that God is not only with you wherever you go but actually goes *before* you.

Yes. For knowing that will make you strong and courageous, you know. And you are welcome (encouraged, actually) to head to Joshua 1:9 and Deuteronomy 31:8 if you don't believe me. Seriously, I won't feel bad at all.

Maybe it's your year to take courage, secure in the truth that God's mercies and compassions are indeed new every morning. The fact that God's overwhelming love for you is both unconditional *and* unfailing . . . may just be the fuel you need . . . to take courage this year. Maybe.

Beloved, when I read these words, they stuck with me straight through to the end . . . "But in the seventh year . . . Jehoiada took courage." (I included the dots for pauses, for that's how I read it, amen.) Yes.

Beloved, maybe it's *your* seventh year. Maybe.

Now as you go . . . remember . . .

Your journey is under the watchful eye of the Lord. No weapon formed against you shall prosper. When faced with temptation to stop believing, you return to Who you know God to be, you hear me? OK, then.

Now, I'm gonna give you a few purposefully placed dots for you to consider and ponder this question . . .

Is *this* my seventh year?

{2 Chronicles 23:1}

ENOUGH!

When will Enough be Enough?

I reckon it depends on how you read that. Did you read it as Enough, as in an adequate amount to meet a need or desire . . . or Enough, as in, "That's *enough*!"

As I read the story of two sisters in Genesis, both desperate to beat each other in the game of "Giving Birth to the Most Kids" (who knew such a contest existed?), I'm still not exactly sure who "won." I'm not sure they ever really knew either, and frankly, my guess is they were eventually *both* pretty worn out from it; babies and toddlers are needy, you know, and apparently Daddy Jacob kept busy doing . . . well, them. And their slaves. And anyone else handed to him, because keep in mind that this guy was used to women telling him what to do. *Hello*, his *mama* was Rebekah. Heck, he was told what to do from the time he reached puberty, probably earlier.

But back to these girls and their chasing of Enough. Unfortunately, the biggest problem with chasing anything or anyone is that a) there's no guarantee you'll catch it/ them, and b) you may be chasing an illusion like an oasis in the desert that's not really there. So yes, that's *one* way to look at Enough.

There's also . . . enough! The sick and tired of being sick and tired that leads to exclaiming *enough*! Which, in turn, often leads to some kind of change that leads to more life. There's also *enough*! As in, there *has* to be *something* we can do; we can no longer sit idly by. Enough! It's why *I love* the story of Esther's Mordecai so much and his all-out *refusal* to put on soft clothes after E became Queen, even though he sure as heck could have. But *instead*, he said . . . No! I don't *want* to get comfortable, not until our people, *all* of our people, E—not just you and me—are completely and totally *free! Enough already*!

Dang, I love Mordy. Jesus would go on to say it too. This one word, *enough*!— complete with exclamation point, which I stinkin' *love*!

Why? Because it shows *passion*. It shows the *opposite* of passivity. It shows that something/someone is *worthy of our energy and emotions*.

And that someone may even be *you*. And that's powerful stuff. And there are *more* ways to look at Enough, but I'm outta room here, so I guess for today, that's enough.

Wink, wink.

{Jacob, Leah, and Rach's story: Genesis 29–30}

HOLD ON AND REFUSE TO LET GO

There's only one way to have the strength and courage needed to go on . . . Hold on to the promises and refuse to let go.

To go on. On from brokenness. On from despair. On from a failed relationship or on from the only land you've ever known. On from hopelessness. On from fear. On from what has left you feeling like there's nothing left for you in the storehouse.

Phooey. The enemy may tempt you to believe that—to abandon the truth that God is Provider, Protector, All-Powerful, that God completes what God begins. But you're not gonna fall for it. At least not on my watch you're not. *You* are gonna remind yourself . . .

It is written. That's right. Every word of your story is written by the Author and Perfecter of your faith from "In the beginning" to final "Amen."

You're gonna remind yourself that Abram, at age seventy-five, was able to leave his homeland and start anew because he *believed* every promise God made to him. *Including* the promise to show him the new land, and make from him a great nation *in* that new land, and *bless* him in that new land, and curse *anyone* who treats him with contempt *in* that new land, and basically-not-basic-at-all . . . *I will take care of you wherever I take you.*

Abram *took* those promises God spoke to him and *believed* those promises God spoke to him and *refused to let go* of those promises God spoke to him, and *that* is why I'm *fully* convinced that Abe had the strength and courage to go on. Well, that, and watching his dad Terah die where he'd settled. And Abe would *need* to hold tight to those promises, not letting go of them once he reached his new land, for they would soon strengthen him *yet again* . . . when God instructed him to climb that mountain with some firewood, a rope, and his only son for a sacrifice.

Beloved, strength and courage arise from our knowing and our *believing*.

Think of it this way: If someone makes a promise to you but you don't *believe* them, then the promise will do *nothing* for you, and it will give you . . . *nothing*. No hope, no rest, no peace, no nothin'.

Ahhhh, but if you *do* believe them. . . . Beloved, God is faithful. *Always*. Believe that. And be strengthened.

{Genesis 12}

CHOSEN

Moses was chosen. Mary was chosen. Jonah was chosen. Jesus was chosen. Ruth was chosen. Rahab was chosen. Esther was chosen. Ezekiel was chosen. Nehemiah was chosen. Noah was chosen. YOU, Beloved, were chosen. Period.

Chosen by God. Chosen for God. Chosen and sent to fulfill the purposes of God. According to the Will of God. Because, hello, God's Will *will* be done, on Earth as it is in Heaven. Amen.

Moses tried to get out of it. It didn't work.

We have no evidence indicating that had young virgin Mary replied, "Ummm, yeah, pick someone else for this," that God would have. Quite the contrary . . .

"The angel greeted Mary and said, 'You are truly blessed! The Lord is with you.' Mary was confused by the angel's words and wondered what they meant."

No doubt. *With* you, Mary. Like literally. ETA nine months for delivery.

Esther didn't ask to be taken into the harem.

Jonah, that poor guy, even *paid* to try to get out of God's call for him, using his own money to pay the ship fare. Sorry, Jonah, no refunds even though you got tossed overboard.

Noah was a farmer, doing farmer stuff, most likely living content on his land with his wife and his kids and watching them grow up and get married and looking forward to retirement. . . . Oh, but wait, guess what? You're gonna make for thyself an ark! Lucky you!

Beloved, you get my point. I know you do. You were chosen for the story written for you by the Author and Perfecter of your faith. A story *filled* with highs and lows and mystery and suspense. And as you know, some of the plot twists will leave you wondering if God really *is* with you. (It's OK. Gideon wondered too.)

Let me assure you that God *is* with you. Emmanuel, remember? And God *is* faithful to complete what God began. Alpha and Omega, remember? Your journey is holy. You were chosen to travel it. And holy is oftentimes . . . hard. Like blood, sweat, and tears hard—just ask Jesus. But you were *chosen* for it. And the God Who *chose* you . . .

Vowed to never leave or forsake you. Vowed to provide for you and protect you. Vowed to see you through every step of the way until you return back home. Amen.

{Luke 1:28–29 CEV}

TRUSTING GOD MAY LOOK LIKE DOING A REALLY HARD THING

Trusting God looks far less like doing nothing and a whole lot more like doing a really hard thing.

That may not be what you were hoping to hear this fine morning, Beloved . . . but I've got a whole bunch of folks in the wings here ready to testify that it's true. I sure do.

For Noah, it looked like building an ark, despite the fact that there was a drought. For David, it looked like continuing to care for the sheep in the field, despite being named future new king. For Abraham, it meant going to a land he did not know, and then later climbing up a mountain with his son Isaac in tow, despite what God asked him to do once he got there. Yikes.

For Rahab, it meant opening the door. For Joseph, it meant marrying Mary anyway. For Hagar, it meant packing up her stuff *and* her son and heading straight into single-mom life. For Esther, it meant going before the king without an appointment . . . and planning a banquet . . . and giving herself time to pray and come up with a plan. For Dan, it meant enduring the den instead of simply refusing to pray his normal three times a day. Yep.

For Paul, it meant continuing to praise in the prison. For Moses, it meant marching his butt off to Pharaoh to demand his people's release. Oh, and did I mention he'd have to do that *more than once*? Oh, and did I mention that he'd then have to lead these now-free people for forty long years while listening to them grumble and complain the whole way? For *forty* years.

I know, right? That's what I'm saying. *Hard things.*

Beloved, if you've been raised or somehow led to believe that trusting God is passive or inactive, then I hope today's panel of guests helps you see, like they did me, that trusting God looks far less like doing *nothing* and a whole lot more like doing a *really hard thing*. For even as I sit here now, I realize something that I reckon is pretty darn huge . . . why would God *so* want me to know that He is with me wherever I go . . . (Joshua 1:9) . . . if I'm actually not to go anywhere? Hmmm.

Beloved, trusting God . . . may look like doing a really hard thing. And perhaps *that* is why God is saying to us . . . be strong and courageous, for I Am with you wherever you go. *XO.*

DROP THE ROCK

Maybe you're exhausted because you've been carrying that rock for so long.

And please, before you hurl it at me, hear me out. Everything in me wanted to write something far easier to hear today. I mean it. I get it.

I've also, however, gotten to the point in my life where saying hard things is much easier, so here it goes: A stone clenched in your fist is not heavy at first. It's not a problem to carry it around for a while; it may even feel empowering. Until it doesn't. Because carrying anything around clenched tight in your hand will eventually cramp not only your hand, but also your style, because walking around holding on to a stone is a really bad look. Amen.

But here's the deal: Perhaps one of the reasons it's so hard to drop it is because a part of us believes that by dropping it we give the victory where it does not—we repeat, does not—belong. Yes. We have reduced the difficulty of this tremendous act of faith by calling it a "chip on her shoulder" instead of what might more aptly be named "a boulder on her shoulder." Amen.

Cuz let's be honest, folks—if it were as easy as flicking a baked Lays off our shoulders, we wouldn't need to be strong and courageous. Amen.

Now I need to tell you how it is I feel even a tiny speck qualified to say these hard words to you, my community, whom I've come to love, so much so that I remind you daily—I've carried stones clenched in my fist ready to fire. And I carried them *way too long*. And when I say "way," I mean "way." And then I slowly began to understand that those at whom we want to hurl our stones are a part of the story too. Yes. I know, I said this was hard.

Beloved, we can't possibly know the plans God has for all God's people; heck, we don't even know the plans God has for ourselves. So instead, we do this . . .

In time . . . we open our hand . . . and we let the stone fall to the ground. And we realize just how exhausting it was . . . to carry it around for so long. Sigh. Yes. Breathe in and breathe deeply, Beloved. God's Spirit within you. His plan still good for you. You are loved, you are loved, you are loved. Don't forget. Amen.

{Inspired by John 8:1–11}

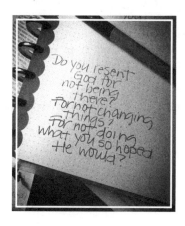

PERMISSION TO NOT UNDERSTAND

Do you resent God for not being there? For not changing things? For not doing what you so hoped He would?

You have permission to grieve. Permission to mourn. Permission to be honest and human. *Yes.* Permission to not understand. Amen.

One of the things I love best about the story of Mary, Martha, and Laz is the realness of those women as they confronted Jesus when He finally showed up and cried out . . . *where the heck were you?* Yes. And perhaps what I love even more is a God Who revealed Himself through His Son . . . as He wept. Yes. No shaming. No guilt. No "ye of little faith" sermon. Nope. Instead, a God Who would show those two women that He *knows* they don't understand. He knows they couldn't *possibly* understand, and so He weeps alongside them *in* it.

You can bring your honest to the God Who knows better than *anyone* that you are human because, for God's sake, He *created you human.*

Permission to bring your whys and your pleads and your begs and your everyday battles and your overwhelming worries and your doubts and your fears and all of your tears . . . to the One Who not only listens but calls you by name and knows the plans He has for you because He wrote them. Amen. Permission to sit with the questions I've penned here and the freedom to be fully honest and human without fear of religious persecution. Permission to be *human* here, friend.

Whether it is something you are currently going through, or you look back on your life and realize that you've been mad at God for a really long time because you just can't understand . . . may you know today that your God weeps alongside you, for your God knows you don't understand. Yes.

Your purpose is holy, Beloved. It is sacred and set apart. The ground you are standing on is too—ground prepared for you by the God Who goes before you. A God Who remains. A God Who is with you. A God Whose love will never be separated from you despite any resentment or grieving or lack of understanding. Yes. You are loved, Beloved. Forever and all time. And if you remember nothing else, remember *that*.

{Inspired by the story of Mary and Martha in John 11}

DON'T YOU FORGET

Don't you forget.

Oh, I mean it. Don't you forget. Don't you forget that the Lord goes before you; the Lord *your* God, by the way. Don't you forget He is with you and for you and will never leave you. Believing that will make you strong and courageous wherever you go.

Promise. Don't you forget. The God Who brought you out led you through. Made water flow and fed you in the wilderness even though you didn't recognize it. Yes. Don't you forget that the Lord your God is bringing you to new land. Flowing with milk and honey land. Land that has been prepared for you and you for the land. Amen.

Don't you forget that God knows God's plan for you—a plan to prosper you and not harm you. And don't you forget that your story's been written and that all things work together for good. And don't you forget that good is defined as sufficient to meet the purpose. Amen.

Don't you forget, cuz there are plenty of times the plan won't seem good as we seem to define good. Amen. Don't you forget that God healed before. That God restored before. That God made a way when there was no way before. Because *remembering* that God did it *before* will strengthen you to believe God will do it *again*.

Don't you forget the woman who suddenly stopped bleeding after twelve long years of loneliness. Or the woman who suddenly stood up straight after thirty-eight years hunched over. Or the guy who suddenly picked up his bed and walked after paralyzed years. Yes. Don't you forget that water was once turned into wine. A boy's lunch was turned into a feast. A ram was turned into a sacrifice, saving poor Isaac that day. Yes. Don't you forget.

Don't you forget that God's Will will be done. That worrying won't add even a speck to your life. That nothing you face today will fall outside of God's sovereignty. And above all else, Beloved . . . don't you forget you are loved. With an unfailing-unconditional-imperishable-everlasting love. You are seen, you are heard, you are known, and you are God's. Forever and for all time, and nothing on Earth *or* in hell can change that. Amen. Don't you forget. That God is near. As close as the breath that He gave you to breathe so that you would never forget. Whew.

Don't you forget.

IF TODAY IS GONNA BE HARD

If you know today is gonna be hard, thank Him for yesterday. It will strengthen you for today.

And if yesterday was hard, go back as long as it takes until you reach a day that wasn't. *Yes.* Go back—and draw from—the well of yesterday and use it to rehydrate the dry doubt within you that is beyond ready to just give up. Rehydrate her. Her as in your soul that needs to dance and get her groove back. Give her some food. Cuz hangryness is real, yo. Revive her by returning to a time when God blew her stinkin' mind. And if that seems impossible right now, well, then, good news—the folks of Scripture wouldn't mind if you drew upon theirs. I asked 'em.

Return to that woman at the well, although you'll no longer find her there about noon, because despite the fact that for years she went at that time (for a multitude of reasons, in my opinion), she no longer has reason to hide. *Word.* Return to Esther. You'll find her in the palace despite the fact that for years she too also hid . . . who she was . . . out of fear. But not anymore. BAM. Return to Sarah rocking her baby to sleep despite the countless—and I do mean countless—nights she thought to herself . . . "I guess it's just not meant for me." *Until it was.* Return to visit the bleeding woman, except she goes by a new name now, not simply an adjective describing her condition, *and it's about time.* (Seriously—can you imagine if we were all named by our ailment? Ugh.)

Beloved, if today is gonna be hard, thank Him for yesterday. And if yesterday was hard, go back further. Go back to a day when God did what you never thought God would do and allow it to strengthen you for *today.* Let the miracles of the past put a spring in your step for the future, for nothing-is-impossible-for-God-and-if-you-don't-believe-me-I-will-kindly-redirect-you-to-the-folks-I-fore-mentioned-*whew-and-amen.*

If you know today is gonna be hard, or if you get partway way in and realize it is . . . thank Him for yesterday—whatever yesterday that is—for truly I tell you, Beloved, it will strengthen you . . . for *today.* And strength for *today* is all you need. Yes. And *you,* Beloved, can talk to *your* God whenever you'd like. *That* is the beauty of a God Who lives within the walls of your very being. It sure is.

TELL JESUS YOU'RE OUT

Tell Jesus you're out of wine.

I'm not a wine drinker, but that sure as heck doesn't stop me from telling Jesus I'm out. Amen. Out of wine? Tell Jesus. And then remember back once upon a time in a place called Cana when a group of people ran out of wine and Jesus's mama told Him—"They're out of wine."

Yes. Tell Jesus you're out of wine. And yes, you've got a million things to be thankful for—but you're out of wine. You're ready for some transformation, you're ready for some new.

Tell Jesus you're out of wine. Tell Jesus you're out of oil.

A widow once did long, long ago, and before she knew it, she had plenty and then some. Amen. Tell Jesus you're out of sustenance. You're surviving but barely, and you're certain that life is meant to be more. And then prepare to be fed. Yes.

Big Note: It may not look how you think it should look, or how you want it to look, but it is provision—bread from heaven—and seeing it that way and naming it as such will allow you to see it for what it truly is—provision. Yes.

Tell Jesus you're tired out from your journey. Just like He was when He took a seat at that well so when that woman got there that day, she could have someone to relate to instead of being threatened by. Amen. And while you're there, tell Jesus you're thirsty. Tell Him you're sick and tired of feeling dry and depleted, not to mention exhausted from trying to live up to some ideal of what the right woman should look like. Oh, heck yes. Amen.

Beloved, tell Jesus you're out of wine. And then live with your eyes wide open, OK? For truly I tell you, you can be right next to a miracle and miss it if you refuse to see it and name it a miracle. Amen. Just ask the Pharisees. Right. And listen, closing our eyes doesn't make something go away; it just prevents us from seeing it. Amen. And those eyes of yours are the lamp of your whole body, so remember that.

Beloved, in your lack, in your loss, in your desperation for restoration, renewal, rest, and some serious reigniting . . . tell Jesus. And then believe. And don't you stop believing, because that believing is what's giving you life. Amen.

{John 2:1–11}

THE MOMENTS YOU WISH NEVER WERE

You will come to see God most clearly in the moments you wish never were.

And truly I tell you, Beloved—*this* is most certainly true. Let's recap and realize how much. Amen.

The famine for the Israelites. Heck, the famine for all kinds of folks. The flood that threatened to take Noah and his fam right out. The den of hungry lions. The furnace that was literally blazing hot. The sea that was so stinkin' huge there was no way someone could cross it. Until a whole bunch of someones did. Amen. The woman who bled for twelve long years. The one who spent eighteen hunched over. The guy who laid by a pool for thirty-eight waiting for some-kind-of-healing-please-thank-you. Right.

Elisha as he watched his beloved Elijah being swept up away from him. Abraham as he lifted the knife. The Shunammite woman who never thought she'd give birth, only to lose the son she was granted, but then watch him come back to life. Right. Mary and Martha as they stood there sobbing. Esther when she was orphaned. Nehemiah when he got the news that things were really, *really* bad back home. Right. Jonah in the guts, Paul in the prison, Joe in the well, you-get-my-point-I-think-I-can-stop-now-amen. . . . Right. Oh wait, one more—the prodigal son. Amen.

Beloved, hear me, hear me, hear me say—if for no other reason than to save you from believing that the Lord your God is against you—you will come to see God most clearly . . . in the moments you wish never were. Yes.

It is in the dark that you will come to know God is light. It is in the drought that you will come to know God is water. It is in the hunger that you will come to know God is bread. Daily. Without fail. Amen. It is in the deepest pits that you will come to know that God is with you . . . even when no one else is. That's right. I've said it before, and I'll say it again—your God will take you to places you don't want to be and place you in moments you desperately wish weren't in order to show you exactly who your God is.

Provider. Protector. All-Powerful. *Amen. With* you. *For* you. *Before* you. *Behind* you. *Beside* you. *Within you revealing Himself to you in those very moments. Amen.* I love you. That's enough for today.

WHEN YOU WANT LIFE TO SLOW DOWN

Have a seat for a sec if you want life to slow down . . .

Geez, Louise, scooch over, make room. Apparently, there's a *whole lotta people wanting life to slow down.*

Welcome. I'll start by saying that I'm fully aware that I hold no special or mystical powers, and I'm certainly not Mother Time. But I have been pondering this for some time, and I've learned over time that taking time to ponder often reveals pieces of the puzzle—the one we call purpose, pieces we thought missing, fallen under the table. If you want life to slow down, here are simply a few suggestions, a few things I've learned . . .

Go for a walk. String your own lights instead of buying pre-lit. Wash the dishes by hand once in a while—you wouldn't *believe* the lessons I learned in *that.* Don't rush to Google the minute you can't think of that one singer's name from the 1980s and it's driving you and your friend/spouse/whoever totally nuts. Go to the grocery store once in a while instead of always defaulting to pick-up. Because here's the thing—someone in an aisle may need your friendly smile, and you may need a friendly smile in one of those aisles. Yes.

Sit for a bit with the God within you each morn before the rest of the world awakes and talk about the stuff that's hurting you, piercing you, seriously bugging you. For truly I tell you, Beloved, in doing so, the God within me has asked me questions like, "My Daughter, *why* is this bugging you so much?" And this has led to some really deep, heartfelt, drawn-up-from-the-pit conversations that led to some desperately needed rehydration, not to mention resurrection and redirection. *Amen.* Go ahead and ask God to move the mountain, but if God doesn't, then know there's a reason God doesn't, and make the decision to climb it instead of continuing to circle it.

Beloved, I'm wondering if the reason we all feel more and more as though time is literally flying by . . . is because we're rushing past every opportunity to slow down, to wait. And if the Bible is true and strength will rise as we wait upon the Lord . . . then perhaps never waiting is why we all feel so weak.

Food for thought. *XO.*

{Isaiah 40:31}

JESUS WEPT, YOU CAN TOO

Jesus wept. You can too. Jesus felt. You can too. Jesus slept. You can too. Jesus kept. You can too.

Jesus didn't apologize for His tears. You needn't either. Jesus didn't justify His emotions. You needn't either. Jesus didn't feel the need to prove He had done enough stuff in order to earn an afternoon nap. You needn't either. Jesus didn't live a life here on Earth free of trials, tribulations, Earthquakes and storms, mountains and valleys, betrayal and hurt and anger and pain and grief and sorrow and every other part of the human experience that sucks . . . and yet . . . He kept. Kept the truth handy. Buried within. A truth that arose from the well—the springs of life—and reminded Him that His purpose was secure and His calling was irrevocable.

Yes. A truth that reminded Him that He was *never* alone, that God was *with* Him, that He would make it through, and He would return home after His time here on Earth was complete and His mission fulfilled. Yes. A God Who came down in the flesh . . . and showed us what humanness looks like. It looks like crying at times and rejoicing at times and feeling all the things and sleeping when you need to sleep because there's-a-reason-why-sleep-deprivation-is-deemed-cruel-and-unusual-punishment.

Yes. It looks like understanding some things but not understanding all things. It looks like walking and occasionally falling and getting back up and helping others back up when they fall, cuz you know what it's like to fall. Exactly. It looks like getting angry at times and after honestly asking yourself *why* you are angry, deciding how you will spend that emotion, for truly that's what it is, a source of energy. The question is, where will I *spend* it . . . cuz it *can* be used for good, you know.

Beloved, Jesus wept. Jesus felt. Jesus slept. Jesus kept. He also knelt and dealt, and you will too and already have a bazillion times because the journey you are on is not easy. But it *is* under the watchful eye of the Lord. A God Who collects the tears that you shed. A God Who never sleeps so you can without fear. A God Who knows you are human and thus whispers to you, "I Am *with* you, *wherever* you go." A God Who came down with the name Jesus, "God Saves," and perhaps during His stint here on Earth, Jesus reminded Himself of that on the regular.

You can too. *XO.*

WHEN YOU KNOW GOD COULD

She prayed, knowing God could . . . and hoping God would.

I am fully aware that God *could*. That God *can*. That part is not up for debate. Not only does the cloud remind me, but my own life has shown me *plenty* of times, as well. I know God *could* . . .

Roll away the stone that stands in the way. Restore what's been broken down over time. Resurrect what has died. Renew what needs renewing. Rebuild what's been destroyed. Raise up what needs raising up and lay to rest what finally needs to just rest already.

Yes. I know God could. I know God can. And that's what at times actually makes knowing God . . . *hard*. Mary and Martha concur. They knew that Jesus (the God Who came down) *could*, in fact, heal their bro Laz if He would just *come down already*.

But He didn't. And that's what made it so hard for those two back then, and that's what *still* makes it so hard for folks like you and me today. *Amen*. Knowing God *could*, so why the heck *doesn't* He?? But see, here's the thing—M & M didn't know what was about to go down. They didn't know that His arrival would come according to God's will, not theirs. They didn't know there was a *purpose and reason* for the wait.

And *that*, my friends, is so often where we are, too. And that's where the second part comes in. The part about *hope*. God, I know You *can*, and man, I hope You *will*. Yes. I hope. And yes, Lord, I'm fully aware that I don't understand what Your plan is; I couldn't possibly. But what I *do* know is *this* . . . You *gave* me hope. So I could use it to pray. To believe. To be strengthened and have light in the tunnel and a thread to hold on to. Yes. You gave me hope, and that hope is as steady and secure as an anchor, which is good, cuz sometimes the storm is rocky, to stay the least. But when it is, Lord, I always think back to that story where You're waiting on the shore with breakfast already goin'. I love that imagery. I use it often.

Beloved, pray today knowing *and* hoping, trusting *and* believing, asking *and* accepting that you won't always understand what the heck's goin' on. And *when* that's the case, here's my advice: Return to who you know God to be. Remember all God has done. Recite "I am loved" . . . repeatedly. *XO.*

{John 11}

YOU ARE NOT ALONE

God told her, "I will never leave or forsake you." So she could say with confidence, "The Lord is my Helper. I will not be afraid."

And she'd repeat it as many times as was needed for her heart, mind, and soul to believe it. She'd say it with confidence knowing it's true. Knowing her God doesn't lie. Knowing that her God knows the plans that He has for her because the Author always does. Amen. She would take the words her God spoke to her, words spoken from Parent to Child, words that would forever remind her that no matter her storm, her season, her circumstance, her struggle . . . she would *never, ever* be alone. Ever.

And when she'd forget, she would stop. She would take a deep breath. She would remind herself that the breath within her was the breath of God, her holy guarantee here on Earth for the tent she was given, a breath that would remain with her until her time on Earth was complete. Yes.

God told her, "I will *never* leave or forsake you." So *she* could say, with a confidence that would strengthen her heart, mind, and soul of hers . . .

"The Lord is *my Helper*. I will not be afraid."

For her story's been written. Her purpose secured. Her call irrevocable. Her God as close as the breath that sustains her. And she'd remind herself often, for it's good to do, because Jesus was right, you know—in this life there will absolutely be trials and tribulations and all of the things.

And *you* are not alone, Beloved. Not even for but one single second. And you are loved beyond what words can express. Drench yourself in that today, OK? And read Hebrews. *XO*. And amen.

{Hebrews 13:5b–6}

I CAN'T DO IT ALL

She cried out to God, "I can't do it all!!"
God answered her, "Oh good, you finally got it."

Beloved, there will be times you need to seek, really seek, like missing-cell phone seek . . . in order to see God in the answer. There'll also be times you pick up your DRB (daily reading bible) and realize there's only like two highlights, cuz the whole thing is just a rattling-off of a bunch of folks whose names you can't pronounce that Dave appointed to do all the work that needed to be done, cuz building a giganto palace ain't no joke. Whew.

And then you smack your head as you hear God chuckle while spitting out, "Oh *good*, you finally *got it*." Cuz God is funny like that and pretty dang good at getting a point across even if it takes us a while to get it. Right.

One of the gifts I'm gleaning since reaching my fifties is the ability to own my crap. I'm a work in progress, of course, but progress is progress nonetheless, and ironically, it's the work that'll set a girl free. Psst . . . read that again.

Truth: I can't do it all. *I want* to do it all. *I love* doing it all. Heck, I love the *all*. But see, asking? Asking for help, assigning and appointing, allowing someone else in this great beautiful text we call life to share in the work . . . that's not *weakness*. It's *wisdom*.

It's a woman whom God has taught to number her days, and now that she does, she's gonna do everything she can to *live* those days . . . *fully, abundantly, freely. Amen.* She's learned that what humans *really* want from one another . . . is permission to be human.

And what we truly want from *God* . . . is permission to ask again and again not only because we know we are heard . . . but also because God *knows* we're human . . . and because we trust the answer will somehow-someday-someway come . . . from the Parent Who loves us without fail and will do *whatever* it takes to show us what we need to see, hear, and experience in order to gain that heart of wisdom.

A Parent Who will make you lie down in green pastures to rest even though you're kicking and screaming. A Parent Who will bring you to your knees in order to finally get your attention. A Parent Who whispers, "You're gonna make it, and there's not *one second* I won't be with you." Amen. Asking is Wisdom.

UNFAILING WEAPONS OF WARFARE

The weapons of her warfare were the unfailing words of her God.

The weapons of her warfare were the words that rose up within her to protect and defend her. Unfailing words spoken by an unfailing God, words that would grab doubt by the throat and choke the life right out of it, replacing it with life-giving hope. Words she heard that sounded like . . .

"You listen to Me, young lady. I *know* the plans I have for you because *I wrote* the plans I have for you *long before I sent* you, and *I am telling you* they are good. They are sufficient to meet My purpose for you on this Earth because *yes*, you have purpose, in case you forgot. I Am with you and for you. I *myself* go before you, and as soon as you actually *believe* that, then *you* will be strong and courageous. Everything, *everything* your soul needs to survive while on Earth is found in the knowledge of Who I Am, so don't *ever* quit seeking to know Me more and more and do *not* be surprised when I take you places you do *not* want to go because I do that so I can *show you* a *new aspect of who I am.*"

Exactly.

"Would you have ever known I was the Provider had I never brought you to lack? And listen, My Girl, I *know* you are human, I know you can't *possibly* understand every word of your story, every step of your journey; so don't forget I Am *here* to talk to in prayer. It's why I *gave* it to you and why My Kid taught the guys how before He came back home. So *talk* to Me. Talk it out. And don't worry, I've heard it all. You'll feel *so* much better *and*, perhaps as you do, the answer you're so desperately wanting will come out of our conversation."

And . . . "Lastly, My Daughter, before you go, don't you forget that My unfailing words placed within you are your weapons of warfare. Use them to take captive every thought that *dares* to set itself up against the knowledge of Who I Am. For I Am *all*-Powerful. *Nothing* is too hard for Me, and Impossible ain't in My dictionary. Now you *go live this day believing that.* And don't you *dare* stop believing, because it's not only keeping you *going*; it's also keeping you *belting it out* as you cruise. Rock on, My Girl. For did I also remind you? I Am your Rock."

(Well . . . I certainly wasn't expecting all *that*, but hot dang I'll take it. Amen.)

SHE BELIEVED

She believed. And that was enough.

Amen.

Much like her faith-daddy Abraham, she simply *refused* to stop believing that God was *absolutely* able to do *exactly* what God had promised. Yep.

She believed. She believes. She believes that God calls into existence things that don't yet exist; she believes God gives life to the dead. After all, she's seen it. She's witnessed it. She's watched as God has rolled away stones before she arrived, parted seas allowing her to walk through them. She's watched God bring forth beauty from ashes and breathe new life into bones that looked as though they would never dance again. But here they are . . . killin' it.

And, much like daddy Abraham, she didn't weaken in her faith when she considered the fact that her body was more than fifty years old, because heck—according to Bible standards, she's *just getting started. Amen.*

Beloved, words written only have power if we believe them. Words spoken to us only have power if we believe them. Case in point—I could tell you right now that you're a mighty warrior, a force to be reckoned with, strong and courageous and brave. But if you don't believe me. . . . Exactly. Nada.

Ohhh, but if you do. . . . Exactly again. Power.

She believes God makes all things right; she believes God redeems all things. She believes God knows the plans for her because God wrote the plans for her as the Author and Perfecter of her faith. She believes that at times her humanness won't possibly be able to grasp her holiness, so at times there'll be blood and sweat and tears. She believes God is sovereign, and that's a mighty big word. So if you haven't looked it up in a while, you may want to. Yes.

She believed. She believes. And because the God *within* her continues to sing "Don't Stop Believin'" *to* her . . . she'll never stop. For she who believes . . . has what she needs . . . to live fully . . . abundantly . . . effectively. Yes.

She believed. And that was enough.

{Romans 3:21–5:21}

WALK INTO NEWNESS

Beloved, confidently walk into the newness.

See, the thing about us hanging out, Beloved, is that because I leave my Notes-to-Self all over the dang place, you have no choice but to see them. But maybe today . . . yes . . . maybe today catching a glimpse of my Note-to-Self is the note that *your* self needs to see. God only knows.

But since you're already here, I'll explain why I wrote it to *me* . . . and if it helps/encourages/causes-you-to-break-out-into-your-own-rendition-of-"Girl-on-Fire"? . . . Well, just invite me to the party, OK? Seriously.

So here's the thing, Sis—not only do I feel as though I'm entering a season of newness, but I also know myself enough to know that because new is scary. . . I turn to Scripture to remind me . . . that *I was created to confidently walk into the newness of life* . . . and yes, the all-caps were on purpose.

I am *alive* because the Spirit, God's Spirit, the Holy Spirit, is *in* me giving me breath. Reviving me. Reminding me. Who I am. Who God is. A God Who brings new—the new that we ask for, plead for, beg for. And then when God *does* . . . we're scared out of our flipping minds. Yup.

But see, *scared doesn't stop the Spirit.* Thank God, or I'd never move an inch. Exactly. No, instead the Spirit within rises up from the well and does what it does so darn well. . . . It performs CPR. It gives me a drink. Sometimes it takes me into the darkness—not as punishment but as provision because what I *really* need is just a minute, please. Yes.

Beloved, if you need this Note today like I do, then I pray you hear my words as a Sis alongside you—not only cheering you on, but fully ready with arm outstretched, if you just need some help taking those first few steps.

Into *your* newness. Whatever that looks like. Knowing who you are. Seen and heard and known and loved—a fulfillment of the plans God has for you and has had since before the foundation. You are chosen and called, equipped and empowered to walk into newness knowing you are never alone. God goes before you. Allowing you to confidently go. Into your newness.

Walk on and rock on, Mighty Warrior. *XO.*

REST. RETURN. REMEMBER. REMIND.

Rest. Return. Remember. Remind. Result? Resurrection.

Oh *good*, you're still *here*. I thought for *sure* I'd lose you at . . . *rest*. Right. Cuz if you're like me, that word looks really great on paper today, but seeing as though it's seated next to the right hand of your to-do list, it's also not looking likely.

Right. But what if the very things we fight in our lives . . . are the very things meant to help us? Like rest—body, mind, soul. Like eating wisely—body, mind, soul. Like moving and stretching to release and let go of what's too much to carry, not to mention the fact that stretching keeps us from shrinking.

In more ways than one, take-it-deep, folks. Yes. What if the reason a mama makes her toddler lie down when he or she is upset and restless is because that's just it—he or she is rest-*less*. Right.

What if it isn't because she's into cruel and unusual punishment but because she knows what her child needs in order to rise anew? New attitude. New smiles. New life. Right. And what if our Parent in Heaven does the same for us for all those same reasons? Whew . . . I know, right?

And what if we take resting and apply it to our soul for that soul-rest we crave more than anything else? What if we *rest* . . . in our *knowing* . . . the *rest*? Yes. The *rest* of the story. Not the details—the outcome. What if *that* . . . the resting . . . is what allows us . . . to rest? I know, right?

Beloved, I know you're busy. I know this week has been hard. So here's some R's for you, should you need them—cuz you know I'm all into alliteration, amen.

Rest in your knowing. Return to Who God is. Remember all God has done—every promise of new, every vow to never abandon or forsake. Remember that graves don't contain . . . cuz they can't. Remind yourself that it's no coincidence that wait and weight sound exactly the same, because both are really, *really* hard to bear. Right. And then while you're at it, remind yourself that both *strengthen*. Mmhmm.

Result? Result of the resting and the returning and the remembering and the reminding? Resurrection. Right. Renewed. Refreshed. Ready.

Rock on.

STAND FIRM

Woman, stand firm.

Yes. Stand firm in the truth that you were fearfully and wonderfully created in the image of the One Who formed you and knit you together by hand. Stand firm in your beauty, your uniqueness, the treasure you carry within that shines like a million stars in the sky, even though most of the time you don't see it.

Woman, stand firm. Stand firm in who you are—chosen and called, set apart and sanctified, sent to this Earth with a purpose that no devil in hell *or* on Earth can prevent, for God doesn't lose. Amen.

Woman, stand firm. Stand firm in what you know to be true while also allowing yourself to continually learn things anew. Yes. Stand firm, not rigid. Not unwilling to move or to shift, but rather firm in your resolve to never give up because you *know* that your God has *got* you, and there *is* indeed a reason for everything under the sun, even when we can't understand it. Yes.

Woman, stand firm in Who your God is—an unchanging God Who chose you before the foundation of the world and vowed to never leave or forsake you. And listen—you're gonna wanna remember that.

Woman, stand firm. Don't forget who you are. Don't forget the power you have been given—the power of the Spirit dwelling within you, supplying your very own breath. Yes. Don't submit yourself yet again to a yoke of slavery that tries to force you to "stay in your place" instead of freely seeking out new lands and new space.

Woman, stand firm. For nothing can separate you from the love of the One for Whom all things are possible and nothing is too hard. So don't you *dare* stop praying and asking and even begging for all that you need and all that you want, trusting that what it is that you desire most was *not* placed within you on accident.

Woman, stand firm in who you are. In Who God is. Provider. Protector. All-Powerful Always. The God Who *sees* you and calls you by name—Beloved. Yes.

Woman, stand firm. For the God Who is *with* you also goes *before* you so you have nothing to fear. Your story's been written and declared to be good. Believe it and "Don't Stop Believin'." *XO*.

{Galatians 5:1}

BELIEVE YOU WILL GROW AGAIN

Despite all that's been taken from you, Beloved, believe today that you will begin to grow again.

We get our hair cut and don't think much of it, because without overthinking it or even thinking about it at all for that matter, we believe without even having to say it out loud that it'll grow back. History tells us that.

We deadhead our flowers throughout their season to bloom because we want there to be room . . . for new blooms . . . yup. And see we know these things and we do these things, and yet I have to wonder when it comes to so many other things . . . do we forget that *we* are *made . . . to grow . . . again*?

Oh good, maybe now we won't miss it.

Beloved, what if today you believed that you will begin to grow again? Thrive again? Survive again? Bear fruit again? Give birth to new again? Smile again? Laugh again? Love again? Live again? And I mean really live again, not just go through the motions of life while muttering, "'nother day, 'nother dollar . . . " Right.

What if you believed today that despite all that's been taken from you, all that's been cut off, plucked, perhaps even taken in order to feed others . . . what if today you believed . . . that you . . . will begin . . . to grow . . . again?

Would that again in fact be a gain? A gain for your strength? A gain for your faith? A gain for your hope, perseverance, and endurance? Would it?

Because *if it would* . . . then dare to believe it. I mean it. And don't stop believin'. I mean that too. I also love you like crazy, so there's that. *XO*. And amen.

{Judges 16:22}

BECAUSE YOU'RE A WARRIOR

Because she was a warrior.

She defeats kings and overcomes things she never thought she'd defeat/overcome . . . because she is a warrior. She climbs mountains big and small, some appearing like giant piles of laundry or stacks of dishes or that hill of paper she's not sure what to do with but is pretty sure she should hold on to . . . because she is a warrior.

She arises each day and drinks coffee and takes time to nourish and strengthen her mind, body, and soul because she knows what the day may demand from her, and therefore she knows what she'll need . . . because she is a warrior. She looks ahead to the future, believing there is still much land for her to possess, and asks/begs God to give her the courage she needs to go and possess it . . . because she is a warrior. And that's what warriors do.

She views victory as what is best for all, not simply for her, because that's how a true warrior thinks and . . . because she is a warrior. She looks for the light at the end of the tunnel, even if it is the low-gas light flickering at her as she drives . . . because she is a warrior. She believes with every ounce of her being that she is fearfully and wonderfully made, and she's gonna own that because *that*'s how much she believes it and . . . because she is a warrior. And that's how warriors think.

She rests when she needs to rest and cries when she needs to cry and sweats when she needs to sweat while thanking her God for the ability to do all three as a way for her soul to process all that it's carrying . . . because she is a warrior.

She asks God again and again and again for what she needs and what she wants, and as she does, she trusts with all she's got that she's heard because she knows darn well her God hears her and . . . because she is a warrior. A warrior with fight left in her and a passion that may just take her places she never thought she'd go. A warrior who dares to believe and refuses to stop believing. A warrior called by name. A warrior seen. A warrior known. A warrior empowered and equipped for all she will face on this Earth.

So yes, she will press on . . . because she is a warrior. *And so are you. XO.*

{Joshua 17:1}

TRUSTING THE ANSWER WILL COME

She begged God to help her with her decision. And then she took a deep breath and trusted the answer would come.

It seems as though we're always trying to make a decision. Some are so easy and so everyday that we don't really even think about 'em. Like regular or decaf. C'mon now.

But then there are others. Ahhh yes, the *others*. Those we grapple with, wrestle with—those we so desperately don't want to get wrong. Those that often look like . . . Should I stay or should I go now? (Permission to sing it—I did!) Should I let go or should I hang on? Should I say yes or should I say no? And whichever I choose, is it revealing my real and truest desire or my hate-to-admit-it fear?

Funny, isn't it? We spend our childhood desperate to make our own decisions, and then we reach adulthood and beg God, "Just show me! Show me what to do/which path to take/tell me what my answer should be!" Perhaps it's because by the time we're here, in the hood we call Grown-Up, we're a bit "decisioned out." Like when the fam asks you what's for supper and you look at them like, "IDK, you tell me."

But truth be told, here's what I love best about begging when it comes to our God—it's intimate. It rises up from this visceral place within and reveals this deep relationship in which you know you are safe to beg. And the *reason* you're begging is because you so desperately want to hear from your God, and at least a *part* of you believes God will answer you, which is why you're begging in the first place. Yes. So we beg. Because we're God's kids. And we can.

So for the one begging God today to help him or her decide what to do or when to do it or how to do it . . . let me get you a fresh cup of joe; don't worry, it's the good stuff. Cuz see, I see you. I'm sitting beside you, which is awesome because now you and I can *each* take a deep breath and remind one another that we can trust our God Whose steadfast love endures forever and Whose faithfulness *never* ends . . . until the answer comes. Cuz we believe it will. One way or another. Some shape, some form, somehow.

And hey, until it does, you and I've got each other. And our good cups of joe.

IT'S OK TO PRAY LIKE MOSES

There will be times when you pray like Moses. It's OK to pray like Moses.

Amen. I'm tempted to stop there, but you all know that ain't happenin', so instead I'll say a bit more. Or a lot more. Whatever.

Moses was named the humblest person on the face of the Earth. (I'm not making that up, by the way—Numbers 12:3.) And to be humble is to *understand that you are human.* Yep. And with that, let me say this: Permission to be human here. I mean it. Moses cried out to God with words like *why* and *why* (twice on purpose, cuz that one's a biggie) and *you promised* and *I can't carry all of this. It's too heavy for me.* And some of you are praying like Moses right now, I just know it. And it's OK. It's *more* than OK.

Now, wanna know how God responded to Moses after this most-real-human prayer? God *listened to Moses.* God let Moses know he was heard, know he was seen, know he was not alone in his holy that was *seriously* heavy and hard. Folks, the guy was responsible for six hundred thousand people on a journey by foot that took years; some of us can't even handle a two-hour car ride with two or three kids asking, "Are we there *yet*?" without losing our mind. (Just to give some perspective here before you start letting your mind dis Moses for not sounding "proper" or "devout.") Mmhmm.

The truth is, sometimes *trust* . . . looks like *asking.* Exactly. God listened to Moses and responded to Moses, which let Moses know he was heard, and *this* is how God responded to him in this case: God told Moses to gather some help.

Yep. God knew the journey wasn't over. God knew He wasn't going to suddenly pick up all these folks and transport them to the Promised Land in a wink. No, there was still much land to travel.

Yes. Friends, that help that was gathered was daily bread. And much like our pals the Israelites, we too often call God's provision manna . . . because we don't always recognize it. *Fact.* (And y'all know how I absolutely love that manna translates as "What the heck is *this*?" Seriously, it never gets old.)

I guess what I'm trying to say among all of these words today is this: There will be times you pray like Moses—not because your faith is *weak*, but because it's *so strong* that you know you *can.* Yes. One hundred percent.

{Numbers 11}

IF YOU GIVE A GIRL SOME HOPE

If you give a girl some hope . . .

She may just change the world. Or her mind. Or her clothes, because she finally feels like she's got something worth caring about . . . *her*. Yes. If you give a girl some hope, she'll have something to hold on to, to believe in, to look forward to.

If you give a girl some hope, she may just have the courage to rise up and walk into this day, even if it's at a snail's pace, because she reminds herself that even slow moving is moving—amen—despite how hard her yesterday was or the unspoken fear she has of what today may just hold.

Yes. If you give a girl some hope, she may just try again. Get up again. Go for it again. Trust again. Believe again. Ask again. If you give a girl some hope, she will be fed with the bread that feeds the soul, and in turn strengthens that soul to live abundantly.

Yes. If you give a girl some hope. It doesn't have to be much. Just the hem of the robe will do; she doesn't need the whole thing. No. She needs only a thread to hold on to because an incredible woman from the cloud reminds her . . . *I promise* you, girlfriend, a thread is enough.

If you give a girl some hope, her day will look different because hope can't sit still; it's always looking ahead. It's more than just the light at the end of the tunnel; it's enough light to make your way *through* said dark tunnel. *Yes*.

If you give a girl some hope, she may just smile again, and dare I say even laugh again. Sarah concurs. She'll tell you it was worth getting her hopes up no matter how risky because believing is what keeps our soul fully alive, and a fully alive soul sounds pretty darn good to us. It sure does.

If you give a girl some hope, she'll do her thing—no matter how mundane she may think it is—with a glimmer in her eye as she does. She sure will. And when you see that glimmer, you'll know that she's doing her thing while at the very same time believing her God has *so* much more in store for her . . . and she can hardly wait. If you give a girl some hope. *XO*.

{Luke 8:43–48; Genesis 18:12}

WHY WE ASK OTHERS TO PRAY

Why do we ask others to pray?

Because they're so much more well-spoken? Because God hears them more? Because we think our voice alone isn't enough to reach the throne of the One? No. Cuz see, if we know God hears all and sees all and knows all and resides within each one of us and is literally as near as our very own breath . . . then why ask others to pray at all?

Here's why: Because the burden is too heavy for us to carry alone. Yes. (Permission to exhale, Beloved.) Because we want to know that someone is standing beside us in our "this" because two is better than one. Yes. Because prayer connects us. It unites us. It awakens us to the needs of another, and that is really helpful when it comes to realizing we were made for one another. *Amen.* Yes. Because it strengthens us to believe . . . yes . . . believe one more day, cuz now we know we're not believing alone. Yes. Because we're tired. Because we're worn out from praying, and so although we can barely eke out the words . . . somehow, we do.

One of my most favorite hidden gems in Scripture (I call it hidden cuz I don't think it gets nearly enough airtime) is when Moses climbs to the top of the hill during battle, along with his buddies Aaron and Hur, and he knows he must pray if they're gonna prevail, but dang it, he's tired and weak . . . *word.* So Aaron and Hur (oh, this is *so* good) take a big stone and put it under his butt so he can sit down . . . and then . . . with one of them on one side of Moses and the other on the other side . . . they lifted Moses's arms in prayer . . . *for him.* I know, right? And *that* is why we ask others to pray. It sure is.

So ask someone to pray. Summon your Aaron and Hur. For in doing so, *you* will be reminded that you are not alone. Yes. And that reminding is gonna strengthen you to hold on to the hope—the hope that you're losing your grip on because your hands have just grown so darn weak and weary from battle—the hope that's gonna see you through. Yes. Amen. I love ya. *XO.*

{Exodus 17:8–13}

Day 29

THEN COMETH JESUS

"Then cometh Jesus . . ."

When I saw these words, I was up past my bedtime. But if these words end up helping even *one* person—like at *all*—it was totally worth it.

Cuz see, when I saw the words written like this, which I understand is nothing more than a simple spacing issue, I couldn't help but read it like it's written, complete with a dramatic pause between each word.

Then . . . cometh . . . Jesus.

Read it again. Slow like that. Yes. And now picture it. I mean it.

Then . . . cometh . . . Jesus.

Into my mess. Into my hurt. Into my sadness. Into my hard.

Then . . . cometh . . . Jesus.

Into my storm. Into my battle. Into my troubles. Into my fears.

Then . . . cometh . . . Jesus.

Into my struggle to decide what to do. Into my questions and doubts. Into my pain and into my worry and into all of my yuck.

Then . . . cometh . . . Jesus.

Yes. With me. For me. Got me. Always. Yes.

Then . . . cometh . . . Jesus.

{Matthew 3:13–17}

REMEMBER WHO YOUR GOD IS

Listen to me, this is how you're gonna get through this—you're gonna remember right now Who your God is.

Yep. You're gonna stop right now and remind yourself that the God Who knit you together and wrote your story in full is the same God Who loves you and is with you to the final amen. You're also gonna allow yourself to question God, "Why??" Because Moses did it all the time, and he seems like a pretty good role model. Right. Cuz see, Moses didn't ask to be where he was, and he sure as heck didn't want go through his "This" . . . but FYI: God is God, and so guess what? Exactly. Moses was doin' the thing. And it was *hard*.

So Moses talked to God about the hard, and he didn't sugar-coat it either. Moses cried out to God using his *own* words in his *own* way, and aren't those the truest and most real prayers of all? The ones born from the most desperate places? The ones birthed from the madness? The ones that cry out, "*Why, God? Why* am I here? *Why* did You send me? *Why are You doing nothing at all* ??*"

And God answered Moses. And, thankfully, someone took notes so you and I can refer to it in the midst of our very own "This." Note: I expanded it based on other awesomeness about who our God is . . . yes.

I Am the Lord. I Am making Myself *known* to you through This. I *hear* you. I *will* free you. I *will* deliver you. I *will* redeem you. I *will* see you through *this*, and I *will* be your God, and *when* I do—you're gonna *know* that I'm your God. I'm gonna free you from the burden you're currently carrying, and I know you don't understand why you're carrying it in the first place, but I *promise* you that it has *purpose*. I Am gonna bring you *out* and bring you *to*, and you're just gonna have to take Me at My unchanging Word on that.

I have *never* forgotten you, and I *promise* you that I will be *with* you wherever you *are* and wherever you *go*, and let Me just remind you, sweet child of Mine—not *one* of My promises has failed. I Am your Redeemer. I Am your Rescuer. I Am the One Who makes *all* things right in due time. I Am your faithful companion as you journey through "This." I Am.

{Exodus 3–4}

GOD WILL MOVE YOU

God will move you in ways you don't always like to get you out of places that aren't for you.

Yes. Amen. But now please, if you will, repeat after me, because renaming is the most powerful tool we've got. Amen. (Read that again in *all caps*, please.) Ready? God is *making room* for me. Ahhh . . . see how much better that feels, how much sweeter it tastes on the tongue? Seriously.

Thanks, Isaac and crew. Yep. Isaac was asked to leave the land where he was by the king at the time, because, and I quote, "You have become too powerful for us." And dang, I hope at least a part of Isaac smiled at that. I sure did. So Isaac did. Depart. Camped in the valley. And *dug in the valley*. Because FYI, sometimes there are springs of exactly what you need in the valley where you don't want to be. Read that again and grab your shovel, please.

Yes. Isaac and his guys dug, actually, *re*-dug, the wells his father had dug because the enemy had filled them all in—nasty buggers. *And* he and his crew hit pay dirt—a.k.a., fresh spring water. To which, of course, the enemies returned and said, "Hey! That's *our* water!"

Whatever. Isaac named the well Contention (seriously) and moved on and dug another one. Yup. Same deal. So Isaac named that one Enmity. And so he moved on and dug yet *another* one. He sure did. Except *this* time, there was no quarreling over it. And so, Isaac named *this* well . . . room. Yup. Saying, "*Now* the Lord has *made room for us*, and we shall be *fruitful* in the land."

I know, right? So hmmm, let's see, what can we take from this super cool story on this ordinary everyday day?

God will move you in ways you don't like (enter contention and enmity) in order to get you out of places that aren't for you, and what God may *actually* be doing . . . is *making room for you*. I know, right? And I can attest. One hundred percent. Been there, done that, lived it—yes.

Oh, and before you go, shall we take one *more* fab bite from this dang-good-bread story? Sure, why not. *Keep digging in the valley you're in, cuz you may just find what you're looking for.*

{Genesis 26}

AND YET

And yet . . .

"Who would've ever thought that at my age I'd be up in the night with a newborn? And yet, here I am, desperately trying to get baby Isaac back to sleep."—Sarah.

"Who would've ever thought that not only would I walk out of the garden that day, but that I'd actually be named Mother of the Living? And yet, here I am, doing my thing and trying my best to keep my kids from killing each other. (Note: I don't always succeed.)"—Eve.

"Who would've ever thought that after all those miserable relationships and the shadow it left on me, that I would actually meet the Light of the World at the well about noon for a drink that would revive me and give me what I didn't even know I needed? And yet, here I am, preparing to preach a kick-butt sermon this weekend if you wanna come hear me."—The Woman at the Well.

"Who would've ever thought that I'd actually get out of that huge fish belly after swimming around in its innards for three days? And yet, here I am, doing what I didn't wanna do, cuz the call of God really *is* irrevocable even when we don't like it."—Jonah

"Who would've ever thought that I'd get called out of that grave after three long stinky days? And yet, here I am, freshly showered and lookin' like a sharply dressed man."—Laz.

"Who would've ever thought that instead of my past defining me it actually refined me *and* prepared me for all God had *for* me? And yet, here I am, killin' it. Crazy, huh?"—Moses, Matthew, Rahab, David, the list goes on and on and on.

Beloved, your story on Earth includes your very own written-for-you *and yet.*

Yes. The story written in full for you by your Author and your Perfecter. And truly I tell you, your story on Earth may be filled with pages and perhaps even entire chapters that you don't like or can't make sense of. *And yet*, every word of your story was written with purpose and ends with *one* word—*amen*—that is preceded by *three* words . . . It. Is. Finished. I believe that with every fiber of my heart, mind, and soul. *And* remember, Beloved, your story includes the language of miracles, the language that says . . . *and yet.*

LIVING AFTER

Eve lived after. Adam did too. Noah lived long after the flood, and Naomi long after the famine. Jonah lived after, and Daniel lived after, and Esther lived after, and heck—even Isaac lived after. Beloved, they lived after. And so will you.

Years ago, I was hired by a woman I'd never met who lived states away to be her private Bible tutor via calls and apps. After I don't know how many sessions, as we determined she'd "take it from there" on her own, I asked her what her favorite verse had been. I was expecting a Bible Biggie—you know, the ones sprawled all over Pinterest and pillows and really cool wall hangings and made into memes that get shared a whole buncha times.

But it wasn't. It was a verse I've never seen sprawled out anywhere, and I'm thinking maybe it should be. Yes. It was a verse that included five simple words, and those five simple words were . . .

"After the flood Noah lived . . ."

Yep. That was her fave. And what a great pick, by the way. Because see, this woman needed to know that people live *after* their floods, *after* their wars, *after* their famines and time spent in cells, and *after* the thing they at one time never thought they'd live *after*. And like Noah, I bet we know the day that the "fountains of the great deep burst forth," and it felt less like the "windows of heaven being opened" and more like all hell breaking loose. Word. So now I'm gonna tell you something *else* big we can take from our pal Noah: Noah and his fam climbed into the ark that he built on the very same day that all the aforementioned took place. That's right.

So, Beloved . . . make yourself an ark. I mean it. A refuge, a fortress, a place you can go in your heart, mind, and soul when the flood waters come. Oh, and keep this in mind . . . Noah lived after. So did Adam and Eve and Naomi and Jonah and Daniel and Esther, and heck—even Isaac. That's right. They lived *after*. And so will you. You sure will.

{Genesis 9:28}

KNOW GOING IN

Know going in . . .

That your journey won't always be easy, that at times the road you are on will seem way too long, and you just won't understand why. Know going in that to bring forth new, there is almost always some level of pain involved—blood, sweat, and tears too.

Know going in so that when it comes to fruition you won't feel as though God is picking on you and is instead *using* you to bring forth the new. Know going in that God created all things *including* the serpent. And *no* you don't have to like it, but it might help if you remind yourself that the serpent *too* takes orders from God and answers to God. And you can read Genesis or Job to concur. Yes. Know going in that your journey may include pit stops in fish guts and waterless pits and dens of lions who haven't eaten for days.

Cuz see, if you know going *in*, then when you find yourself in those said places, you won't be as surprised, and you can return to Who you know God to be, just like the folks who found themselves in those places. *Yes.* Know going in that waiting isn't punishment; it's a form of strength training. Get it? *Weight*s and *wait*s.

Right. Know going in that God planted the garden *before* placing Adam in it, because it's gonna help you immensely to know that God goes before you preparing the place that you'll be *before* you get there. Yes. Know going in that there will be sleepless nights. The new often brings that too. Just ask parents of newborns.

Know going in that not everyone who follows you is cheering you on, and then give thanks that the Bible used the ongoing saga of Jesus and the Pharisees to show us that. And then remind yourself that Jesus kept doing Jesus things because if they wanna watch, sweet; it wasn't gonna alter His purpose. Know going in that not everyone will make room for you; nod to Mary and Joe. That sometimes you'll beg God to calm the waters, and instead God will call you to walk on them, and sometimes God *won't* move the mountains before you and instead instruct you to climb them.

Yes. Know going in that you're not alone, and that you were built for your journey.

STEPPING INTO THE NEW

She had no idea what she was about to step into . . . but she knew her God went before her . . . and that was enough for her . . . to keep going.

And I hate to break this to you, Beloved, but you don't either. That's right. Cuz to quote our guy Sol using ole' King James wordage . . . We deviseth our way . . . but God directeth our steps. Mmhmm. And indeed. (Also, King J, you should know— spellcheck don't like you, but no worries. I got you.) And I digress.

Cuz see, you and I, Beloved, we have no idea what we're about to step into. Oh, we may *think* we know, but we don't reeeeally know, ya know? Right.

But here's what we *do* know: The Lord Himself goes before you; He is with you and will never leave you. *Therefore* (since all *that* is true), do not worry, do not be afraid, do not be discouraged, do not be dismayed . . . God will not fail you *or* forsake you (say some translations), but however you hear it, the message is clear . . . God goes *before* you. Yes.

As you leave behind what was and walk straight into what will be, you bid adieu to what lies behind you and, with the passion of Paul, press on to lay hold of that for which Christ has laid hold *for* you. *Heck yes.* (And then you thank Paul for hanging out in the cloud, cuz sometimes you need a hefty dose of his passion and fortitude.) Word.

Beloved, God goes before you. And I don't know about you, but if I'm stepping into the scary unknown, I'd just as soon have the God for Whom all things are possible and for Whom nothing is too hard and to Whom everything else is simply a speck because He's just that freakin' *huge* . . . go *first*. Amen to that. Seriously.

And so, on that note, the note that perhaps can serve as the very first note of the new song you'll sing. . . . Here's to the *new*. And to the God Who is already there.

{Deuteronomy 31:8}

Day 36

RENAME YOUR DARK

Rename your Dark and call it the Start.

Yes, and amen. I'm-Not-Kidding-I'm-Sure-As-Heck-Not. Now let's get started, shall we? Great.

The womb, the tomb, new life springs from both—not to mention each new day that comes. Right. Because let's not forget, dear sweet friends of mine, that the day doesn't start when we get out of bed; it starts at *midnight. Amen.* Right. Rename your Dark and call it the Start.

Read the opening lines of Genesis if you need reminding . . . that the great big world you live in, Darlin', *started* with nothin' but darkness. Right. Rename your Dark and call it the Start. And then talk to Joe, the one with the fancy coat. He'll tell you that the dark pit his bros threw him in was simply the start for him. (Plus, do read the story, cuz the fact that his same bros end up needing his palace-assistance is priceless.)

Right. Ask Danny if that dark den was the end. FYI—it wasn't. Ask Jonah. He's got a whale of a tale to tell ya. (Sorry, I couldn't help myself.) Ask Mary and Joe about the dark of that stable, or ask Nehemiah what it was like to scope out all of those ruins in the darkness of night . . . as he thought to himself . . . this ain't the end, this is where we *start* . . . to *rebuild* . . . amen.

Rename your Dark and call it the Start. And while you're at it, here's something else that might help. . . . Remind yourself that it's not Dark to the One Who is Light. That's right. The One to Whom all things are known, and all tears are kept, and no secrets are hidden, and no dark can hinder one darn thing cuz it just ain't dark to Him. Amen. Right. The One Who will kindly remind you as you sit in your dark . . .

I Am right here, My Beloved . . . and *dark* . . . is where . . . *I start.*

And if you're lucky, He may even throw in a bing-bang-boom. Just sayin'. Rename it, Beloved. I mean it. Big love.

WHEN IT JUST DIDN'T GO LIKE YOU PLANNED

When it just didn't go like you planned . . .

You call in folks who can relate, because although it is what it is, it's also nice to know that you're not the only one whose "is what it is" wasn't what you thought it shoulda been. Seriously, if your own personal book title right now could be *Emotions Entangled like Christmas Lights*, you might want to read on, cuz I've got some peeps here dying to chime in . . .

Mary's up first: "Ummm, this is *not* what I had planned for my life. What about my dream wedding? The aspirations I had? What about all the stuff I wanted to do before graduation?"

Joe: "I'm supposed to marry this girl even though she's preggo (and not by me, by the way) *and* return to my hometown, which I obviously left for good reason. *And* when I get there, I get to be reminded *why* I left when my own people can't even spare one small room?? Wow."

The shepherds: "Listen, we were just out doing the whole shepherding gig—leaning on our staffs and crackin' jokes to burn the midnight oil—when all of sudden we thought we were goners. I mean, who the heck has a big scary angel appear to them in the middle of the night? And you *do* know that we had to take all those sheep with us, right? Exactly. We're *good* shepherds, *hello*, so of *course* we didn't leave them alone."

The wisemen: "Herod *told* us what to do. Go find the baby, he said. It'll be fun, he said. We did what he said, only to be warned in a dream after we got there that we best find a new route back home because Herod was *hot* and not havin' it. Umm . . . what??"

Joe again: "After all *that*—you guys won't believe this—*another* angel interrupted my much-needed sleep and told me to load up Mary and the newborn and flee to Egypt because Herod was on the hunt for us. Yeah, *that* was a fun road trip . . . with a newborn . . . *not*."

Beloved, if today's devo allowed you a breather and even a grin, it did its job. Now, let's hear it for today's cast, who did a pretty sweet job of reminding us that things don't always go as planned.

GOD'S WORKED IT OUT

Just think—right now you're worried about something that your God has already worked out for good.

Tera's Tip: Write yourself notes.

You do it for everything else—from your grocery list that you then forget at home on the counter, to your to-do list that you add things like "wake up" and "get out of bed" to, just so you can proudly cross them off. You're smiling cuz I'm right. I got you.

So today's note to self, the one you may want to borrow or share or screenshot is this . . . Just think—right now you're worried about something that your God has already worked out for good. Yup. (Pause to recall and remember that we've all agreed that "good" is defined as sufficient to meet the purpose, and psst, FYI—we all know *Whose* purpose. Amen.) Proceed.

Beloved, I don't know what the something or host of somethings is that you're worried about right now, but I'm willing to bet my last regular-not-decaf coffee pod (and that's saying a lot, by the way) that you are in fact worried about *something*. Right. And your God? Your God, Who not only created you before the foundation of the world but also wrote your entire story start-to-finish and loves you wholly and completely and forever will no-matter-what? *That* God has already worked out the Something for good, because God leaves no stone unturned. Amen.

God leaves no stone that needs rolling unrolled . . . leaves no stone that needs to find its way into a slingshot lying on the ground . . . leaves no stone clutched in pious fists undropped. Amen-and-how-bout-them-apples.

Beloved, take a deep breath. Remind yourself that it's God Holy Spirit within you. Remind your worry Who your God is. And lastly . . . be brave enough to pray and be strong and courageous, for your God really *is* with you wherever you go. (Refer back to the breath thing.) Amen. Your God has already worked it out. Believe it today. And don't stop believing tomorrow. Big love. Far more than I can fit into this space.

WITH YOU AND AHEAD OF YOU

God is both with you and ahead of you.

Whew. Seriously. Cuz that's the thing about God—God is Spirit. So, therefore, in fact, God is . . . E-v-E-r-Y-w-H-e-R-e. No limits, no bounds. Thank God. Amen. *With* you . . . as you don't understand why it has to be the way that it is, why *this* storm or why *this* drought and why God, why right now? Why am I here in this place and why aren't *You* here, "Lord of all"???

God *with*. Yes. A God Who is *with* you to hear you and listen and give you compassion that is new every morning and never runs out because, hello—He *knows* you're not going to understand; you couldn't possibly. You didn't write the script. *right*. A God *With* you . . . so you're never alone . . . and always have Someone. The One. Yes. *And*. A God Who is *ahead* of you. Thank God again. No doubt. *Ahead* of you . . . preparing the palace to receive you . . . as was the case for both Esther and Joe. *Ahead* of you, warming up His vocal cords in order to call forth life from the grave . . . as He did for our friend Laz. *Ahead* of you, orchestrating the Earthquake that's gonna set you free . . . like when He did it for Paul and for Silas and for all the rest of the prisoners, for that matter, as their cells broke open that day. *Yes*.

Ahead of you, rolling away the stone like He did for the Marys or providing a ram in the thicket like He did for Abe and his kid. Yes. Or positioning an angel in the den of lions you're about to find yourself in or a great fish in the raging sea you're about to be tossed into. Yes again.

Whew. Beloved, truly I tell you, God is both *with* you . . . *and* . . . *ahead* of you. Near *and* far. Thank God. Close enough to surround you and hold you and cover you and capture every word, every thought, every tear that falls, giving it *all* value and worth . . . *and* . . . far enough ahead of you to prepare and provide and protect and to make it all count. Absolutely. Every amen. Big love.

I'LL BE BACK

Repeat after me, "I'll be back."

Physically. Emotionally. Mentally. Spiritually. Say it in your best Arnold S. voice, if you want. But say it out loud—this is important—because I not only want *you* to hear it, but I want to hear it *too*. I'll be back. Send the message to your heart-mind-and-soul that where you are or where you need to go is a temporary trip, a temporary stay, *not* permanent residency. So yes-dang-right you'll be back. Absolutely. I'll be back.

Beloved, I *love* Genesis 22. The tale of a guy and his boy and a major trip to a mountain and up a mountain after God told said guy to slaughter his boy on the top of said mountain.But said guy, Abraham, cool as a cucumber based on *refusing to let go of the promise God had made to him to give him nations and generations from this said son* . . . wakes up early in the morning after receiving the command the night before and says . . . . "Let's go." You bet he did. And he brings two young guys along with him and his boy. Why? Cuz see, Abe needed his boy Isaac to hear words that were spoken confidently and calmly to others by the one he trusted most in the world.

"You guys stay here with the donkey. The boy and I will go over there to worship; *then we'll come back to you.*"

We will come back to you. *We* will be back. And off the guy and his boy went.

And as the boy is carrying the wood up that mountain and sees his dad with flint and fire in hand and realizes they have nothing with them to place on the altar and asks the question, "Hey, Dad, ummm, where's the lamb for the sacrifice?" . . . his dad responds, still calm, still cool, and still fully collected, "God Himself will provide the lamb for the burnt offering, my son."

And spoiler alert—God did. Just like the guy named Abe knew he would. So Abe named that place, "The Lord Will Provide." And I'm willing to bet it's a day that the guy and his boy will never forget.

Beloved, repeat after me . . . I'll be back.

{Genesis 22}

HEALING TAKES TIME

Yes, the Word of God heals. But Bible verses aren't Band-Aids. So I'm sorry for all the times someone slapped one on your bleeding because it was far more comfortable than sharing your rough cloth. Healing takes time. No, there is nothing "wrong" with you, Beloved—you are human . . . and healing takes time.

I don't always know why I'm compelled to write what I do. But whenever I place pen to paper and watch what pours out as ink on a page, I'm convinced that it is with good reason and purpose—that some*one* some*where* is longing for something he/she can hold on to, from a fellow human being upon this great Earth. So here we are. And me saying what yet again feels like a hard thing to be said . . . Bible verses aren't Band-Aids. The same goes for Christian clichés. Or stupid memes that encourage us to "let God in" to do the healing, as if we "let" God do anything.

News flash: God is God, and we are not. And because God is God, and God is love, and God looked at all God had made and called it Good . . . out of God's great mercy and compassion and understanding of the way we were formed . . . God gives us . . . *one another.* To be close to the brokenhearted. To bind up wounds. To stop, look, and listen, amen. To remind one another that . . . healing takes time. Amen.

God went as far as to give us an earthly body of flesh that is capable of bruising and bleeding and breaking, amen . . . and then show us how in each of those cases . . . the length of the healing is based on how severe the bruise/bleed/break . . . yes. Read that again. Deep wound? It will take longer. Paper cuts sting, but not for long.

Beloved, I'm not only sorry for all the times someone slapped a Bible verse on your bleeding like a Band-Aid; I'm even more sorry if it caused you to in any way feel as if something was "wrong" with you because you weren't immediately healed. Beloved, you are *human. And healing takes time.* You are loved, amen. I promise it's most certainly true. Oh, and Beloved? Forgive them, for they know not what they do. *XO.*

WANTING TO BE WHERE GOD IS

Here's the thing—when you know Who God is, you just wanna be where God is.

There are words that have been spoken to us here on Earth that we hope we never forget—along with, of course, those we can't forget soon enough. This story is the former.

My now-teenage son was around three or four years of age. I was doing what I have been doing every morning since I was forty; I was curled up in my chair with both coffee and the Word in my hands. Sacred time. Precious time. *Me* time.

Just then, in the dark of a very-early morn, I heard little footsteps making their way down the stairs. Being Mother-of-the-Year, I thought . . . "Excuse me, little person coming down the stairs—this ain't Christmas mornin'. Please, oh please turn your tiny butt around and go back up." He didn't. Instead, he made his way to me without saying a word and nudged himself right between me and the arm of the chair. Still tired, as hard as he tried to remain upright, the poor dude's head kept nodding to the side like a bobble head.

"Honey," I whispered, "Why don't you go lay on the couch. You'll be more comfortable."

And that's when that tiny human looked up at me and said the words that I pray I never forget . . .

"I don't wanna be comfortable. I wanna be close to you."

Knowing who I am to him, he wanted nothing more than to be close to me, regardless of any discomfort. That's what happens when we know who God is—we just wanna be where God is.

It reminds me of two guys who were following Jesus. He turned to them and asked them, "What are you looking for?" They replied, "Where are You staying?"

That's right. Cuz we wanna be where You are. *That* is why we are following You. Climbing a mountain? Let's go. Skipping lunch to talk to someone alone at a well? Here we are. Stepping away from the crowd for a bit to just have a minute with God? Perfect. We're all in. Even if the crowd can't understand it. Time to wash feet? Time to embrace the new land You have for us, Lord? OK, sounds good. We're just glad You go *first*.

{John 1:38}

Jesus told Pete he could walk on water, and Pete did great, until he doubted himself, until he forgot who it was who told him he could. STORMS WILL DO THAT. amen.
—teriejean
#iwasonline
christianjourney

Day 43

STORMS WILL DO THAT

Jesus told Pete he could walk on water, and Pete did great, until he doubted himself, until he forgot Who it was Who told him he could. Storms will do that.

I think we often forget that Pete *asked* to walk on water that night. Yup. Pete said words to Jesus that I myself have said to Jesus, and just like Pete, I absolutely meant them and felt the full crux of them when I said them. . . . Lord, if it's You, bid me to come to You. Knowing full well, by the way, that Jesus was walking upon the water, which means if I'm gonna go to where He's at—well then, I'm gonna need to walk on water too.

And just like Pete, I can. And just like Pete, I have.

It seems impossible until you're actually doing it, strengthened by the truth that you can, spoken to you by the One Who told you that *you can. And* just like Pete, I do great. Until the storms arise, and the strong winds blow. For nothing throws our boats off-kilter like some nice, strong winds blowing against them.

But I'm happy to see that I'm stronger than I once was. I'm able to ride out the storms better than I once could. For this I know—storms will arise in the stories of our *lives* as well. Just think how many you've survived already. Each one strengthens you for the next one that comes. Each one teaches you a bit more. Each one reveals to you something you never knew before that storm arose.

I hear the words of Jesus, whispering to me through those winds . . . You keep your eyes on Me, young lady. Don't you forget who I Am, and don't you forget who *you* are, who I created you to be . . . a girl who can survive storms. A girl who can stand when the strong winds blow against her. A girl who can walk on water when I bid her to come.

And I'll tell ya what—when God speaks to a girl like *that* . . . she believes it. She sure does. She believes every word of the One Who has told her she can walk on water, knowing that One is *with* her.

{Matthew 14:22–33}

EVEN THERE

You listen to me, Beloved—God can show you favor wherever you are. Yes, even there.

There in the pit. There in the prison. There in the place you never asked to be in. There in the flood. The flood of bad news. The flood of Why Me? The flood of Are You Freaking *serious*, Lord, *again*?? Not to mention the flood of emotions that occasionally (and sometimes more than occasionally) rises up with a force we're certain will drown us. Yes, even there.

There in the belly of a great big fish. There in the den full of lions. There in the door of the tent that day as you overhear some guys tell your hubby that you're gonna be a mama at ninety. There as you climb that mountain. There as you cling to hope. There as you cry out to God, "*Why* is this a part of my life??" There in the dismissal. There in the divorce. There in the diagnosis you never saw coming. There in the workplace you're not sure you should be in or stay in as you croon out the classic . . . "Should I Stay or Should I Go"?

Yes, Beloved, even there. There in the place that makes no sense—the place that feels more like punishment than part of some glorious plan for your life. Yes, even there.

Now, listen—if you don't believe me, that's fine. We can totally call in the great cloud of witnesses. And if it's OK with you, Joe would like to go first. Cuz see, this guy will tell ya that whether he was in the pit or the prison or even in the grip of Pot's wife's evil plan. . . .

God showed him *favor* in all of his *theres*. And I bet He'd *also* like to sing you a little ditty as you go today. Maybe you've heard it?

Dream on. Dream until your dreams come *true*.

Joe did. And although his journey included twists and turns and detours that, at times, totally and royally *sucked* . . . Joe will tell you that wherever he was, God knew his *there* and saw to it that Joe be given favor, right there in his *there*. Now believe it for *you*, Beloved, and for the love of God, don't stop believin'.

Day 45

FINDING YOURSELF

She would often find herself in Scripture.

One thing about the Bible is that unlike a casual read on the beach (which I highly recommend, by the way), it's not the kind of book you're gonna lose yourself in. You're not gonna read it in a day. Your head may explode if you do. But what I've come to realize over the past fourteen years in this chair is that what I *do* do . . . is *find* myself in it. And much like occasionally *losing* yourself, I can't *begin* to tell you the value in *finding yourself.*

I *find* myself in Scripture. I find myself in the stories of these people who are like *me*. I find myself in the woman at the well, the woman hunched over, the woman exhausted from climbing the same mountain year after year of begging God for the same thing. I find myself in Martha as she runs to pound her fists on Jesus's chest while screaming, "Where *were* You when we *needed* You??"

I find myself in the guys in the boat when the great storm arose on the sea as they found Jesus taking a *nap* of all things, which caused them to shake him and scream, "Wake *up*!! Don't You *care* about us?!" I find myself in Peter as he bravely asks to walk on water. I find myself in Paul as he speaks with a level of passion that some just don't understand. I find myself in Jonah when I try to run from what I know darn well is God's plan for me, but I'm just so scared to death that jumping overboard seems like a better option than actually just going with it.

I find myself in Sarah as she gives birth to new after menopause, in Hannah as she asks God for what she *wants* and not simply what she needs, in Anna as she abides in that temple day after day after day . . . each day awakening and confidently declaring . . . *today* is the day. And when it's *not* . . . she arises the next day and declares the *same thing. Yes.* Cuz truly I tell you, Beloved, *that's* where I'm at. A girl with a passion that feels like a fire that began as a spark all those years ago. Beloved, read Scripture. And *find* yourself in it.

THE BEAUTY OF HOLINESS

The beauty of holiness . . .

There I was—mindin' my own business, sippin' on my third cup o' joe, and reading the Psalms that make the whole world sing—when suddenly, these four words reach up and grab me by the hem of my coffee-stained robe and cry . . . *write about us.*

So here we are. With the beauty of holiness.

Beloved, you are holy. Your life is holy, set apart for the good purpose of the God Who not only *created* you for holiness but also *wrote* every word of your holy story. Amen. And perhaps each one of us has the same story title despite all of our varying chapters . . . *The Beauty of Holiness*. And the beauty of holiness may at times look like royal robes and crowns and jewels and makeup that's totally on point . . . but there are *also* times, *so* many times, when the beauty of holiness will look more like . . . blood-sweat-and-tears. Just ask Jesus.

Journeying through the desert for years on end trusting that bread will continue to fall from Heaven each day, even if you *are* calling it manna. Making your way through a crowd knowing full well that everyone *in* that crowd knows about your "issue," but at this point, you're totally spent and got nothin' left to lose. The beauty of holiness.

The single mom with her child in tow and not a clue where to go, and of *course* the kid is crying. When suddenly her God reminds her that He sees *and* hears both her *and* her kiddo . . . and in *that* moment, she names Him *the God Who sees me.*

The beauty of holiness. It may look like barrenness. It may look like loneliness, at least for a while. Like standing at the edge of the cave of chaos desperate to hear the still small voice of your God. Like spending three days and three nights in the rock bottom gut of a great big fish with time to think and assess some life choices. Like traveling countless miles on foot with your pregnant wife, all the while thinking . . . I never signed up for this.

Yet here you are, smack dab in the beauty of holiness and set apart with great purpose.

{Psalm 29:2}

EVERY STEP YOU TAKE

She who is unwilling to take the steps won't get very far, amen.

Can you imagine how different life would've looked for Naomi, not to mention Ruth, if she hadn't been willing to take the steps back to Bethlehem? For one thing, she wouldn't proudly be sporting her "Grandkids are the Chocolate Chips in the Cookie of Life" tee. Just sayin'.

Or how about Esther? Let's ask her nation of people if they're glad that she took those scary steps down the palace hallway that day, marching her brave butt right into the throne room of the King, despite no sign of an outstretched scepter—not to mention what it did for Esther *herself* as she realized *she could do hard things. Amen.*

Or how about the widow with her last handful of flour and last drop of oil? I bet *she's* glad she took the steps that were laid out to her by the prophet that day—not to mention her "Mom, I'm *starving-to-death*" son.

Or how about Hannah as she tearfully, repeatedly took the steps up that mountain? Or Rahab as she courageously took the steps to hide those two guys who were spies? Or a woman who obviously loved her family deeply as she took those steps to the well each day about noon? Or how about the women who took the steps to the tomb that day . . . prepared to anoint a dead body and instead witnessed a life resurrected?

I know, right? *So* dang good. Their stories *never* get old. The steps. Every step. All the steps. The steps we take that position us to *see* God *be* God. *Yes.* To see God be the Provider, to see God be the Protector, to see God be All-Powerful in ways we *never* expected. And *those* kinds of moments not *only* leave us *breathless* . . . they *also breathe new life into us* . . . to *keep on believing* for the next time. *Yes.*

Now C'mon, how stinkin' *awesome* is that?

THE SMALLEST OF SIGNS

It is often the smallest of signs that deliver the most-needed messages.

Like waking up to the lightest dusting of snow after recently discussing with someone that despite how much the "no snow" thus far during that season had been swell, our worn and weary land was crying for nitrogen. The smallest of signs that delivered the most-needed message . . . I will provide.

Like the sign of a fist-sized cloud, the one that appeared to Elijah in the midst of the drought. Like one single ram in the thicket for Abe (not to mention Isaac), or that one single drop of oil for that one widow and her only surviving son. Like a small piece of wet fleece on dry ground for Gideon, or a small piece of dry fleece on wet ground for Gideon, or the emergence of the smallest baby bump for Hannah as she clutched her belly with joy and excitement. And speaking of babes . . . how about one small baby wrapped in swaddling clothes and lying in a manger? One small baby with the most-needed message . . .

God Saves. Yes. Jesus. God is with us. Yes. Emmanuel. God *provides*. Yes. Always. In due time. The most-needed messages . . . through the smallest of signs. Like a still, small voice. Like a longing fulfilled.

Like one lone paper clip there on the sidewalk as she walked her usual route after searching every junk drawer in the house just that morning for one, cuz hello—there's *always* a paper clip *somewhere*. But alas I had none. So onto my list it went. But first I went for my walk. And there she was. All alone. On my path. For me to find. With one great big message to give me . . . My Daughter, I will provide. And do you know that to *this* day, I hear that message *every time* a paper clip unexpectedly appears to me.

Beloved, it is often the smallest of signs that deliver the most-needed messages. Don't dismiss or disregard them.

YOUR TIME WILL COME

Now Elizabeth's time had come . . . Elizabeth. Sarah. Hannah. Hagar. Ruth. Mary. The list goes on. Women whose time had come . . . and Beloved, yours will too.

"Now Elizabeth's time had come. . . ."

I read the words, Beloved, and the best way I can describe it to you is that it felt as though my soul quite literally leapt for joy within me . . . much like I imagine Elizabeth's did when she heard her young (and also pregnant) cousin Mary's greeting to her.

Yes. Elizabeth's time had come . . . to deliver. Read it again. Elizabeth's time had come . . . to be delivered. Read that again too. Because it depends on which translation you ingest, and since I *stinkin' love 'em both*, both are gonna be on my plate for breakfast this mornin'. Now Elizabeth's time had come . . . not a minute before, not a minute too late. Her time to deliver, to be delivered . . . had come. And so will yours. And how about "to *be* delivered"? That time . . . will *also* come. To be delivered of what hurts you, pains you, weighs so heavy upon you—that thing within that you're longing to be delivered . . . from. Yes.

Now, Beloved, here's the thing—in all of this I write to you, none of it will do a *darn thing* for you unless you *believe* it for *you*. For you are *worthy of your own believing, you know*. You sure are. Because without believing . . . they're simply consonants and vowels positioned together on a page. So *believe* it, Beloved. Breath for your soul, remember? Fueled by faith, strengthened by hope, alive and ready to take captive any thought that *dares* to set itself up against the knowledge of who your God is. A God Who when the fullness of time had come . . . was delivered into our world by being born of a woman.

Beloved, you are living the Scripture written for *you*. You are living *your* story right here, right now. Let these women who now reside in the cloud inspire you . . . encourage you . . . remind you . . . that their time came. And yours will too.

{Luke 1:57}

STRENGTH TO BELIEVE

For the one who could use some strength to believe and some hope to hold on to . . .

It takes strength to believe. It takes strength to endure and persevere. It takes strength to ask. It takes strength to hold on to hope when hope feels more like a thread and less like an anchor. So for the one today who could use some strength to believe and some hope to hold on to, I give you the following, praying that it will strengthen you even a bit, sustain you even if for a moment, by providing you an oasis in the desert—a place of respite, relief, rest, peace.

Beloved, agony has been known to give birth to new. What has been buried has been known to arise. Life has been known to walk out of death despite how long it's been in the grave . . . for *both* wombs *and* tombs have been known to bring forth new life.

Redirections have led to new beginnings. Detours have provided new things to see. Donkeys have been known to talk in order to stop us and finally get through to us. Seas have been known to part, and stones have been known to roll. A fist-sized cloud has been known to appear in the sky in the midst of a drought that seemed like it'd been going on for like *ever* . . . and that single fist-sized cloud amidst that great big sky was enough to hold on to. *Amen again.*

Beauty has been known to rise from ashes, and joy has been known to emerge from mourning. Mountains have been known to be tossed into the sea *and also* been known to stay put . . . so that they can be climbed and conquered while at the same time strengthening the climber every step of the way. *Amen yet again.*

Beloved, the best way to care for our flesh is to support it. To care for it and nourish it and support it with what is good for it. The same is true for our *soul*. So care for it, nourish it, support it with what it needs to survive and believe, to ask and endure, to persevere against all odds.

Strength to believe. Hope to hold on to. May it be yours. *Today.*

WHAT YOU MOST NEED TO HEAR

Paul knew what the Thessalonians most needed to hear, and maybe today, Beloved, you do too.

It's during the hard things of life that we most need to remember, because that's when we tend to forget. Hard things like illness and persecution like the Thessalonians faced—things that *you* may be facing today. Or maybe it's divorce or despair or an unsettling feeling within you that you can't quite explain, but it's there, and you're not sure what it means. Maybe it's realizing your life is changing because your season is changing, and you're not only not crazy about it—you're scared to death of it. Maybe your world feels like it's spinning out of control, and there's not a dang thing you can do about it, and you may be right . . . but what you *can* do is stop and remember. Or in today's case, let me remind you.

Paul wanted his peeps in Thessalonica to *remember*. Remember who you are. Remember Who God is. Remember who everyone else is. *And*, Paul would add, keep going . . . by stopping and reminding yourself of some unchanging things. Stop and breathe and remind yourself that the breath within you belongs to the God Who created you, and it will be *with* you until you head home as a reminder that you're never alone.

Find peace *within* you because *that* peace can't be taken from you, for it is safely kept in the sanctuary of your soul, the inner room, the holiest of holies. Seek to do good cuz you'll feel better when you do. Help the weak and keep in mind that sometimes the weak . . . is you. Be patient, knowing and trusting and believing that the God Who calls you is *faithful* to fulfill *every word* of the story He penned for you. Pray without ceasing. Ask God again and again, even if you've been asking for years. For asking keeps us connected to the One of Whom we're asking and is the very best way to be awake and expectant.

Beloved, hard is hard, and slathering it with whitewash doesn't help anyone, so you can count on me *not* to do that. What I *will* do though . . . is remind you . . . that you are seen, heard, known, and loved—that God is *with you* and will see you through.

Day 52

LIVIN' YOUR LIFE

She would live the life.

Yes. She would live the life her God had assigned to her, the life to which she was called. The life that at times didn't make sense to the world or even to her, for that matter, but then again, why would it?

She would live the life, remaining as she was when she was called instead of desperately trying to *change* who she was by morphing into another sister on Earth, making good use of her *very own* present condition, for who she *is*, is *exactly* who her God created her to be, and God wants her to run her race . . . free from anxiety. *Yes.* So she would run her race without the hindrance of forgetfulness when it came to the God Who had sent her for such a time as this into the very life ordained for her before the foundation of the world.

And as she ran, she'd look back at her younger self—and all those younger than her, for that matter—and she'd tell them, "You don't have to catch up. I started long before you did." For she wished that once upon a time someone before her would've spoken those words to her. Yes.

She would live the life. She would live *her* life. She would run her race, resting in the knowledge that *all* things are from God, even the stuff she didn't like or couldn't make sense of. She'd trust that all things have purpose, because she knows if she doesn't, she'll never make it outta this thing we call life alive—not to mention the fact that if she doesn't, there's no way she'll be able to truly love her neighbor as herself. Right.

She would live her life. Her holy whole life. The life scripted for her by the Author of her Story and Perfecter of her Faith long before she had lived out even Day One . . . and she'd oftentimes pause to remind herself . . . that *perfect* means whole and complete. It sure does. She would live the life . . . *her* life . . . and be grateful for it. For it seemed to her . . . a pretty great way to live. Amen.

{1 Corinthians 7–9}

BRING IT ON

Beloved, God will bring you to uncomfortable so you can see what needs to be done.

What kind of God would intentionally burn your craw and break your last straw? Gee, I don't know . . . perhaps a God Who is *stoking your fire or forcing you to finally get off the camel*? Just a thought. Because I've been there. So has Gideon. And Mordecai. And a whole host of others now residing in the cloud cheering us on.

Beloved, as I've said before, because God's ways are *higher* than ours, they're *different* than ours—meaning they're not always the ways *we* would choose. And when God brings us to *uncomfortable*? Well, we rush right past it. Cuz we don't like it. Rough cloth sure ain't silk.

But what if we take the uncomfortable and reframe it . . . seeing it as God's way of showing us something we need to see . . . thus allowing us to rename it and actually call it a gift instead of some kind of punishment?? I know, right? Game. Changer.

Now before I go, let me add this—you will hear it said that "nothing good comes out of your comfort zone." And to that, I call bull. Here's why: Our comfort zones are often indicators of our truest gifts and callings. For example, while the majority of the population fears public speaking over dying, I feel most *alive* when I speak, when I write. Exactly.

So how about instead of clinging to a phrase that I think can do more harm than good, we quit resorting to either/or and start embracing the "and." Good things can come out of my comfort zone—*and*—God will at times bring me to uncomfortable in order to show me something I need to see so I can ask myself what I can do, what needs to be done, so I can sit with it long enough to ask God, "Why did You bring me here?" and then go from there.

Beloved, the prayer I wrote this morn is this: "O God, Giver of Life, Give me Life, in this New Stage of Life." Yes.

And if it's the uncomfortable of new for me that brings about even *more life*? Well then, bring on the uncomfortable.

BELIEVING LIFTS

Nothing will lift you up out of the pit or raise you up from the dead faster than believing.
Amen. Believing that God will make all things right. Believing God will provide. Believing there is more in the storehouse for you. Believing it just hasn't yet been your time. Believing that God is with you, goes before you, and has chosen you for the callings God's given you. Believing that God still rolls away stones and parts seas and calls forth life from the grave and completely transforms what was into something brand new, even naming it A New Thing. Believing that you are worthy not because you belong, but that you belong because you are worthy. Believing that your current sufferings can't even *compare* to the glory that's about to be revealed to you.

My mind goes to two sisters at their brother's tomb who had *no* idea they were just moments away from witnessing a miracle. And maybe, Beloved, *you are too.* And that's why you don't stop believing. And as a result, you keep on asking your God for what it is that you need, what it is that you want. And you do it because your faith, not your fear, reminds you that *you can.*

It *also* reminds you that you're talking to the One for Whom all things are possible and nothing is too hard—not to mention the One Who has vowed to love you forever and never leave or forsake you, *ever.* The One Who wrote your story, complete with a calling that is irrevocable, so maybe it's time to make peace with it. And live fully into it. Trusting God through it. Reminding yourself that you can trust God and still not *like* every part of it, despite what stupid Christian memes tell you. Psst . . . your humanness does NOT negate your holiness, and *please* for the love of God hear *that* in all caps.

Beloved, should you find yourself in a pit of despair, or in a valley that feels much like death . . . believe. That where you are is not where you always will be. That God's plan for you is good all the way through to the end. That you are loved without fail and always will be by the One Who created you by His own Spirit—the One Whose very breath gives you life.

PROCEED TO THE ROUTE

The Word of God taught her that she didn't need to compete in order to win. She didn't need to prove anything in order to be worthy. She didn't need to make sense of every twist and turn and redirection of her journey in order to proceed to the route.

She learned that not everyone who follows her is cheering her on. Jesus used the Pharisees to show her that. She learned that Judas is as much a part of God's plan as John.

She learned that Earthquakes have been known to roll away stones that stand in the way, and strong winds have been known to part seas. She learned that twists and turns and redirections are a result of her God going before her, knowing which way is best for her . . . even when she can't understand why and complains "Are we there yet?" every few miles. Just like her ancestors did. She learned that daily bread doesn't always look like daily bread according to what she thinks a good loaf of daily bread should look like. So again, like her ancestors, she ends up calling it Manna, which of course means, "What the heck is *this*??" She learned that she has permission to speak for herself. And for any "that's not biblical, Tera" folks in the crowd, I'll kindly direct you to my reading today, specifically Acts 26:1. Amen.

She learned that mountains are for climbing and building up strength, not some kind of punishment from a God Who hates her guts. She learned that waits . . . are . . . OK. Yes. She's learned a *lot*. About who *she* is . . . because of who her *god* is. The One within her giving her breath. The One Who will never leave or forsake her. The One Who is with her *wherever* she goes. And *that's* why she can be strong and courageous.

Beloved, life is short. And God is good. Sit with the One Who fearfully and wonderfully formed you . . . and discover who you always have been. Loved. Cherished. Worthy. Packed with power and purpose and sent to this Earth to fulfill every Word your God wrote for you.

I could go on, but I reckon I've kept you long enough. You are seen, you are heard, you are known, Beloved. And don't you forget it. Amen.

REMEMBER

She had to remember . . .

And maybe today, you do too. Yes. You *have* to remember if you're gonna keep from drowning, keep from receding, keep from being completely swept off your feet—but not in the good way like on TV. Right.

She had to remember that God used storms to show her she could walk on water. Used Earthquakes to roll away stones. Used strong winds to part the seas, creating a way for her to cross safely. She had to remember that God speaks through fire and leads using clouds and is Creator of both—yes, *both*. Light *and* dark, day *and* night, which means there is dang good reason for each of 'em. Yes.

She had to remember. She had to remember that stretching often brings healing and climbing always brings strength. She had to remember that God has been known to send angels into dens of hungry lions and into guarded prison cells made of cement and into stinky smelly tombs that held the sleeping. She had to remember in the heat of her day, her week, her month, her year, that the very best thing she can do in those times is to take a seat at the well and talk it all out with Jesus. Cuz see, she had to remember that self-care without soul-care isn't self-care at all . . . for to be human is to be *both* flesh and soul. Yes. She had to remember in the midst of all that she could *not* understand . . . that it is all for *something* . . . because Purpose is God's middle name. Yes.

She had to remember. That joy comes in the morning and after the mourning. That beauty really does rise from ashes. That all things really do work together for good and that the final word of her story penned by her Author really and truly is "Amen."

Yes. She had to remember. And maybe today, Beloved, you do too.

GOD IS ALWAYS WITH YOU

Joe was sold. Esther was orphaned. Moses was sent downstream. Naomi was widowed. Jonah thrown overboard. Hagar kicked to the curb. But God was with them all. And, Beloved, God is also with you.

Beloved, if I do *anything* in this space, I hope it's to feed your soul enough daily bread that you actually feel revived and alive, even if just for the day, or the moment. I mean it. Those names above that you just read? There could have been a *ton* more. Seriously. Folks from Scripture who couldn't *possibly* understand every word of their human-existence story, especially in light of their very real realities. No doubt. And, of course, you and I could add our names too. Amen to that.

Beloved, let their stories feed you, strengthen you. Let them remind you that you aren't alone. Let them cheer you on when the words in *your* story don't make sense either . . . or flat-out royally suck. Job is free if you need someone to talk to. Word. Hang out with these peeps as they tell you their stories of adversities and troubles and trials and places they didn't want to go and circumstances they didn't want to be in and situations that were about as close to hell on Earth as you can get. And then . . . stay with them as they finish their stories. Listen to them 'til the end. Hear from them how despite every obstacle and challenge they faced in the plans their God had for them . . . God never left them. God was always, always *with* them.

Yes. And *because* God was with them, they overcame. They rose again and persevered again and prayed again and believed again. And their stories were one for the books. Or at least one. (Grin.)

Beloved, hear me loud and hear me clear and hear me knowing that I wouldn't say it to you if I didn't believe with every ounce of me that it's true. God was *with* them. And God—their God, *our* God, our Providing and Protecting and All-Powerful God—is also, *also* with *you*. Amen. And Amen. And every Amen on Earth as it is in Heaven. Amen. I mean it.

{Acts 7}

POWER IN THE WAIT

We want to know when . . . Jesus reminds us, you won't know when . . . but you will have power in the wait. Hallelujah.

The apostles wanted to know, "Lord, is this the time when you will restore?" Is it Lord? Is it?

And see, you and I, we get that. We too wanna know. Jesus would answer the apostles, which is great because now we know too. . . . You won't know when. It's not for you to know the times or periods that God has set by God's own authority. What, not the answer you were hoping for? I hear ya. But see, that's why we read on. Cuz there's gotta be more, right? Indeed.

You won't know the *when* . . . but you *will* have *power* in the *wait*. Thank. God.

Power in the wait. Power to trust and believe and return to the truth that God has worked all things together for good. Power to be still and know that God is God and there is no other, and then remember that same said God is Provider, Protector, All-Powerful. And if there's a wait, then by golly there's a dang good reason for it. Right. Power to live in the wait and plant in the wait and build in the wait and love one another in the wait and not delay living in the wait because history tells us through Scripture that the wait may, in fact, be a while. Yup.

Power in the wait. For God vowed to never leave you or forsake you, and that promise *also* holds true in the wait. Yes. You have *power* in your Wait for the When . . . because the Holy Spirit Breath of God within you is *giving you life*, yes and amen. We don't have all the answers. But what we *do* have . . . is *power in the wait*. The power within us . . . reminding us that redemption always comes . . . resurrection is to be expected . . . reality seriously bites sometimes, but there's always, always a reason . . . even if we can't understand it. Yes.

Power in the Wait. To trust that indeed there is good reason for the Wait and believing that we will one day look back and realize just what that good reason was.

{Acts 1:6–8}

THE PEACE OF JESUS

"My peace I give to you."—Jesus

The peace of knowing that all things have been worked together for good and knowing that good means sufficient to fulfill the purpose, and then knowing Whose purpose we're talking about. The peace that arises each time you remember that God is with you, *within* you, giving you God's own breath as a holy guarantee so that your heart needn't be troubled during your stint here on Earth.

The peace that calms you in the midst of the storm that won't seem to end, when you remember that God speaks to you from the eye of the storm, which means God is not only *in* your storm *with* you . . . God is also speaking to you *from* the calm . . . because God knows what you don't . . . I Am gonna see you through this. The peace of knowing that all storms eventually end, all seasons eventually change, and all droughts eventually see rain. The peace of knowing that there won't be one single second today when God has given up sovereignty.

Friends, today as I read, I couldn't help but hear Jesus, like *really* hear Jesus—the tone of His voice, the urgency, the realness and rawness that causes someone to *really* believe what the person talking to them is saying.

"Peace I leave you, *My* peace I give you."

My peace. The same peace I have. The peace I have about doing all the things I've been sent here to do, even though I didn't like all the things, even though I begged God to bring it about a different way, pleading with God in the garden that day so that *you* would know that *sometimes you'll feel that way too.*

And *when* you do, Beloved, you'll know I did too. But that didn't change the script written for me or the purpose for which I was sent. And the same is true for you. The whole and holy script written for you, including all of its joy and all of its sorrow, all of its pleasure and all of its pain, is the work of the Author and is one that *you*, Beloved, have been sent here to live. Yes, your story *really is* that powerful. And guess what? There's peace in knowing *that* too.

{John 14:27}

YOU WILL RISE AGAIN

She who believes will rise again and again and again.

Because believing resurrects. It sure does. It rolls away stones and brings forth life from the grave. Thank God. It awakens the part of her that has fallen asleep. And sometimes she'd welcome the wake-up call. Other times not so much. Right.

So in those times, she'd remind herself of the Who and the Why . . . and that reminding gave her the strength and the zeal to rise . . . again. Believing all God had spoken through the One Who was sent would prove to be life to her soul, pouring new life into her spirit each time it felt like it hadn't quite reached its daily living water goal. And some days, most days actually, her bones would dance and her voice would sing . . . because resurrected life will do that.

And each morning would be a new chance to dance. A new birth to behold. A new opportunity to believe. And rise yet again. For after the dark of the mourn . . . comes the morn. Yes, *after*. Not before, for mourning deserves its time too. Time to mourn the loss of what is no longer, whatever that death may be. It could be the death of a marriage, relationship, job; a goal you had put on a deadline; a dream you once had that you've decided is best left to slumber . . . and you're OK with it, actually, because new dreams have come. That happens when we sleep or when things die—*new* comes from those times. Yes.

Beloved, she who believes . . . will rise again . . . and again . . . and again . . . because believing is breath to the soul. It revives, it restores, and it resurrects. It's really reeeally good. Believing. That God is Provider, Protector, All-Powerful. That God is sovereign over *all* things. That God wrote the Scripture known as your story and will be with you until the final "Amen." That your calling is irrevocable, and your power is undeniable because the One Who created you gave you both. That your purpose can't be altered or thwarted by anyone or anything because your purpose ain't up for grabs. Heck no. It's secure. In the hands of the One Who calls you Mine.

And today, Beloved, you're gonna *believe* that. And *rise. Again.*

{John 11}

ALONE WITH JESUS

Alone with Jesus . . .

Where she'd be reminded of her value, where her soul felt its worth. Alone with Jesus . . . where she'd come to learn that her story is a vital part of the overall book. It's also where she learned about Who'd authored her story in full, from "In the Beginning" to final "Amen" before she had lived even day one and was perfecting her faith, making it whole and complete, as each page written for her unfolded. *Yes.*

Alone with Jesus . . . where she could cry and He would cry with her, knowing she couldn't possibly understand all of God's ways because they, of course, extend far beyond her human reach. Alone with Jesus . . . where she'd hear words of empathetic compassion such as, "You don't know what I Am doing right now, but someday you will." And at least that gave her *some* comfort. Or at least helped her not feel as dumb in her wondering/questioning, especially as a number of Christian-folks said stupid stuff like "You *should just . . .* " or "What you *need* to do is . . ."

Beloved, today in John 8, I read again the story of yet another "*the* woman." You may know some of the others. *The* woman at the well. *The* woman hunched over. *The* woman with the issue of blood. Today's daily reading was *the* woman caught in adultery. *Which*, by the way, the KJV translates as *taken* into adultery . . . which, my-my-my, doesn't *that* put a different spin on this story. *Amen. It sure does.* But again, another time.

The woman. Alone with Jesus . . . where *she found her own voice.* Where she was Named, not referred to as Less-Than. Where she was lifted up instead of beaten down. Where she was freely given the space to ask questions, give answers, and *not* be condemned for it. *Hallelujah*-no-wonder-we-love-this-guy-Jesus.

Alone with Jesus . . . where she was fed the words of life from the Bread of Life, and she ate them up because they tasted so much better than what the majority of the world is serving. Yes. It was *soul* food. *Filling* her and *fueling* her and causing her *not to forget* who she is. . . . Reminding her she belongs here. Amen.

{John 8:1–11}

A TIME FOR EVERYTHING

Not one thing will happen in your life before its time.

Not. One. Thing. Not one word will be revealed to you until you get to its page in your story, and not one thing will happen before the words "Now it came to pass . . ." precede 'em. Right.

Ya know how sometimes when you're reading a book, you just wanna "get to the good part"? And although you can skip ahead if you want, it doesn't change the placement of where the words are in the story. Or ya know how when you go to the movies, and there's what you think is a slow part, so you get up to go potty cuz you already drank your large Diet Dew, and when you return, you whisper to your companion, "Did I miss anything?" Either way, "the good part" you're waiting for is gonna come whenever the writer has written it into the story.

Beloved, truly I tell you, not *one* thing in your life will happen before its time because, to put it frankly, you ain't the Author. You didn't write the powerful full-of-purpose story written for you before the foundation of the world. I didn't write mine either. So see, you and I can't possibly be privy to all that will unfold for us as each word is revealed, each paragraph is lived, each chapter is finished. And let's face it—our humanness couldn't possibly make sense of it anyway; it'd be like turning to a page near the back of the book, reading one sentence, and wondering why it makes no sense. *Hello*, why would it when all words preceding them are necessary to get us to them?

Beloved, not one thing in your life will happen before its time. *And* (not but) . . . it doesn't mean that at times you won't hate the wait. Or despise the dead spots. Or even begin to wonder if it's such a great book after all. It doesn't even mean you have to love the thing when it actually *does* come to pass, because every one of us has things come to pass that we so desperately wish wouldn't. Fact. What it *does* mean . . . is that our story is written . . . by the Author of our story . . . and *that* Author says . . . This is *My* book . . . with whom I Am well pleased.

ASK GOD FOR LIFE

She asked God for life . . . and God gave it to her.

It came in the form of new mountains to climb and the strength and the confidence she would gain by climbing each one. It came in the help that was sent from the sanctuary of Heaven above through those who walked beside her on Earth . . . and the angels who were sent to roll away stones that stood in the way of the path carved out for her. It came in the Word made flesh as she ate of it each morning while hearing the Voice that she knew without doubt heard hers . . . This is My body . . . given for you . . . take . . . and eat.

And she did. And when she did, she remembered. And that remembering . . . was life. Yes. Remembering that God was within her, that God went before her, and that God would never leave or forsake her. Remembering that God had written her story in full before the foundation of the world, including every word she couldn't possibly understand and every chapter she wished would've never made the Final Cut. But of course . . . they all needed to, because every paragraph had purpose, and every syllable would sing of God's unfailing presence, and that was a song worthy of singing. Yes.

It came in the form of water poured out for her as she asked for a drink, knowing full well it was living water that she would intake. It came in the form of the truths she would never abandon and the promises she'd never give up, for she knew that they were both life. True life. Real and raw and full-of-all-the-joys-*and*-all-the-sorrows life. Abundant life. Whole life, not half-life, because half-life would never again be enough—not after experiencing whole. Life in the form of words that would never pass away but instead would become a part of her very DNA. Life that would sustain her.

She asked God for life . . . and God gave it to her. For with every breath that she took, she knew . . . You are here. You will *always* be here. Until I breathe my last. And come back home to You.

Beloved, ask God for Life.

CLOSE TO THE ONE

She prayed without ceasing for one simple reason. She wanted to be close to the One.

Years lived and wisdom gained had taught her it wasn't about getting her way. It wasn't about overpowering the hand that had written her story along with everyone else's on Earth. It wasn't about understanding every word written for her or for others, for there were some she would never understand.

But that's not why she prayed without ceasing. She prayed without ceasing for one simple reason: she wanted to be close to the One.

The One Who held her, covered her, consoled her . . . especially on those I-just-can't-understand days. The One Who bends an ear to listen to her, the One Who would comfort her as she cried and collect all her tears, reassuring her they'd be put to good use, for wasting them wasn't an option. The One from whom no secrets are hidden, all things are known, and not even the darkness is dark. The One Who once rolled away stones that stood in the way and *still does* . . . so she wants eyes wide open to see and recognize Who it is that is doing the rolling. The One Who controls the winds and the waves and commands the sun to rise and to set and to sometimes even stand still. The One Who prepares feasts in wildernesses and meets women at wells worn out from their journeys, nodding at them with a smile while seated himself as he whispers, "Me too, girl." Because empathy is a powerful thing. Indeed. It reminds us we aren't alone.

Close to the One for Whom all things are possible, and nothing is too hard. The One Who repeatedly says, "Do not fear"—not because there aren't things to fear in this world, but because *I Am with you and I Myself* go before you *wherever* you go, and *that* is why I tell you to be strong and courageous because knowing I Am with you . . . you *can*.

The One Who is indeed Provider. Protector. All-Powerful. The One Who is Sovereign over all things, *all* things, and all means *all*. Amen. Close to the One Who is *as near as her very own breath. That* is why she prayed without ceasing. She wanted to be close to the One.

THE WAIT YOU HATE

What if the wait that you hate is actually the gift of time from your God?

Lord, as I once again wait . . . I know it has purpose. And that purpose could very well be . . . the gift of *time*. It sure could.

The time I've begged You to slow down, and now that You have, I'm torked off about it. (sorry bout that, by the way). Time to think and to process and to sort things out. Time to get other stuff done. Right. Time to ponder, consider, perhaps even change my mind like folks sometimes do when they're waiting at the salon, like, ya know what? Maybe I *will* go blonde. Just sayin'.

Time. Time for things to take root. Time for things to heal. Time for things to work together for good according to God's purpose in Heaven. Time to make some decisions without feeling rushed. Time to calm some of the fears. Time to wrestle with You, Lord, in the midst of the wait . . . to build up my strength for the next steps I'll take. Time to toss and to turn in the dark of the night, in the storm that won't seem to end . . . and then to remember that You are asleep in the boat, reminding me that I too can rest, knowing full well that You control every wave that crashes and every strong wind that blows. Amen.

Time. Time to breathe and be still and remind myself . . . wait a minute, I *know* Who my God is. I *know* God is here. I *know* God is real. I *know* that I *know* that I *know* that God wastes *nothing*, including every *wait* I endure, and I *know* that God loves the world without end. Amen. Dang right.

So today, Beloved, maybe you'd like to join me in considering. . . . Could the *wait* you *hate* . . . be a *gift*?

WRITE WHAT YOU KNOW

Write what you know.

As I was fervently writing out all the things I didn't know, all the questions I have that I'm eagerly (and impatiently) awaiting answers to . . . *this* is word-for-word what I heard . . .

"Tera, write what you know."

Yes. Write what you *do* know in the midst of all that you *don't* know; I *assure* you it's the best thing you can do. So I did. I wrote what I know, and here's what I wrote . . .

"Lord, I know You are with me. I know You are for me. I know You Yourself go before me. I know You know the plans that You have for me because You wrote my story in full before I lived even day one. I know my calling is irrevocable. I know there are no returns or exchanges. I know that my purpose is holy, and therefore oftentimes lies far beyond what my humanness can grasp. I know that You are good and that Your steadfast love endures forever and that nothing can *ever* separate me from it.

"I know You are Provider, Protector, All-Powerful, and that You will indeed reign forever. I know that the enemy is under my feet and that You are above all things. I know that believing is breathing for my soul, keeping it alive and excited and expectant for what still remains in Your storehouse for me. I know there is a reason for everything under the sun, and I know that sometimes I won't like the season I'm in. I know that the waits that I hate are strengthening me, and the mountains I'm forced to climb are building endurance and perseverance within me. I know that at times my journey will make me sick, because twists and turns will do that. I know there will be dead ends and detours, and so I'll expect them and rename them Redirections.

"I know Wisdom will call out from the streets I travel, and I know listening to her will be beneficial. I know, Lord, that You listen, and I know that You care, and so I will continue to cast all my worries upon You. I know that my tears are precious to You, which is why You collect them, and I am convinced You will use them to water the land You're next taking me to. I sure do. *XO.*"

DON'T STOP

Don't stop praying. Don't stop hoping. Don't stop believing. Don't stop. Period.

Jesus told his peeps: Don't you stop praying. That's right. Don't you stop. Don't you stop asking God day and night for what it is that you *need*, what it is that you *want*. Don't stop praying.

Don't you stop hoping. I mean it. For hope is the means by which you'll move forward, and forward is the direction you're going. And should your hope begin to wear thin . . . you stop and remind yourself that a thread is enough to hold on to. Don't stop hoping.

Don't you stop believing. That there is more yet to come. That there is good to behold. That God will, in fact, provide and protect and perform miracles right in your midst. Yes. Don't stop believing.

Beloved, don't stop praying. Ask God, beg God, talk to God however it looks. Don't stop hoping. It's fuel for your soul, and just like your car, you need it to go. Don't stop believing. Believing is like breathing, it keeps you alive, opening your eyes wide like a child eagerly waiting to go downstairs on Christmas morn.

Yes. Don't stop praying. Don't stop hoping. Don't stop believing. Don't stop.

Because truly I tell you, Beloved, and in the words of the seriously amazing Aerosmith . . . You really *don't* wanna miss a thing. Amen.

{1 Thessalonians 5:17}

EVEN IN THE DROUGHT

Today might be a really good day to remind yourself that even in the drought, God provides.

That even in the desert, bread from Heaven continues to fall. That even in the pit, there is already a plan in place for the rescue. That even in the wait, there is something to hold on to, a little thing called Hope, which is both the greatest thing you can hold on to and the hardest thing to hold on to the longer the wait. Yes.

Today might be a really good day to remind yourself that even when things don't go as you planned, go as you wanted, go as you dreamed that they would for as far back as you can remember, God *still* provides in those places because Provider is Who God *is*, and God is not limited by location on Earth, thank God. Hallelujah. Amen. Yes.

A Provider God Who hangs out in hospital rooms and the floors of public restrooms as you're hurling your guts out. A Provider God Who sends angels into dens of lions and really good peeps on the side of the road when you find yourself broken down there. A Provider God Who sends a big, massive fish into big, stormy seas to not only save you from drowning, but perhaps more importantly, to give you some time to think. Yes. A Provider God Who places a creek to sit beside when you're feeling about as tossed out as last week's trash . . . so you can peer into it, see your reflection, and be reminded of just how truly valuable your life on Earth is as you see the face of God looking back. Yes.

Beloved, even in the drought, God provides. Even when we don't recognize it. Even if we don't call it what it is—daily bread. Even when instead, we name it what our ancestors the Israelites named it—Manna. Best translated as, "What the heck is *this*?" Exactly. (And also seriously one of my fave OMG-moments over the years, which is why you've seen it here in this space before.) Yes. Because it's so dang true. Amen.

Beloved, today might be a really good day to remind yourself that even in the ____, God provides. For truly I tell you, this knowing will in fact open your eyes to *see* it. *XO.*

GROWING STRONG

The place you don't want to be is the place you will grow strong in spirit.

The wilderness. The desert. The pit you were tossed into. The den full of lions. The guts of a fish. The storm to end all storms. The flood that just won't end. The side of the creek all alone. The endless rows of barley to glean. The well that feels more like a hellish reminder of just how bad your life sucks. The hard places. Yes. The places you don't want to be. The places you're tempted to name "Maybe God's Not with Me after All."

You know those places. Those hard places. Scripture is *filled* with peeps who know those places. And lest you've forgotten all that is stored in their stories, check the cloud. I mean it. Cuz see, the cloud will tell you something that may just encourage you. Big time. They will tell you that in those places where they *never* wanted to be . . . was where they grew *strong in spirit*. That's right. *And* they will tell you that in hindsight, they realized they *had* to be in those places, to *strengthen their spirit*, because they would *go on* to be *used mightily*, and they would *need a strong spirit* to do it. Amen. Absolutely.

Beloved, today's post was sparked, as it oftentimes is, by just a few words, and those few words were these . . . "The child grew and became strong in spirit, and he was in the wilderness until the day he appeared publicly . . ." Referring to our guy John. But again, check the cloud. They'll concur.

Beloved, if you find yourself some place you don't want to be but have no choice but to be there . . . rename it. I mean it. Call it "The Place I'm Growing Strong in Spirit." And believe it. I love you. Amen.

{Luke 1:80}

WHEN THE TIME IS NOT YET

According to the clock, the time was not yet.

What if we adopted this new way of answering the question of "When?" . . . when we're not seeing what we wanna be seeing? Not yet. Yep. What time is it? Oh, let me check my watch. It looks like the time is . . . *not yet.*

Beloved, today's reading included the story of Jesus and a fig tree. The NRSV was "OK," but holy mother of Moses, I just wanted to buy Ole King James roses when I read his translation. Seriously. Cuz see, my NRSV said, "for it was not the season of figs"; which is all fine and dandy, but the KJV ? The KJV put it *this* way . . . "for the time of figs was not *yet.*" And you guys, the "yet" was even italicized. I know, right?

So to recap the story: Jesus was hungry. The disciples were with Him. Jesus knew that when the disciples were with Him, it was *all* about training them—which is why it included hard things, cuz training is hard. He comes to a fig tree with leaves but no figs . . . because the time of figs was *not yet.* Exactly. With his guys within earshot, Jesus says to the tree, "No one's ever gonna eat from you." And they all go on their merry way.

The *next* day, as they're passing through, there's the fig tree, all withered up. And leave it to Pete to say something. Pete says to Jesus, "Hey, look! There's that fig tree you told yesterday would never bear fruit. It's all withered up."

Ding, ding, ding. Someone get Jesus a disco ball, please.

Cuz see, in true Jesus fashion, he had set the stage for a teaching. Cuz see, right at that moment, Jesus says to the guys, of all things . . . "Have faith in God." Except I think it sounded more like, "Have faith in *God.*"

Not in the words spoken to you from a world that can't possibly understand that the reason you aren't producing figs at this moment is because the time for your figs is *not yet.* Exactly. Have faith in God. In God's timing. According to God's purpose. Because you know what, Beloved? Do you wanna know when you'll see figs? When it's the *right season for your figs. Amen.* Exactly.

{Mark 11:12–26}

IT ONLY TAKES ONE

It only takes one.

If I decide to go on a hike in the wilderness and I get lost, do you know what I'm gonna call the voice of one crying out in that wilderness? *Enough.* I sure am. *One* voice crying out when you're alone and you're lost? Exactly. *Enough*, Baby, we call that *enough. Cuz one is enough.*

One drop of oil and one scant cup of flour when your cupboards are like Old Mother Hubbard's. One tiny cloud way up in the sky when you haven't seen raindrops for months. One sack lunch when you're like seriously starving, and there's a whole gaggle of you that are like seriously hangry, cuz I mean, it's been like a whole buncha hours since you've eaten, hello?! One thread on the hem of the robe. Enough to grab on to. One whisper from God calling you by name so that you can name that voice just like Hagar did . . . "The God Who *sees* me." . . . Oh, yes. Sees me all alone here . . . with my crying child . . . not knowing what in the heck I should do.

Yes. One is enough. One seed so tiny you can hardly see it. Enough to produce an entire tree that will protect you and provide for you in ways you haven't even imagined. One move into the palace like Esther. One call to head home like Nehemiah. One field to glean where you will be noticed showing the faith you have gleaned just like Ruth. Indeed.

One call. One text. One afternoon nap. One day away. One day spent at home. One chance meeting that wasn't by chance at all that is now sending you in a supercool new direction. Yes. One undeniable OMG-encounter like Thomas . . . with the One Who formed you, knit you, calls you by name, and wrote every word of your story from "In the beginning" to final "amen," not to mention Who is also *perfecting* (making whole and complete) the faith you've been given every step that you take. Amen. I'm not kidding.

Beloved, it only takes one. One is enough. To keep hoping and believing and trusting and not forgetting . . . that the God Who is Parent, Provider, Protector . . . is absolutely with you and for you. *XO*.

{Mark 1}

HOLD ON TO THE AFTER

After the suffering . . .

If your heart grabbed hold of the *after*. . . . Perfect, then you didn't miss it. Cuz see, that's what our heart-mind-soul-strength needs to hold on to in times of suffering . . . the *after*. Absolutely. Knowing and trusting and believing that there will indeed be . . . an *after*. *Yes*.

After the suffering. After the flood. After this war finally ends. After the trauma. After the storm. After the time in this den of lions that look like they're seriously ready to eat. After the heartache. After the headache. After the ache we're not even sure how to name. After the change we never wanted. After the change we literally begged God for. After the change that comes as sure as the seasons, whether we like it or not.

Yes. After. After the trial has ended. After the summit's been reached. After the thing you've been dreading or the thing you are living through right now is finally, *finally* behind you. After the wait for God's sake. Yes. After the suffering.

Beloved, I want you today to hold on to the *after* . . . knowing and trusting and believing that there *will* be an After. For just as all those who have gone before us . . . *after* . . . is a part of our story. For it is written. It sure is. I love you. Amen.

*Bonus Content: Did you know that one of the definitions of "after" is "the stern of a boat"? *And* did you know that when the disciples were caught in a storm they thought for *sure* would completely wipe them out, that *that*'s where they found Jesus sleeping? Huh. You don't suppose Jesus was showing them that they could find rest in knowing that there is an After and that He is in fact already there . . . do you? *Just sayin'*.

YOUR BACKUP PLAN

Her backup plan was she just knew that God would somehow provide.

Once upon a time, a girl arose early. Approximately thirteen minutes before the birds began to sing—belting out their songs, making plans for their day. She grabbed her journal along with her coffee, for both were a big part of her daily habit. And after those first few sips in the dark, she grabbed her pen and became a psalmist. *Yes.* She poured out on the page all her fears, all her doubts, all her worries, and the realest reals of her realities, holding nothing back, cuz why bother when talking to the One Who knows you right down to the number of hairs on your head.

So there she sat, pouring out her realities onto the page, knowing there was no reason to hide or to fear. And then, she poured out all of the ways in her current realities in which God was good indeed *and* in deed. Yes. And after she did, she felt a weight lifted—actually, balanced would be the far better word. The scale before her, her worries about her current realities on one side, and all the ways God is currently providing *in deed* on the other. For see, in becoming a psalmist, she had learned to balance her song with just the right mix. And so, with song in soul and the scales of justice before her, she wrote out these words . . .

Her back-up plan was she just knew that God would somehow provide. Cuz that's what a Provider does.

Then she set down her pen and picked up her Bible, eager to read today's readings. And lo and behold, she would start the book of Ruth. A story drenched in the incredible ways God provides. And see, it's in *those* moments, moments just like that, when God becomes not only *real*, but real to *you*. A personal God Who reaches through the chaos of your world and grabs you by the shoulders while looking into the eyes that He made and says . . . *I see you*, and I will *provide*.

Friends, that once upon a time was this morning. And that girl was me. God *will* provide. Hold on to that. And keep singin' your song. *All* your songs. And *all* your psalms. God is far closer than you think. And God sees you in *all* your realities. *XO*.

THE SEDENTARY SOUL

Is your soul living a sedentary life?

Experts say that a sedentary lifestyle is killing us. All the sitting and scrolling instead of standing and strolling is having a significant effect on our bods, so I have to wonder. . . . Because we are human and because being human means we are both body *and* soul, today's question to consider is this . . .

Is your *soul* living a sedentary lifestyle? Is *that* why you feel like you're simply going through the motions robotically instead of owning and using your aliveness fully? To move mountains perhaps. Or climb them. Or finally quit circling 'round them.

For truly I tell you, Beloved, a soul that is alive and active produces *that* kind of faith. It sure does. It sings "Don't Stop Believin'" all day long, and that singing reminds the soul what to do. It marches and marches and marches some more until something finally starts to give, and the wall comes tumbling down. It does what *looks* to be impossible. But with God, all things in fact *are* possible. And that word *all* sparks the soul even more, and you just can't hide that kinda spark, not even under a bushel. No.

I did a quick search of the signs of a sedentary lifestyle—let's see how they translate to our souls, shall we? Great. You're moody. Short of breath. You find yourself tossing and turning at night because you haven't spent any of your energy. So no wonder it's ready to party. OK, I totally tweaked that last one, but am I right?

You find yourself forgetting stuff. Your tank is always low. You don't have the drive to get up and go, so you go ahead and keep it in park and then get mad that you're not seeing new sights. OK, I totally added that one, but hello, again, am I right?

Beloved, believing is to your soul . . . what breathing is to your lungs. You need *both* to fully live. Ya know the verse that says how faith without works is dead? I don't think we need to read that as a stern shaking of the finger, but more as a very calm matter-of-fact fact. We are indeed human, my friend. Which means we are both body and soul. Let's keep both alive, OK? Cuz we've got *so* darn much light to shine.

THE NEW YOU ARE LONGING FOR

The new you are longing for may not align with your calendar.

On the last day of the month, I got up and did what I do. I started the coffee, drank my water, let the dog out, and headed to the BFJC (Big Fat Jesus Chair.) I journaled, I penned, I prepared to preach this weekend and next. And then, I picked up my DRB (daily reading Bible), for this too is what it is that I do.

"Huh," I said to myself, "I start the New Testament today."

Just like that, the old has gone, and the new has come.

"Gee, God," I said, "too bad it didn't come *tomorrow* on the *first* day of a new month instead of *today* on the *last* day."

God interrupted. Hey, I took no offense, because God knows He has to if He's gonna get a word in edgewise with the Chatty Cathy He so fearfully and wonderfully formed. *Word.*

"Oh, my Girl," He said, "*that's* the point—My *new*, the *new* you are *longing for*, the *new* you have been asking Me for, at times *begging* me for . . . won't always align with your calendar."

I know, right? And then, what was *really* amazing is that I heard what sounded like a crowd at an '80s rock concert all belting out in unison the lyrics to their song, and from what I could make out, the lyrics were . . . "Amen to *that*!" Turns out, it was the Crowd that is the Cloud, and frankly, I'm just glad there'll be '80s rock playin' when I get there.

Beloved, I know you get what I'm saying today. And I know because God made it as clear as the opposite of clear as mud. The *new* you are longing for . . . may not always align with your calendar. So we have to ask ourselves, or at least I think we should: Is the new we are longing for . . . worth sacrificing the comfort attached to our calendar?

I know the answer for me. And I'd bet hard cash money it's the same for you. Amen. Rock on. And *XO*.

SEASONS CHANGE

Are you in a season you hate? Hear the good news: Seasons change.

You don't have to love where you are.

Isn't it nice to have someone say that out loud? It's like it relieves some of the pressure you feel to pretend to love where you are because that's what a good Christian does, gimme a break and amen. Seriously. As a matter of fact, you can hate where you are . . . *and* . . . still rejoice and get excited about what's coming next. Yes.

Currently in a season you hate? Good news—seasons change! Exactly. (Squeals in her bring-on-the-pumpkin-spice-voice.) Now, is the transition always easy? Please, ask your allergies. But the season you are in will, in fact, *not* stay the same because seasons change and that's *gotta* be why God designed it to be that way—to show us that very cool fact. Amen. *Yes.* So just think, this most basic of truths—seasons change—may be *exactly* the very thing you needed to hear today. And if so, I'm so glad you're here.

Beloved, seasons change, and we change with the seasons. It's why we write letters to our younger selves and wish our younger selves would've written letters to us. Seasons change. The promises of God . . . *remain.* Throughout the seasons. Throughout the ages. Throughout the eons and eras. I Am with you. In *every* season. *Every* season has *purpose*, even the ones that you hate. I will see you through. I will love you to the end. Seasons change, and you will change with the seasons, but I Am unchanging, so I guess you know where you can go when you need a breather of stability. Yes.

Friends, you know how on Good Friday each year we say, "Sunday's a'comin'!"? It's because we know that after Friday comes Saturday, and after Saturday comes Sunday. Cuz it *always does*. Right. If the season you are currently in feels like Good Friday, know this: a new season is comin'. It always does. *XO* and amen. I love ya.

{Ecclesiastes 3:1}

WHEN YOU'VE LOST SIGHT OF WHO GOD IS

Maybe you've just temporarily lost sight of Who God is . . .

So here's a fun fact: Mental stress can affect your eyesight. I guess that explains the twitch. So can dehydration and reduced blood flow. So, Baby, I'm here today to hopefully get your blood flowin' and pumpin' and groovin' and dancin'. Amen. And *hopefully*, the result will be a slight respite from your stress desert, where it appears that neither the water or blood seem to be flowin'.

Beloved, when I read these words this morn in Zephaniah, "Walk like the blind, because they have sinned against the Lord" . . . I kid you not, I literally exclaimed, "That's it!!" And what I meant by that exclamation is this—I think the feeling we get that mimics walking around like the newly blind . . . is a result of *losing sight* of Who God is. To lose sight of Who God is . . . is to separate yourself (even temporarily) from the truth of Who God is . . . and truly I tell you . . . it seriously sucks when that happens.

So today, Beloved, if you find yourself in that sucky place, that place where you feel like you're walking or stumbling around . . . have a seat. I'm gonna loan you my readers. (And if you keep 'em, it's totally fine cuz I lose 'em all the time.) Here's the eye chart. Oh, scratch that. Here's the "I" chart.

I Am Provider. I Am Protector. I Am All-Powerful. There is nothing too hard for Me, and *nothing* lies outside of My sovereignty. I Am the Way, the Truth, and the Life, and I Am rolling away stones and moving mountains right now that you don't even know about. I Am with you and for you, go before you, stand beside you, and yes, I bring up the rear. I Am Daily Bread. I Am Living Water. And I bet that sounds pretty darn good in this heat, right, My Daughter? I Am making all things new. I Am restoring in secret dark places. I Am in your midst. I Am your breath . . . so breathe. *Yes.* I Am able. I sure Am. And . . . *I love you.* Yesterday, Today, and Always. Amen. Now, don't lose sight of that, OK? OK.

I love you too. Amen.

{Zephaniah 1:17}

Day 78

PARTING GIFTS

Leaving is hard . . . even if it's right. Keep in mind that parting gifts may include peace, joy, a renewed sense of worth, a spring in your step, and more.

Parting gift: a gift given when you leave, a "leaving" gift. Usually given as a consolation prize on a game show to contestants who aren't the big winners.

Ahhhhh, but *see*, Beloved, God's Kingdom don't play by those rules. Hallelujah. For see, *your* parting gifts, the gifts *you* receive as you leave—an unhealthy situation/relationship/workplace/land-where-you-dwell/mindset-of-worry-and-fear/addiction-you-quit-ignoring-and-start-addressing-because-it's-already-taken-enough-from-you-plus-you're-such-an-awesome-human—you're-simply-not-healthy—so-what-do-we-do-when-we're-sick?-we-go-receive-the-treatment-we-need-*yes* . . . or any other person/place/pick-your-noun that you find yourself leaving, whether by choice or not.

Yes. Keep in mind that *your* parting gifts may include . . . peace, joy, a renewed sense of worth, rest, a spring in your step . . . and more. Yes, *more*. Like a new robe so you can finally ditch the prison clothes you've been wearing, cuz, Baby, orange ain't your color.

Beloved, leaving is hard. Even if it's right. And I'm not gonna insert my big "But" here cuz it don't belong. What *does* belong, however, is perhaps a spot of encouragement, a light in the dark of your tunnel, a sip at the well in your dry dusty desert, and if nothing else . . . someone who gets it . . . another human being like you. Yes. The place where God is taking you—physically, emotionally, spiritually—that you maybe don't want to be could be the very place where God *rescues* . . . and *redeems* you. That's right, Beloved. It just might be.

I love you. I see you. I mean it. Amen.

{Micah 1:14}

WHEN YOU THINK YOUR LIFE IS OVER

Sarah. Hagar. Hannah. Esther. Naomi. Ruth. A woman who bled. A woman hunched over. A woman who lies sick in her bed. A widow with only one drop of oil. A woman begging for crumbs. Women who thought their life was over . . . and were wrong.

Dang, I love callin' in the bomb squad. Cuz these women are the *bomb*.

Beloved, you and I have the chance to take some really good stuff from our gal pals who've gone before us. We get to listen to 'em one by one as they tell us their stories *and* all as one massive tribe as they shout out, "Amen, Sister, *Amen!*" So thanks, God, for knowing we'd need 'em and using 'em to form clouds so we'd never forget 'em.

So the list is fantastic, right? It's also—a *partial* list. Women from the stories of Scripture and other women we've read about over the years or heard speak somewhere and they completely blew us away, or women in your *very own life* who showed you what it looked like to persevere against all odds and to keep on believing, despite there being but a thread or a drop or a tiny seed of hope left.

I'm addressing the woman here today . . . who is being tempted to believe right now . . . that her life is pretty much over, that there's no way there's any new left to come, I guess that's all God wrote for me, so I guess God doesn't like me too much . . .

Enter the rumbling of the cloud. Cuz see, you can't keep a good woman down, not to mention an entire dance floor of 'em. And who knows, maybe the rumbling *is* a giant dance party under a super fab disco ball. Those who've gone before us felt the way we feel; they experienced discouragement, despair, disappointment, worry, fear, anxiety, heartache and heartbreak, and the very same question that still plagues our hearts most today, "Why, God, *why?*" Yup.

So let's listen to the ladies, OK? Let's sit with 'em and have a great cup o' joe or dance with 'em under the disco ball while belting out "I Will Survive." Let's let *them* remind *us* that at one point in their lives they *too* thought something seemed impossible . . . and yet.

GOD'S UNSTOPPABLE PLAN FOR YOU

It doesn't matter who's praying against you. Nothing can stop God's plan for you.

Today's entry is courtesy of, and specifically written for, the beautiful young woman who sat behind me one morning at a hotel breakfast. Because while I was down at the hotel breakfast where the coffee beans flourished, a young woman and her two friends sat directly behind me. And *because* they were directly behind me, I could hear their conversation. The young woman shared with her friends for the first time her need to have surgery soon, telling them because she knows that they'll pray for her. Perfect.

But then she said this: "I'm not telling other people, cuz you know there's people out there who'll pray *against* you, and I don't want nobody praying *against* me, cuz then who *knows* what?"

Dear Beautiful Young Woman Who Sat Behind Me . . .

No one praying *against* you can stop God's powerful plan *for* you. No one on Earth holds the pen or the Wite-Out. No one can alter the words of the story written for you—a story packed with power and purpose, by the way, and don't you forget it. Amen. Don't live in fear of what others may say, of ways they may plead with God to conspire against you as if they have that kind of power. Cuz truly I tell you, Beautiful Young Woman Who Sat Behind Me . . . they don't. They sure don't.

The God Who wrote your story is Author. That same God is also Perfecter. And perfect means whole and complete. Your story is of immeasurable worth. And *you*, Beautiful Young Woman Who Sat Behind Me . . . have been sent here to live it. And I'm so grateful for that. So be strong and courageous, OK? Be brave enough to pray based on every promise God ever made.

And although I agree with you about not telling everyone everything, it's not out of fear for ways they may pray *against* you, cuz they can try all the live-long day to do that and it just ain't gonna happen, OK? OK.

P.S.: I'll be praying for you.

WHEN GOD THROWS DOWN MOUNTAINS

The shaking up of your life right now . . . may be God's way of throwing down mountains that stand in your way.

I don't know if it is or it isn't, but *if it is* . . . wouldn't it give the shaking up some *value*, wouldn't it make it *worth* something? Wouldn't it mean that although you may not have *wanted* the shaking, or maybe you even *despise* the shaking, that at least it's not all for *nothing*?

And what's *more, becuz* God knows that we're human, *becuz* God knows we can't *possibly* understand all of God's ways, God says to us . . . *I Am with you*. I Am *within* you. My Spirit, your breath, is My holy guarantee until you return home to Me. I Am with you *wherever* you go, and it is *that* truth that's gonna allow you to be strong and courageous wherever you go. I Am *close* to you when you are brokenhearted because I *know* you don't understand. I sit upon your bed and remind you, assure you, promise you . . . that your story's been written in full, and as the *Author* of your story, I *know* how it ends, and I can tell you that all things really *do* work together for good.

And here's when I'll remind you, My child, that good means sufficient to meet the purpose . . . and then I'll remind you of Whose purpose . . . Mine. And see, *I know* that your humanness can't *possibly* understand the crux of your holiness. I'll remind you that I know the plans I have for you because, *hello* . . . *I wrote* the plans. Every chapter, every paragraph, every sentence, every word . . . and every period, comma, and exclamation point, too. I sure did. I'll remind you that once upon a time I used a great quake to roll away a stone. And another one to split open the Earth, changing it for all time. I'll remind you that even the *shaking* has purpose . . . and I'll remind you that you're gonna get through it.

Beloved, as always, I don't have all the answers. None of us do. But what if we could see it anew? What if the shaking up in your life right now . . . is God's way of throwing down mountains that stand in your way?

ARE YOU LISTENING?

My Daughter, I am speaking. Are you listening?

Body-Mind-Soul. It's what makes us gloriously human. All three in one. And all speak. Our flesh cries out "Headache!" And we know what to do. Our flesh screams "Hunger!" And we *definitely* know what to do. Our flesh interrupts our regularly scheduled programming with "We're done here folks," and lays itself down. *or . . .* decides *not* to pay attention. And we all know what happens when we don't pay attention to where we're going, right? We run smack dab into walls. This is also known as "*I hit a wall*," and perhaps you've heard that before . . . heck, perhaps you've *said* it before. Perhaps already today.

So yes, our flesh speaks. Our mind does too. And sometimes our mind speaks its mind. And sometimes we like what we hear, and sometimes we don't, but we'd be wise to pay attention to the words that we speak because the mouth speaks what the heart is full of. Yes. *So*, what do you hear yourself saying? Are there things you say every day that you don't even realize? And what do those words reveal about what's going on deep in your heart?

Beloved, the conversations we have with ourselves are the hardest of all, which is usually why we try to avoid them at all costs. But truly I tell you—and here's what I've learned—it is *those* conversations—those honest, real, raw, no-one-can-hear-you-so-you-might-as-well-be-honest conversations—that will rock your world. And maybe your life could use a little rockin' and rollin'. After all, those newly-hydrated, previously-dry bones need a playlist to dance to. Our soul speaks too. Like our flesh and like our mind, it lets us know when it's hungry or thirsty or tired or overwhelmed or all of the above. Amen.

Ya know, this morning I read about ships being heavy-laden, and in turn sinking, and I had to *stop and think about that*. Because picture it. You're a ship. You're cruising along on the water and soakin' in the sun, when suddenly you notice you're starting to sink . . . *because you're carrying too much stuff.* Just think about it, OK? *XO.*

NO MAGIC FORMULA

There is no magic formula. Life at times will be hard.

Abraham. Sarah. Noah. Rebecca. Hannah. David. Daniel. Esther. Job. Naomi. Ruth. Jeremiah. Ezekiel. Nehemiah. A Woman who bled. A Woman who cheated. A Woman who just needed to escape from the crowd. A Woman hunched over. A Woman thrust to the dirt. A Woman begging for crumbs. Moses. Mary. Mordecai. Paul. The Guys. The Gals. Those who traveled with Jesus. Jesus. Exactly.

Beloved, there is no magic formula. Life at times will be hard. And you know that. And you've struggled as you've tried to figure out what you could have *possibly* done to deserve the hard you've endured. You've wrestled with God to the point where you're completely worn out and utterly exhausted. You don't have the answer to the question that's plaguing you, perhaps that's been holding you hostage for years . . . Why, Lord? Why??

Created human, and human we shall be, and with our humanness comes our inability to fully understand the whys and the ways of our God. This, however, does *not* diminish our holiness. Thank God. And what we *can* do . . . is return to the center. Return to who we know God to *be*. Return to every promise made to us before the foundation of the world . . . I Am with you. I will *not* abandon you. I will *not* forget you. I have engraved *your* name in *My* hand as a sign of My faithfulness to you. I will be *with* you wherever, yes *wherever*, you go. Whether you are in the dark or the light, the desert or the plush pasture, the highest mountain or the deepest valley or the pit on Earth that feels like hell . . . *there* with you I shall be. Your story's been written. I know how it ends. Your very last word is one Big. Fat. *Amen.* My thoughts toward you are good, and My plans for you are good, and don't you forget what good means. Sufficient to meet the purpose. *My* purpose, My Girl—*My* purpose. A purpose that will not always make sense to you, but a purpose that is *packed* with value and worth just like *you*. Yes.

And see, folks, *that's* why I hang out with God like I do—cuz I need those kinds of reminders. And maybe today, you do too.

THE FIRE THAT IGNITES

What if the fire is not meant to destroy you . . . but ignite you?

And what if the story of Moses talking with a burning bush is to show us that sometimes God speaks to us through fire? And what if it also shows us that we can *be* on fire but not *consumed* by fire? And what if God takes the fire and uses it to ignite one of our purposes, one we didn't even know we had, setting us ablaze to do the thing we had no clue we'd be doing? What if the fire is God's way? What if *that's* why God used fire to lead all those Israelites by night as they journeyed . . . to show us that *fire* . . . is *also* . . . *light*. It opens our eyes to stuff. It *also* opens our eyes . . . to *self*. What if fire can be *both* a deadly force *and* a lifesaving one? Oh, that's right . . . it *can*. What if the fire is one we don't want? We didn't ask for this fire, and yet here we are?

Hear this good news—you don't have to like it. Nope. You're not the Author, therefore you don't know your full story, and the One Who is the Author is also perfecting your faith as you live out each page. And so darn right you're not gonna like every word, cuz you can't *possibly* see the whole thing.

Now the flip side—the fire within may be what's keeping you alive and living fully ablaze. The fire that's not only keeping you hot but keeping you fed as well. The fire within you that is *so* lit you're singin' "Disco Inferno" while cruisin' the strip.

Beloved, fires can destroy. No doubt. Fires can also *ignite something* within us. We've seen folks all over our world face fires in their lives they never *ever* wanted to walk through, tragedies and deaths and heartbreaks they *never* wanted to endure. And they *took* that fire that was now within them, the fire they never asked for, and used it for *good* in our world. And oh, how we love those stories. They remind us that God really *does* use *all* things for good.

Sit with the fire a minute, Beloved. Remind yourself that God is *in* it and that you can trust your God.

Day 85

EVERY STEP AND EVERY STOP HAS PURPOSE

God is leading you. God is guiding you. You won't love every step you take or every stop you make—but you can trust that every step, every stop has purpose.

God is. God sure is. God is leading you, and God is guiding you, and sometimes it doesn't feel like it, and sometimes you don't like where you are or where you're sent or where you've been. And sometimes, like Ezekiel and a whole host of others, you find yourself crying out, *Lord, what the heck?* Or worse. Cuz hell on Earth ain't no joke. Fact. Every step—purpose. Every stop—purpose. Trust that, Beloved. *Return to that.*

Listen as the cloud of witnesses share their stories with you . . .

Mary and Martha—Why did You lead us to this smelly grave, Lord? Are You trying to make our grief worse?

Hunched-Over Woman at the Back of the Temple—Why are You calling me up front, and right during church, and in front of everyone?? Geez Louise, why the heck do You think I was standing in the *back*?

The Woman who Bled—No kidding, Lord, I echo the last gal who testified. I mean, calling me out in front of that entire crowd that looked at me like I had a major case of the cooties?? Seriously, Lord??

Moses—Lord, You picked the wrong guy.

Mary standing next to Moses—Ummm, *no doubt*, Lord. In case You didn't notice, I'm an unwed teenager . . . hello?!?

Abraham with son in tow. Esther at the palace. Joseph in the well that day. The woman who met Jesus at one about noon.

You get my point, Beloved. And hey, if along the way you cracked a smile? *Score.* Cuz God *is* leading you. God *is* guiding you. God really *hasn't* forsaken or forgotten you, cuz a promise is a promise, amen. And you don't *have* to like every step you take or every stop you make . . . to trust . . . that every step . . . and every stop . . . has purpose. Amen.

P.S.: And the next time that where you are or where you're going or where you've been makes no flippin' sense at all . . . go park your butt under the cloud. They'll tell ya. *XO.*

YOU DON'T NEED TO DENY YOUR REALITY

You don't need to deny your reality.

Job didn't deny his reality. David didn't deny his reality. Jeremiah didn't deny his reality. *And you don't have to deny your reality.* For truly I tell you, Beloved, in the words of Manhattan SVU Detective Olivia Benson, "Sometimes life sucks." Amen, Liv, amen.

Beloved, you don't need to *deny* your reality. You don't have to gussy her up to take her out. You don't have to scooch her out of the way in order to *recall your God in the midst of your reality,* for *this* is your rescue. Amen.

When your reality is draggin' your heart around despite your endless singing, begging it not to . . . put your soul to work. Tell that soul of yours to summon to the forefront the truths you need to hold on to if you're gonna get through this time in your life.

In the midst of your lamenting (which you have every right to do), call to mind *this* . . . The steadfast love of the Lord never ceases. And then say *never, never, never* out loud a whole buncha times, cuz you *really* need to remember that. God's mercies *never* come to an end. They (steadfast love and mercies) are new *every* morning. *Every morning.* Yes. Great is Your faithfulness, Lord. Great as in *huge and massive, and therefore covering me and the entire world, and I'm gonna need to remind myself of that great faithfulness,* especially when *it feels like you've taken off, Lord.* Right.

The Lord is my portion. The truth of who God *is* . . . is my enough for today. It's gonna see me through, and *therefore—becuz* all of the above is true in the midst of my reality that is *also* true—I will hope in God, in Who I know God to be. I sure will. The *one* thing that's a constant, the *one* thing that won't change, the *one* thing that remains no matter *what* else is taken or stolen or lost . . . the steadfast love of the Lord *never* ceases. God's mercies are new *every* morning. *Great* is God's faithfulness. Yes.

Those truths are *enough* for me today. So *that* is where my hope shall be. Heck yes and amen. Beloved, in the midst of your reality, recall your God.

{Lamentations 3:22–23}

FREE TO LAMENT

What do you do when you hate God's ways? You lament. Yep. You lament.

And at least *part* of you is glad that *someone* out there decided to pen a whole book—Lamentations— about it and include it in *this* big book we call the Bible, because it means that at least *one* other person in history lamented, and so hallelujah—you have permission to, too.

And as you do, you realize you don't have to apologize for it, and thank *God* at least *someone* else totally gets that, so you know you're not the only one . . .

Questioning why. Bawling your eyes out. Wishing things could be different. Yes.

You get to *own* your humanness, not sacrifice it on the altar of holiness by somehow pushing it aside "in the name of the Lord." There *will* be times when you hate God's ways, which makes perfect sense, by the way, because they're not all *meant* to be comprehended by us. Exactly.

What do we do when we love our God but don't love all of God's ways? Well, I reckon we have two options: We can take off, although many have tried, and few have succeeded. Or we can return—return to Who we know God to be. *Yes.*

God is my Provider. God is my Protector. God is my Parent, amen. God is gonna see me through this thing and not let go in the process. God *knows* that I'm human. He *created* me this way, uniquely designing both my flesh *and* my soul to release what is too heavy to carry. Yes. Tear ducts to pour out my heart like water. Sweat glands to work out the anger. A big fat mouth to talk to God *and* to God's people on Earth, because talking things out *helps*.

Beloved, if you're in a part of your story right now that has you lamenting . . . lament. I mean it. Give yourself the space you need to lament over what you wish wasn't. And please, please don't sacrifice your humanness as you do. Please know that you don't have to. And as it all pours out, draining you and dehydrating you, return to the well. Drink some water. Restore and replenish what has been poured out. Sip by sip *drink* of this water, this *living* water, that it may restore you, that it may revive you. *XO.*

EVERY JOURNEY HAS PIT STOPS

The next time you find yourself in a pit, remind yourself, "I'm on a journey, and this is a pit stop."

Never thought of it that way? Well then, Beloved, starting today, I pray that you do. I *sure do*. Reframe and Rename. I mean it. Because have you ever once thought about the fact that when you go on a long road trip that you need to make pit stops? And how up until now, you've never once given any thought at all to the fact that you actually call it a pit stop? Or the fact that you know when you stop at said pit stop that it's gonna be . . . temporary? I know, right?

That was me in my chair this morning as I made that connection. And you know your girl Tera *loves* a good OMG connection. And even now, the thought expands, the lightbulb gets brighter, the loaves multiply . . . as I realize just how powerful I believe this connection is, or could be, for someone who right now finds himself or herself in a pit they believe they will never, ever get out of.

But now they've got this. This tool to survive, this weapon of defense, this new way to see it that's gonna rescue them from utter hopelessness. And truly I tell you, Beloved, ain't *nobody* wanna be there. Fact. They're going to reframe and rename the place where they are, the pit they are in, and they're gonna remind themselves that a *pit* . . . is a *pit stop*. And when they do, their countenance changes, and they find the courage and strength that they need to endure the pit until it's time to continue the journey.

And then, their soul goes a step even further, exceedingly and abundantly more if we wanna use Bible lingo, and brings up the story they heard once upon a time about a guy named Joe who found himself in a pit that was actually a pit *stop* . . . on his way to the palace. *Amen.*

So, Beloved, in a pit? Tell yourself *today*, no matter how many times you have to say it or how many sticky notes you need to use to line the walls of your pit . . . this is a pit stop. This is a pit stop. This is a pit stop. *Amen.*

GOD USES OUR STRUGGLES TO SPEAK TO US

Oh, oh, oh, Sweet Child of Mine, I Am using your struggle . . . to speak to you.

Your struggle. Your storm. Your umpteenth night in a row wrestling all night with God. The emotions, the feelings, the thoughts, the worries, the fears . . .

Beloved, I *gotta* sit with 'em a minute. I *gotta* give 'em space to breathe. I *gotta* ask God . . . Are You *using* these things to *speak* to me? Are You? I mean, You gave us our bodies to tell us stuff, so I guess it makes sense. And often we don't pay attention and listen until it's to the point where we really have no other option. I mean, *that's* when we go in and get checked out, right? When something's *not* right, something's *not* working as it should, something's in pain or off-kilter or throwing us completely off game? Right.

God wasn't kidding with the whole wonderfully *and* fearfully formed thing. Sometimes it's wonderful . . . and sometimes it scares the crap out of us, but we gotta admit it got our attention. So, could it be that the countless stories about how God speaks in the storms and the cisterns and the cells and the fill-in-your-own-dreaded-places . . . are to teach us that God *speaks* to us through our struggles in those places? I'm guessing that's a big fat *yes*. We cry out, "Teach us to number our days that we may gain a heart of wisdom!" But we forget that being taught to number our days *more often than not* comes through the things we hate. Amen.

Beloved, I am convinced God speaks. Through our flesh, our battles, our times of peace and quiet, and our times of raging internal wars. So I sit with it. I name it. I talk to God about it and tell God I hate it. And then I ask God—are You *telling* me something? Are You *speaking* to me *through* this? Cuz if so, Lord, give me ears to hear it . . . and a two-by-four wouldn't hurt either. Cause me to sit with the struggle long enough to hear Your voice in the midst of it . . . showing me what's best for me . . . leading and guiding me through it.

RESTORATION PROMISED

Restoration promised.

If today's daily bread were to consist of only two words—would those two words be enough? I bet they would. Take 'em, Beloved. I mean it. Take 'em. Eat 'em. Keep 'em. Believe 'em. Rest in 'em. Yes.

Restoration *promised*. Not suggested, not recommended, not "we'll see how she does first based on how she handles today/this week/this month" . . . No. *Promised.* Restoration promised . . . from the One for Whom no promise has ever failed. Like *ever.* Restoration . . . *promised.*

Now . . . stop and inhale the breath your God gives you . . . through ancient words God still speaks . . . I will restore you . . . Your wounds I will heal . . . I . . . Am going . . . to save you. I have loved you with an everlasting love, and therefore My faithfulness to you will continue. I will build you, and you will be built. Again you will dance, and again you will sing, and again you will know I Am with you and for you. There is *hope* . . . for your *future.*

And someone in the room right now just realized that if there is hope for her future . . . then *this ain't the end, amen.* Yes. And she's gonna believe that. And live like it's true. Because she knows that what she *believes* . . . determines how she *proceeds* . . . and she wants to proceed . . . believing that every word spoken for her will indeed come to be. Cuz they will. Yes. So she will proceed believing . . . that restoration is part of her story. That redemption is too. For the One Who authored her story is both Restorer and Redeemer, so that's *exactly* what she can expect. Whew-Hallelujah-Heck-Yes.

Beloved, two words. Given for you. Take and eat. This is bread broken and given to you . . . from the One Who stands before you and says . . . *do this* . . . to *remember me.* Yes.

Restoration *promised.*

{Jeremiah 30–33}

SERPENTS, SERVANTS, AND SOVEREIGNTY

This much she knew—even the serpent is God's servant.

Yup. That's what she knew. Which was good, because she'd need to return to that knowing time and time again, and when she did, she'd pour out her heart to her God about just how much she freakin' hated it. The serpent, that is. And God understood. God knew she was human, after all. It was with good purpose she was created that way. And in that safe place, she was reminded that she didn't have to like all things in order for all things to have purpose . . . and you can bet your bottom dollar that she would rather err on the side of *God is sovereign over all* . . . than for *one second* believe that God had somehow lost control.

And honestly, if she's being frank, that's what makes faith at times . . . *hard*. The *knowing*. The knowing that God *can* . . . so what the heck, God? What gives? Why am I going through this? Why does it feel like the enemy is winning and that the weapons formed against me *are* actually prospering, hello?? Why? And that's when she'd stop. In the midst of the storm that swirled about in her mind, she'd head to the sanctuary. She'd return to *this* truth that would see her through the times when it felt like the serpent had somehow out-arm-wrestled her God—even the *serpent* . . . is God's *servant*. *Yes.* And then she'd give herself grace for sometimes forgetting, cuz *dang* those two words are *close*. She'd remind herself that God's ways are far beyond her comprehension . . . but *at least God's still in control*. Whew.

And that right there, Beloved, is somethin' you're gonna need to return to time and time again in order to get through stuff. Amen. So, at the end of the day, she resigned herself to this—no matter what is happening, God knows. And God is gonna take what was intended for evil and use it for *good*, for *God's* purposes.

And God loves me. Knows the plan for me. Fearfully and wonderfully formed me. And (thank God) will always be with me. Whatever it is will pass . . . but God will *still* be here. Still in control. Because God is *sovereign* over all . . . and *all means all, amen.*

Day 92

WORTH THE RISK

Hope is worth the risk.

Of course, there *are* potential side effects. You might get your hopes *up* and then be let *down*, but truly I tell you, every second you *hope* is a second you're *up*, and that's a pretty fab place to be. And although Hope in and of itself doesn't disappoint, the outcome you're hoping for might. Right.

Some of y'all never did get the pony. Or the job that you reeeally wanted. Or the diagnosis that said "all clear." Or the answer you soooo wanted to be "yes." All those things you hoped for did *not* come to fruition . . . so why get your hopes up again? Because, Friend . . . Hope keeps us looking *ahead*. Hope is the means by which we move *forward*. Hope fixes our eyes on what *might be* and keeps us heading toward that oasis in the midst of our desert.

Once upon a time, there was a gal who was scared to get her hopes up again. She laughed it off with a "Yeah right, like *that'll* ever happen." Laughing stuff off is a powerful defense mechanism, you know. It's our way of trying to show others we "don't care," "it's no big deal," "I'm fine with it." And we *do that* because getting our hopes up again and admitting it . . . seems to set the stage once again for potential disappointment, so laughing it off it is. Even though . . . you *so* want to believe this time will be different, because why *not* this time?

Her name was Sarah, by the way. Sarah had resigned herself to the fact that at *her* age, there was *no way* she could bring forth any new . . . *but secretly* . . . Sarah never stopped dreaming, never stopped believing, never stopped hoping that maybe, just maybe . . . And so when three visitors showed up (despite her not having her monthly visitor for *years*) with the news that she was going to conceive and bring forth *new* . . . Sure, she laughed it off at first . . . you and I would've too . . . but I have no doubt . . . that in that moment . . . what Sarah *really* thought was . . . *could it be?*

P.S.: This time, it was.

{Genesis 18:1–15}

ASK GOD TO BREATHE NEW LIFE INTO YOU

What's stopping you from asking God to breathe New Life into you? That's right. Nothing.

Nothing can stop you from using what may just feel like the only breath you've got left . . . to *ask God to breathe new life into you.* Because maybe, Beloved, just maybe, that's what you need this very day of this very year—a breath of fresh air, new life, amen. Maybe. And although you have no idea just *how* God will breathe new life into you, you know that God is the One Who gives you God's breath, so Who better to ask than the source, amen? Amen.

Ask God to breathe new life into you. . . into the depths of your soul that feel dead . . . into the parts of your heart that are in desperate need of reviving . . . into the areas of your mind that the buildup of dust known as doubt is thick, and the cobwebs of worry have taken up residence, and it was so gradual you never even noticed Charlotte over there spinning her web. Yes. Ask God to breathe new life into you. Get *excited* about what that new may bring as it is delivered from you. Ask God to breathe new life into you because somethin's gotta give around here, or you just might break. Ask God to breathe new life into you because you can actually feel yourself slipping into "another day, another dollar" mode, if you aren't there already. Ask God to breathe new life into you because new seasons require new vision, and you can't seem to get your eyes off what was, and so you desperately need help looking ahead at what is to come.

Ask God to breathe new life into you *because you can.* And then know that that breath might arrive as a gentle whisper that caresses the side of your cheek . . . or a mighty wind that dang near knocks you off your feet . . . but either way . . . it'll be *God's* breath . . . breathed into *you* . . . breathing *new life* . . . into *you.*

{Job 33:4}

THUNDER AND RAIN IN THE DARK

There's just something about thunder and rain in the dark.

And I love it. It feels like God to me. And I reckon it's because I know that it is. A God Who commanded the rain to fall before beckoning the sun to rise. Yes. It feels like provision to me, it feels like . . . I *see* you, My Daughter. I know you feel like you're gonna *break* . . . so I'm gonna go *first* . . . and break open the heavens for you . . . and gush drops upon drops of rain upon you . . . I'm gonna use the storm . . . to help you. To let you know I Am near. To let you know that I heard you last night in your weariness and this morning before your eyes even opened. I Am *sending* this rain to break up the heat, to green up the grass, to feed your crops what they desperately need, and *when you see that*, My Girl . . . I want you know that it's *Me*. And that I do the same . . . for *you*.

I allowed the sun to sleep in, because sometimes the dark isn't scary, is it? Sometimes it's permission to rest. It's a refuge, a wrapping of My arms around yours that reminds you that I Am actually the One Who carries the whole world in the palm of My hand . . . not you. Yes. I'm gonna roll out this thunder, My Child, and *you* . . . are gonna hear . . . *Me*. And you're gonna call it My Voice and know that indeed I Am the One . . . speaking to you . . . because I've heard your prayers desperately asking Me to let you know that I hear you. And for the record—I do. Yes.

I Am the One Who knows what you need, and this morning, My Girl, I think *this* is just what you need. A reminder that I Am above you, watching over you and hearing every word spoken by you and every thought that never quite caught breath. I Am *providing* for you. I Am *protecting* the soul I created within you. I *promise*.

Oh, and the occasional lightning you see? Yeah, that's Me too. Giving you light. For that's who I Am. I love you, amen.

SOMETIMES GOD WAITS TO TELL YOU

My Daughter, there are things I waited to tell you 'til now.

I was so caught off guard. There I was, just hummin' along in the book of Isaiah, when suddenly, I ingested a chunk of daily bread I had clearly never before digested. And it was through *those words* that I realized . . . OMG, there are things You *didn't* tell me before Lord, not to *punish* me, but to *protect* me. Wow. You weren't holding out on me because I wasn't deserving. You were holding back because You *knew* I wasn't anywhere *near* ready to understand, comprehend. For *this* is what a good parent does. Indeed.

Here's a bit of the Scripture I read . . . . "before today you have never heard . . . so you couldn't say 'I already knew . . . '" And it's about that time that my teenage self *totally* got it. Right down to the eye roll. Parents of teens—you get this. You're talking to them, and their response is rehearsed and interrupts you mid-sentence sounding something like this—"I know, I know!" Mmhmm.

I read on. "You have never heard, you have never known, from of old your ears were not opened . . . because I *knew* you would . . . " and from there the fill-in-the-blank options are endless.

Beloved, I don't know if any of this means a darn thing to you, but for me? For me, it allowed me to take times of silence, times when I've wondered, "Why aren't You telling me???" . . . and Rename it. *Yes.* And realize that what it always has been . . . is *protection*. It was, and will forever be, the *love* of a Parent for a Child. A love that protects and makes things known *when* the child is ready.

Beloved, if you feel like God is holding out on you, purposely not telling you stuff that you're dying to know, you may be right. Rename it . . . and call it Love. A love that protects and provides. And rest in the truth that in due time . . . all that is to be made known to you . . . will be made known to you . . . for *that* is how great the love for you.

{Isaiah 48:6–8}

THE HARD IS HOLY

The hardest part was . . . she knew. She knew the hard was on purpose. She knew that it was holy.

She knew there was no changing what was written in her story. She may one day understand the why, but until that day, she'd have to make peace with the hard . . . knowing it was holy. The hard that was planned for her long ago, the mountains and the valleys and the long stretches of wilderness that were purposely placed in her path. The obstacles, the trials, the tribulations. The hard that was holy. The times when she realized why Jesus, in the garden that night, tired and worn out from it all, was crying to the point that the tears had run out and had literally switched over to blood.

Maybe you've been there, Beloved. Maybe you are there now. If so, let's hop in the car, OK? Road trips are more fun with a friend. You grab the snacks, and I'll crank the tunes, and we'll return to the truth that the hard has *great purpose,* and therefore is *serving* us, and that sounds *so* much better than defeating us. *Dang right.*

It's not harming us; it's helping us. It's not weakening us; it's strengthening us. This hard we've been given is *holy* for God's sake, so you better *believe* we're gonna *call* it that. We sure are. And then we're gonna remind each other that breakdowns on the side of the road are bound to happen on long road trip journeys; we're at times bound to run out of gas, burn through all our midnight oil, overheat, and need to cool down. *When* those things happen, we'll remind one another that our God is as near as our breath. That crying only makes sense when the heavy we're carrying needs to be unloaded from the car, cuz it's seriously too much to carry and is weighing us down. So we'll sit on the side of the road, and we'll cry. And we may yell and scream too, depending on our mood, and a full-on tantrum ain't off limits either. And then I'll grab your hand and say, "It's time to get back on the road. I know *just* the song to play."

Beloved, the hard you're enduring is holy. That doesn't make it any easier to endure, but it does give it *purpose.* Amen.

KEEP LOOKING

If you can't see God in it . . . keep looking.

I mean it. You look until you find, you hear me? You search and seek as if on a rescue mission, cuz in essence, Beloved—you *are*. For *you*. *Yes*. God won't always be easy to see . . . in the storm . . . in the sweltering heat of the desert . . . in the suffocating loneliness of the valley . . . in the stress of the battle. Ain't it the truth. But see, you're gonna look like Joe did until he realized, "Wait a sec, sure I got tossed in this massive deep well. But it's *waterless*. I'm not gonna drown."

Or Jonah, similar experience, no doubt, except of course he was sitting in the guts of a whale. Or great big fish. Or whatever. Or how about Ruth? Look like she did. As she's working in that field after losing her husband and wanting nothing more than to provide for her and her mother-in-law. I wonder if on about the tenth long row, while being protected from all the menfolk so she could do what she came to do, she thought to herself as she reached down into the dirt, "OMG, these are handfuls of *purpose* I'm scooping up." So cool. Love that story.

Or how about Job in the midst of his mega storm; everything around him swirling and whirling and crashing and burning, and suddenly, he hears God speak. To *him*. Yup. Do you suppose right then and there that Job had his own "Wait a Sec" moment as he realized, "OMG, if I can *hear* You, You must be *in this storm with me*." And the fact that God was speaking from the *eye* of the storm, the *calm* of the storm? Big fat bonus, IMO.

Beloved, if you can't see God in it . . . *keep looking*. I mean it. Keep looking until you *do* see God in it. It's also a really great way to put your stress and worry to work for you. Seriously. Look like it's your last cent to spare. Look like it's the last drop of oil. Look like it's your *cell*. I know, right? Look like *that*. If you can't see God in it . . . keep looking. And don't stop looking until you do. Amen.

PEACE LIKE A RIVER

Lord, if I'm gonna need to go with the flow here, give me peace like a river, OK?

Ask God for what you perceive you might need, based on what you perceive just might be a need. I know it's a mouthful, but what can I say—they don't call me wordy for nothin'.

But also—do it. I mean it. Take a look at your day, your week, your current battle, the war you know is before you, the thing you are so looking forward to or the thing you wish you didn't have to face, but ugh, alas, here you are . . . and then *ask God* for what it is you might need. *This* by the way, is the equivalent of "Give us this day our daily bread," for those looking for a reference point. Amen. Yep.

I can look at my schedule and perceive that I may just need to go with the flow in at *least* a few places this week. So I'm asking God to give me peace like a river because I *can*. I sure can. I can ask for daily bread. Jesus says so. I can ask for what I need, or even *think* I might need, should my plans pan out like I think they might, and *certainly* like-totally-for-sure if they don't. (Sorry folks, you can take a girl outta the '80s but . . .)

Beloved, God's Will is gonna be done today, just like every other day that ever has been and ever will be. And *you*, as God's own child who carries the promise that you will never be forgotten, never forsaken, never disowned . . . can *ask* for *whatever* it is you might need . . . to fully live while that Will unfolds.

So today, if you're like me, and you look and see that you potentially may just need to go with the flow in some places this week, and you tend to be (ahem) the bossy freak-out-a-bit-when-things-don't-go-like-you-think-they-should-go type— well then, Darlin', you may just want to ask God for peace like a river too.

Or *whatever* it is that you need. Cuz you *can*. Cuz you're heard, and you're seen, and you're more precious than all the jewels in the palace and don't you forget it. Amen.

BELIEVING IS THE KEY

If you don't believe it, it doesn't matter how true it is.

Beloved, if I were to have you over for coffee (how fun would that be, by the way?) and asked you if you believed that Jesus healed a guy with mud made from His spit mixed with dirt, or if Jesus multiplied some kid's sack lunch, or if Jesus beckoned Pete to walk on the water and Pete actually *did*, or if Jesus turned a whole buncha plain water into really fab wine so the party wouldn't have to end early, what would you say?

I'll tell you what you would say: "Well, of *course* I believe it, Tera. I mean, it's God's Word, after all."

But see, then I'm gonna look you right in the eyes, my gaze firmly planted on you, and say, "Sweet. Now do you believe it for *you*?"

Do you believe that God will part seas for *you*? Do you believe that *your* fields still have much fruit to bear? Do you believe that there really *is* more new to come despite your age? After all, remember Sarah? Naomi? Noah? The list-goes-on-and-on-*hello*. Do you believe that *you* are seen like Hagar was, that *you* are heard like Hannah was, that *you* are known like Mary was, and therefore carry something *mighty within you—do you*??? Do you believe you will love again? Feel good again? Experience amazing things again? Witness miracles again? Do you?

Because *if you do*, Beloved, there ain't no stoppin' you. You're alive—your *soul* is alive—the part of you that carries the faith you've been given is *alive*, and hallelujah-thanks-be-to-God it don't take much. A mustard seed. A drop of oil. One single cloud that appears in the midst of the drought. One sign that flashes like a neon billboard—one that only you can see—one that says—*I told you I knew the plans for you.*

And you smile. Because you know it's for you. You *believe* it's for you. And that *believing*, the very definition of faith, is what's gonna keep hope alive. And nothing—*nothing*—strengthens and revives us and excites us like hope does. All things are possible, my friend, for the One for Whom all things are possible. Believe it—for *you*. And for God's sake, don't *stop* believin'. *XO.*

GOD, SHOW ME SOMETHING

God—show me something.

Something that will feed, nourish, revive. Something that will excite and stir and strengthen my resolve to keep on believing. Amen. Something I haven't seen that it's time to see and then give me what I need to see it and make sense of it and do something with it or about it. Yes. Show me something in Your Word. Something in Your World. Something similar to the sea-partings or fishes-and-loaves feast would be great.

Show me something that will blow me outta the water, or how about this—since You're living water, bring to the surface what I am to see, and then bring me into position to see it. Show me something that's missing but not really missing, just hidden until this very moment—reserved for me and now ready to show itself to me. Show me something that will heal and comfort, protect and provide, remind me of Your faithfulness and new mercies every mornin'.

God, show me something. Something big, something small, something in between because I'm not sure in this case that size matters much at all. Show me something that will show me *You*. The truth that You still see me. Still hear me. Still know the plans You wrote for me. Still have more in the storehouse for me. Show me it's not too late. It's not over. Show me there's more. Show me that burning bush again and remind me that it's totally possible to be on fire and yet also fully alive. *Yes.* And for the record Lord, I love that one.

Show me something that will let me know You're in the valley, the desert, the wilderness, the storm. And I'll do my best not to forget the next time I'm in any of them—again. Show me something. A door opened for me. A stone rolled away. A something that will leave me breathless in the best kind of way. And God? I'm calling all this Expectant Hope. Based on who You are. On Who I know You to be . . . Provider. Protector. All-Powerful. Potter. Author. Creator. The One Who fashioned me according to Your purposes for me. I love You. And I'll be watching.

THE STRENGTH WITHIN YOU

Without mountains to climb, you would never know the strength that lies within you.

I was talking to God this morning about my last mountain—the one that had now moved on, in a sense. I told God I found myself missing this mountain that came in a form I never expected or thought I wanted, and God chuckled and said, "Don't worry, Girly, there'll be more." And then I heard *this* as our convo continued . . .

"My Daughter, without mountains to climb, you would never know the strength that lies within you, and strength not realized is wasted. Your life on Earth is an unfolding of the story I wrote for you—a revealing day by day of the plans and purposes I have for you. The mountains, My Daughter . . . are *for* you. Do you know why I had Moses climb up and down that mountain so many times when I was doing the whole stone tablets thing? Because Moses didn't believe he had it in him, and I wanted him to see that *he sure as heck did.* Joe could say the same about the pit I placed him in, and Dan could say it about the den, and Jonah about the whale, and Ruth about the fields, and Esther about the scary position I brought *her* into—and, well, I think you get it, right?"

And God *was* right. I *do* get it. Without mountains, I would never know the strength that lies within me, and strength not realized is wasted. Without hurdles in this life, I would never know I could jump. Without challenges that feel like never-ending marathons, I would never know that patience and endurance lie deep within me just waiting for me to behold them. Without things that stir me from placidness, I would never speak from the depth of the well, and without times of testing, I would never know what I know . . .

That my story's been written. By not only the *Author* but also the *Perfecter* (Whole and Completer) of my faith. The faith given to me as a seed that continues to grow and protect and provide, thank God. And day by day, page by page, word by word, as my story unfolds, I discover who I am and what lies within me.

Dang. What a great morning. Behold your mountain, Beloved. *XO.*

THE MORE THAT IS FOR YOU

Maybe your discontent is actually the Holy Spirit stirring you up so you know that there's more for you.

Maybe it is. Maybe you've been so busy trying to convince yourself that you're content (because, after all, that's what a good Christian does, right?). That if *you* do feel even a *hint* of it, your enemy, Shame, from just down the street, barges in for an unwanted visit and claims the win for the day. And so, therefore, you dare not speak of it, *or* if you *do* admit it, even if just to yourself, you feel like you'd better pray for at *least* a good hour and ask for all kinds of forgiveness.

Anyone?? Well, OK then. Beloved, have you stopped to consider that perhaps the discontent is actually the *Holy Spirit within you stirring you up so that you know there's more to come for you?*

Hey, just a thought. Cuz see, I'm not talking about never being satisfied. That's its own deal, and King Sol was right—it's like chasing the wind. I'm talking about a restless desire or craving that *keeps you going and seeking and excitedly, expectantly praying and believing, and maybe that's the point, amen.* Maybe *that's* the *purpose* of your discontent. Maybe you're *not* a spoiled brat after all. It's just that you *so* trust God, you *so* know Who God is, and you *so* know what God has done over thousands of years, and so you *dare to believe in what may just be possible for you.* Yes. Whatever it is that is stirring you, even if you yourself aren't quite sure what that is, and yet all of a sudden God brings to mind the guy who couldn't walk laying by the edge of the pool *waiting for the waters to be stirred . . . in order to heal.* I know, right? Good stuff.

Beloved, sit with your discontent long enough to have an honest convo with God about it. Ask yourself a whole buncha questions and see what honest answers arise. Know that there really *is* a time for everything under the sun, and so maybe, just maybe . . . your time to rename your discontent and call it Holy Spirit Stirring . . . is *now.* Cuz who knows? A spin like that may just turn the beat around, turn it upside down, and I'd love to hear it.

LET'S TALK LAZINESS

Let's talk laziness for a sec . . .

King Sol warned his kiddo against it when doling out all his advice. And since we're in a time in history when a sedentary lifestyle is being called the new smoking, well then, I guess the Bible really *is* still relevant after all. Mmmhmm.

Now, to be clear, I didn't say tiredness. That's its own deal, thus its own word. We'll liken laziness to an attitude, a mindset that convinces your body, mind, and soul that they're "too tired" to do whatever it is, in turn providing an excuse not to do it. Yikes, did I just say that? Us fifty-somethings really gotta mouth on us, don't we? But what if we're lazy not because we've done too much (again, that's tiredness), but because we haven't, in fact, done *enough*? We *haven't* moved our body/mind/soul, we *haven't* manifested the energy we carry, we *haven't* stirred ourselves up, and we literally haven't "gotten up and got going" despite nearly every morning telling ourselves, "I'm fine once I get up and get going." Right.

So unlike tiredness, which God gives us to indicate it's time to rest, laziness is an enemy *against* us, whispering in our ear that we're too exhausted to do whatever it is when, in fact, if we're honest with ourselves, we haven't even come *close* to expending enough energy to actually be exhausted.

I remember learning years ago how exercise actually *gives* you energy. I remember being mind-blown by that. Until I realized, "Wait, that makes sense! We actually manifest our own energy as we move, and so *no wonder* mornings are so hard on folks. We just need to get up and get going!" Right.

Tired. Lazy. Two different words. Be honest with *you*. You deserve it. *XO.*

PRAY FOR MORE PEACE

Today I pray for you more peace.

When our daughter was just a tiny tot, my parents took us all to the Omaha Zoo. And if you haven't been there, truly I tell you, it's *huge*. And after hours and hours at that great big zoo, we headed back to the car to call it a day. It was at that moment that this sweet little girl raised up her arms to my dad and said, "*More* zoo, Grandpa, *more* zoo!" Cuz see, that's what happens when you really love somethin', amen? You just want *more* of it. Right.

So today, Beloved, I pray for you *more* peace. Yes. *More* peace. More peace in who you already are, more peace in who you once were. More peace in the challenges that lie before you, more peace in all that you've already endured. More peace as you stop, more peace as you wait, more peace in your decision not to wait anymore as you realize you've circled the mountain long enough and it's time to climb the darn thing already.

Yes. More peace. More peace in the decision that needs to be made, more peace in the questions that need to be asked, more peace as you navigate your way through the storm, and more peace as you serve out your stint in the wilderness, trusting that it too has good purpose. Yes. More peace. More peace in the relationships that mean *so* much to you and more peace in putting up boundaries for those that are not serving or treating you well. More peace in finding a new place to sit if the one you are at requires altering who you already are every time you sit down. Yes. *More* peace. In the results. In the course of action. In the moments between those two things that feel like a lifetime. More peace as you trust that there really *is* still *so* much for you in God's storehouse. *Yes.*

Beloved, today I pray for you *more* peace. May it be yours. In *abundance*. And may you guard it . . . because it truly is . . . *that* valuable. It sure is. I love you. Amen.

HEAL ME AND CALM ME

Lord, please heal . . . and calm fear.

I was praying for you this morning, Beloved. Asking God to heal. Heal what is broken . . . hurting . . . heal what's in need of help or repair. Heal what is tearing you up and tearing you down and robbing you of life, not to mention good sleep. Heal what has been destroyed by disaster, damaged in shipping, dehydrated from all the tears shed. Yes.

Lord, please heal. And. Yes, Lord . . . *And.* Lord, as You heal . . . calm fear. Yes. Settle her spirit, give her a drink, meet her at the well or the side of the road or right there on the edge of her bed as You rub her back gently, reassuring her that everything's gonna be alright. Yes. Calm fear. The fear that is seeking to kill, steal, destroy her. The fear that's trying to name itself king. The fear that's doing its very best to cause her to forget just Who her King *is. You,* Lord, *You* are her King.

Calm fear. The fear that looks like a flood or a famine. The fear that resembles a desert or drought. The fear that has her convinced that the door will never open, the stone will never be rolled, and the mountain will never ever be moved. Yes, Lord, *that* fear. Calm it. Calm *her.* Look her straight in the eyes while clutching her shoulders and remind her that You are both with her *and* for her, and *You* are gonna see her through this thing she is going through *right now* on her journey back home to You. Yes.

Lord, please heal . . . *and* calm fear. Oh, and one more thing, Lord—tell her she's loved, OK?

Day 106

MAY YOU SEE IT

Today may you see it.

It's my prayer for you today, Beloved. I mean it. Today may you *see* it. Yes. Today may you *see* what it is that you are so desperately longing for, what it is that you have been so patiently or impatiently waiting for. Today may you *see* it and see it *so* clearly that your only response mimics Thomas's when he realized it really *was* his Savior right there in the flesh standing right in front of *him* . . . Oh . . . *my* . . . God. And you'll mean it. You sure will.

Today may you see it. The prosperity, the favor, the massive cloud rolling in to shield you from the sun's intense rays, and as you do, you'll whisper, "Oh my God . . . You are *here*."

Beloved, today may you see it. May you *see* the stone roll away, the mountain move, the sea part, the prison doors fling open. Today may you *see* God's hand lift you up out of the pit. Today may you *see* it. *See* what is right in front of you and name it Purpose. *See* what is behind you and name it Look How Far I Have Come. *See* what is within you and name it I Am Not Alone Amen and Amen. Today may you *see* it. The goodness of God in the land of the living, cuz FYI, that's where you're currently living. Today may you *see* it . . . and *know* . . . it really *is* . . . God. Yes. Fulfilling God's purpose for you and providing for you every step of the way, in ways you like, and in ways you absolutely despise, but it's because your humanness can't possibly grasp the crux of your holiness. Yes.

Beloved, today may you *see* it. The love of God *in* you. The love of God *for* you. Letting *you* know . . . you are *seen*. XO.

{Psalm 128:5–6}

WAIT A SECOND

Slow down enough to say, "Wait a second . . ."

If God parted a humongous sea for my journeying ancestors as they reached the edge of it, then who's to say that God won't part the sea of how-in-the-heck-am-I-gonna-get-through-this for *me*? If God made sure there was a great big fish in the raging waters to swallow up thrown-overboard Jonah and save him from drowning, who's to say God won't save me from drowning in my very own fear of going where I believe God is calling me?

Hmmm. Wait a second. Naomi is over there rocking her grandbaby despite the fact that she lost her husband *and* both her sons. So who's to say that God won't do what looks seriously impossible for me too? Wait a second. Sarah's moved from Kotex to Poise, and yet here she is in the maternity section at Target. So who's to say that God won't deliver New out of *me* too? Wait a second. There were thousands of hungry peeps that one day, and yet some kid's lunch was all that was found, and so Jesus took what was in that kid's hand and multiplied it and put it in His disciples' hands, and then *they* fed all the peeps with it. So who's to say that God won't take what's in *my* hand and multiply it and do the very same thing?? Wait a second. God provided a ram in the thicket at the top of that mountain, and no one was shouting "Hallelujah!" louder than Abe. Except Isaac.

Wait a second. Wait. A. Second.

Beloved, slow down long enough . . . calm down long enough . . . fear not long enough . . . to say to yourself . . . "*Wait a second.*" For truly I tell you . . . in that space of a second . . . Possible arises . . . bringing with it all of the strength and the hope that Possible possesses . . . providing what it is that you need . . . to believe one more day. The portion you need for *this* day, this day we name "Today." *Yes.* Wait a second.

Day 108

NEED A LIFT?

Need a lift?

Picture it. Your car breaks down in the middle of nowhere in the hundred-degree heat, and you have no choice but to hoof it ten miles to the next stop for help, and of course your cell is dead because, hello, it's always dead when you actually need it. You're walking. In the heat of the day. A friend out of the blue (one of my fave expressions) pulls up alongside you and says, "Hey, need a lift?" Hallelujah-Sweet-Jesus-*yes* you need a lift.

Now, Beloved . . . imagine it is your *soul*, not your flesh, walking down that road, out in the sweltering heat, and Jesus—yes, Jesus (out of the blue, of course)—pulls up alongside you and says to you, "Hey, need a lift?" To which, of course, your soul cries out, "*Heck yes, I need a lift. I've been through a lot, and this road is endless, so scooch over. I'm gettin' in.*"

Amen. And you climb in beside Jesus. And Jesus . . . as you cruise down that highway together . . . lifts your *soul* . . . by reminding your soul just Who your God *is*. Yes. Jesus glances over you at you while keeping His hands on the wheel and says calmly to your overwhelmed, exhausted, worn-out soul . . . Your God is Provider. Your God is Protector. Your God is all-powerful, and your God is gonna see you through this. Your God is water, your God is bread, your God is light and shelter and shield, and your God is your strength. Yes.

Your God is with you and for you and knows you are human, and so, in turn, knows that you can't *possibly* understand every *why*. But truly I tell you, you can *rely* on the God Who formed you, created you, and *sent* you to fulfill God's purpose *for* you on Earth. Your God raises and lowers and helps and defends and will never, *ever* leave or forsake you. And that's when Jesus stops the car and looks you straight in the eye and says, "I'm not kidding—don't *ever* forget that." And you promise Jesus you won't. And you won't. Until you do. And then Jesus will remind you again, cuz He's super awesome like that. Like totally.

Beloved, need a lift? You might. Cuz life is a highway. I love you. Amen.

GOD IS POSITIONING YOU

"My Daughter, I Am positioning you."

I started my reading for today and kept stopping to put Ms. Sharpie to work, scrolling out all kinds of stuff that I knew I'd want to write about. But then, upon reaching the end of my reading, I found a note I had written at the end of this date— long, long ago in the year 2020. You may know it as "Oh, *that* year." Right.

"My Daughter, I Am positioning you."

And when my eyes saw it, all my heart-mind-soul could rise up and say was . . . Write *that*. Tell 'em *that*. Share *that* because *that* might be exactly what someone needs to hear today, because she's calling it something *else* and has *never* considered it *this*, and maybe if she considers it *this*, it'll change the way she *sees* it, allowing her to *reframe* and *rename* it. Amen. Whew. Maybe.

Beloved, maybe our God is saying *this*, these *very words*, to *you*, *today*: *"My Daughter, I Am positioning you."* Positioning you to witness a miracle, or maybe even partake in one. Positioning you to do a hard thing and giving you the strength and courage to do it—that's why you've had weights and waits lately—strength training. Ohhh . . . right. Positioning you to receive help, receive favor, receive real love on this Earth.

"My Daughter, I Am positioning you."

To see. To hear. To know without doubt, cuz you were *there*. And then, like Thomas-who-gets-a-bad-rap, you too will exclaim, "OMG . . . it's *You*!" Positioning you to move to a new land or expand your existing land or Lord knows what else because God is God and God knows the *plan* . . . for *you*. Amen.

"My Daughter, I Am positioning you."

Go ahead, say it out loud; it feels really "real" when you do. Holy-Spirit-provided-breath will do that, you know. It sure will. It'll also help you . . . *believe it*. I mean it. *XO*.

GOD'S WAY IS OFTEN THROUGH

Recalling would remind her . . . whether she liked it or not . . . that more often than not . . . God's way was through.

I was so shook when I read these few simple words today. Shook in what we call a good way, I guess, because it reminded me that although I can't always understand *why*, God's way is most oftentimes . . . *through*.

"Your way was through the sea . . ."

Through. Through the sea, not around it. Through the mighty waters, not an alternate route. Through the desert and through the wilderness and through all the things. OMG . . . it's *You,* God, isn't it?? It's *You* that chose the way of *through*. Through the day. Through the night. Through all the stuff that we *so* wish wasn't, and yet that's the way we're to go. *Through.*

Suddenly, I saw a flashback as the Spirit recalled to me . . . The hunched-over woman in the temple that morn walking though all those pews to get to the hands she believed could help her look up again. The woman who made her way through that crowd of people, leaving drops of blood as she went, but at that point, she didn't give a rip what they thought because this was her last shot at healing, and she *knew* if she could just get to that hem . . . The woman was dragged through the dirt and thrown to the ground only to have the One Who could rescue and save her from the stones set to destroy her . . . meet her in that place and defend her. Esther walking through that palace that day on her way to confront and challenge the King. Hagar now-single-mama with baby on hip wearily trudging her way through the great abyss of abandonment. Naomi bravely and boldly and courageously wading through the grief and realizing as she did . . . I need to go home.

And I could go on. But by now you get the gist of what I'm saying to you, and I pray in some way it meets you, Beloved . . . as you go through . . . whatever it is and however it is . . . you are going *through*, remembering that you are not going *through* it . . . alone.

{Psalm 77:19}

WHEN THE WAIT ABOUT DOES YOU IN

We know God will make it all right . . . it's the waiting that about does us in.

Because sure, we know that God is the One Who makes all things right—but we also know that it'll be in God's time according to the plans that God has for us. We know that God *will* . . . eventually . . . it's the *waiting* that about does us in. And causes us to cry out, "*When?*" Amen. We know that God *will*, but we want God to *now*. The waiting about does us in.

So what do we do?

While we wait, we return. We head to the inner sanctuary. We hike it back to our soul. We return to the part of us that cannot be shaken because we're shaken enough, thank you very much. Yes. We return to the truth that God *will*, and we trust that there is good reason and purpose for the wait, *even if we can't understand it*. And then we take Sol's advice, and we refuse to lean on our own understanding, cuz I'll tell ya what—it's weak.

Here's what *else* we can do . . . We can head to the Psalms. We can wait with Dave. We can even borrow a few of his words if we want; he won't mind. And because I love alliteration like I do rhyming, I couldn't help but lift from the pages today some of the R words our guy Dave uses . . .

The first one is Rejection. So if that's where you're currently situated, Beloved, Dave feels ya. But after *that* R word came *these* R words, and if you're like me, you may want to jot 'em down. Yep. They are verbs that Dave asked God to *do* . . . and they are nouns that Dave used to remind himself Who God *is*. Restore. Repair. Rescue. Rally. Repay. Rock. Refuge. Rest. Rich Feast. *Rejoice.* Sounds like a pretty fab progression to me—*so* fab, in fact, that I think I'll offer up one of my own. Rock on.

Beloved, as you wait for our God to make it all *right* . . . *return* to Who you know God to *be* . . . and ask God for what you *need* . . . as you *wait.*

{Psalms 60–63}

BEAUTY WILL ARISE

Beauty will arise out of the hell you've been through.

And today, Beloved . . . you're gonna believe that. You sure are. You're gonna get up when you're done reading this, and you're gonna go take a good look at yourself in the mirror, no matter how tattered or torn or beat up you feel after the ride you've been on, and you're gonna tell the person looking back at you . . . "You listen here, young lady—God wastes *nothing*." *And if*, in fact, you've been to hell and back, then, Baby, you're gonna focus on the *back*. You sure are. And then you're gonna go ahead and lift a few of Dave's words, cuz you're friends now, so it's totally fine . . .

God *will* save. *And* rebuild. And you're gonna say it just like that. You sure are. And then you're gonna add your own tagline, cuz after all, you're a Psalmist too. *And* . . . I'm gonna *live again*. That's right. After all, Noah lived after the flood, and Daniel lived after the den, and Joe lived after the stint in the pit—and heck, he even ended up in the palace, *amen*. And let's not forget about Jonah; he's got a whale of a tale to tell (*grin*).

But also—*heck yes*. You're gonna head to the well within you and draw up a big hefty gulp of *beauty from ashes*, Baby, and you're gonna lap up that living water like nobody's business, cuz dangit—you're *parched*. Trips to hell and back will do that, you know. And then, since we've made it this far together, you're gonna indulge me by repeating after me, OK? Great.

"Beauty will arise . . . out of the hell I've been through."

And now you're gonna repeat that over and over and over again until your heart-mind-soul actually *believe* it. And it's gonna be awesome, cuz then Journey's gonna start croonin' . . . quiet at first like at the start of the concert . . . and then building up to the point of total rock-out. . . . Don't Stop Believing. Don't Stop Believing. Don't Stop Believing. *Amen.*

{Psalm 69:35–36}

THE BIRDS KEPT SINGING

The birds kept singing.

I sat in what seemed like the darkest of morns. I listened to the thunder as it rocked and it rolled and to the lightning as it, well, thunderstruck. It was loud. So loud. I wondered if those in my house would wake up, but I hadn't yet heard a peep. But what I *did* hear, above it all, was the birds of the air. The birds kept singing. I wrote those four words in my journal right after the words "thunder" and "lightning" and realized that what I was doing was penning my very own psalm.

The birds kept singing.

Suddenly, I was transported back in time, and I found myself walking alongside Jesus and the guys on one of the many field trips He led. I blended right in. There was no need to draw attention to the fact I was there. After all, lots of women followed Jesus. Word up and amen. And as we walked, Jesus talked and pointed things out, cuz that's what a good field trip leader does. He stopped us at one point and directed our eyes to the birds in the trees, and then He calmly said (or at least it's what I heard Him say) . . . "Friends, the birds aren't worried. They're not striving to earn God's favor because they know they *already have it.* They're not reaping *or* sowing *or* hoarding away all their stuff into barns, because truly I tell you . . . they *know* that their God will feed them."

And then He reminded us that worrying won't actually tack on any days to the story that's already been written for us, so it really is a waste of our precious, incredibly valuable time. He sure did. And then at that moment, as He laid down the mic and vanished from our sight, I realized I was back in my chair. And the thunder was still thundering, and the lightning was still lightning, and the rain was actually even much heavier than it was before. But the birds? The birds kept singing. *Knowing will do that.* And because knowing is intimate . . . no *one* and no *thing* can take it from you. *XO.*

{Matthew 6}

BRINGING FORTH GOOD WINE

How's this for a Reframe It, Rename It: Whatever or whoever is trampling on you is actually helping you bring forth good wine. I know, right???

I'm not saying that's what's happening, I'm saying, *what if you believed that's what's happening?* Just sayin'. Would it not breathe *life* into words like . . . "No weapon formed against you shall prosper." I have worked all things together for good. I know the plans that I have for you. Or how about the words Joe spoke to his bros after they sold him off and then came crawling back to him needing his help . . .

"But as for you, you meant evil against me; but God meant it for good, in order to bring it about as it is this day, to save many people alive." *OMG exactly, amen.*

Or how 'bout what wise King Sol taught us in his little book of proverbs . . .

"The Lord has made everything for its purpose, even the wicked for the day of trouble." *Yup.*

Beloved, you *know* how passionate I am about this. How on fire I am about it. Here's *why*: It's because I *so* strongly believe . . . that the power we've been given . . . is the power to decide . . . *what am I gonna call it?* (And if I have my way on it, someday God's gonna take me all across the land talkin' about it, cuz *dang*, if it's just not *so* stinkin' powerful. It sure is.)

Feeling trampled upon, Beloved? Reframe it and Rename it. And *call* it—*bringing forth good wine.* Heck to the y-e-s and amen. *XO.*

{Isaiah 54:17; Romans 8:28; Jeremiah 29:11; Genesis 50:20; Proverbs 16:4}

THE FIRST STEP TO FREEDOM

Being truly honest with yourself about yourself is the first step to freedom. Amen.
And FYI—it takes courage and bravery and a whole lotta guts, so don't equate this exercise to some small thing or you'll treat it as such. Amen. Yes. Freedom begins with honesty. Be honest with *yourself.* Like *really* honest. Like gut-wrenchingly honest, cuz remember how much better you feel when you're sick and you wrench out of your gut what is not serving you well. *Right.*

Where am I at? Where am I going? Why does this bother me *so* much? And your "this," of course, could be a full range of things. Ask yourself: Why is this affecting me so much? Cuz here's the thing, Beloved, getting to the heart of the matter is just that—getting to the heart. Your *own.*

Example: Someone says something to me that stirs me from placidness (which is a nice church-girl way of saying revved my engine hot, amen). If my engine is hot, I have to ask myself—*why* is this causing my engine to be so hot? This, of course, is the antithesis of allowing my engine to backfire right there on the spot. Been-there-done-that about a million times, and if I myself am being honest—at times I still do. But hey—work in progress, amen?

Here's the other thing about honest uncovering—as you discard the layers, you may just discover what makes your heart go tick-tick-boom, and the world could use your good tick-tick-boom, you little firecracker, you. Something may cut you deep because you're the one God is gonna use to bring healing. Something may break you because God is going to use your brokenness to feed the hungry. Something may stir you from your own placidness and hurl you right into the wilderness because God needs your wind to show others the way out.

Beloved, honesty is hard. Honesty with *self* is hard. It includes taking time to take stock, and asking yourself hard questions, and then answering those hard questions with the truth instead of anything else. It's what I've discovered as a gift of my current decade that I've lovingly named "Owning My Crap." I knew you'd like that.

Beloved, your life awaits you. Begin with being honest with self. It's the gateway to freedom. Let's go. *XO.*

RAISED FROM THE DEAD

How did she know that people really do rise from the dead?

Easy. She was one of them.

So are you, Beloved. Proof right here on this Earth that someone can take a trip to hell and back and survive it. That someone can be burned and yet arise from the ashes. That someone can have dried up bones and yet get her groove back and dance once again. Someone whose hard didn't weaken her, but in fact *strengthened* her to do all that the Lord her God *still had for her to do.* And it actually makes total sense . . .

When you join Martha on that dusty road way-back-when on the day Jesus *finally* showed up, too-little-too-late, to heal her bro Laz, as she thrusts her fists into Jesus's chest while screaming . . . "Where *were* You??" Which, by the way, seems the most appropriate outcry when the One you *know* to be Healer . . . doesn't show up to heal. Exactly. But see, in that moment . . . Jesus tells M Who He is, and then asks M the question that would stop her in her tracks and cause her to think.

Martha, I *Am* the Resurrection. I *Am* the *life. Do you believe this?*

Beloved, here's what I know—the *truth* of *Who God is . . . raises me* from the *dead.* Yes. It raises me up. It lifts me out of the pit. It calls me out of the grave and tells me that I can walk. It restores my soul. It revives my spirit. It *raises* me . . . from the *dead.* Fact. This is my story, this is my song, and this is about the *eternal soul within me.* The Spirit that gives me breath and the hope that serves as CPR for my soul. *Yes.* A CPR for my soul when my soul feels dead within me, telling me with every thrust upon my chest . . . *Don't stop believing. I Am* the Resurrection. I *Am* the Way out of this pit. *I Am* the Truth that's gonna set you free. I *Am* the *Life . . . your* life . . . *within* you. Now, My Beloved . . . *arise.*

So . . . How did she know that people *really do* rise from the dead? Easy. *She was one of them.*

{John 11:17–44}

SECTION BY SECTION

Repairing section by section. It's a process, Beloved.

You want the repairs to happen overnight. You don't wanna wait. You despise the fact that repairing happens section by section, and if you called the shots, there'd be one giant roll of endless duct tape—no other supplies needed, thank you very much. Because quick fixes are our favorite. Just ask Insta or Facebook or whatever new thing is on the scene. Right. But see, *repairing*, just like *rebuilding*, is most oftentimes not done in a day. The whole Rome thing, remember? Right. Repairing what has been torn down or trampled on or broken or burned happens section by section. It sure does. One glance through Nehemiah 3 will teach a gal or guy that. Psst . . . it also teaches you the importance of who is standing next to you, and that's *big*.

Beloved, I don't know what's in need of repair for you. I don't know what's been torn down or trampled upon or what's been broken or how you've been burned. What I *do* know is this—

Rebuilding takes time. Repairing takes time. It happens section by section.

Why does our God do it this way? Hey, I don't have all the answers, but I have to ask myself: Is it because God loves me *so* much that I'm actually given the time to witness it and not miss it, behold it and actually believe it, play an active role in the repairing and rebuilding so that I can then stake my claim in it and guard it, protect it, defend it? And *if* that's the case, and based on who I know God to be, I think there's a pretty good chance that it could be . . . then perhaps I really *can* trust the process . . . as each section is repaired. Rock on, Beloved. Section by Section. *XO.*

{Nehemiah 3}

GOD IS DIRECTING YOUR STEPS

She took great comfort in knowing—that God directed her steps.

For this is how she'd survive in the midst. Yes. The knowledge of who He is before her, standing strong between her and the battle ahead. She needed to put Who she knew Him to be before her own mindset that tried to convince her . . . it's too late, there's nothing you can do, you're not strong enough, you can't win . . . and so many more . . . Sigh, yes so many more. The thoughts that gathered and seemed to gain strength, worry and fear at the top. Anyone? I know, sister. I know, brother. I know.

Beloved, take heart, the Lord Himself goes before you. Yes, *before* you. And *yes*, you may be walking into battle, and if not today, there will come a day, for our battles seem to provide mighty opportunity to watch Him move . . . and defend . . . and strengthen . . . and save . . . and provide . . . and deliver. Amen.

Name your battle. And then remember the name of your God. And put *that* in front of your own understanding, your own thoughts of fear and of worry. Yes. The name of God is I Am. *Hallelujah.* I Am Protector. I Am Defender. I Am all you need. This I promise. I Am your Shepherd. I Am your Father. I Am always with you and for you. I Am. I Am Sovereign. I Am Just. I Am Love and I Am Mercy. I Am working all things together for good . . . even now when you just can't see it. I Am.

The unchanging truth of who He is, beautifully positioned between you and the battle you face. You are not alone, Beloved. Not even for a moment.

{Proverbs 16:9}

WHERE YOU ARE IS WHERE GOD IS

Every place you find yourself today will be a place God also is.

Sure, it may seem like the simplest of statements. But also . . . it's true.

Beloved, every place you find yourself today will be a place God also is. The boardroom. The courtroom. The waiting room. Your living room. The drive to work. The trip to the store. The appointment you're dreading, or the one you're so hoping is gonna bring you some much-needed good news (or at least some answers). Yes. The divorce hearing. The annual review. The "same ole shift" you've been working for years. The nursing home. The funeral home. The laundry pile on the table in your dining room. You know the one. In your cubicle. On that line. Every prayer that whispers, "Lord, I'm begging You, please, help me just one more time." Yes.

On your journey. The one to better health, because lately as you get older, you've been thinking about that a whole lot more. Physical, mental, spiritual, you name it— you're all in. Yes. The pit you're trying to claw your way out of. The mountain you so desperately wish God would move so that you don't have to climb it, amen. The desert of what feels like endless disappointment. The wilderness you've been wandering in for far too long. Your storm. Your still. The green pasture He's made you lie down in. The victory. The defeat. Every ugh. Every drudge. Every gladness. Every sadness. Every praise. Every cry. . . . Yes. God. There.

Truly I tell you, Beloved, every place you find yourself today is a place God also is. Ask Him to show you. You can do that, you know. Ask Him to show you and bless you and keep you and make His face shine upon you and be gracious unto you and give you His peace. Cuz I reckon that's what you're looking for, amen. Beloved, God Himself goes before you. *Believe it.* For as you do, you will look for Him *in* it. Every place, every stage, amen. And *you* will know . . . you're not alone. *XO.*

Day 120

KNOWING GOD KNOWS

There was a certain calm about her, not because she had it all figured out, but because she knew that God knew . . . and that was enough.

I'm talking about an inner calm that has come with knowledge and time, one that's arrived as the journey has continued to play out, one that has deepened (thank God), and I pray will continue to. Because here's the truth, friends—God knows. Yes. *God knows.* God *knows* what's goin' down—behind the scenes, behind the doors, behind it all—every thought/word/deed for or against you. God knows. Every tear. Every "Why?" Every "Where are You?" And every "When is it gonna be over, Lord?"

Yes. God knows. And that *knowing God knows* is oftentimes gonna need to be enough. To get you through. To get you over that mountain and across that sea and sustain you in the wilderness while you are there. To get you through that sleepless night. Hey, we've all been there. The truth that God knows coupled with the truth that God makes all things right, that all things in fact work together for good, that God knows the plans He has for you, cuz He wrote every word reminding you that every syllable has power and purpose, amen . . . and that He's perfecting your faith all the way through it—even when we don't like it or can't see it.

Yes. God knows. Every hurt. Every worry. Every pain that's so internal it can't even be properly named. Every wonder. Every dream. Every wish you make upon a star and every one you don't because you figure what's the use anymore. Yes. God knows. And there's a certain calm that comes with that—a peace. Yes. A calm and a peace that knows that God knows, and since God is for us, then really, who can be against us? Right.

Beloved, God rescues us by reminding us. Read that again. God *rescues* us . . . by *reminding* us. That He is Parent-Provider-Protector-All-Powerful. That He will never leave or forsake us. That His compassions are new every morning and that

His mercies are too. That His grace is amazing. That His love is unending. That He is All-seeing, All-hearing, All-*knowing*. That *you* are not alone and never will be, and *that* is a promise you're gonna wanna hold on to. It sure is. *XO.*

THE WEIGHT OF EVERYTHING MATTERS

The weight of everything . . .

. . . is recorded. Because it matters. That's why it's recorded. Amen. That's why when you go see the doctor, the nurse asks you to step on the scale while jotting it down in your chart because the weight of everything matters. *Yes.* The Doc will then look at that number and assess if what you are carrying is negatively affecting your life, if it's causing you to struggle, if it's causing you pain, and if it's preventing you from doing things you could otherwise do. *Now apply that to your heart, mind, and soul, amen.* Honestly, I don't think I'll ever get over how stinkin' cool it is that God designed our flesh to teach us so dang much about our soul. At least I hope I never do. The weight of everything . . . matters. It plays a significant role in your ability to move and breathe and have your being.

My mind races ahead from Ezra to Hebrews as I hear the Spirit within rise up and whisper . . . *Throw off that which entangles you and run the race set before you.* Easier said than done? That's an understatement. Like a *humungous* understatement. *Or is it?*

What if I throw off my forgetfulness of Who God is? And what if, as I throw off that forgetfulness, I return to Who I know God to be in the midst of the weight that I'm carrying? What if I return to the soul sanctuary where holy truths are guarded and sacred, and upon seeing them I remember . . . wait a second . . . God *is* . . . Provider. Protector. All-Powerful. Not to mention my Parent. God has a history of raising up what remains—heck, even raising up what's long gone. God is known for rolling away big giant stones.

And see, when I'm in that sacred-grounds-soul-space barefoot and free . . . I remember how God multiplied those loaves. I remember how the oil didn't run out in the drought until the rain started falling again. I remember how even post-menopause, God showed a woman way-back-when that there was still *new within her for her to deliver. Amen.*

The weight of everything . . . matters. *That* is why it's recorded. *XO.*

{Ezra 8:34; Hebrews 12:1–3}

THE WORK CAN RESUME

Just because the work on the house stopped, doesn't mean it can't resume.

You hop in your car. You take off for work or for play or whatever. You get to the stop sign. You stop, put it in park, turn off your car, get out, and plant your butt on the asphalt, for apparently this is your new permanent address.

Oh wait, you *don't* do that? Why not? Is it because *the stop is not the end of your journey but instead just simply a part of it?* Gosh, I love your grin.

Beloved, you're the house. You're the temple. The Spirit of God resides within you, and lest you don't believe me or lest you've forgotten, go ahead and breathe in and breathe out for a sec . . . yup, there it is. Talk about an awesome ongoing reminder. Nice touch in our design, Lord. So *yes*, maybe the work on your house *has* stopped, but that sure as heck doesn't mean that the work can't *resume*. Bing bam boom. Grin. Also—it's *true*.

Maybe the work has stopped for some of the same reasons it was stopped back in the Ezra days. . . . Maybe you were deceived. Or discouraged. Maybe your plans were frustrated by the hands of another or a whole bunch of others or even your own, for that matter. Maybe the work stopped because you needed a break from the work, but just like *at* work, there is a time limit, you know. Now see, there's that grin again for the win. Maybe the work has stopped because it seems too overwhelming. And so instead, you've decided to settle with what you've got, despite secretly longing for more, and then ugh, in turn feeling guilty for wanting more because you're afraid the watching Christian world will call you ungrateful for wanting more—*geesh, what a cycle of crap. Get off that bike stat.* Gosh, that's the third grin this mornin'. I'd better stop while I'm ahead.

Beloved, just because the work on the house *stopped* doesn't mean it can't *resume*. It doesn't mean you can't *renovate*. It doesn't mean you can't *rebuild*. It doesn't mean you can't *regrow*. And it sure as heck doesn't mean you can't be *resurrected, amen*. Stops are stops. But see the thing is, you're not out of gas. Last grin. And I stinkin' love it. Let's cruise.

FREE TO REBUILD

Captivity has ended. You are free to rebuild.

Captivity has ended. You are no longer bound. The wait is over, and you hold in your hands the remnant of what remains . . . After. Yes. After the relationship has ended. After the job has ended. After the diagnosis is realized and the plan to heal is in place. After the help you received broke chains that at one time you never thought could be broken. After the treatment did its thing. After the time spent in prison—either the actual one with iron bars that the world can see or the actual one with iron bars only you and perhaps a handful of others can see. Yes.

Captivity has ended. And now . . . you are *free to rebuild.* And *you*, Beloved . . . are now a *survivor. Yes.* A survivor set to rebuild. A survivor whose spirit is stirred beyond even your own comprehension, which in turn is strengthening you to do what you never thought in a million years you'd be able to do . . . Rebuild. Yes. Rebuild from the remnant. Oh, I'm sorry—*rebuild from the remnant.* There we go. Rebuild . . . from what . . . Remains. Because see, you know darn well that this big book we love tells us over and over again that it's not the size of the remnant that matters—it's the fact that . . . a *remnant remains.* Bing Bam Boom. Yes, indeed.

One tiny seed. One drop of oil. One ray of light. One hem of a robe. *One shred of hope, amen.* What is a remnant? *Enough.* Enough . . . to Rebuild.

And don't you forget it. And don't you stop believin'. I mean it. I'm cheering you on. I'm here to assist. I suck with a hammer, but I do OK with words. And I love ya. Go. Rebuild. From the Remnant. And read Ezra. *XO.*

I WILL

I will.

Rise again. Begin again. Be restored once again. Amen. I will believe again no matter how long it's been, since I truly like-absolutely-zero-doubt believed—like to the tips of my fingers and the soles of my feet and the depths of my soul believed. Yes. I will battle again. I will succeed again, and I will fail again. I will ask God again and again and again cuz I *can.* I sure can.

I will seek again—like really seek—not like a teen asked to find something in his or her room. (In their defense, have you *seen* their rooms lately? I digress.) I will look ahead again while also occasionally looking back again in order to remember just how far I've come. I will build towers in the wilderness and hewn-out cisterns in the desert because I know there are blessings to be found in those places, and I want to *see* them and *draw out* every one of them. I will heal again. Recover again. Regain my strength and my might and my hope once again. I will sleep again. I will *believe* that I will sleep again. I will go to bed knowing that the sun will rise once again, bringing with it new mercies, new compassion, new grace. And I'm ready for all of that new. I sure am.

I will be taken new places and given new mountains to climb, not as some sort of punishment, but as a gift from my God so that I can discover what it is I'm truly made of. Yes. I will face giants. And I will defeat them. I will endure wars. And take booty from them. I will grow. I will gain. I will regain. There may be pain. I will be replenished again, and my dry bones will dance again, so someone cue the '80s station. I mean it. I will *survive.* So someone cue that song up too. Seriously. I will.

So the question is this, Beloved: Can two really small, reeeally small words, hold power? You tell me.

IS IT TIME?

Beloved, ask yourself, "Is it time?"

Is it time to come out of hiding and take courage? Is it time to begin to restore? Is it time to start to put things in place for you to rebuild what has been destroyed, torn down, taken from you? Is it? Is it time to speed up, or is it time to slow down? Is it time to rest, or have you rested long enough? Be honest with yourself. This is key. And remember . . . God knows. Which is good, cuz it means you can hash this out honestly with this God of yours. The One Who just happens to be the One Who fearfully and wonderfully knit you together and is also supplying your very breath at this moment. *Yes.*

Is it time? Is it time to look back and gain strength from it? Is it time to replenish dry bones? Cuz word on the street is it's possible for those dry bones of yours to get their groove back, and I've got the boombox loaded and ready to hit Play when you're ready. Is it time? To take possession of the land you've been given instead of spending one more day believing you're not cool enough for you to possibly even step foot in it?

Beloved, ask yourself, "Is it time?" Wrestle with God, if that's what it takes. Set that heart dial of yours to Seek so that your eyes are as wide open as they can be so you're sure not to miss it. Be brave . . . enough . . . to pray. Ask God if it's time. And if God has *already* shown you it is, well then I reckon right now your mouth could catch flies. Beloved, the Lord your God is with you wherever you go. And that's the truth, not just one chick's early morning ramblings over coffee. Sol was right, you know, when he wrote about there being a time for everything under the sun.

So ask yourself, "Is it time?" And then sit with it a minute. Be still and know. That God is God. And whether the time is now, or the time is not now, or the time is spread out over a wingspan of time . . . you will *never* be alone in that time. And that's a fact. I love you. Rock on.

{2 Chronicles 21–24}

BRAVE ENOUGH, STRONG ENOUGH

Her heart was courageous, brave enough to build, and strong enough to remove and tear down what needed to be removed and torn down, so she could live fully . . . abundantly . . . free.

Yes. Finally. Amen. She strengthened herself against that which sought to kill/steal/destroy her, by placing forces of truth, the truth of Who she knew God to be, in the fortified place of her soul she calls sanctuary. She would return there when the battles grew hot, when the wars just wouldn't end, and she'd ask that God of hers for exactly what she needed, no holds barred, amen. She took note of Who stood beside her and made adjustments as necessary. She sought the Lord because she knew the Lord always won—even if she didn't always agree with the Lord's definition of won. She envisioned her heart with a great dial upon it, and she turned that dial to *seek*. Yes. For seeking *keeps* seeking . . . *until* . . . it *finds*. Yes.

She cried out when she needed help, knowing her God would help her. She periodically stopped and checked in with herself, asking herself, "Have you considered . . . ?" When she was afraid, she would pray and remind herself of just Who her God is, recalling every miracle she's witnessed up to this point, every stone rolled away, every moment that had blown her mind causing her to exclaim, "OMG!" and absolutely meaning every word. Like Thomas when he finally realized his God really was . . . *alive*. Yes.

She would remember that praise reroutes the enemy, and so even if it took some mustering, she'd do it, because she wanted the enemy to flee. She believed in the Lord her God to the depths of her desperately-in-need-of-a-spring-pedicure toes, and because of that, she was established. She would remember that battles yield booty, sometimes so much it takes three days to haul it all home. She remembered that there are blessings to be found in the valleys. And she remembered that through it all, the God Who created her and had written her Scripture was with her and for her and fulfilling His holy and powerful purpose for her. *Amen.*

A PLACE TO REBUILD

Maybe what has been torn down . . . is giving you a place to rebuild.

And how would it affect your strength and your zeal and, heck, your overall attitude and mood if you believed that in fact this was true? Like *really* believed it? Like no-one-can-convince-you-otherwise believe it? What if today you believed that what has been torn down is for your *benefit*? That it is actually *providing* you space that is clear and free, space no longer at war, space that is calling out to you, "I'm a blank slate, let's do this thing!" *What if?*

And what if you hold up that "What if?" Making it front and center and calling it good instead of evil. Allowing it to fill your heart-mind-and-soul with all sorts of possibilities because now *nothing* is off limits. After all, you're dealing with the Lord your God, the Creator of All, the One for Whom all things are possible and nothing is too hard, the One Who gives beauty for ashes, not to mention the God Who *raises the dead to life*, amen. And *heck yes*.

What if *empty* really *isn't* the end? What if it's really . . . the *beginning*? What if what has been torn down, despite not being easy and-that's-an-understatement—what if the *empty* that *remains* . . . is *beckoning you to begin again*? To rebuild again. To restore again. To make new again. Yes. New . . . that will serve you . . . even *better* than before. And what if *today* . . . you *believed* that? And you let me and Journey (the band, as well as your own) serenade you through? *What if?*

Beloved, I swear to God, I hope what you receive from me in this plot of land is this—the ability, the strength, the courage and fortitude and support and cheering-on needed . . . to help you *reframe* . . . and *rename*. Yes. For truly I tell you, it *may* just help you . . . *regain*. Your hope. Your peace. Your strength. Your zeal. Your light. Your flame. Dang, I hope so . . . cuz watching you shine and set the world ablaze . . . is my favorite.

YOUR OWN EASTER STORY

You've got your own Easter story—and no one can take that from you.

The Easter story that is yours—the story that no one gets to dispute. Four gospel accounts written by four different guys, and although their details differ, one thing remains the same—He is risen. Indeed. And see, Beloved, you've got your own story, yes—your own story of how it went down, how you got to that tomb. The place that perhaps you felt as if you yourself were as good as dead and buried. The place you never thought you'd arise from . . . and yet . . . here you are.

Maybe there was an Earthquake in your story, something that although it shook you to your knees, it also rolled the giant stone away, and for that, you will always be grateful. Maybe you went by yourself to that place, that place you didn't want to go but knew that you had to go, or maybe others accompanied you. Maybe you were worried as you went. Or scared. Or excited. Or all of the above because the beauty of the soul-sanctuary is that it is equipped to carry more than one emotion at any given time.

Your own Easter story. How you got there. What you saw. The emotions it invoked in you and how those emotions fueled you and moved you. Yes. Your own Easter story. One that may sound like Matt's or Mark's or John's or Luke's or may not sound like any of them, but instead is filled with details that are uniquely your own, details you're not soon to forget. Thank God. Cuz someone needs to hear 'em.

Your own Easter story. A story of tears and laughter. Battles won and battles lost. A story filled with moments of great panic and fear and moments of overwhelming, undeniable joy. A story that recalls your own death . . . *and* resurrection. A story . . . of *life. Yours.* Given to you by the One Who gives you God's very own breath every moment of every day that you're here . . . so that you will *never* forget . . . You *belong* to Someone. You are *connected* to Someone. The very same Someone Who penned your very own Easter story. A story of *endless love* . . . and *victory*. Hallelujah. Indeed.

KEEP LOOKING

He was trying to see Who Jesus was, but on account of the crowd, he could not, because he was short in stature.

And if you currently can't, for whatever the reason, Beloved, I urge you . . . keep trying. Zaccheaus was more than a wee little man. He was a man desperate to see Who Jesus really was.

Maybe you're like Zacchaeus. Zaccheaus couldn't see Him. The crowd was thick, he was short, the reasons were valid, amen. *Yours are too.*

The marriage has failed; you can't see Him. The checkbook is drained; you can't see Him. The loss is real, and you feel it so deep that you're not sure how you're supposed to go on; you can't see Him. The pain continues, and the promise seems light-years away; you can't see Him. The desire to throw in the towel is so fierce at this point that it's whipping you like a wet one in the junior high locker room, and man it stings; you can't see Him.

And you're desperate to see Him. See Who He *really* is. See He's Provider. See He's Protector. See He is Parent and Friend. See how He plans to turn this thing around because you know that He can. You're just not sure why He hasn't, and it's causing you to feel like He won't.

"He was trying to see Who Jesus was, but on account of _____, he could not."

Maybe you're like Zaccheaus. If so, keep listening, friend of mine, for I've got some good news to share . . . Zaccheaus refused to give up. Desperation would serve him, not destroy him. (Please read that again.) Zaccheaus saw Jesus. And Jesus saw Zaccheaus. Jesus called Zaccheaus by name. Jesus called Zaccheaus to Himself. And after that, Zaccheaus was not the same. For he saw Who Jesus really was. A God Who sees him and calls him by name, a God Who calls him to Himself, amen.

Beloved, if you can't currently see Him, first off, I'm so sorry—pain and heartache and struggle are real; secondly, I urge you . . . keep trying. For truly I tell you, just like our new friend Zaccheaus, God sees you. And calls you by name. And to Himself. To show you Who He really is. Amen.

{Luke 19:1–10}

MOURNING LOOKS TO MORNING

Mourning looks . . . to morning.

Mourning also . . . mourns. Yes. It gives itself the space it needs to spread out, flail its arms and legs, shake its fists, beg for what it needs to rise . . . yet again. And *as* it does . . . it *looks* . . . to morning. Because that's what hope does. It forces us, thank God, to look ahead, to behold what remains to be seen. Yes.

We mourn. *And.* We look to morn. We do *both*. We allow the feelings and emotions we have to coexist, allowing them to make peace with one another instead of vying for the title of "most important," or worse, believing that one is more "holy," thus denying your own human existence. The existence you were created to possess, by the way. And a guy-God named Jesus Who came in the flesh—just like you—to live out that humanness, including every one of those human emotions, so you could see *that it's OK to experience them too.* They're part of your DNA. Yes.

Mourning . . . looks . . . to Morning. It sure does. Through the tears, we look to the dawn of a brand new day, to a sun still commanded to rise. Through the grief, we look to the empty of what is, and the resurrection of what just might be. Through the sadness, we look to the joy set before us . . . believing that there is indeed some joy set before us . . . set aside just for us . . . and it's just up ahead. We mourn, as Paul says, *with* hope. We hold on to hope *as* we mourn, and we don't ditch the mourning in the "name of what a real Christian would do." Gimme a break.

We mourn *with* hope. Yes. A companion to our mourning, hope whispers to us in the darkest pits, in the darkest caves, in the darkest most solitary graves . . . "New is coming." And we believe that, because we're so desperate to believe it that we can't help but believe it . . . and that in itself is perhaps yet one more reason why desperation can be the very best thing to happen to us. Yes.

Mourning . . . mourns. *And.* Mourning looks . . . to Morning.

YOUR SCRIPT IS BEING FULFILLED

Beloved, your script is being fulfilled.

So own it. I mean it. Because it's *yours*. Yours to make notes on as you go and be confused about various stage directions, and yours to fill with tear and coffee stains when the nights are long and the dawn just won't come. Your *script* is being fulfilled. It is written—three words Jesus repeated to the enemy when He was tempted to forget Who God is. Protector. Provider. All-Powerful. Amen.

It is written. And there will be pages when you find yourself in the garden of Gethsemane, and you too will find yourself on your knees and begging God for it to be any other way. There will *also* be lines that surprise you in really cool OMG ways, and sentences where you literally LOL because the Author knows laughter is medicine. There will be times you're on stage front and center, and other times you're off in the precepts, because guess what? There are others in your script as well. Those who surround you and cheer you on . . . and those who don't. But you return to what you know about the Author, the One Who wrote your script from In the Beginning to final Amen, the One Who assures you that *all* things have been worked together for good.

It is written. And that assurance keeps you going, living out your story, especially when you remind yourself that good means sufficient to meet the purpose. The *Author's* powerful purpose for your life that no human can take and no enemy can kill/steal/destroy . . . because it is written. *Yes.* A purpose you won't always understand, or like. A script filled with every emotion played out through plot twists you never saw coming. A life given to you and fueled by God's very own breath until you breathe your last.

Beloved, your script is being fulfilled. And as it is . . . remember that it was written in full by the One Who fearfully and wonderfully created you, knit you together by hand, and vowed to never leave or forsake you. Return to that truth when you desperately wish the script said something else . . . pray continually . . . and remember to rejoice and celebrate every word that you just can't believe gets to be a part of your script. *XO.*

ASKING IS WISDOM

She cried out to God, "I can't do it all!" God answered her, "Oh, good—you finally got it."

There'll be times you need to seek in order to see God in the answer. There'll *also* be times you pick up your Bible and realize there are only like two highlights, cuz the whole thing is just a rattling-off of a bunch of folks whose names you can't pronounce. And then you smack your head as you hear God chuckle while spitting out, "Oh *good*, you finally *got it*." Cuz God is funny like that and pretty dang good at getting a point across, even if it takes us a while to get it.

One of the gifts I'm gleaning since reaching my fifties is the ability to own my crap. I'm a work in progress, of course, but progress is progress nonetheless. Truth: I can't do it all. I *want* to do it all. I *love* doing it all. But see, asking? Asking for help, assigning and appointing, allowing someone else in this great beautiful text we call life to share in the work . . . that's not *weakness*, it's *wisdom*.

Ya know, I began to realize after my claim-to-fame (if that's what ya call it) post "Ask Him Again" back in 2019 hit the streets, that perhaps what humans *really* want from one other . . . is permission to be *human*. And what we truly want from *God* . . . is permission to ask again and again not only because we know we are heard . . . but also because God *knows* we're human . . . and because we trust the answer will some-how-someday-someway come . . . from the Parent Who loves us without fail and will do *whatever* it takes to show us what we need to see, hear, experience . . . in order to gain that heart of wisdom. A Parent Who'll make you lie down in green pastures to rest even though you're kicking and screaming. A Parent Who'll bring you to your knees in order to finally get your attention. A Parent Who whispers, "You're gonna make it, and there's not *one second* I won't be with you." Amen. Asking is Wisdom.

CARRYING YOUR HOLY

God helped her carry what was hard . . . what was holy . . . what was hers.

And that's the *truth*. Amen.

It's hard to make sense of the story in the OT where God burst out against the guy who was trying to steady the cart that the Ark of the Covenant of God rode upon . . . *until you keep reading . . . and realize . . .* (wait for it . . . you know I love a good mind-blown moment) . . . you can't steady the cart for the Ark to ride *upon* . . . you need to *carry* the Ark yourself . . . *within*. Dang, I love this book.

Beloved, God . . . helped . . . the Levites . . . who were *carrying* the Ark of the Covenant. Yes. Oh, and a few verses prior, it tells us that they *carried* it . . . *on their shoulders*. I know, right? Cross to bear, anyone? Right. God helped her carry what was hard . . . what was holy . . . what was hers. To *carry*. So then, I reckon it should be no surprise that Dave would go on to then instruct his peeps . . . Seek the Lord and His strength; seek His presence *continually*. Right.

Because we all continually carry *something* . . . amen? The hard, the holy, the parts of our story we wish never would've been written, the blessings, the favor, the moments we wish would never end, and our *God*, the knowledge of Who our God *is* . . . helps us carry it. Yes. Reminding us that God will provide again and protect again and show us His power again and will *help us carry what is ours to carry*.

I love you. I love you. I love you. Amen.

{1 Chronicles 13–16}

BEHOLDING AND WEEPING

He beheld her . . . and wept.

Palm Sunday. A day known for its rejoicing. A day associated with a great parade as the King casually-yet-valiantly strolls in on a colt not yet broken. Yes. But sometimes, a girl just has to seek more. Indeed.

This morning before heading to my regularly scheduled reading, I wanted to head back to Jerusalem for a day in the life of that day. And as I did, I noticed something I *hadn't* before, and you *know* how that lights this girl up.

"And when he was come near, he beheld the city, and wept over it."

And I'll tell ya what, it struck me just right as I envisioned Jesus beholding . . . and weeping. *Again.* Yes. And are you ready for the definition of behold? To *see. Really see.* I know, right? Jesus beheld her, the city He loved, and wept over her, knowing what was to come. Wow. What a visual.

Now this may be a good time to mention that in my journal prior to reading, I wrote this—Palm Sunday. Lord, connect my daily reading somehow to this day, OK? Now, seeing as though I was in the Chronicles, I wasn't sure how that would work, especially since the majority of it I can't pronounce—but hey, a girl can ask her Abba anything. So I did. And it was *there* . . . that I then read *this* . . .

David resided in the stronghold; *therefore* it was called the city of David. I realized, Beloved . . . I am the city of Tera. It's where I reside. You are the city of _____. It's where *you* reside.

And our God beholds us. Sees us. *Really sees* us. And weeps over us every time He knows what's to come next in our powerful story of purpose that will cause us pain, discord, sadness, fear. Yes. That's love. A love that doesn't force you to understand, but instead covers you with its very own compassion poured out in tears. Ackkkk, I know, right? Incredible. I swear I'll never get sick of this story. *XO.*

{Luke 19:41–42; 1 Chronicles 11:4}

THE NEW YOU DIDN'T WANT

What do we do when the new we awaken to isn't the new we had hoped for?

Here's what I wrote in my journal—"Storm turned blizzard overnight." Such is life, amen? Oftentimes what we awaken to isn't what we had hoped for. So then what? What do we do? We're still for a moment, giving ourselves time to recapture the breath within, the One we call Holy Spirit, and that still-for-a-moment does more than simply slow down our anxious . . . it strengthens us to then move from that place of still . . . to a place of go. We acknowledge our disappointment and sadness over what we had *hoped* our eyes would awaken to . . . a new-so-much-better day. We allow ourselves the full gamut of emotions instead of burying them deep out of fear that those said emotions somehow mean we don't fully trust God. Gimme a break.

And then we *use* that still, that stop, that pause . . . to remind ourselves that tomorrow . . . will bring with it *more* new. We remind ourselves that all storms eventually end. And we remind ourselves of all the storms we've survived up to this point, some of which we never thought we would. But we did—so either we're built stronger than we realize, or hell really did freeze over. We remind ourselves that just as the seasons battle . . . we too will battle at times. Especially during change of seasons. *Word.* We remind ourselves. . . . Such is life. And as simple as that sounds, it's true. It is life, with its trials and tribulations and jaunts through the wildernesses, deserts, and valleys— and with its wins and its victories and its smiles and its laughter, and as corny as it sounds, its rainbows after the storms.

So what do we do when the new we awaken to isn't the new we had hoped for? We are still. And we know God is God. We acknowledge our humanness and don't make excuses for it. We allow the still to strengthen us. Revive us. Refresh us. Resurrect us from believing that the whole of life sucks. Cuz it doesn't. And lastly, we believe in the *next* new we'll awaken to . . . and believe that it'll surprise us in a really fab way. And of course, we don't stop believing.

"PRAY" ISN'T THE ONLY VERB

"Pray" isn't the only verb in the Bible.

Imagine a whole book dedicated to revealing Who God is and how God uses the works of God's hands to do God's work on God's land, the Earth that God made. So Pray. Yes-Absolutely-Save-the-Hate-Mail-I'm-not-saying-don't-Pray. I'm *saying* Pray *and.* Yes. *And.*

Let me tell you a Tera-able, like a personal parable that just happens to be pronounced "terrible," but I assure you, it's not. Actually, you can be the judge, I guess. Once upon a time, a girl named Tera got up and prayed and prayed and prayed and then proceeded to sit and sit and sit instead of doing what needed to be done and done and done, when suddenly, God interjected, disturbing her sitting, for she was clearly done praying . . . "Excuse Me, young lady, I didn't just strengthen you to sit." I know, right? The audacity. But also—*dang*—talk about a God Who knows God's kids to a fault. Seriously.

So, am I telling you *not* to pray? Gimme a break. If you've been here more than five minutes, you should know me better than that. What I *am* saying is—pray *and.* Yes. *And.*

And ask. And seek. Do justice. Love kindness. (The uncomfortable kind, by the way, not simply smiling at someone today and calling it good-I-think-were-done-here-I've-done-my-part.) I know, conviction sucks. Move. Plant. Make a change. Do the thing. Heck, do *some* thing. Walking by faith still involves walking, you know. (I know, right?!) Go. Stay. Try. Make. Find your voice that's been stirred by what you wish never had been and use it for God's sake. And for the sake of God's peeps. Cuz we need you.

Turn if you need to turn. Dig if you need to dig. Rest if you need to rest. Rise up if you've sat long enough and, as the old adage goes, "are sick and tired of being sick and tired." Tear down what needs tearing down and build up what needs building up. (Psst . . . what needs building up may be you, by the way.) Remind yourself Who God is, who you are in light of Who God is, and who everyone else is in light of Who God is. Yes.

Beloved, pray. *And.*

IS IT NOT WRITTEN?

Now the rest of her story—how she fought and recovered, survived and gave birth to new, rebuilt and restored, was defeated and rose again—is it not written?

It sure as heck is. And, Beloved, *so is yours.* So you listen to me. The next time you find yourself being tempted in the wilderness to forget Who your God is the way Jesus was—well then, you just go ahead and serve it right back with the same three words Jesus used, the same three words that are gonna whip Satan's butt back to darkness, amen.

It is written.

That's right. Every defeat and every victory. Every uncontainable smile and every uncontrollable tear. Every battle you've fought, including those you are fighting *right now*, and every time you did the impossible—rose again. Amen. Every cry that has ever stained your pillow when the nights were so long and the dawn just wouldn't seem to come. Every pang of hunger when it seemed as though the famine would never end. But it did. And if you are in that famine right now, it will again. Every storm you survived and grew stronger and smarter as a result of surviving it, preparing you and equipping you for when the next one comes. Which it will.

It is written. Every word of your story, your incredible story, born from the purpose that the Lord your God Who calls you by name and loves you unfailingly has for you . . . which is a holy story, by the way, and holy means "set apart," so quit expecting it to look like another's . . . written by the Author *and* Finisher/Perfecter of your faith. *Amen.* Which is the final word of your story, you know.

Now the rest of her story—how she fought and recovered, survived and gave birth to new, rebuilt and restored, was defeated and rose again—is it not written? It sure as heck is. Beloved, grab hold of the *and*s of your story . . . and just *look* at how *far* you have come. *XO.*

NEW LIFE FROM DEATH

New life may arise from something that has died in your life.

And maybe that something is something you know needed to die, and so you're grateful and gushing out praise to your Maker. And maybe not. Maybe what died was a job or worse, a career; or maybe it was a relationship—a friendship, a marriage-ship, a partnership—a ship you weren't ready to watch take off and set sail. And if that is the case, permission to mourn what has died. For that's what humans do, and it's good to do so. And as you do, you mourn with hope. Cuz see, mourning and grieving *with* hope look far different than mourning and grieving without it. And today as I read words that've clearly been here from the beginning, yet apparently I never saw as highlighter-worthy 'til now . . . they sparked the words you're now reading. Here's what I read . . .

As a man was being buried, a marauding band was seen, and the man was thrown into the grave of Elisha. As soon as the man touched the bones of Elisha, he came to life and stood on his feet. I know, right? Quite a story from a guy whose name we're not even told. But then, I have to wonder if that *too* doesn't hold purpose. Allowing us to *be* that man, thrown down, left for dead . . . and a God Who used what had *died* . . . in order to restore him to *life*. Yes. And that life restored may look like a new fire lit from within and ready to no longer hold back but go out in this world and change what needs changing. It may look like a new compassion and empathy for others birthed from your own despair. It may look like discovering a new part of yourself that you didn't even know existed 'til now . . . and you're sure as heck not gonna waste it.

Beloved, new life may arise from something that has died in your life. And just think how different today will look . . . if you *believe* that . . . instead of resigning yourself to the grave.

{2 Kings 13:21}

BATTLES CAN BRING VICTORIES

Keep in mind that God may bring you to a battle so you can experience a victory.

Beloved, God may bring you to a battle so you can experience a victory. That's right. Now . . . let's read it again with proper emphasis so you can get your juices flowin'/engine revved/whatever, shall we? Great.

God may *bring* you to a *battle* so *you* can experience a *victory*. Which of course, will *strengthen you for the next time you're faced with a battle.*

Because you'll remember. That's right. You'll remember that you've battled before, and you've been victorious before, and so there's absolutely no reason to believe that you won't be victorious again. Yes, *again*. And as I've said, believing that, *believing* that . . . is what's gonna strengthen you to *battle* again. Because see, now Possible is within city limits. It's clutched in your fist, and you're not letting go. It's tucked safely and securely away deep within the crevices of your soul and rises up and calls from within . . .

Remember last time? Remember how you battled and how you were victorious? Remember how through the course of that battle *you* realized just what was *in* you? Remember the fight? Remember the fire? Remember that flame that refused to go out? Right.

Beloved, I don't have the answer to the Why of your battle. But perhaps today I can help you reframe and rename it. Look at your battle. And believe something *else*. Don't name it punishment or a set-up to fail. Name it opportunity. An opportunity to be *victorious* . . . and realize just what you're made of. *Yes*. Name it. Claim it. Believe it. It'll strengthen you. I mean it. I also love you. Big time.

THERE IS PURPOSE IN THE LACK

As hard as this is to hear—I promise you there is purpose in the lack.

And let me be the first to say, yet again, you don't have to like it. You are welcome to cry and scream and throw yourself on the ground while yelling out, "Why??" . . . and I'll be there with tissues and dark chocolate to listen. Because your *humanness* doesn't negate your *holiness*. Read that again and tuck it away for the next time someone tells you it does. And call me for backup if need be.

Beloved, there is purpose in the lack. The widow of Zarephath in my reading today is just one of a million examples. Look how she referred to God *before* God showed her provision . . . "As the Lord *your* God lives," she told the prophet Elijah. Right. A widow with mouths to feed and nothin' left in the cupboard sure as heck ain't gonna be feelin' God as Provider. I mean, this God may be *that* guy's God, but *clearly* this God ain't *mine.*

But desperate does what desperate must do, and so she does what Elijah instructs after receiving *this* promise. Notice *also* how E refers to the Lord as "the" God, careful not to say "my" God, allowing the woman to consider that *perhaps* this God was *her* God too. I know, right? Good job E.

Update: The jar of meal *wasn't* emptied, and the jug of oil *didn't* run out, until the rain fell. Just as God had said through E. It wasn't enough for the woman. She needed *more* proof of this God whom E claimed to be Provider/Protector/All-Powerful. (Dang, I love the three P's.) Her son became ill. No breath left. The woman now had some ammo . . . See! I *told* you God wasn't all that and a bag of chips. See! E went to the boy. Stretched himself over him, covering him to heal him (ahem, that's another whole sermon), and the boy's breath returned. And *guess* what the woman said *then*? "Now I *know* that you are a man of God, and that the word of God in your mouth, is *truth.*"

Beloved, there is always purpose for the lack. It may be to show you something. It may be to draw something out of you. Whatever the case, it has *purpose. XO.*

YOU WON'T ALWAYS UNDERSTAND

Your God is fulfilling His will for you. Believe me, you will not always understand.

"So the king did not listen to the people, *because it was a turn of affairs brought about by the lord, that he might fulfill his word . . .*"

Word. And oh good, you caught that. Beloved, I mean it when I say that what I believe trips us humanfolk up the most is trying to understand the ways of God, despite the forewarning that they are much, so much, and I mean *so much* higher than ours. Higher as in beyond our comprehension no-doubt-understatement-amen. And again, I don't know if you can hear the cloud of witnesses chanting, but I assure you they are.

I can hear Ruth. "I had no idea why things had to go down like they did, but they ended up landing my butt in Bethlehem and marrying my boss Boaz. It was crazy! I went on to find myself in the family line of Jesus!"

I hear Esther. "I thought God had abandoned me not once, but twice—first with my parents, and then with my amazing cousin-turned-adoptive-father Mordecai. But it turned out that I was being brought into a position as queen that would ultimately save thousands of people! Wow! I *never* saw that coming!"

I hear Mary. (The Jesus-mom Mary in this case, cuz truly I tell you, there's a whole bunch of Marys, amen and wink wink.) "I could *not* figure out why in the *world* God would choose *me* over my older-married-devout-did-everything-right relative Elizabeth to carry His Son, the Savior of the World, no less . . . but now looking back, I bet it was so everyone would *be clear about who the father was.*" Sorry, Maury Povich, we're not gonna need you for this one.

Beloved, my point is this—your story, the one written in full for you from In the Beginning to final Amen, was written by the Author *and* Finisher/Perfecter/Completer of your life. So . . . *return to that knowing when the turn of affairs doesn't make sense. XO.*

{1 Kings 12:15}

BEAUTY FROM ASHES

People may burn you, reduce you to ashes, but you listen to Me—there is beauty to come from those ashes, cuz you can rebuild.

And see, now you've got a holy fire to work with, because maybe, just maybe, one of those ashes still had one remaining ember, and baby, you're gonna use it to relight the fire, *amen.* And *heck yes.* And that holy fire is gonna light up the joint so you can see what it is that you need to rebuild, and it's gonna give you the warmth you need for when the cold nights grow long, and it's gonna serve as the perfect place for you to heat up your food and eat, because did I mention you're gonna need strength for this build? *Whew—amen—you sure are.*

Beloved, my post this morn is not gonna be quite as long as my norm (and some of y'all are thinkin'—Hallelujah, praise God), cuz I reckon the words I scratched on the page are enough for you to sit with a minute . . . amen?

Hey, a girl just knows. Cuz see, people may burn you, reduce you to ashes, but you listen to me—there is *beauty* to come from those ashes, cuz you can *rebuild.* You sure can.

Cuz lest you've forgotten, your God is your supplier, stocked with a storehouse that never runs out. Like *ever.* Believe it. Ask for what you need. And build. Or *rebuild.*

I love ya. Amen.

{1 Kings 9–11}

WHAT'S MEANT FOR YOU WILL BE YOURS

If it's to be yours, it will be yours.

And permission to live out your humanness if it's not—despite how desperate your want. Yes. Permission to cry and to scream and to mourn. And if it *is* to be yours, the same is true—permission to live out your humanness. Permission to rejoice and celebrate and exude your gratitude all over the place.

My point, Beloved, is one you already know, but as I've mentioned about a bazillion times before, I believe there is power in simply stating the truth of what is. Sometimes it will be yours. The position, the placement, the win, the whatever. And sometimes it will *not*. And whichever way the coin the lands, the wind blows, or whatever other famous phrase you wanna insert, you get to be fully human in your response. Cuz see, I'd rather have my tantrum and get it all out before the God Who I know loves me . . . than to carry it around, letting it fester, mixing with every other emotion in there and baking into one hot mess of bitterness and resentment, amen. Been there. It sucks. Movin' on. And doin' my best to grow up. (Don't worry, I have hard convos like that with myself all the time; I've learned that big-time transformation is the result.) Note: it's not easy, but dang, as we sang in the eighties as John Mellencamp crooned . . . hurts so good. Right.

Beloved, at the end (or in this case beginning, I guess) of the day, here's the truth: If it's to be yours, it will be yours.

Solomon was to be king. One of his bros decided he was gonna be king instead, so he did all the things and gathered a buncha peeps and threw this big party and everybody was chantin', "Long live the king!" *Except* . . . he wasn't anointed or appointed to be king. Except in his own eyes, of course. So God used a woman you've probably heard of, Bathsheba, to speak up and say what was right. *Right. Solomon* was to be king. Cuz God said Sol was gonna be king. So despite all the efforts his bro had made to name himself king . . . he wasn't king. Cuz Sol was to be king. Amen.

{1 Kings 1:1–27}

WHAT AUTHENTIC FAITH DOES

The famine continued. And year after year, David asked God, "why??" Because that's what authentic faith does.

It sure does. It also knows it may or may not like the answer, but by asking and inquiring and begging and continually seeking to *know* that answer . . . it stays connected to the One for Whom nothing is too hard, everything is possible, and from Whom no secrets are hid, so you might as well be honest and come right out and ask/ inquire/beg/question, *amen*. I wonder how often we dismiss what we might consider to be "no-big-deals" when it comes to our God? For example, could it be that part of the reason God sent Jesus to ask a whole buncha questions . . . was so that *we would know that we can ask a whole buncha questions too?*

Maybe. Because truly I tell you, Beloved—a real faith, an authentic faith . . . asks questions. It wrestles with God at night while sobbing and crying out, "*why???*" It sure does. And as *hard* as that is . . . it's also the very thing . . . that makes it *real*. Makes it *whole*. Makes it not some distant fairy tale but down-in-the-dirt nitty gritty. Yes. Something we can hold on to and feel between our fingers as we grapple to understand our place in this great big world. As we struggle to not only discover our purpose but then come to terms with it if it's nowhere near what we hoped it would be. It keeps us up at night but also provides naps during the day as we resign ourselves to the fact that despite the truth that we will *never* have all of the answers . . . our faith allows us to keep on asking the questions. Yes. Even the hard ones. Amen.

Friends, my words today were sparked by Dave, cuz the guy was seriously lit. (Sorry, couldn't help myself.) The Script today tells me that the famine lasted three years, and *year after year, David inquired of the Lord: Why?* Because a man, a woman, a child after God's own heart . . . knows that he/she . . . *can*. Amen. Amen. I'm not kidding. A million amens.

{2 Samuel 21:1}

WHEN ONE IS ENOUGH

What do you call one remaining ember? Enough.

To rekindle the flame. To spark what remains. To see in the dark and not completely freeze to death in the cold. Yes. One ember remains. What do you call it? *Enough.* That's right and amen. So don't you dare quench it. I mean it, or I'll show up at your door and light a fire right under your butt, and I mean that too.

The wise woman in my story today (the Bible is *filled* with them, wise women, FYI) uses this beautiful wordage that I don't reckon I've ever thought about or taken note of before. She defines the hope she has left . . . as "one remaining ember." And oh, how true it is, amen? Not enough to light the whole path but enough to maybe take one more step? Not enough to prepare a whole feast but enough to not starve to death? Not enough to cling to with both hands but enough for maybe one pinky finger to carry and feel the singe, and although it hurts, it reminds you the fire is still alive *so you'll take it.* Yes.

Beloved, what do you call one remaining ember? Now see, that's not fair, I've already told you. No worries—all A's for everyone today. We call it . . . *enough.* Just like one thread of the hem, one drop of pure oil, one kid's sack lunch, one flicker of light at the end of the proverbial tunnel. *Enough.* To keep going. Keep knowing. Keep believing. Absolutely.

So you listen to me, don't you *dare* quench it, OK? Don't you dare quench the spirit within you. Fan it. And watch it grow. And then you get your fiery butt out there and set the world ablaze, would ya? Sweet. See ya there. *XO.*

{2 Samuel 14:7}

THERE WILL STILL BE WARS

A woman after God's own heart still experiences wars.

And they will take their toll on you. And they will tire you out. And you will sometimes win, and you will sometimes lose. And you will take treasure from them. And you will grow stronger because of them. And you will not always understand the reason for them. And you will wonder if somehow it's payback for that thing you did back in high school or college or whenever. And you will also wonder when it will end, because at times it feels like it's lasted just shy of a lifetime. Yes. There will still be wars. Even if—yes, even if—you are a woman after God's own heart. There will still be wars.

I tell you this, Beloved, because I don't want you to believe for even *one* second that if you experience war you are somehow doing the whole after-God's-own-heart thing *wrong.* (And please, I beg of you, shake the dust off your sandals and keep going, lest any overzealous self-proclaimed religious thinks-he/she-knows-it-all tries to convince you otherwise under some self-satisfying guise of trying to "help save your soul from hell.") Gimme a break. Cuz see, a man or woman after God's own heart . . . will *still experience wars.* Just ask Dave. Amen.

Beloved, a woman after God's own heart will still experience wars. And they will be hard. *And* she will not fight alone even when she feels alone. And there will be tears. *And* those tears will not be for naught. And there will be times when she feels like she just can't battle another day. *And she will.* Because as long as she has breath in her lungs, she remains. Here. And believes. Now. That the plan her God wrote for her is filled with *such* an incredible magnitude of power and purpose that she can't even *begin* to comprehend it all. And she's goin' with that. *Cuz she can.*

THE PLANS GOD STILL HAS FOR YOU

Believe in the plans God still has for you.

Still. Still as in, well, let's consult our friend Dictionary dot com. Still, as in, "even, in addition to, yet." Still, as in, "in the future as in the past." Still, as in, "to a greater distance or degree," and yes, Dic said greater, so thanks Dic. Yes.

Beloved, believe in the plans God *still* has for you. Believe that God's storehouse is, in fact, filled with all of the abundance your God *still* has for you, trusting that it will be given to you at just the right time. Yes. Believe that. Because there is strength in believing, and even if you never actually *see* it, you *believing* that you're gonna see it is what's gonna strengthen you and stir you and comfort you and take care of you and protect you when you're in the pit known as "Well-I-Guess-This-Is-It-For-My-Life." Oh, you've been there? Me too. But don't stay there, OK? Cuz it sucks there. Amen. And Believing? Believing raises you *outta* there. Yes, amen, and every Hallelujah. Right.

Beloved, believe in the plans God *still* has for you. The plans that include words we stinkin' love, like "hope" and "future." The plans we envision as, well, as we say in the '80s, like totally awesome. The plans that await us that'll blow our minds, and we seriously can't wait 'til they do. Yes.

Beloved, believe that there is *so* much more to come for you that your humanness can't even begin to imagine it but, dang it all, you're sure as heck gonna try. Cuz that's the stuff dreams are made of, and if you ask me, dreams are highly underrated. Yes. Believe today. Believe tomorrow. Believe every day that the sun continues to faithfully rise and faithfully set. *And don't you dare stop believin'.* I mean it. Cuz the pit sucks. And you deserve better. *XO. XO.* And *XO.*

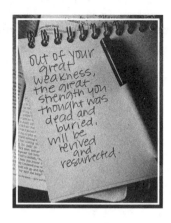

Day 148

REVIVED AND RESURRECTED

Out of your great weakness, the great strength you thought was dead and buried will be revived and resurrected.

The idea is that when you're at the end of your rope, you hold on even tighter, in turn strengthening the very hands that are holding on to hold on longer.

David and his peeps were worn out. Weak. Scripture actually describes it as them reaching a point where they didn't even have enough strength . . . to weep. And maybe you're there too. Maybe your soul is ready to call it a day, toss in the towel, call it quits. Dave was there too. He also knew he was gonna need to get through *and* get his peeps through, and so David, and I quote, "strengthened himself in the Lord his God." David strengthened himself with the knowledge of Who the Lord . . . *his* God . . . *is*. I can picture Dave there at his absolute weakest, talking out loud to himself as he feeds his own soul, thus reviving and resurrecting it with bites of bread like . . .

Wait a minute, *my* God is my *Provider*. *My* God is my *Protector*. *My* God is *All-Powerful*. My God is the Author and Perfecter of the *plan* God has for my life, and there ain't no enemy in *hell* that's gonna be able to *alter that plan, amen and take that*. And I imagine that's when Dave realizes that the strength within him that was dead and buried . . . could *also* be *revived and resurrected*. Sound familiar?

How do you think the woman with the issue found the strength to make her way through that sneering crowd? How do you think the woman who had been hunched over for nearly two decades found the strength to make her way to Jesus at the front of the temple? How do you think the woman at the well found the strength to *run* back to the people in her town, the very same people she did her best to avoid, because she just *had* to tell them who she had met?

Beloved, *out of great weakness can arise great strength*. Out of a place of "I just can't take one more step up this mountain," a faith that can not only move it, but hurl it into the sea, can emerge. Strength out of weakness. Hold on.

{1 Samuel 30:4–6}

NOBODY CAN STOP GOD'S PLAN FOR YOU

Blessed is she who knows and believes . . . that ain't nobody on the face of this Earth can stop God's plan for her life.

Word up. Mic drop. Amen. I mean it. But because I'm a woman of *many* words, not few (hey now, I see that smirk), here are some more. Words.

Here's the story: The same Saul who loved and adored David at first had come to seriously despise him because jealousy kills-steals-destroys-and-*that*-just-may-be-the-biggest-understatement-ever. But I digress. Right. So because of his jealousy, our guy Saul was out to kill his perceived threat—David. So he sends messengers to kill Dave. But when they got there, God threw them into a prophetic frenzy. One today might say (or perhaps it's just me) that God threw them into a tizzy. Right.

So Saul sends a second group of messengers. Same thing. So Saul sends a third group. Yup. Same thing. So Saul decides he best go for himself, and if you know where this is going, well then, you might just be a prophet yourself. Right. Same thing. God sent Saul himself into a frenzy/tizzy. What's my point? *Exactly.*

Beloved, truly I tell you, there ain't *nobody* on the face of this Earth who can stop the mighty and holy plan God has for your life. *Fact.* Believe it. And don't you stop believin' it. And now, I'm just gonna go ahead and lay the mic down over here in case you wanna *pick it up and use it.* Amen.

{1 Samuel 19}

HOW TO BATTLE AFTER BAD NEWS

Battling after bad news . . .

How do we muster the strength needed for battle after receiving bad news? Because truly . . . isn't that when we need strength the most . . . after we receive bad news? Isn't that when we need the strength to battle, to rise, to persevere, to endure? Isn't that when we need strength most of all? I reckon it is. So how do we muster it?

—Prepare. Yes. Prepare for the battle by taking stock of what your new reality holds and how this is gonna look moving forward.

—Find Your Armor-Bearers. Yes. Those who will not only come alongside you, but they're also fully prepared to cover you if your covering begins to wear thin.

—Taste Some Honey. Yes. Amidst all the sour vinegar you've had to ingest, taste some honey—some good news. Look for it until you find it, if that's what it takes, but taste some honey. You'll be surprised at how it can brighten not only your face but your day, and hey, even a moment of respite is worth it.

—Hype Yourself Up. Yes. Be your own huddle and count down from three as you holler out, "We got this!"

—Return to Who You Know God to Be. Yes. This actually goes hand-in-hand with the last point because God is your "We" there, amen.

—Worship the Lord Your God. Yes. Worship—find your *worth* in the God Who not only created you but sent you to live out God's holy purpose.

—Remind Yourself That the Battle Will Pass. Because all battles eventually do.

Battling after bad news. Is it possible? You'd better believe it is. Now on three. We got this!! That's right. You are not alone as you battle, Beloved. I promise, I promise, I promise. *XO.*

{1 Samuel 13–14}

THERE WILL BE TIMES YOU ARE DEFEATED

There will be times you are defeated.

I *swear* I had something else all written out on the page that felt a whole lot better than this, but a nagging, yes I said nagging, voice within kept rising up . . . "Tell 'em the truth. There's power there, and it sets people free." So here we are. I can't help but believe that there is tremendous value in speaking what's true without trying to pretty it all up with a bunch of religious flare that we'll call yeast, instead simply acknowledging it completely unleavened so we know that when—yes, I said *when*—it happens, and it will, we know we aren't alone . . . instead of believing that we obviously lack faith or we somehow don't trust God "enough." Gimme a break. For the record, I trust God completely, *and* I've also been defeated at times. And so have you. And maybe you're even there now.

And so instead of throwing a big "But" in here (ahhh, the visual), let's get our big "But" out of the way and make room for our friend "And" on this journey. Yes. Let's. Now let's practice.

I am defeated, but I trust God. Ah, ah, ah, get your but out of the way.

I am defeated *and* I trust God. *Yes.*

Because the truth is—there *will* be times I'm defeated. Now, does defeat equal destroyed? No. When a team plays a game and is defeated, do they quit playing the sport? No, of course not. They play the next game on the schedule. Exactly.

Beloved, there will be times you are defeated. Your ancestors the Israelites are screaming from the cloud, "Sorry, it's true!" *And.* Your God is still with you and for you. *And.* Your God will not leave or forsake you. *And.* Although you don't understand the reason for the defeat, I *guarantee* there is one, because God wastes *nothing*, and *all* things have value and purpose and worth cuz that's just God's jam and M.O., amen.

And. Defeat does not mean Destroyed. It means defeat. Which means you can rise again. Soar again. Be restored and renewed again. *Yes.* Because you are more than a conqueror. You're a warrior.

{1 Samuel 4:2, 10}

YOUR JOURNEY IS UNDER THE WATCHFUL EYE OF THE LORD

What I can tell you is this—your journey, the mission you are on, is under the eye of the Lord your God.

Will the "it" you are praying about turn out exactly as you hope? I don't know. Will you succeed in the way you define success? I don't know. Will there be equal amounts of tears and laughter as you go? I don't know. I don't know, Beloved. I don't know the answer to the questions that are plaguing you and perhaps even paralyzing you.

What I *do* know is *this*, and truly I tell you, ain't nobody or nothin' on the face of God's green Earth is gonna change my mind, so don't bother for those who think they might . . . your *journey*, your *mission*, your *purpose* played out as you breathe *life* into every word of your rich story written uniquely for you . . . is under the eye, the *watchful* eye I may add, of the Lord *your* God. That's right. Amen. Cue the lights to slowly dim cuz we're done here. I jest—but also—I'm serious, Beloved.

Your journey is under the watchful eye of your God. (The same is true, by the way, for your kids, grandkids, great-grandkids, great-great-you get the idea.) You are never *not* seen. Because the journey you are on, the mission you are on, is under the eye of the Lord your God. Oh, yes. Which means, of course—you are not alone on the journey you are on and the mission you are on, and not only are you not alone, but it is the God Who created you and vowed to never leave you and is with you and for you and, heck, goes before you that is with you. *Hallelujah. Can I get an amen?* Seriously.

Beloved, every breath you take. Every move you make. Every bond you break. Every step you take. And if you are singing right now, I swear you're my people, amen. God is watching you. And your God? Yeah, your God is your Parent. Your Provider. Your Protector. Your God is All-Powerful and don't you forget it, amen, cuz *that* is the God Whose eye you are under. I mean it. I love you. Now go sing.

{Judges 18:6}

PROVISION IN UNEXPECTED PLACES

God will provide in the midst of unexpected places.

A feast in the wilderness. A handful of food to feed over five thousand. A large-bellied fish in the midst of a roaring, really ticked-off sea. A rock in the desert that spouts out water. Bread for the journey falling from Heaven despite your constant complaining. The absence of water in a really deep well. An angel in a furnace of fire. A eunuch who truly cared, put in charge of the harem. A much older cousin who went first in her pregnancy so she could give you the lowdown of what's about to go down—literally. Another much older cousin who would adopt you as his own and raise you to be strong and brave, courageous and bold—reminding you that you were created on purpose, and when the time is right, you'll be brought into position for such a time as this. Yes.

Beloved, God will provide in the midst of unexpected places. Like a big rusty paper clip in a gas station lot. Like a woodpecker high up in the tree—not only heard, but visibly, powerfully seen. Like a full night's sleep at a seventh-grade overnight retreat. I know, right? Talk about unexpected.

Beloved, God will provide in the midst of unexpected places. In breakdowns and detours and in hospital hallways. In droughts and in famines and in encounters with strangers. In storms and in silence. In peace . . . and in war. God will provide. Watch for it. Name it. Provision. It'll make a big difference. Love ya, mean it. Amen.

THERE IS A STRONG TOWER WITHIN YOU

Beloved, there is a strong tower within you. Return there for refuge when the world is simply too much and regain the strength that you've lost.

There is a strong tower within you. A place to find refuge and regain your strength, because I know that the battle has taken quite a bit out of you. There is a strong tower within you. A place hidden deep, safe and secure, a place around which your fearfully and wonderfully made flesh was formed—your center, your core. Yes. There is a strong tower within you. A place where you can retreat and know you are seen and know you are heard. A place where your tears can freely fall without fear of judgement or shame. There is a strong tower within you. A place that knows you by name and is so glad you came as it fetches you a drink from the well. And you can actually sit for a spell. Because you need to, and because there's no guilt in this place, so you can.

There is a strong tower within you. A place that reminds you just how powerful you are, because I think perhaps you've forgotten. Call it a hunch. A place where you can be reminded of who you are and Who your God is, and there is nothing, and I do mean *nothing*, better than that to relight your flame and refill your shaker and send you back out in the world again. And from that place, that strong tower within, you will be restored, and from that place of restoration, you will crush the skull of the enemy—the enemy that dares to step foot near your strong tower, forgetting just how strong and powerful you are. *Yes.*

There is a strong tower within you, Beloved. A strong tower that cannot be shaken. So don't you forget you can go there. *Amen.* So much love. So dang much love. I mean it.

{Judges 9–12}

YOUR LAND MAY INCLUDE ENEMIES

Just because enemies remain in your new land doesn't mean it's not your land.

One verse. Daily bread. A chunk of enough. Yes. Strength in knowing. Peace in knowing. Perseverance awakened from a dead drooling sleep as a result of now knowing. Yes. A knowing that will allow you to keep going instead of giving up when the going gets tough, amen. Yes. Because knowing is powerful. And will bring you to back to life like nothing else will. Fact.

And today's knowing is this, gleaned from one verse from one chapter from one book amongst sixty-six . . . Just because enemies remain in your new land . . . doesn't mean it's not your land. That's right. And as you read those words and claim those words for your very own self and exhale knowing you don't have to question every life decision you've ever made . . . I want you to listen to Josh as he encourages you (and I join my voice to his, by the way) . . .

Be strong and courageous, Beloved . . . for the Lord your God is *with* you . . . *wherever* . . . you go. That's right. Don't forget. Love ya, mean it.

{Judges 1:19}

YOU COULD BE THE NEXT FIRST

Beloved, who is to say that you won't be the next first?

The first survivor of whatever it is. The first to receive or achieve what until now has been named Impossible. The first to do the thing, conquer the thing, defeat the thing, overcome the thing. The first to defy all odds.

Beloved, who is to say that *you*, yes *you*, won't be the next *first??* *I mean it.*

The Red Sea was the *first* body of water God parted. But it wasn't the last. Five thousand-plus people seated on grassy land were fed with what seemed like a little. But they weren't the last. Laz was the first guy raised from the dead. But he wasn't the last. Just ask two gals who headed to a tomb one morning, with spices and oil in hand, all ready to do their thing. Right.

Or how 'bout the man born blind from John 9? (FYI—I freaking *love* this guy.) The guy whose eyes a man called Jesus opened. He flat-out says to those who don't seem to believe that this could've *possibly* actually *happened* . . . "*never*, since the *world began*, has it been heard, that *anyone* opened the eyes of a person born blind." And yet, dear Pharisees . . . *boom, here we are, amen.*

Beloved, as per my usual, I could go on with a bazillion more examples, but you've got your day to go live . . . *believing* that *you*, yes *you*, may in fact be the next *first*. And frankly, Beloved, why *not* believe it? Exactly. Start singin', Baby. You know the song. *XO.*

THERE MAY BE BATTLES IN YOUR AFTER

It may be after you cross over when the real battle begins.

I say it out loud so you know going in, or perhaps you're already there. God brought you to the land, and that's all fine and dandy *except*—excuse me, Lord, but how come I'm not being served milk and honey while soaking in the rays? I wasn't expecting there to be a battle once I *got* here? And so enter today's words scratched out on a page . . . from one small town girl . . . who refuses to stop believing. . . . It may be *after* you cross over when the real battle begins. And I tell you that so *when* that happens or *if* you are there right now, then *you* can have even a shred of peace knowing that *just because there is a battle here doesn't mean you're in the wrong place. It just means there's a battle here too.*

And you may or may not understand Why, because as I've said a bazillion times, we are not always going to understand Why because we're living one word of our story at a time, and God knows every word to the end, cuz that's the benefit of being the Author. Amen. So *yes*, there may be a battle. But *also yes*—you are *armed for it.* Cuz see, you watched God do what God did to get you to that place, that land. And just like Moses instructed his little Israelites in Deuteronomy, you may need to periodically stop and *remember that.* Right.

You may have to pull out the words, "The Lord Himself goes before me; He is with me and will never leave me, therefore I will not worry or be afraid." Right. And you may want to couple that with, "Be strong and courageous, for I Am with you wherever you go" . . . emphasis on the *wherever.* Right.

Beloved, there are days more and more the older I get when I'm convinced that part of my deal here on Earth is to say things that may be hard but indeed help . . . even if they're just to give voice to what *is* so someone out there knows they aren't alone. And that God hasn't abandoned them. Or forgotten them. Or forsaken them. When they find themselves . . . in the hard. *XO.*

{Joshua 4:13}

KEEP ASKING, SEEKING, AND KNOCKING

Listen to me—You keep asking, you keep searching, you keep knocking til your knuckles are bloody if that's what it takes. I mean it.

And if I sound loud and bossy, it's because I'm loud and bossy. Amen. And . . . because I mean it with every ounce of my marrow, and I pray my very real confidence gives you some very real strength. To keep asking. To keep searching. To keep knocking on that door that won't seem to open . . . with even the tiniest mustard seed of faith believing . . . that in due time . . . God's time . . . it will.

Yes. For truly I tell you, Beloved, although I can't venture to guess why God reveals what He does in the timing He does, I do know your story is secure in the hands of the Author Who penned every word. So if there's a wait . . . or a weight . . . there is purpose for it. A mighty one. For could it be that the One Who vowed to perfect (complete) your faith here on Earth is doing just that as you endure the wait . . . or weight? Could it be that when His Word cries out . . . "those who wait upon the Lord will renew their strength" . . . that in fact the purpose of the wait . . . or weight . . . is actually revealed? Yes. *Renewed strength.*

Beloved, if I were speaking before you, you'd hear every ounce of what I believe to be true pour out with a passion that is birthed from a knowing that's real. You sure would. And as I've said before, I often pray that one day, one generation of offspring of mine . . . will pick up this book at just the right time . . . and discover this note I've left behind . . . And in God's perfect time, it will be just what he/she needs to hear . . . to keep . . . Asking. Searching. Knocking. Trusting. Believing. And today, Beloved, perhaps these words are for you. Perhaps. Big love.

{Matthew 7:7–12}

RENAME THE REMOVING

Rename the removing and call it relocating. It wasn't punishment; it was positioning.

I've been removed from places I've lived that I didn't want to leave. I moved a few times in my childhood. And in my adulthood, I've been picked up and plucked out of places I thought were places I'd stay . . . after all . . . I was bearing good fruit. But see, I realize now that in both of those cases, God wasn't removing me because I had done something *wrong* . . . God was relocating me because the time was *right*. According to God's plan for me, which sometimes I stinkin' love, and sometimes I seriously don't and roll my eyes at and say, "*Really, God*??" And there are even times I throw a full-on toddler temper-tantrum, cuz that's how I'm feeling, and hey, Jesus told me to be like a child, can I get an amen? Right.

Cuz see *now* I know, that it wasn't *punishment*; it was *positioning*. And doesn't that sound, like, wayyyy better? Like totally gum smack, amen? Right. So . . . does God Relocate? Replant? Repot? Of *course* God does; read The Book. So have you stopped to consider that despite the fact that you're bearing good fruit where you are . . . that perhaps the Lord *your* God is relocating you because you've *outgrown your space and have more fruit to bear*? Have you considered that perhaps the Lord *your* God is relocating you despite the fact that you don't want to go, because God has gone ahead to where you are going next and actually has something for you to give *and* something for you to take while you're there? Read it again, whew and amen.

I *mean it*. Have you stopped to consider it? Or if you stop and consider it *right now*, then do you suppose that maybe today you can rename it and call it what it is based on Who you know God to be? And lest you've forgotten, no worries, I got you—Provider. Protector. All-Powerful. *Always*. In *all ways*. I mean it. And I love ya. Big time.

THE WILDERNESS WILL REVEAL WHAT YOU'RE MADE OF

God already knows what you're made of, but God may send you into the wilderness so you can know what you're made of.

Cuz see, God could've come down the mountain and talked to Moses face-to-face . . . instead of asking Moses to climb the mountain multiple times in order to have the conversation. God could've picked up the hundreds of thousands of Israelites and set them down around the milk-and-honey fountain with a feast of fresh fruit for dipping . . . instead of allowing them to journey their way there. Or how 'bout the woman who bled for twelve years? Do you think grabbing the hem of Jesus's robe was the hard part? Heck no. It was making her way through a crowd of her very own people as they whispered, "Ewww . . . there she is, don't touch her! Cooties!" Right. But see, then she got to Jesus, and Jesus called her out. He not only wanted to show the *crowd* something that day, but also show this woman . . . *what she was made of.* Faith. Courage. Bravery. Endurance. *Amen.*

Or how about the woman hunched over at the back of the temple the day Jesus served as pulpit supply. Do you think the hard part was going to the service that morning and blending in at the back of the room? Heck no. It was having to make her way to the front when Jesus saw her at the back and called her forward, and so there she was, taking one slow hunched-over step at a time while the congregation no doubt murmured, "OMG! Hurry up! Don't you know *Jesus* is preaching today?" Right. Until she got to the front. And realized that she had done it. And I can't even *imagine* the eye contact between her and Jesus at that very moment. A look that no doubt said, "You did it! *Look* at what you are made of, My Girl!" *Yes.*

Beloved, here's what I know—*God* already *knows* what you're made of. It's a fringe benefit of being the Creator. God may *also* send you into the wilderness, *however that wilderness looks for you,* so that *you* can know what you're made of . . . before you take the next step in your journey. Cuz God is just that good.

THE WOMEN WHO CHANGE THE WORLD

Women who take a stand . . . and dare to speak . . . change the world.

Esther will tell you it's true—after all, she's still got her head. And her crown. Amen. But you *may* not know five *more* women from Scripture, sisters actually, who changed the world because of their courage. Their bravery. Their bold willingness to say something that *needed to be said.* Wanna meet 'em? I knew you would. Tirzah. Mahlah. Milcah. Hoglah. Noah. Cuz these five women deserve all the space here to have their names brought to light because *they* brought something to light that *needed* to be brought to light, because oftentimes that's what *brings change, amen.* Yes.

Cuz see, these five women were the daughters of a guy named Zelophehad. Their dad Z died, and they had no brothers. *Uh-oh.* What about Z's land? What about Z's possessions, all of his stuff? I mean, the law clearly states it goes to the boys, but what if there *are* no boys? Now what?? And *that,* my friends, is when five bold women we rarely (if ever) hear about (or perhaps even knew about until right this very moment) . . . took a stand. Literally. The Word says they stood before Moses *and* the priest *and* the leaders *and* the *entire* congregation . . . and said what needed to be said. *They sure did.* "Why should the name of our father be taken away from his clan because he had no son? Give it to *us.*"

So Moses took their case before the Lord. (*Thank you, Moses.*) And the Lord said . . . "They're *right.*" *Yup.* Read it yourself. So good. So good. But wait, there's *more* . . . Cuz see, the Lord went on to say that from that point on, should this happen again, well then to the daughter(s) the inheritance shall go. That's right. Change as a result of what's been brought to light.

Five women. One voice. Changed the world as they knew it. Amen. Amen. So-Dang-Good-Amen.

{Numbers 27:1–11}

FALLING FLAT ON YOUR FACE

Scripture would teach her that falling flat on her face wasn't the worst thing . . . for it was often when the glory of God would appear.

For a big book that talks a whole lot about falling on faces, we as humans sure do everything we can to avoid it, amen? I mean, I totally get it. After all, who the heck wants to fall flat on their face? It sucks. It *also*, however . . . reminds us we're human. And perhaps being reminded of that from time to time is a really good thing, because it allows us to send our superhero cape off to the dry cleaners. Cuz see, when we fall flat on our face, we come face-to-face with the ground from which we came. We're reminded that we actually *don't* have to always get it all right, and we *won't* actually always get it all right, and that it's actually OK when we don't *always* get it all right.

And there's freedom in that. Because when we fall flat on our face, we are free to cry without apology, and who knows . . . perhaps our tears will water the ground we're now lying on, and that ground may just bring forth some new. Let's believe that, OK? Falling flat on our face brings us face-to-face with our humanness, and the older I get, the more I'm realizing that our humanness seems to be the one thing we carry the most shame about . . . which is ironic, because it's also the one thing we can't ever change. We were *created* human.

One day, I sent out a group email. The next morning, I realized it included wrong info. Face-plant. But you know what? I realized my error, and I sent out a *new* email with the right information. And if I'm *really* being honest . . . I gave God a nod and said, "Thanks for showing me. I guess having a full plate sometimes leads to stuff falling off of it."

Folks, God is *that* personal. Scripture is *that* personal. I can't tell you what it's saying to you because I have no idea what you are saying to God. But you do. Just remember, falling flat on your face isn't the worst thing . . . for it's often when the glory of God appears.

{Numbers 20:2–6}

WHEN YOU FEEL LIKE MOSES

Moses often felt like he couldn't catch a break. There will be times you feel like Moses.

And I don't know what it is—but isn't just saying stuff out loud and speaking it raw and unfiltered refreshing? Moses often felt like he couldn't catch a break. Times when he wondered and flat-out cried out, "What the heck, Lord??" Times when he was angry. Times when he was over it. Times when he no doubt muttered to himself, "Ummm *hello*, Lord, this is *exactly* why I told you to *choose someone else for this*." But alas, God chose Moses for this holy. And Moses's holy was far from easy.

Beloved, Moses often felt like he couldn't catch a break. Going from one wilderness to another. One ugh to the next. One step forward, two steps back on this way to this land that God had promised them, which is why in the heck I reckon it took so darn long. But do you know what *else* Moses did? Moses talked to God about his hard. Moses talked to God about his weary. Moses talked to God and repeatedly cried out *why* because he knew that he *could* . . . And there's power in that. *Power in knowing that God would hear him.* That God would remind him that he was the one to do this hard thing and that he was not alone as he did it. That God would see him through his hard holy . . . the hard holy Moses never would've chosen . . . but the hard holy God had chosen him for. And our folks in the cloud chime in, "Hey, we can relate!"

And there's power in that too. In knowing that others feel the way you do . . . like if others are feeling it . . . then maybe you don't have to feel so horrible for feeling it. And *when* we feel like Moses did, we're actually *grateful* that at times he did . . . because then we can see what he did . . . He talked to God. He cried to God. He screamed at God—not because he didn't think God couldn't hear him, but because he simply needed to scream and let go of what was too darn heavy to carry, amen. And we can too. Thanks, Moses.

THIS ISN'T THE END OF YOUR STORY

Abigail's story didn't end after being married to a fool. Just sayin'.

Jonah's story didn't end after the stint in the fish. Naomi's story didn't end in Moab. Neither did Ruth's, by the way. Dan's story didn't end after his time in the den, and Esther's story didn't end after she was orphaned *or* after she was taken into that harem. Moses's story didn't end after he was placed in that river among the reeds, and Sarah's story didn't end after decades of negative pregnancy tests, and Mary's story didn't end after one positive one, and Dave's story didn't end after the *plethora* of times he no doubt thought that it had. And don't even get me started on Job.

Beloved, their stories didn't end after what they thought might be the end of their story. Please kindly read that again—*amen*. So how about *today . . . you believe . . .* that the *same . . .* is *true . . .* for *you*? And listen, if it helps to picture a fifty-something-year-old gal cheering you on with pom-poms in hand and a megaphone up to her lips . . . well then, go for it. Anything for a friend.

Beloved, my guess is that while Abigail was married to Nabal the fool, she probably thought that's where her story would end. But if so . . . Ab was wrong. *Just sayin'.* Beloved, what you *believe* today will either *help* you or *harm* you. You decide. So look to the cloud if you need reinforcement, and to me with my cheer gear if you need a giggle, because laughter really *does* help, and decide today what you're gonna believe. Rah to the Rah Rah Rah. *XO.*

CITIES OF REFUGE

Beloved, the land you've been given includes cities of refuge. Seek them out when refuge is needed.

Beloved, the land God has given you is not void of refuge and rest stops. You know what they look like, even if at times they seem only to be a mirage. These are the places that rehydrate your dry bones, renew your heart and your mind, refill your soul. And *again*, hear me when I say . . . there are *more than one* of these sacred spaces . . . in the land that *you* have been given. These cities do not all look the same. They vary. This is God's gift to you, so please, don't get stuck on the notion that they all look the same *or* like somebody else's. These sacred grounds may look like the place you're avoiding . . . but now that you've learned that sometimes *healing* comes from *going* . . . you may be more apt to increase your goings. For truly I tell you, Beloved, *people* are God's *provision* to us . . . so as the song says . . . Can't we all . . . get along?

One of your cities of refuge may look like a long walk outdoors—just you, your God, and the birds that keep singing no matter what. Another may look like a kitchen complete with all of the best ingredients needed to whip up something fabulous that'll make your recipients drool. One of your cities may look like grabbing your camera and going out into this great, big, beautiful world to catch one of those incredible, mind-blowing shots. Another may look like a planned nap on the couch or a short unexpected one out in the spring sun. One may look like a girls' night out, and one may look like a night spent at home doing absolutely *nothing* at all—guilt-free.

Beloved, you get my point. And I hope that you feel *seen*. For the land you've been *given* . . . includes cities of *refuge* . . . Seek out these cities . . . as needed. For God *gave* them to you . . . as part of the land you've been given . . . out of God's *great* love and care for you. Yes, you are truly *that* loved.

{Joshua 20}

WHEN HOLY IS HEAVY

Sometimes holy is heavy.

So what if instead of glossing over the reality that sometimes holy is heavy, we acknowledge it and say it out loud, and in doing so allow the One Who is in the midst of *their* heavy holy to know they are seen . . . and what if also in doing so, we actually see them . . . and in turn help them carry their heavy holy? Cuz sometimes holy is heavy. Things of great magnitude often are. The weight of an unexpected loss. The weight of an answer you didn't want. The weight of the wait. Yes. It's not that you don't know the weight is holy. You do, it's just that you're also human, and frankly, you're sick of apologizing for that. *Word.*

News flash—your Creator could've created you to be anything and actually chose human—so you don't need to apologize for that. God knows that sometimes holy is heavy. Like a cross on your back made of wood that feels like the whole darn tree. Exactly. The things we go through, the things we endure, the things we wish weren't, because we just don't understand, cuz we're human . . . these things can be both holy *and* heavy. Yes. *And.* They are not exclusive and are actually paired together quite often, and perhaps that's why words I had previously highlighted reached up their arms to me this morning like a toddler desperate to be picked up . . .

. . . "the care of the holy things that had to be carried on shoulders" . . .

Because truly I tell you, as hard as it is, sometimes *that* is how holy is carried. On shoulders. Sometimes holy is heavy. And because I don't feel right leaving you there in that truth . . . I'll also add this: The heavy *is* holy. It bears weight because it is valuable. It has worth. It has purpose. It is more precious than rubies or diamonds. And *you*, as God's forever held and eternally loved Human, are allowed to cry and rest and slow down and sometimes even all-out stop . . . before taking your very next step. Yes. God is with you, Beloved.

{Numbers 7:9}

YOU WERE BUILT FOR YOUR BATTLES

You were built for the battles assigned to you.

Beloved . . . *you are covered. Yes.* You are covered in the battle you wish wasn't your battle. Because battles are hard. And that's an understatement. And because in our humanness we often can't understand the purpose of the battle, we're forced to pull out our walking stick, the one we've named Trust, and keep going, literally walking by faith and not sight because we can't possibly see the purpose in the midst of what we're enduring. Naomi couldn't either. Or Esther. Or the one at the well, or the One Who bled, or the One Who was down to her very last drop of oil. But see, what they didn't know at the time was that they were built for their battles. And thankfully, they now reside in the cloud, so we can hear them as they whisper to us . . . *You are too. Yes.*

We are built for the battles assigned to us, and we are covered in each battle we're in, and, *and*, there are those who help us in the battles. Those ready to stand beside us like Aaron and Hur did for Moses as they raised his hands *for* him because he was so . . . worn out . . . from his battle. Those ready to fight on your behalf because you've got no fight left, and those ready to do what they must to defend you when the enemy's about to pounce on you because you're at your weakest, and as I've said before . . . you are *never* more tempted to forget Who your God is . . . than when . . . you're at . . . your weakest. *Nod to Jesus, Who purposely fasted in the whole wilderness-with-Satan story so we could get that.*

Beloved, you were built for the battles assigned to you . . . by the One Who fearfully and wonderfully made you. The One Who not only wrote your story in full before you lived the first day but also reminds you, lest you've forgotten, "Ahem, I Am the Beginning *and* the End." You were built for the battles assigned to you, and you are *covered* in those said battles. You will never be *anywhere* that God is *not* because the tent of meeting lies *within you, amen.* Don't forget that, OK?

LOVING THE LORD WITH ALL YOU'VE GOT LEFT

Loving the Lord your God "with all of your strength" sometimes looks like using all of the strength you've got left to love the Lord your God.

A God Who includes the words "all your strength" in addition to your heart and your mind because, yes . . . there will be days. Days that are hard. Days that are really hard. Nights that are long. Nights that are really long . . . or so short you're not even sure you slept. The moments or passages of time when, despite the fact that you know just how *real* God is, it takes every ounce of the strength you've got left to continue to love that God—that God you know is yours—and yet, a part of you questions, like Gideon . . . then *why*, Lord? Why? Yes.

Beloved, I'm not exactly sure why I'm writing these words right now at this moment, but I reckon it's because I wonder if someone may need to hear them. Hear that it's *not* always easy to fully and completely love the Lord your God with all your strength, because the word itself—strength—lets us know that something is gonna be hard.

So if today is hard for you Beloved, and you feel like you're using every ounce of the strength you've got left to keep loving, keep trusting, keep believing, keep hoping, keep asking, and keep going . . . then I just want you to know that I see you. And although hard is hard, and using all of your strength is hard at a whole 'nother level, the Lord your God *still* goes before you. And God *still* knows you're human and *still* weeps alongside you on those days when tears are the truest and sincerest of prayers, and the strength used to love and trust has literally drained you right down to your knees. Yes.

Beloved, you are seen, you are heard, you are known, you are loved. And *you* . . . are gonna get through. *XO.*

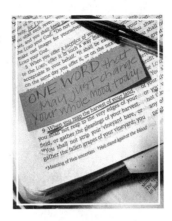

ONE WORD THAT CAN CHANGE YOUR WHOLE MOOD

One word that may just change your whole mood today . . .

When. One four-letter word that is a welcome change from the one you've been muttering lately. Hey—I got you. I get you. But today, we welcome this *new* four-letter word, this word we didn't realize held so much power, but dang if it don't, and we're so glad it does.

When. One four-letter word that may just strengthen you enough to keep going today. Or allow you to rest today. Depending on which it is that you most need. One four-letter word that may just give you enough light at the end of your tunnel to endure the dark spot that you're in. One four-letter word that, although it has but one simple syllable, carries with it the meaning of a much bigger word—*Promise.* Yes.

When. When you reap the harvest of your land.

Wait. Did You say *when*, Lord?

Yup.

When I *reap*?

Yup.

You are gonna *reap*.

Wait a sec again, Lord—I'm gonna reap a *harvest*?

Yup. You read that right, Darlin', and we ain't talkin' slim-pickings.

OK, Lord, sorry, one last thing—I'm gonna reap this harvest in *my* land? The land that You *have* given me *and* all the land You *continue* to give me??

Righty-O again, Sweet Child of Mine.

Mood-changer, Beloved? You tell me. But if nothing else, I hope you had some fun and cracked a smile. I love ya.

{Leviticus 19:9}

WHEN YOU'RE SCARED TO GET YOUR HOPES UP

Maybe you're not allowing your mind to go there because you're scared to death of getting your hopes up.

Up for consideration today, folks, is this: Maybe you're not allowing your mind to go there . . . because you're scared to death of getting your hopes up. Maybe. Because, of course, you're likely not admitting that out loud, and that's OK, because God knows, and so you can actually rest (or wrestle) with that truth. So I ask you—if you are 100 percent honest with yourself right now, are you refusing to let your mind "go there"—to that good place, that promised land you always hear preached about, that fruitful dang-this-tastes-sweet spot in the garden? Yes, *that* place. Are you not allowing your mind to go there because you're scared to death of getting your hopes up? Maybe. I'm actually convinced that's why Sarah laughed . . . when she heard the news that she'd be needing a crib despite no longer needing to buy plugs and pads . . . just sayin'.

So again, I ask you, Beloved, are you refusing to let your mind go there . . . because you're scared to death of getting your hopes up? Because if so, let me share with you what came to my mind as I thought about the visual of getting our hopes up . . . Getting them *up* means lifting them. Raising them. High above our heads, which is good because our heads often have a tough time understanding what the heck God is doing, amen. What if getting our hopes *up* is actually good for us? What if the weightier the hopes are that we raise . . . the stronger we become as we wait? What if we could picture a weightlifting bar with our hopes attached to both sides, and then imagine ourselves raising that bar up high, thus literally getting our hopes up??

I know, right? This kinda stuff makes me giddy. Because the more I think about it, even if the specific hopes that I raise up are not realized . . . *I will be stronger for having lifted them.*

Beloved, if right now you're smiling because a part of you is daring to believe . . . Sweet. That is *exactly* where I hoped this would take you.

ASK YOURSELF WHAT YOU CAN DO

Ask yourself, "What can I do?"

The woman whose issue just happens to be bleeding for twelve long years: "Well, I guess I can stay here in my box, isolated one more day, *or* I can finally say, 'Screw it! Enough is enough!' and have the audacity to go for it. After all, I've got nothing left to lose, and I wanna see Jesus too."

The woman who had been painfully hunched over for the past eighteen years: "Well, I can stay home for the 937th Sabbath in a row, *or* I can just plan to leave early and slowly make my way to the temple. After all, I wanna see Jesus too, and I heard He's preaching today."

The chief tax collector, we'll call him Zach for short (no pun intended): "Well, since I'm so short, there's no *way* I'm gonna see Jesus in the midst of *that* massive crowd, so I guess I could stay home, *or* I could run ahead and climb up into a sycamore tree, cuz those babies grow 30–40 feet tall, and after all, I wanna see Jesus too."

Beloved, truly I tell you, our lack has the power to *drive* us. It's what *gives* lack value and purpose. Lacks and Limits are *opportunities* to reach deep within yourself and discover a strength and a determination you never thought you had.

I was recently talking to a group of teen girls. I told them to imagine that we were on a killer road trip to NYC for an all-expense-paid trip to do *whatever* we wanted upon arrival. I told them to imagine us cruising and belting out the best '80s classics and munching on the very best snacks when suddenly, halfway there, we reach a dead end. Do we park there and call it good? Do we turn around and head back home, forgoing all we had planned? *Or* . . . do we *find a new way to get there*?

Beloved, in the midst of all that you *can't* do, for *whatever* reason, ask yourself *this:* What *can* I do? For staying stuck may just be robbing you of the full, abundant, all-that-remains-for-you life you so desperately want. And when you *are* tempted to let your "I just *can't*" rule the roost, well then, baby, you let *these* fine folks sing you their cock-a-doodle-doos. *XO.*

MAKE THYSELF AN ARK

Your testimony to Who you know God to be resides in the ark that saw you through your storm.

Beloved, do you know why I think God commanded Noah to "Make for thyself an ark"? *Because Noah was gonna need an ark to see him through the storm.* Do you know why I think God commanded Moses to instruct the Israelites to *make an ark*? An ark covered and overlaid and protected to the *n*th degree to keep the covenant in? *Because it's worth protecting.*

And Friends, let us also pause here to recognize that God didn't *give* Noah an ark. God gave him what he needed to *build* it. Same with the Israelites. And I have to wonder if it's because it is *through the process of building that we come to know more and more of Who God is.* Hey, just a thought. I wonder if it's because *the building itself actually strengthens us, not to mention binds us to what we have made, because now it's personal to us—the work of our very own hands/heart/mind/soul.* Again, just one girl's thoughts.

Beloved, I've said this before, but dang-it-all if I don't think it's huge. . . . Make for thyself an ark. *Yes.* Construct it using the truths and promises of who you know God to be. Cover it. Protect it. Remind yourself that it's layered in gold and that there are angels above that are woven right into it. An ark that serves as a refuge and shelter for your heart, mind, and soul for when the storms that are bound to come . . . come.

Beloved, I don't even have to know you to know that your testimony to Who you know God to be resides in the ark that saw you through your storm. And if that storm revealed to you the need for an ark . . . then make for thyself an ark so you're ready when the next storm comes. Make sure to remind yourself that whether it was Noah or whether it was Moses . . . *neither* of them was alone when it came to their arks. And neither are you.

{Genesis 6}

HARD ROADS CAN LEAD
TO BEAUTIFUL REDEMPTION

Really hard roads can lead to really beautiful redemption.

And in typical Tera-fashion, I certainly don't expect you to take my word alone for it. The Israelites are happy to visit with you and share their story about how their really hard road led to really beautiful redemption as you sit and enjoy some fresh fruit and honey and a really tall glass of milk. Esther would love for you to join her at one of her killer banquets and share with you about her life as a child, losing her parents, having her name changed, being kept hidden in a foreign land as a way to stay alive, being forced into a harem and chosen as Queen, which you would *think* would be awesome, except that her new royal position would bring with it the biggest decision of her life. Whew. Spoiler alert: It ends well. For her. Not the bad guy. Redemption.

Naomi and Ruth are happy to chat with you about what it was like to travel as two single gals after both losing their husbands, and Ruth will tell you all about working the fields so they wouldn't starve. Second spoiler alert: Also ends well. And Naomi is busy chasing her grandson around. Redemption. Sarah could tell you about a really hard road. The woman at the well could talk your ear off. The gal hunched over for eighteen years and the one who bled for twelve will tell you *all* about their walks of shame . . . *that led to beautiful redemption. Yes.*

Why do I share this today, Beloved? Because maybe *you* are on a really hard road. And I want you to know that really hard roads don't always lead to really hard places. Sometimes, they lead to really beautiful redemption. Just talk to the cloud, cuz there's a whole bunch more with their hands raised. *And* how different would it look for you if you *believed* that your really hard road is leading to a really beautiful redemption? Would it give you the strength to keep going? Would it give you the courage you need to press on? Would it—dare I say—even make you *slightly* smile if you believed that it'd all be worth it? Maybe.

Beloved, I've said it before—faith is to your soul what food is to your flesh. Feed *both*. I love ya. Amen.

HOW TO CALM THE STORM WITHIN

How to calm the storm within . . . rebuke the winds and waves. Jesus taught her that.

Sometimes the stars align. Sometimes my daily Scripture readings do too. Both are so cool when they do. A storm. Jesus would intentionally send His disciples into one, personally accompanying them on this short hop-across-the-lake voyage to see what they had gleaned from what He had just taught them. Which of course, they hadn't. Not fully anyway. For how would they know, until they were *in* it? How would they know if it'd *stuck*?

So Jesus *took* them. And Jesus *showed* them. In real time and in real life. For that's how they would need to go on and teach others.

So off they go, and a storm arises, a purposefully sent storm for teaching purposes, because visual aids are often the best way to learn, *amen*. And as the strong winds are blowing and the waves are raging, Jesus is catching some Zzz's in the boat. Panicked, they wake him up. And Jesus's reply to the awaking? *Hello . . . where is your faith?*

Guys, remember how the seed, that is, the Word of God, when it's in good ground and when it's held on to and as it endures with patience . . . produces fruit? Tell me . . . *Why are you waking me up for this? Where is your faith?* Is it hanging out on the path that was trampled on? Is it somewhere that it lacks moisture? Is it dwelling among the thorns and therefore has choked the life right out of you? *Where is it?*

Use it. Use it to calm the storm within you. Use it to rebuke the winds and the waves that feel like they're gonna take you out. Rebuke by Remembering. I Am with you. I Am for you. I will *always* be with you, even to the end of the age, *amen*.

Now, Beloved, you may be wondering, what do I mean when I say my daily readings aligned like the stars? Well, my Psalm today was 42. So should *you* be battling a storm within, first read this cool storm story in Luke 8:22–25 (yup, just four verses!) and then head to Psalm 42. And quiet the storm within you by rebuking the winds and the waves . . . by remembering where your faith is. *XO*.

GOD'S GOT A PLAN

Do not be afraid. God's got a plan.

And please, I don't mean to sound corny or kitschy or any other adjective that makes you cringe; you know that's not my style. I simply want you to stop right now, in the midst of your struggle, your fear, your panic, your storm, your worry, your war, your raging sea . . . and hear me across our cups of piping hot joe, as I look at you, directly and right into your eyes, your eyes that say so much, and with every fiber that I've got, I say this . . . "Do not be afraid. God's got a plan."

A plan that includes your rescue and your redemption. A plan packed with purpose and might. A plan that starts with steadfast love and never ceases to remain in that love, because love is Who God *is*. A plan that will include pages that you love and pages that you vehemently hate. A plan that includes ups and downs and roundabouts that leave you wondering *why* . . . not to mention sick to your stomach. A plan that includes your purpose revealed on this Earth. A purpose that's holy, set apart, which would explain why it oftentimes doesn't make sense.

Beloved, I don't say it lightly. I don't say it to somehow gloss over your hurt, making it one more stupid Christian meme out there that does more harm than good. I say it for the same reason Moses said it to the Israelites when they couldn't understand why in the world God would finally lead them *out*, only to allow them to be pursued once again. Ugh. But see, Moses knew what they did not. He knew God had a plan. A plan that would free them while simultaneously showing the Egyptians (who God also loved, by the way) that He really *was* God.

Beloved, I don't know what you stand in need of today, or if your journey has you some place you'd rather not be, or you simply can't wrap your head around the big giant "*why*??" . . . But wherever you are . . . if you are feeling afraid . . . I hope these words give you respite. Even if but for a moment. Do not be afraid. God's got a plan.

THE BATTLE'S BEEN WON

She would fight her battles, knowing they were from God and knowing they were already won.

She sure would. She'd also remind herself that she was allowed to cry out whenever she needed. And that freedom to scream and to cry and to question would arise from reminding herself that the God Who created her and wrote her story in full is fully aware that she was made human, and therefore can't possibly understand all His ways, which is why He *also* repeatedly tells her "I Am *with* you," so that she can be strengthened by the fact that not only is she not *alone*, but it's *God* for God's sake Who is with her . . . *whew*.

Beloved, what do you suppose allowed Moses and Aaron to keep doing the thing despite every plague that *God* sent? I'll tell ya what—it was knowing that the battle had already been won. *Yes*. God had told them that the day would come when the peeps would be feasting on honey and all sorts of awesomeness, but first He had to do some stuff so that the Egyptians *too* would know He was God and the Israelites would come to respect Moses as their leader. *Exactly, amen*.

What do you suppose it was that allowed little David to voluntarily take on big Goliath? It was knowing that the battle had already been won. Encouraging himself, strengthening himself, hyping himself up really by reminding himself that *God* for God's sake was with him and so, seriously, how could he lose?

Beloved, there is only one way I know how to fight the battles that come my way, and it's this—it's knowing they are *from* God, and therefore knowing they've already been *won*. I don't have to *like* the battle. God knows I won't. But we don't have to like something in order for it to have purpose. I can get tired because battling takes a lot out of a gal. I can cry because crying is a really great way to release what is too heavy to carry. I can rest because even in war, there are times of rest. Yes. I can fight without understanding why I'm enduring the battle . . . and I can do it by knowing the battle has already been won . . . by the One Who knows the outcome and has declared it . . . Holy.

REMEMBERING IS YOUR SUPERPOWER

Listen—this is how you're gonna get through this—you're gonna remember right now Who your God is.

You're gonna remind yourself that the God Who knit you together and wrote your story in full is the same God Who loves you and is with you to the final Amen. You're also gonna allow yourself to question God, "Why??" . . . because Moses did it all the time, and he seems like a pretty good role model. Cuz see, Moses didn't ask to be where he was, and he sure as heck didn't want go through his This . . .

So Moses talked to God about the hard, and he didn't sugarcoat it either as he told God, "I'm not exactly the most eloquent speaker, Ya know." Moses cried out to God using his *own* words in his *own* way, and aren't those the truest and most real prayers of all? The ones born from the most desperate places? The ones birthed from the madness? The ones that cry out, "*Why, God? Why* am I here? *Why* did You send me? *Why* are You doing nothing at all*??*" And God answered Moses. And thankfully, someone wrote it down so you and I can refer to it in the midst of our very own "This" . . . Note: I expanded it based on other awesomeness about Who our God is.

I *Am* the Lord. I *Am* making Myself *known* to you through This. I *hear* you. I *will* free you. I *will* deliver you. I *will* redeem you. I *will* see you through *this*, and I *will* be your God, and *when* I do—you're gonna *know* that I'm your God. I'm gonna free you from the burden you're currently carrying, and I know you don't understand why you're carrying it in the first place, but I *promise* you it has *purpose*. I Am gonna bring you *out* and bring you *to*, and you're just gonna have to take Me at My unchanging Word on that.

I have *never* forgotten you, and I *promise* you that I will be *with* you wherever you *are* and wherever you *go*, and let Me just remind you, sweet child of Mine, not *one* of My promises has failed. I Am Redeemer. I Am Rescuer. I Am the One Who makes *all* things right in due time. I Am your faithful companion as you journey through *This*.

UNSPOKEN FEAR

Scared to "go there"... but have never actually said it out loud? A God Who speaks life into unspoken fear, "Don't be afraid. I'll go with you."

There's no question I love Scripture. It's why I eat it every morning for breakfast. Cuz I learned long ago that if we feed only our flesh and not our souls, then a part of us is gonna be dead. P.S.: For those who feel like they're already to that dead place, hear the good news: God resurrects.

Ya know what *else* God does? Speaks life into unspoken fear. The fear that you've never actually said out loud because a) admitting that fear is the reason you're not "going there" ain't easy, and b) if you say it out loud, it makes it more "real," so it's best to just pretend it's not there. But see, the super cool thing about an *All*-Knowing God is that All means All, which means God knows, which is why God is able to speak into that which has remained unspoken, and truly I tell you, Beloved, that's when all of a sudden, as you're reading your daily reading and come across words that feel so dang "I'm *talking to you, girl*" personal that you can't help but actually smile and sigh..."*Fine, I get it.*"

Jacob never said out loud, "I'm scared to go." But God knew. So God spoke. God spoke life into unspoken fear. And God started by calling Jacob by name. And Jake listened and heard exactly what he needed to hear..."I am God, the God of your father; do not be afraid to go down to Egypt, for I will make of you a great nation there. I myself will go down with you... and I will also bring you back up again..." And upon hearing those words of life that bred strength... Jacob set out. Despite his age. To go where he was scared to go.

Beloved, I don't know where your "there" is. It may be a place or an internal desire. It may be a hard conversation or something within you that is begging you to at least try. Whatever the case, hear God's words to you this day: "I Myself... will go *with* you."

{Genesis 46:1–4}

IT WAS GOD

There will be times in your journey when you look back and are actually able to forgive what you never thought you would, because you'll realize it was God.

Joseph will tell you that it's *one hundred* percent true . . . and your girl Tera Jean will too. Beloved, there will be times in your journey when you will stop and look back and realize . . . *OMG* . . . that was *God*. I may not have liked God's *way*, but I sure as heck can't deny it was God.

Ask Joe if he liked being tossed in a well, sold into slavery, and thrown into prison after being falsely accused of rape. But he's over here ready to tell you that *he gets it*. He gets what it's like to go through a buncha crap, wondering where the heck God Almighty is while simultaneously crying out "*Why me???*" Joe gets you. Joe gets us. Thanks, Joe. But after all the crap Joe went through . . . when he saw his brothers bowing before him, begging for food because the land they had stayed in was in *such* a deep famine, Joe realized . . . *OMG* . . . *that's* why I'm here. *That's* why I was brought here. As much as I'd like to continue blaming my bros, *God brought me into this position for such a time as this. As Esther chimes in, "Amen, Dude!"*

Beloved, like Joe, it took me a while to realize that the parts of my story that included taking me from places I didn't want to leave . . . into an unknown land I didn't want to *or was afraid to enter* . . . was all along God Who was whispering to me . . . but it took years to hear, because anger and bitterness and resentment are loud . . . I *know* . . . the *plans* . . . I *have* . . . for *you*. Yes. Will they always make sense? No. Will we always like them? Heck no. Will faith, hope, and love protect and provide for our soul as we journey . . . like food, water, and shelter protect and provide for our body? Yes.

God has brought me to where I am today. With purpose. And Beloved, God has brought you to where you are too. With purpose.

TRANSFORMED THROUGH THE HARD

Jacob was transformed through the hard. You will be too.

My guess is you already have. *And* my guess is, you will be again. Me too. Jacob needed to break free from some stuff. Maybe you do too. He needed to see God in the places he didn't want to be so that he knew that God really was with him in those places he didn't want to be. Maybe you do too. He needed to work through some really hard stuff and wrestle with God about some really hard stuff and walk through some really hard stuff that he didn't want to walk through because *the process of transformation is hard.*

Yes. We know it for our flesh, right? Ask anyone whose flesh has ever been transformed if it was easy. I *guarantee* he/she is gonna laugh out five words . . . "*heck no it wasn't easy.*" . . . to then likely be followed by another five words . . . "*but it was worth it.*"

Transformation is hard. It involves refining and defining and sculpting and since *hello, God is the Potter and you are the clay* . . . you're gonna have to trust that God knows *exactly* how your transforming will take place. *And* Beloved, how's this for the opposite of artificial sweetener—*it's gonna be hard.* And God *knows* it's gonna be hard for us, and therefore, just like with Jake, God tells us again and again . . . I Am *with* you. I Am *for* you. I Am *within you,* which means you can talk to Me and cry to Me and heck, even scream at Me, cuz I *know that you're human. I'm the One Who created you human, hello.* The One Who gave us sweat glands and tear ducts and every other orifice to release what is too heavy for us to carry, *amen.* Talk about good design. Seriously.

Beloved, Jacob was transformed through the hard. You will be too. *And* . . . the Lord *your* God . . . will be with you every single step and phase of your transformation, amen. Believe it.

STOPS IN HARD PLACES

Your journey will include stops in hard places.

And like our guy Jacob, you too may dream at night that there's a mighty stairway to heaven (song break), not so much to admire the beauty of its gorgeous gold steps . . . but more so to scream at it *get me the heck outta here, Lord.* Your journey will include stops in hard places. Places where, again like our pal Jake, we are left so destitute that we feel as though a rock is our pillow and our lack-of-sleep raises her hand to testify.

Your journey will include stops in hard places. And there's absolutely *no* way I'm gonna start the next line with *but* here, because I absolutely *refuse* to let a big *but* take away or diminish the reality that *your journey will include stops in hard places.*

And . . . your God reminds you, just as God reminded Jake in his hard place . . . I *am* the Lord, the God of your *entire* family tree, and I *Am your God too.* And then God goes on, knowing that Jake needs a bit more to hold on to if he's gonna get through this and hello-so-do-we, so let's listen . . . "Know that I Am with you and will keep you wherever you go (ahem, Tera's interjection here—if God is saying He'll be with him wherever he goes, then clearly Jake *won't always be in this place, amen*) and will bring you back to this land; for I *will not leave you until* I *have done what* I *have promised you.*"

Right. Jake woke up. This convo had taken place in the night, and I realized something, let's call it a light(bulb). Could it be that God comes to us, stands by us, and whispers to us in our dark . . . because God knows that it's in the dead of our dark nights . . . that we are most desperate for some life-giving light? Just a thought. Jake woke up and thought one thing . . . *OMG! God is in this place . . . this hard place in my journey . . . and I didn't even know it.* Again, Tera's translation.

Beloved, your journey will include stops in hard places. *And* . . . God will be there too.

{Genesis 28:16}

THERE'S ENOUGH FOR YOU TOO

Hey, Sisters! Listen, when God stops for one of us—to bless, heal, set free—it doesn't mean that there won't be enough left for you.

God doesn't run out of blessings. God doesn't run out of power. God doesn't run out of bread or water or the ability to break chains and set people free. God doesn't run out of grace, compassions, mercies, love—pitch your tent toward the sunrise if you're prone to forget. God can stop for *one* of us and not use up all God's *stuff*—so go ahead and *take a breath* and quit secretly envying your sister. *Ahem.*

Once upon a time, a father came desperately to the feet of Jesus and begged Him to come to his house and heal his one and only daughter. Off they went. *Except.* In the midst of the mob that followed Jesus on His way to heal that girl, another girl, this one a bit older, was *also* desperate for healing. She was probably *also* grateful for the mob-crowd at that moment—easier to blend in, go in unassuming, and touch the hem of that robe. And she did touch it. But not unassumingly. Dang. Cuz see, Jesus decided to up and proclaim—Who touched Me? *Someone who believed touched Me, cuz I could feel it.* Yup.

So, knowing she wasn't gonna get outta this thing, she fell before His feet, shaking in fear, and laid it all out to Him *and* to the crowd that surrounded them. She told them her *why.* And then told them *how.* How the minute she touched that robe, she felt better. Her issue no longer defined her. She felt free for the first time in *twelve* years. *Hallelujah, what a relief.*

But wait. What about the *young* girl? Wasn't Jesus on His way to heal *her*? Now what? Word came. Too late, Jesus. She died. Maybe you shouldn't have stopped for that older gal. Maybe *then* this young girl would've made it. Jesus told them not to fear. He continued on His way to her. They laughed at Him, thinking He was crazy. He wasn't. He knew He hadn't run out of power or blessings simply because He had stopped and bestowed them on *one.* Jesus took that young girl by the hand and whispered . . . Arise. And she did. And she ate. For there was *enough for her too.* XO.

{Luke 8}

FOR THE MAMA WHO WORRIES

For the mama who worries . . .

How did I know that would get your attention? Two words: Mamas worry. Whether their child is still in diapers or whether they're all grown up and gone . . . Mamas worry. At least at times. Some more than others. They sure do.

As the story goes, Sarah was barren and "well stricken with years," a.k.a. *old*. She wanted to give her husband an heir, so she offered up her slave girl, Hagar. Hagar did as she was told and indeed conceived and ay ay ay yi, once it got real, our girl Sarah turned on Hagar faster than you can say *hey-lady-this-was-your-idea*. Right. Hagar ran away. Came back per an angel's instruction. Gave birth. Sarah *also* conceived and gave birth. Surprise! And when Sarah saw *her* son playing with *Hagar's* son, she told her hubby, *That's it! She's gotta go!* So after the Lord assured Abe it would be OK, he packed up Hagar and their son Ishmael and sent them on their way. P.S.: I *promise* I'm getting to the worry part, bear with me.

After her provisions were all used up, with no water left in the skins and no bread left to feed her and her son, Hagar put him under a bush . . . and left him there . . . and went a good way off . . . for she just couldn't stand the thought of watching her son starve to death. And as she sat and as she wept, she lifted her voice, and then Scripture says *this* . . . God heard the voice of . . . *the boy*. I know, right? You thought it'd say Hagar. But Scripture instead tells us that God heard the voice of *the boy*. And then—OMG, this *so good*—God said *this* to Hagar . . . "What troubles you Hagar? Do not be afraid; for God has heard the voice of the boy *where he is*."

Yes. Where he is. So for the Mama who worries . . . God sees your child. God knows where your child is. God has written your child's story, and God's steadfast love extends from generation to generation. I promise, amen. *XO*.

{Genesis 21}

GOD WILL PROVIDE IN THE MIDST
OF YOUR WAR

God will provide in the midst of your war.

As a matter of fact, provision was already in place for you before your war even began.

Read that again. Now granted, it should be noted, that sometimes provision in the midst of war is not always easy to see. Confusion surrounding the Why of it all combined with the sheer exhaustion of it all, not to mention the fear that pitches its tent in the crux of your soul and just won't seem to leave . . . can make provision in the midst of your war hard to see. And yet . . . *it's there. Yes.* The provision prepared for you before your battle even began. Read that again too.

I was reminded today in my OT reading, the part where Moses instructed those whom he led, to *not* destroy the trees in the land they were warring with, for the trees were there to *provide for them.* Yes. Instead, he instructed them . . . to employ them in the siege.

Hold on—*employ them in the siege. Yes.* (I stinkin' *love* that—thanks, ole King James!) Put them to work for you. Eat from them. Take shade from them. Find shelter under their leaves. And if they are *not* producing anything for you, *then* chop 'em down and use the wood to build stuff like ladders or towers or things you may need. *Yes.*

Beloved, God will provide in the midst of your war. A field with just enough grain left on the ground for Ruth to scoop up and feed her and Naomi. A fish with a belly big enough to house a guy trying to escape from his calling, giving him three days to think. A single cloud in the midst of the drought, just enough to bring enough hope to believe that maybe, just maybe, this drought will finally end—today.

Beloved, I could go on. For hours, I'm sure. God *will* provide for you in the midst of your war. Look for it. Behold it. And know that the Lord your God is with you *in* it. *XO.*

{Deuteronomy 20:19–20 KJV}

YOU CAN BELIEVE AND QUESTION

Abram believed God and questioned God. Because you can believe God and question God.

Ahhhhhh the sound of chains breaking, seriously one of my favorite choruses right after the Hallelujah one. It sure is. Beloved, you can *believe* God . . . *and, and, and . . . question* God. That's right. And the truth shall set you free. Not to mention close the gap. Big time. And I want to apologize right now on behalf of anyone who has ever told you or led you to believe otherwise. Amen.

Abram believed God. And questioned God. Hagar believed God. And questioned God. Job believed God. And questioned God. Mary believed God. And questioned God. You get my point, and I hope it's lightening up that burden of guilt you've been carrying around, cuz that sucker's heavy.

Beloved, you can question God. Question God not as in *doubting* God, question God as in *asking God questions*. Right. Beloved, do you know what Google will tell you if you ask her the best way to get to *really* know someone? Save yourself the time; I already asked her. I know you're busy. Here's what she said—*ask genuine questions*. And it makes sense, right? I mean, if you're in a relationship and never ask any questions of the one you're in relationship with, how could you *possibly* get to *really* know them? In the words of the Fonz . . . Exactamundo.

So, if the question today is this—can you believe God *and* question God, keeping in mind that the word *question* here refers to *asking* not doubting—well then . . . I reckon our answer is . . . a *big, fat heck yes*.

Beloved, may you get to know your God more fully . . . through the questions you dare to ask . . . while playing and replaying the anthem of your heart-mind-and-soul so that you can't *possibly* forget it. That's right, you know the one . . . Don't Stop Believin'. Rock on. And Amen.

THERE IS NEW TO COME AFTER

There is new to come after the flood.

That's right. New. *After.* And to quote the verse . . . "These are the descendants of Noah's sons, Shem, Ham, and Japheth; *children were born to them after the flood.*" *Hello?!?!?* Right??? So good, so good. *New. After.* A thousand amens and someone please cue the Hallelujah Chorus.

Beloved, there is *new* to come *after* the flood. Yes. After the flood. After the fire. After the raging storm. After the strong winds stop blowing. After the divorce. After the loss. After the thing you thought would completely destroy you, and although it may have done that in part . . . you hold on to this word Rebuild . . . defining it as Opportunity . . . for New.

There is New to come after the flood. After the famine. After the separation. After the letting go that felt less like a beautiful release and more like someone forcefully prying open your fiercely-desperate-to-hold-onto bloody hands. There is New to come after. There sure is. And God shows us.

Beloved, as I sat here and tapped out these words, there was well over two feet of snow outside my window . . . and yet . . . I know that beneath that hefty blanket of frigid cold white . . . lay new. New in Waiting, we'll call it. *Yes.* New waiting to burst forth through the ground, waiting to bud, waiting to replenish the Earth with its new. And Beloved, that may just be where you are at too. In waiting. But knowing. Or *now* knowing as you read these words and tuck them away into the deepest part of your soul knowing what you now know . . . thanks to a few simple words . . . found in Noah's cool story . . . children were born to them . . . *after the flood.* New. After. Believe it, and don't stop believin', Beloved.

{Genesis 10:1}

GOD GAVE YOU POWER

He gave her power.

Power to tread over serpents and scorpions, reminding her they were under her feet. Power to overcome the enemy, the one that usually posed as fear/worry/doubt and came only to kill/steal/destroy. Power to take captive every thought that arose within her and *dared* to set itself up against the knowledge of Who her God is. Yes. He gave her power. To hope when all seemed lost. To trust when the path all-out sucked. To keep going despite all the unscheduled and unwanted stops, for there must be *some* reason for them. Yes.

He gave her power. To *believe* . . . over and over and over again . . . reminding her *that* was her superpower. And went as far as to give her a song for her lips to sing, lest she needs that reminder, amen. Yes. He gave her power. To tear down and to build. To drive out and to take in. To add and to remove. To pull herself up out of the pit or to cry for help to be lifted. Yes. He gave her power. To see others. To hear others. To be in community, where unity can be found. Indeed. Comm*unity*. He gave her power. To ponder in her heart what it all might mean. To persevere by praying continually, thus reminding herself she was never alone. In fact . . . the Lord her God was with her . . . *giving* her such power.

The God Who stayed when others fled. The God Who remained, regardless of the trouble she was in or the trial she was currently facing. The God Who whispered to her from the eye of her storm in the deepest and darkest part of her night . . . I will be with you . . . all the way to the end. Yes. He gave her power. To want more for her life without apologizing for it. To desire more of what it was that made her soul come alive. To live her life each day as if she was steps away from a miracle, *cuz who knows? She just might be. Amen.* Yes.

He gave her power. And she *sure* as heck wasn't gonna waste it.

WHEN YOU SIT WITH JESUS

If you're too busy to sit with Jesus for a few minutes, you're missing out on the good part.

And if you *don't* sit with Jesus? Then what? The truth is—your day will still move forward. God will still provide. You'll still be seen and still be heard and still be fully known and called by name and completely and totally loved without fail, no exceptions, amen.

But you'll miss out on the good part. The part . . . where you *know* it. You *know* you are worthy of God's time and attention as you sit there with coffee in hand. The part where you hear your *own* name being whispered as you read or as you pray and beg God to answer. The part where you're holding your God in the word-made-flesh and realize as you commune with Him that He really *is* right there *with* you. The part where you see that you are *so* precious and *so* valuable, and your God knows you *so well* that even the number of hairs on your head have been counted, even the gray ones and the ones you have lost, amen. That the tears you are crying are being collected. That the hurts and the pains, every want, every need, are out in the open as you sit with the One Who weeps alongside you, knowing you can't *possibly* understand the depth of the purpose of the plans He has for you.

Yes. The good part. The part on the *inside*. For anyone can take the first bite of bread, but they'll taste only the crust. The good part is *for* you. The good part is *there*. The good part can't be *taken* from you, because knowing is *personal* and resides deep within you. The good part is *set apart*, so *please* don't leave it on the table in your rush to get out the door. The good part is your *opportunity* . . . to finally *sit* for a few minutes . . . and realize what this brief life on Earth is *really* about . . . while being *reminded* of your immense value in this land you've been given to *live* in and not simply exist.

Yes. The *good part*. The part where you not only know God is *real* . . . you know God is right there with *you*. XO.

{Luke 10:42}

WHY WE PRAY

She didn't pray thinking she'd change God's mind. She prayed to open her own, to process her own, to calm and strengthen and comfort and remind herself that she wasn't doing this life here alone.

She prayed to process what had been, ponder what is, and mentally prepare for what may or may not lie ahead. She prayed to talk, to get it all out, even if it was through her pen, lightening her burden with every stroke. She prayed through complaining and grumbling and bawling her eyes out and literally begging God to show her the purpose, show her the plan . . . knowing of course that it was not for her to know . . . but instead be revealed to her as she went . . . knowing that her journey was under the watchful eye of the Lord . . . the One Who vowed to never leave or forsake her. *Ever.*

She prayed, pleading and pounding her fists on some mornings, and rejoicing and praising on others. She prayed exactly as she was, for she knew that her God knew who she was, and what was *really* going on both within her and around her, so there was no use trying to filter it through fancy words or pretense. She prayed boldly at times and exhausted at times, for she knew that her God bent an ear to listen to her at all times, regardless of her current condition.

She prayed because she *could.* Yes. She could pray whenever she wanted and wherever she wanted, and no one could take it from her. For the conversation she had with her Creator was born from within her. She prayed to open her eyes to all that awaited her. To stir up her anticipation and fuel her excitement. To revive her and restore her and send her out with a renewed and strengthened hope not based on blind faith . . . but on a faith that absolutely *refused* to stop believing, amen. She sure did. She prayed. For when she did, she knew she wasn't alone. *XO.*

WHEN GOD DOESN'T

When God doesn't, that also has purpose. The times when Jesus didn't also had purpose.

When God *doesn't*, that *also* has purpose. *And* Jesus came to *show us that.* He sure did. When Jesus didn't rush to the home of His friends Mary and Martha, despite them sending him a personal message to not only do so, but make it right quick, a.k.a., *hurry up.* When Jesus didn't head into town with the guys to grab lunch, and instead had a seat by a well, for He knew that one worn-out-from-her-journey woman would soon be there—about noon.

When Jesus didn't go to the home of a woman who had been bleeding for twelve stinkin' years, or the home of the one who'd been hunched over for nearly eighteen, and instead called them out right in front of their respective crowds. Purpose.

When Jesus didn't keep His disciples on nice steady ground but instead knowingly sent them into what would soon be a storm. When Jesus didn't open His mouth to try to prove who He was, to prove His identity, to prove anything at all—in turn causing Pontius to believe all the more that He was who Pontius now believed that He was. When Jesus didn't let a man named Legion go with Him in His boat, despite Legion's begging and pleading, and instead told him he needed to go back home to the people who had despised him and show them who he now was.

When Jesus didn't call upon God after a long day of healing and casting out demons to DoorDash five thousand ready-made gourmet meals for the hungry among Him, and instead told His disciples—use what ya got. Purpose. When Jesus didn't wash His hands before supper. He knew *that* would get the Pharisees going. He *also* knew it'd be the perfect visual aid to *show them they were missing the point.*

Beloved, I write these words to the one who doesn't understand why God doesn't. Why God doesn't do the thing. Why God isn't doing the thing. Why God isn't doing *something*. God *is*. And it may just be . . . in what God *doesn't*. For even when God *doesn't*, that *too* has *purpose*. Wait in trust. Keep on asking. Don't stop believing. And know that you are held and loved wholly in process.

HOLD FAST TO YOUR CROWN

Hold fast to what you have so that no one may seize your crown.

OhBoomChickaHeckYes. And now I hope *this* may help strengthen your soul enough to actually hold fast to what you've got. Cuz let's be honest, it ain't easy. And after the week/month/year/decade/lifetime you've had, a little strengthening may be needed . . . and welcomed . . . word and amen . . . (and if it's *not* enough, feed and water her more, please.) Yes.

1. No *one* or no *thing* can take your inheritance. Period. God's *will*. Get it? Right.
2. Your *calling* . . . is *irrevocable*. (Note: Sometimes you'll wish it could be. I mean it. Ask Jonah or Job or Joe or Jesus, for that matter, uffda, not to mention a whole slew of others.) I digress.
3. You can *ask God* for what you *need* from God, knowing that God already *knows* what you need, but praying reminds you that you're not alone, and when you remember that you're talking/asking/begging/beseeching the One for Whom nothing is impossible or, for that matter, even too hard, you wouldn't *believe* how quickly Hope comes in clutch. Right? I *love* her.
4. You are royalty. *That's why you have a crown.*
5. God holds your life in the palm of God's hand, which means whatever *you* are holding is *also* in the palm of God's hand. Mmhmm.

And, well, I reckon five is a good place to stop cuz, ya know, five smooth stones and all.

Beloved, hold fast to what you have, so that no one may seize your crown. Read it again, bam and amen. Big love.

{Revelation 3:11}

WHERE YOU ARE

The well. The whale. The wedding that ran out of wine. The fiery furnace. The waterless pit. The tomb that reeked of death. The side of the road, bleeding and hurt. The side of the stream, broken and lost. The side of the sea, starving like thousands of others. Beloved, I don't know where you are, but I assure you, God is there with you.

Amen. And when someone is with you . . . you have someone to talk to . . . even if your tears are doing the talking . . . ask Hagar. Or Hannah. Or a whole host of others, amen. Beloved, I don't know *where* you are, I simply know Who is *with you where you are*. Yes. The God Who throughout Scripture reminds us that no matter where we find ourselves . . . including the depths of our own personal hells . . . we are not alone. That's right. A breath that was given so that our soul never truly forgets—even when our mind can't seem to make sense of it or our heart is nowhere near feelin' it. Yes.

Beloved, where you are has purpose, even if you freakin' hate it. I'm sorry. You know I shoot straight around here. And it's true. So today, wherever it is that you are, I want you to stop, and I want you to breathe. And as you do, I want you to inhale and exhale one name . . . Emmanuel. God *with* us. But please, make it personal or it won't mean a thing. I mean it.

Breathe God is with me. Breathe *God* is with me. Breathe God *is* with me. Breathe God is *with* me. Breathe God is with *me*. Yes. May your breath do the begging on your soul's behalf as you trust the Spirit within you that intercedes for you with sighs too big for words to express and too massive for your mind to fully comprehend, amen.

Beloved, you are seen, you are heard, you are known, you are loved . . . even when it doesn't feel like it, and even in the places you never wanted to be. I promise. Now breathe. *XO.*

YOUR LACK MAY BRING FAVOR

God coulda chose Liz.

I'm gonna say this right off the bat in case we have any dropouts this morning or anyone late to where they need to be—your *lack* may be what brings *favor*. Yup. OK, for those who need to go, have a great day. For the rest of y'all, here we go.

God coulda chose Liz (you may know her as Elizabeth) to carry the Savior of the world. And actually, it would've made a heckuva lot more sense because, quote, "*They* (oh, did I not also mention she was married, and to a priest no less? Pretty holy, eh?) were both righteous before God, walking in all the commandments and ordinances of the Lord blamelessly."

I know, right? Liz *clearly* seems like the obvious choice here. Except, as we know, she wasn't. Could it be that God purposely chose the young and unwed to show us something really big and make a really huge point that being chosen by God to do a holy and mighty thing does not require a list of credentials, amen??? Just sayin'. If God woulda chose Liz for this particular calling, would not the folks at the time—a) have assumed it was her hubby Zach's baby, and b) even if they *did* believe it was Holy-Spirit conceived, believe it was because Liz was so darn perfect in all that she did? I bet they totally would've.

So God chose Mary, and her lack of credentials is the very thing that brought her favor. I know, right? My mouth is open too. Her *lack* was counted as *favor*. Wow. And after I penned all that out in my journal . . . suddenly to what should my wondering eyes but appear . . . but a few women who joined me for coffee . . . and here's who was her: Ruth was here, Esther too, and Sarah chimed in between dozing off, because old people like to nap in their chair. The woman at the well was here, and I was thrilled, cuz you know how much I adore her. The widow with the drop of oil was there too, and let me tell you, she's awesome.

And by now, Beloved, you get my point—don't rule yourself out. Cuz you just never know. God coulda chose Liz. Just sayin.'

{Luke 1}

LOOK AHEAD TO THE NEW

If the right now season is painful and hard, you are free to look ahead to the new.

You sure are. Amen. Not that you need my permission. I mean, who am I? But affirmation is a seriously powerful ditty, amen?

Beloved, do you know how runners get through the races that are gruelingly hard? *They look ahead.* Do you know how women get through the toughest of labors? *They look ahead.* And did you know that in both of these cases, oftentimes what helps them do so is folks on the sidelines/next to the bedside cheering them on with words like . . . "You're almost there! You're so close! You can do this! You're amazing! Keep going! Keep pushing through! You got this!" Right. And to that I say—if it's you, Beloved— Rah to the Rah Rah Rah. I got you.

If the right *now* season is painful and hard, you are free to look ahead to the *new*. Because maybe your right *now* season *is* painful and hard, and here's what I've learned over my years—denying the truth that the *now* is painful and hard doesn't make it *less* painful and hard. It just keeps you captive, held hostage by guilt, and since both of those things royally suck—let's not, OK? Cuz here's the thing about seasons, Beloved—there's always a new one coming. And as long as the Heavens and Earth remain, there will always be seasons. So if the right *now* season is painful and hard, you are free to look ahead to the *new*, as long as you promise me *this*, OK? That you trust and believe that you are held and covered and drenched in mercy-love-grace in the *now*.

And *lest you forget*, I've still got my pom-poms in hand, and I'm not afraid to use 'em, just sayin'. And *if*, Beloved, these simple words of mine today brought even a *glimpse* of a crack of a grin or a smile in the midst of your painful and hard . . . I'm so glad, because a cheerful heart is dang good medicine. Beloved, you are seen-heard-fully-known-fully-loved in every single season that comes. You sure are. And if the *now* is painful and hard, you are free to look ahead, from right where you are, to the *new*. You sure are. Amen.

HOLD AND BE HELD

Rock the baby. Calm the boat.

The boat you are in that won't stop rockin' and rollin', but not in the good '80s-music kinda way . . . more like the I-think-I'm-gonna-throw-up kinda way. Right. The boat you are in that feels like it's never gonna reach the shore . . . never gonna find calm waters . . . never gonna get out of the storm that it's in.

Beloved, if that's where you're at, I urge you . . . Rock the Baby. The *Baby* Jesus. Yes. Hang out with Baby Jesus. Sleeping Baby Jesus. Peaceful . . . Sleeping . . . Baby . . . Jesus. Rock the Baby. Calm the Boat. Cuz see, rocking that sleeping Baby allows your heart-mind-and-soul to relish all that is right and good in the world. It allows you time to sing and coo and imagine all of the possibilities, all of the new, all of the wonder of what might just be. Hold that wrapped-in-swaddling-clothes Baby in your arms and remind yourself that you too are covered and wrapped with the love from which you were sent. *Yes. Hold* the Baby . . . and *be held* in return.

Beloved, *you are held*. So rock the Baby. Calm the Boat. For as you do, you will realize that although you are moving, you are not actually going anywhere . . . which is fine by you, because the constant running is wearing you out. So today . . . stop for a minute . . . or two . . . or ten . . . and rock the Baby. Listen to the hush of the beautiful sighs that inhale and exhale and remind you . . . God . . . is right here . . . *with* you . . . Emmanuel . . . Indeed. Rock the Baby. Calm the Boat. Jesus sleeps. In the manger and in that boat, no matter how bad the storm gets. To remind you . . . you are never alone. And we're gonna get through this thing called life-on-Earth together, you and I . . . we sure are.

Beloved, if you're crying right now, I pray it's because you're letting go of what is too heavy for you to continue to carry. Rock the Baby. Calm the Boat.

REJECTION HAPPENS

The rejection of man cannot stop God's plan for you and what you've been sent here to do.

Rejection is part of the whole hard-holy package on Earth. Jesus not only told us it would be, but actually showed us before His first cry was even heard by His mama and all of those sheep. Yep. Luke 2:7. "And she brought forth her firstborn son, and wrapped him in swaddling clothes, and laid him in a manger; because there was no room for them in the inn."

Now read it *this* way—"And she brought forth her firstborn son, and wrapped him in swaddling clothes, and laid him in a manger; because there was no room for *them* in the inn."

Here's the thing, Peeps—the rejection of *man* could not stop God's *plan* to deliver God's son *into* this world *for* this world *by* this young couple—yes and amen. Jesus Himself. Rejected at the beginning and rejected at the end, and perhaps part of the reason was to show us . . . *rejection happens*. Is it hard? Yes. Does it suck? Also yes. Does God know that it's hard, and it sucks, and therefore continually reminds us . . . "I Am with you wherever you go . . . Don't be afraid . . . In this world there will be troubles and trials, but take heart . . . I will never leave you or forsake you, and nothing is too hard for Me, and I know you don't understand what I Am doing right now, but . . ." Right.

Beloved, the rejection of *man* cannot stop God's *plan* for *you* and what you've been sent here to *do*. A story being lived out in person, a story packed with power and purpose, and sometimes power and purpose are accompanied by pain and rejection. True that. And *when* that is the case, this I implore you—return to Who you know God to be. Return to this story. Remind yourself that the God Who is *in* you, is *there* for you, when rejection rears its ugly head against you. Remind yourself that you are seen-heard-and-known right down to every last hair on your head, even the stubborn gray ones. Because truly I tell you, Beloved, *nothing* can stop God or God's purpose for you here on this Earth. Amen.

Day 197

DIG DEEP FOR HER

Dig deep, Beloved. She's in there.

The soul that's been tattered and torn by the storm—the one that's buried under all of that rubble as a result of the battle, the war. The soul that can still taste the dirt after being thrown to the ground and pummeled with stones that were picked back up after Jesus had left the room. The soul that's been taking her marching orders from fear, and therefore hasn't marched at all, which has her questioning if it's even possible anymore. The soul that is starting to lose her grip in more ways than one, and is ready, beyond ready, to witness some (please, Lord) redemption.

Yes. Dig deep, Beloved. She's in there. And you *knowing* she's in there is what's going to give you the strength to *keep digging*, because let me put it this way—if your son or daughter or, heck, even a perfect stranger were buried but alive under mounds and mounds and *mounds* of dirt . . . you'd keep digging until you rescued the one who was buried and yet still alive. You sure would. And maybe, Beloved, the one who is buried alive, is *you*. So *dig*. Dig *deep*. And don't you stop digging until you find her, for the soul is imperishable, and therefore never dies, so she's in there, I promise.

She may be dehydrated. She may need a drink. She may be starving. She may need a bite. But she's *alive. Yes.* Because she'll *never die.* She's unshakable, despite everything that shakes and quakes around her; she's held, securely, eternally, in the palm of the God Who created her. She may have been buried for a really long time now, but so was Lazarus, so *don't forget that please.* Dig for her, Beloved. Fight for her. Rescue her by the hand of truth, the truth of Who God *is.* Yes. Dig deep. She's in there. Her voice may be small and still. It may be so faint that it's hard to hear without quieting the noise, but she's in there. Yes. Dig deep. Lift her out of the grave, out of the dirt, out of the mud and the yuck. Revive her. Take a deep breath and remind her that *God's* very own breath—that should help. Dig deep, Beloved. She's in there. *XO.*

WHEN IT SUCKS TO BE YOU

Chosen. Destined. Sanctified. That's you. And sometimes . . . it sucks to be you, amen?

There are mornings when I can already hear the backlash because of my word choices. But listen, folks, in the words of P. Pilate—I wrote what I wrote. Amen. As I've said before, I believe there is tremendous value in stating the obvious and not glossing over it, because frankly, that filter is overrated, and it's the raw and real that truly connects us. For example, Chosen and Destined and Sanctified are awesome, and they all describe *who you are . . . and . . .* sometimes Chosen looks like being an unwed teenager nine months pregnant on a donkey, and sometimes Destined looks like Esther deciding if she wants to risk her head for the sake of her people, and sometimes Sanctified looks like . . . well . . . every single one of the folks that make up that cloud of witnesses over us.

Beloved, you are chosen. And sometimes chosen is hard because rejection often accompanies it. You are destined. And sometimes destined is hard because you wish your story looked like somebody else's. You are sanctified. And sometimes sanctified is hard because, well . . . sanctification ain't for the faint. Just look up at that cloud. Right. Beloved, you *are* chosen and destined and sanctified. You *are* royalty, and you are God's *own*. You *are* seen-heard-and-known, you are covered-and-held. You are never alone, not-even-in-storms, cuz your God resides in them and actually speaks from the eye of them. Just ask Job.

You were made in the image of the one true God, and you are reflecting that image here on this Earth. And sometimes it's hard. And sometimes sucks is a better word. And when it is, when it does, I want you to remember two things, OK? The two things I tell my son every morning when I drop him off at school: Remember who you are. Remember Who your God is. The God Who created you securely holds your imperishable soul and is right now giving you His very own breath so you will never, ever forget . . . you are never alone, and you were built for this life. *XO.*

THE JOURNEY IS HARD

Mary was nine months along when she was hoisted onto a donkey to travel ninety miles to a place where she and Joe wouldn't be welcomed to deliver her first baby, sans drugs, in a barn. Beloved, the journey is hard.

Mary was preggo and dang-near set to deliver (the Son of *God*, by the way), when Joe told her they needed to go, so "hop on this donkey here, Mare, and don't worry, it should only take us dang-near a week to get there." And then they arrived to where they were to be . . . and were rejected at the doors of places to stay, and as much as I hate to say this, Beloved . . . that rejection was also part of the plan. (And we may want to tuck that little truth away so the next time it happens to us, we'll know that it's leading us towards God's holy purpose, *amen.*) So there they were, two kids completely unprepared for what was about to happen next, and a stable with hay for a hospital bed. And alas—no drugs. Not to mention the annoying sound of animals grunting and bleating and God-knows-what-else.

Beloved—the journey is hard. And at times (OK, *lots* o'times) it doesn't make sense to us humans who are living our story out a single word at a time . . . but it is *fully known* by the God Who *wrote every word*, from In the Beginning to final Amen. Joe and Mare needed to get to the City of Bread . . . to deliver the Bread of Life . . . into a *feeding trough* . . . to be given for all . . . to nourish and sustain . . . the Soul.

Beloved—the journey is hard. And although the temptation is to write the word "But" here . . . I won't. Because I don't want a big "But" to push aside the reality of the truth. Instead, I will say *this*—God is never lost. And although at times it feels like you're completely off course, alas—you are not. For although it may not make sense to you, and although "C'mon-God-there-*must*-be-a-shorter-easier-way" . . . the God Who goes before you, follows after you, watches over you, and hems you in on every side . . . is not lost.

SOMETHING YOU'LL NEVER FORGET

Perhaps God brought you to this place you don't want to be to show you something you'll never forget.

Like water gushing forth from a rock. Like daily bread falling from Heaven. Like a giant sea parting right before your eyes as you cross over without a need for galoshes. Right. Like watching the stones meant to stone you fall from the hands ready to throw them. Yes. Like witnessing life walk out of the grave. Like seeing those lions' mouths closed shut despite the fact they were ravenous. Yes. Like encountering God face to face. In that desert. In that wilderness. In that fire. In that storm. Yes. For if we stop and think about it, Beloved, the disciples needed to *be* in that storm if they were to see Jesus calm it. Amen. Mmhmm.

Beloved, perhaps God has brought you to a place you don't want to be to show you something you'll never forget. Something you'll take with you for the rest of your journey that will serve you in ways you can't possibly imagine. Ways that will strengthen you the next time you're weak, nourish you the next time you're hungry, rehydrate you the next time it feels as though the well has run totally dry. Yes. And if nothing else, Beloved, it gives you a new way to look at the place you don't want to be . . . through the lens of who you know God to be.

Yes. Provider. Protector. All-Powerful. Amen. Always. Don't forget. I mean it. Big love.

{Numbers 20:4–8}

HOLY CAN BE HARD

Mary knew. In that moment, she knew. The holy that God had chosen her for would be hard. It oftentimes is.

That moment that clicked in her heart-mind-and-soul like it so oftentimes does when the click cries out . . . "*OMG* . . . this is *real*." And I reckon that moment for Mare *wasn't* when she was originally told about her mission, and it *wasn't* as she watched her belly grow bigger, and it *wasn't* even during the delivery itself. My guess is that it wasn't *any* of those moments that truly confirmed it was real. It was when those shepherds arrived and started making known everything they had been told about Who this baby actually is . . . and amidst all the talking and excitement and praise-God-hallelujahs . . . Mary stopped . . . and thought . . . and pondered . . . and realized . . . *OMG this is real.* And *because* it is, if I thought the journey all the way here on that donkey nine months pregnant was hard . . . it ain't nothin' compared to what lies ahead. Whew. My holy . . . is gonna be hard.

And Beloved, *ours will be too.* Because holy is hard. And acknowledging that doesn't make the holy less holy or *you* less holy for acknowledging that, so there's that. Right. Holy is hard. And yet, we can take our lot, even our "a lot," and name it Holy, thus giving it purpose and value and worth. Yes. Pain then has a purpose, and trials then have value, and what we endure then holds tremendous worth, and then at *least* we know that it's not for naught. Thank God.

Being chosen by God to be *you* isn't easy, Beloved, but it is . . . *holy.* And so like Mary, you're doin' it. Like Job, you're doin' it. Like Moses and Noah and Daniel and David and Ruth and Naomi and Hannah and Hagar and need I go on? No, I don't think so. Their lots were hard. Their "a lots" were hard. They were *also* . . . *holy.* And so are yours. And so are you. And God is with you, seeing you through the purpose for which He sent you while whispering, "I will never leave or forsake you." Don't forget that, Beloved. Don't ever forget.

FOR THE WEARY

For the weary . . .

I see you. I hear you. I am you. Desperately wanting to get it all done, and at this point not even sure what "it" is anymore. Longing to give more and more but trying to balance that with your checkbook. And, alas, one side seriously outweighs the other. You're weary. You're worn. You're scared to go into the deep with yourself because the deep is scary and may even dare ask you . . . Are you doing what you're doing because you feel like you've got something to *prove*? I know. Ouch. I told you it was scary.

Maybe you're grieving or desperately waiting for healing . . . of body . . . a relationship . . . a situation you can't even really describe, so thank God the Spirit intercedes with sighs. Seriously. Yes. The weary. If you are among this group, this I-have-no-doubt massive group huddled by the side of the sea, hungry and exhausted and feeling bad to the bone but not in the good rock star way . . . you are not alone. God is near. I promise. Lean . . . on *seated* . . . Jesus. Yes. Seated Jesus. Seated because the work has been done. Seated to show you He's not in a rush. Seated so that, like John at the table, *you too can sit and lean on.* And maybe He'll even hum, "Lean on Me" as you do, cuz He's really super cool like that.

Lean on seated Jesus. Call Him Emmanuel and then take yourself by the shoulders and firmly remind yourself, "That means God *with* you, young lady!" And yes, you may have to be that forceful with yourself so you actually get it. You sure might. And if right now even that seems too much . . . How about a word? One word to grab hold of and refuse to let go of today. Good news, I've got lots of one words. So take your pick—Hope. Light. Peace. Rest. Strength. Healing. Restoration. Rebuilding. New. Better. More. Grace. Not-too-Late. (Ahem, the hyphens make it one word.) *Loved.* You. *XO.*

FLESH-AND-BLOOD JESUS

In the days of His flesh, Jesus prayed and begged and pleaded with God through crying and tears. And maybe right about now . . . you get that.

What we love so much about flesh-and-blood Jesus is that hello-we-are-flesh-and-blood. Right. And when Scripture depicts this praying and begging and pleading though blood-sweat-and-tears Jesus, as much as it pains us, a part of us is actually (big-time, actually) comforted, because *if Jesus felt that way in His flesh, then maybe I shouldn't be surprised I do too.*

Right. Strength in numbers—yes. Comfort in numbers—also yes. The Jesus Who came to live among us in order to show us that we will endure stuff while we are here and how to survive in the midst of it. Yes. Oh, how we give thanks for praying-begging-pleading flesh-and-blood Jesus. A God Who has gone before us, and therefore knows where the road eventually ends, calmly sits on the side of our bed and weeps alongside us while whispering . . . I know . . . I know . . . I'm right here . . . this is hard . . . everything is gonna be alright . . . I know because I Am already there . . . I wouldn't tell you this if it were not true.

A God Who came to Earth to show us that there would be tears. Tears that serve holy purpose, and therefore require no explanation and certainly no apology, amen. A God Who became flesh-and-blood to show us that sometimes our flesh will be pierced, and pierced flesh often draws blood. A God Who decided . . . How 'bout this—I'll give Myself yet *another* name—Emmanuel—which in case you forgot means God *with* us—yes. So *we* will know . . . that *we* are *never without God, amen.* Yes. Flesh-and-blood Jesus. Praying-and-pleading-and-begging-God-for-there-to-be-another-way-and-yet-knowing-deep-down-that-God's-Will-will-be-done Jesus. We love this Jesus. This Jesus gets us.

So, Beloved, if this is where you currently find yourself, I encourage you to hang out with this Jesus. For this Jesus will remind you . . . as the One Who has gone before you . . . Every little thing's gonna be all right . . .

{Hebrews 5:7}

LOOK AHEAD

Looking ahead is crucial to your well-being. So look ahead. Even if you don't know what you're looking for.

I reckon the reason the book of Philemon is so overlooked and underrated is because it's so stinkin' small, you may just miss it. Now, I'm not gonna get into the whole gist of the book—you can read it yourself in like ten minutes—but I do wanna nab some of Paul's final words to his pal Phil, because they're pretty dang good, if you ask this word girl. Paul writes (in so many words) . . . Oh, one more thing, Phil—prepare a guest room for me, for I am hoping through your prayers to be restored to you.

You guys—*hope prepares the guest room.* It looks past the current empty and sees full. So . . . look *ahead.*

Currently in a pit? See yourself in the palace. In a raging storm? See yourself on dry land sipping on something scrumptious. In the dead of the desert? See yourself at the grandest oasis where the water is flowing and the feast just keeps comin'. Look *ahead.* Beyond where you are if where you are is leaving you feeling like things will never get better . . . you'll always be stuck . . . you'll never move beyond where you are, so you might as well just pitch a tent. *Except* . . . tents are temporary, amen and amen, and don't you forget it. So are storms and stints in pits. So is the dead of dry, because eventually the rain starts to fall.

Look *ahead.* To the places your God has yet to take you. To the things that await you that you can't possibly imagine. To the One Who goes before you, is with you, and will never leave or forsake you. Look *ahead.* See yourself laughing again. Having fun again. Feeling alive again. Friends, Paul didn't know if he'd be back to visit his buddy Phil, but he *believed* he would, and that *believing* fueled the hope within that is constantly looking ahead. And so . . . he told his pal Phil . . . Get the guest room ready, Buddy, I'm comin'. I *love* that.

{Philemon}

A PLACE OF BREAKDOWN

What if God brings us to a place of breakdown so we will finally address what it is that is hurting and harming our heart, mind, and soul?

Beloved, what if? What if God brings us to a place of breakdown not to harm us but instead to help us? Dare I say, even heal us? What if God brings us to a place of breakdown so we will finally address what it is that is hurting and harming our heart, mind, and soul? And what if we recognized it as such, and as we did, our given-to-us holy breath rose up and reminded us . . . God is *close* to the brokenhearted . . . the broken down, if you will . . . Yes.

What if we learned to see . . . through the lens of Who we know God to be? Provider. Protector. All-Powerful. A Parent Who vowed to never leave us, forsake us, abandon us, drop-the-ball when it comes to us, the One Who will never stop loving us no matter what. And what if, *when* we forgot such things, we simply eked out one name with the scrap of energy we have left . . . Emmanuel. God with us. *God* with us. God *with* us. God with *us.* Yes. The works of His hands, the bearers of His light, the temples that house the very breath that He gives us, calling it Holy Spirit. The guarantee. Hallelujah.

What if the breakdown is to cause us to stop and address instead of trying to limp on and simply get by? What if God loves us far too much and wants so much more real life and abundance for us, and *that* is why we're stalled on the side of the road? What if? And listen, I'm not here to say either way, or to claim every breakdown looks or feels the same. What I am here today to do in this space is to ask the question—what if? And maybe, just maybe, someone here in this land is broken down on the side of the road . . . and now has a new possibility to ponder in the wait.

GOD, DO IT AGAIN

God—one thing: Do it again.

Unfiltered and raw, God, cuz here's the deal—I've watched You do it before. I've watched You clog chariot wheels on their way to attack, and I've watched You slam shut mouths of lions. I've watched You cause the sun to stand still, and I've watched You move mighty mountains. I've watched You take the tiniest bit in the desert and transform it into a feast in the wilderness. And although I would've preferred a five-star restaurant, You did indeed feed, and I thank You. I've watched You roll away stones, rebuild, renovate, restore, and even do a new thing right in my midst, even if I had a hard time perceiving it.

I know Your work. I've watched You resurrect that which was dead as You called forth life from the grave. I've watched You free prisoners locked within cells even though You chose an Earthquake to do it. But I gotta tell ya, Lord, it did cause me to stop and realize that sometimes things need to be shaken up something fierce if freedom is gonna be realized. I've watched You part seas, heal the hurting, and stay near at the side of my bed as You whispered, "Everything's gonna be alright."

I've watched You. I've cried with You and laughed with You and pounded my fists on Your chest. I've believed You with all that I've got and at times struggled to believe You at all. I've relied on Your grace and mercy to be bigger than my doubt, and I'll forever be grateful they are. I've wrestled with You like Jacob, ran from You like Jonah, and stood in disbelief like Sarah as I nervously giggled like she did as a way to self-protect. Because getting hopes up is risky. Thanks for reminding me it's worth it. Yes.

I've watched Your faithfulness unfold in times of war and Your glory appear like light at the end of the darkest of tunnels. I've watched You. So I know. That nothing is impossible for You. Nothing is too hard, nothing is too big, and nothing even comes close to Your level of power—not even the devil, despite his trying. So, God, here's the thing—I've watched You. And *because* I have, I've got this one plea, this one prayer, this one supplication thing—do it again. *XO.*

YOU SHALL RISE UP

You shall rise up.

Yes. You shall. You shall rise up. You . . . shall rise up . . . again. Like the woman hunched over at the back of the temple when Jesus Himself called her forward. Like Pete's sick mother-in-law lying in bed, anxious to be well and get up and make those hungry men some food, for goodness's sake. Like Ruth after she spent the night at the feet of Boaz, and like Hagar as she got up from beside that stream . . . knowing she was seen . . . and grabbing her baby boy to move on.

And *you*, Beloved. *You* shall rise up. I shall rise up. We shall rise up—amen. For our God is a resurrecting God, hallelujah . . . and we've seen Him do it before, amen? With Jesus for one. And Lazarus. And the woman at the well. And the guy lying next to the pool. Yes. You shall rise up.

And now my guess is, you know someone who *has*, and perhaps that someone is *you*. Or perhaps you know a him or her who desperately needs to hear these words today—these four simple words, amen. . . . You shall rise up. For held within this promise lies the hope that refuses to quit. The hope that keeps us looking ahead knowing He is Author, Perfecter. Yes.

You shall rise up. And now you listen to me—you believe it, OK? For *this* is most certainly true. Amen. And Amen.

{Joshua 8:7}

FAITH MAKES PLANS

Faith makes plans.

It sure does. It's already thinking about after. After the recovery. After the rest. After the restoration. After the reviving of the soul that feels dang-near dead. After the want is realized. After the wait. After the way is made clear. After the shock wears off. After the trial has ended. After the storm *finally* ceases and the strong gusty winds *finally* calm down to a cool gentle breeze.

Faith makes plans because it believes for what is not yet seen, *which* by the way, is a really cool thing. So thank God for giving each one of us a measure of it. Great design. Just sayin'. Faith makes its bed because it deserves a made-bed to come home to. Faith makes a date and like-totally looks forward to it instead of like-totally dreading it. Faith makes plans to party like it's 1999 while *in* the year 1989 because it is *that* certain it'll still be partying in 1999 . . . wearing a raspberry beret . . . and driving a little red corvette . . . just sayin'. Faith makes plans.

In Psalm 25, I read as Dave reminded himself that his eyes are ever toward God, and that God *will* in fact pluck his feet out of the net in due time. And since I can like-totally relate to Dave, I not only *welcomed* his words, but I was also *grateful* for what I heard my *own* soul rise up and say . . . "Sweet! Where should we go *first* after the pluck?" I know, right? God is so cool. Psst . . . you are too, Dave. Thanks for the words.

Beloved, Faith makes plans. It dreams dreams and counts it all gain. Nothing wasted. Not for naught. That's just not what our God's about. And *even when* Faith walks through the shadow of the valley of death, it whispers to self . . . "It's only a shadow; keep walking." Yes. Faith makes plans. It makes plans because it *believes*. And *that* is why Faith's life song is this . . . "Don't Stop Believin'." Amen. It sure is.

{Psalm 25}

GOD IS FAITHFUL IN THIS LIFE

The One Who chose you for this life and called you to this life is faithful to you in this life.

Pause for you to read this at least five times, because I swear to God it's true, and dang I hope my confidence gives you some strength, amen . . . and I mean that. Grin-for-the-Win.

Beloved, the One Who *chose* you *for* this life, and *called* you *to* this life, is *faithful* to you *in* this life. That's right. So now listen to me, *wherever* you find yourself right now, and I do mean *wherever*, I urge you to repeatedly return in your heart-mind-soul (especially in rough patches of which there are many, amen) to *this* place. *This* shelter. *This* refuge. *This* eye in the midst of the chaotic storm. Yes. For this much we know— Chosen doesn't mean easy. And Called sure as heck doesn't either. Ask the Apostle Paul; he has a few words to say about that. Seriously.

Beloved, God *chose* you for *this* life. And *called* you to *this* life. And the promise God gives you because God *knows* it ain't easy to be chosen and called—is *this*: I will be *faithful* to you *in this life*. Yes. In every facet, every aspect. In that which you understand and in all that you don't, which I know is a lot, My child. That's right. I know. *And.* I Am Faithful. To you. Yes, to *you*. The one I knit together with My very own hands and delivered into this world with power and purpose. Yes. I Am Faithful. Always and Forever. Don't forget.

GOD HAS CHOSEN YOU

God has chosen . . . you.

To be right where you are right at this moment, regardless of where it is that you are. To do the thing that you're currently doing, even if it's not what you want to be doing, because what you may not know is that you will never find yourself anywhere that the Spirit of God is not (Pssst . . . breathe if you forget while reciting Job 33:4.) And wherever it is that you are is most likely not where you will forever stay and instead is preparing you somehow and someway for where it is you'll next go. Whew. And all caps *yes.* God has chosen . . . *you.* Now let's remind each another that this super-cool truth in no way translates easy peasy. Or easy street. Or easy anything for that matter. And I've got a whole buncha folks here in the witness cloud who are itchin' with hands raised to shout out Amen. Yep.

Job was chosen. Go ahead and ask him how his story unfolded. Naomi and Ruth were chosen. Ask them about the journey that got them from where they were to where they landed. Right. And speaking of journeys that royally (pun intended) sucked, ask Joseph about his path to the palace. Yowza. Rough is an understatement. Seriously. And how about Jesus? Exactly. So I ask you, Beloved—were these folks any *less* chosen because their roads included major difficulties and not simply amazing triumphs? I'll go ahead and give ya the answer; it's *no.* Oh, and by the way, I could rattle off another hundred peeps, but I know you've got to get ready. Right.

My point is this—God has *chosen . . . you.* That's right. You are holy—set apart. You are loved—unconditionally and unfailingly. You are known—every hair on your head and every tear that falls, whether it's from sadness or gladness or frustration or fear. Yes. *chosen.* To be where you at this time in your story. The story penned by the Author and Perfecter of your faith, amen. That's right. So, you take those words and you own 'em, you hear me? And you live like they're true, got it? OK then, I reckon you're good to go for today. God has chosen you, Beloved. I mean it. *XO.*

{1Thessalonians 1:4}

WAIT FOR IT

Wait for it.

The "it" that will come in due time, in due season, by the One Who makes all things right. Right. And *hold on to that truth as you wait*. Indeed. Wait for it. The sea to split. The stone to roll. The heavens to break open with a sign so obvious there's no way you could possibly miss it. The resurrection. The revival. The renewal you're so desperately longing for. And don't you lose hope as you do. That's right.

But *should* you start to lose that hope, that hope that is yours and was given to you by the One Who created you, not only as something to cling to in every storm but also the means by which you'll move forward . . . I want to remind you where you can look for it. You'll find the babe wrapped in swaddling clothes and lying in a manger, a trough, an ark. Yes. So lest you feel you can't find this hope, or you fear it's escaping you, perhaps you'd like to be a wise man/woman/child and head to the stable to remember that it lies right in front of you . . . and within you. And did I mention a mere thread of it will do? A drop? A crumb? Simply the hem? Yes. Enough. To drink. To eat. To cling to when you feel like you just can't take one more step.

Friends, I found myself in the book of Habakkuk, and these words that I share with you are words that just wouldn't let go—thank God. "If it seems to tarry, wait for it . . ."

Yes. Wait for it. And *as you wait*, grab hold of the rest, for our God is really good at providing a promise right after some killer advice . . . to actually enable/equip us to take that killer advice and do it. And today's is *this*—it will surely come. Hold on to the "it will" as you wait. For every ounce of the wait . . . is strengthening your faith. Amen and amen. And remember—you are wholly loved in the wait. You are covered/clothed in the wait. You are seen/heard/known in the wait. *This* . . . is most certainly true. *XO.*

{Habakkuk 2:3 and Colossians 3–4}

DON'T MAKE ROOM FOR THE DEVIL

Here's the thing—when you forget Who God is . . . you make room in your mind for the devil to move right on in. Don't make room.

I know, right? Visuals help. It's why Jesus spoke in parables . . . *and all the humans-who-struggle-to-comprehend say amen.* Amen. Beloved, picture your mind as a part of your home. Which it is. Maybe the busiest part. The place where roundtable discussions take place over the breaking of bread, perhaps. It's a big room. So . . . forgetting Who your God is, thus "removing" Who you know God to be from the room . . . *makes room for the devil to move right on in, so let's not,* OK? Great.

Cuz see, Who you know God to be takes up a *lot* of room—hmm, let's see—Provider, Protector, Parent, All-Powerful, Light, Peace, Resurrector, Healer, Chain-Breaker, Stone-Roller, Source of Strength, Source of Comfort, Shepherd, Confidant, Wonderful Counselor, Sovereign Creator, Everlasting King, Lord of Lords, Mighty Defender, Hope-in-the-Manger-We-Love-That, Risen, Earth-Is-His-Footstool, Grace-and-Mercy, Endless Supplier, Love, Love, Love, Love, Love, I mean . . . I could go on, but you get the idea.

The truth of Who your God is takes up a *lot* of room (hallelujah), so when we *forget* Who God is, that all-goes-out-the-window-making-room-for-the-devil-to-move-right-on-so-let's-not-forget-amen-and-amen-and-even-go-as-far-as-to-remind-one-another-when-we-forget-*whew.* Dang, I'm wordy. But I mean it when I say—I hope my wordiness helps you. I sure do. Helps you to see things even a tiny bit clearer; sheds even an *ounce* of fresh light.

So, Beloved . . . let's not forget Who our God is, OK? Let's not make room. Cuz doubt and anger and bitterness and resentment and jealousy and all the other crap that stinks . . . really affects the whole house. *XO.*

{Ephesians 4:27}

HOPE IS THE ROPE

Hope is the rope that will save you.

I gotta tell ya, I was surprised when my pen inked this out. And honestly, the minute I read what I'd written, my first thought wasn't, "Wow, that's deep." My first thought was, "Soap on a Rope." Yup. Now, if you reside in my age span, you know exactly what I'm talking about. And if you don't, you may be thinking, "Huh??"—so here's a brief explanation.

Back in the day, fathers and grandfathers all over the land were gifted Soap on a Rope for Christmas. Seriously. Soap on a Rope was soap that was sculpted into super cool things like golf balls or cars or baseball gloves or fish, all sorts of stuff really. That perfectly sculpted soap then hung from a rope that hung in the shower ready for use. Get it? Soap on a Rope. Right.

So as I was thinking about *hope*, I journaled a few things about hope and then picked up my DRB and read a few things about hope, and before I knew it, I had written these words that I hope (see what I did there?) you can make out, but if not, please let me assist—

Hope . . . is the Rope . . . that will save you.

Yes. Save you from getting stuck in the mindset that things will never get better, you'll never find love, the job will never amount to more, the promotion will never come, you'll forever be in debt, you can't possibly lose the weight now at this age, you're too old or too young to do the thing you most want to do, and even if you don't believe that—you're way too scared to even try for fear of what others will think of you. *Whew.* That's a mouthful.

But see, here's the thing—unlike that soap that would get smaller and smaller each time you used it, hope gets bigger and bigger each time you use it. I know, right? Hope builds on hope. Hope gains momentum. Hope gets bigger as we grab it in the shower each morning, mentally preparing us for a brand-new day. *Yes.* Hope . . . is the *rope* . . . that will save you. From the thoughts that seek to destroy you. Hope. Rope. Yes. Amen.

YOUR GREATEST WEAPON

Beloved, your greatest weapon in the wars that you face is the knowledge of Who your God is.

And lest you forgot in the midst of the rat race, or it somehow got stuck in the cesspool of doubt, or perhaps with all that you've got going on you simply don't remember where it was you last saw it . . . Please let me kindly remind you. Your God is Provider. Your God is Protector. Your God is All-Powerful, All-Loving Parent. Your God is Light and sees all and hears all and knows all, amen. Your God brings beauty from ashes and actually sits with you after the fire, reminding you that all things will once again be made beautiful in due time. Yes.

Your God is as near as your very next breath and as far away as the heavens above, and that actually brings you some peace, because deep down, you want a God Who stays close enough to hold your heartbeat and yet far enough away to see everything that's goin' down and actually do something about it, amen. It's OK to admit that, you know. Your God opens doors and closes doors. Your God makes ways where there currently are no ways. Your God rolls away stones and moves mountains and at times doesn't roll away stones or move mountains, but instead gives you the strength to do the rolling and the moving, amen. Yes. Your God resurrects. Revives what is dead. Rebuilds from the ground up what has been demolished or destroyed and sometimes builds something brand new on a plot of land that has yet to be broken.

Beloved, your greatest weapon in the wars that you face is the knowledge of Who your God is. It really is the joy of your strength. It's meeting doubt at the door of your mind and taking it captive and forcing it to come face-to-face with the knowledge of Who your God is, and I'll tell ya right now Who's gonna win. That's right, cuz did I mention your God is also *big*? Beloved, nothing destroys like doubt, which is why I'm constantly singing "Don't Stop Believin'" off-key in your ears. That's right. Meet doubt at the door. And take it out. With the rest of the trash. Amen.

{2 Corinthians 10:4–5}

ASK GOD TO SPEAK TO YOU

Ask God to speak to you—surprise you—remind you He's near.

I talk to God through my pen in the notebook I've got, and some days I talk a *lot*. OK, most days. It is through these prayers-on-paper, knowing God hears me without uttering a word, that I'm very raw/real about what I feel I most need—OK, honestly—what I most want. There are days I ask God to speak to me directly or surprise me ecstatically or to do whatever to let me know that He's near. And then, I pick up my DRB and head to whatever day is today, for today is enough for any one of us, amen, and it's there that I read these words: I want you to be free from anxieties . . .

And truly I tell you, it was as if God was sitting across from me, and we were both just totally chill and relaxed and sipping on reeeally good coffee as He casually looked up at me after listening to me go on and on because that's what love does—it listens—and then holding His mug in His hands looked directly into my eyes, and with every ounce of peace in the world said . . . "My Daughter, I want you to be free from anxieties." So loving. So caring. So near.

And so after I had my moment, my first thought was this—*this* is why I head here each morning. *This* is why the conversation never gets old. Because I am *continually* changing, and so what I hear from the God Who I've come to love and trust speaks to me *now* right where I'm at . . . so it's obviously a different talk than we had ten years ago. Or even last year, for that matter.

Beloved, I don't know what you're asking God for, but I hope you're asking. For asking keeps us believing. Just ask any kid close to Christmas. Oh, and I hope these words I read, "I want you to be free from anxieties," feel like God handing you your own cup o' joe with tender loving words that feel like a hug that maybe you didn't even realize how badly you needed 'til right this moment.

{1 Corinthians 7:32}

EXHAUSTION IS A VERY REAL THING

I believe exhaustion is a very real thing . . .

. . . and that our bodies and souls give us cues, and sometimes even flat-out hit us over the head with proverbial two-by-fours. Which is ironic, since we also often beg God to "give me a sign and make it reeeally obvious God" . . . and then we're kinda shocked when God does. But what if the signs from above don't always look like rainbows or perfectly hued sunsets or an unexpected check in the mailbox on the day you so desperately needed it? What if there are other signs, given by the God Who loves us, not for our harm but for our good? What if they're God's way of saying slow down, enough is enough, yes there is much to do, but the sum of that much does not lie solely on you?

But see, we have a hard time with those words because somewhere along the way we learned that needing to rest meant we weren't a "big kid," and we wanna be a big kid, darn it! We began to associate weakness with being "less than," and so instead of holding up our weakness as opportunity like the Apostle Paul, we hide it in the garden like Adam. We picked up these notions like poisonous potions, and over time, they've killed a part of us.

But alas, resurrection is real. Amen. And so is a God *Who makes all things new.* And a God Who makes us lie down in green pastures. And we do. Cuz we have to. Because cars stop when they run out of fuel. And it doesn't mean it's time for the car to head to the junkyard; it simply means it's time to stop and refuel, amen. And no one blames the car for needing to do so.

Beloved, maybe you just need a day. Or two. Time to stop and be still and listen to your body-mind-soul, no matter how difficult the conversation to see what it is you most need. I am learning that this is not weakness, my friends, but indeed tremendous strength. Today is a new day. Perhaps you need one more day. And that's OK. It really is. I'll save you a seat at the big kids' table. Promise.

GOD WILL STRENGTHEN YOU TO THE END

God will strengthen you to the end.

And you're gonna hold on to that today, OK, Beloved? You sure are. You're gonna grab hold of that "will" . . . and you're gonna refuse to let go. You're gonna cling to it, grasp it, whatever other verb you wanna insert here, as long as you catch my drift. Amen. God will strengthen you to the end, because *God is faithful and you are worthy of strength.* Oh good, you caught that. Feel free to read it again. You may even wanna write it down. Just sayin'.

Beloved, the beauty of Scripture is that it gives us small everyday words . . . words that we not only understand but can completely take hold of/ingest . . . and use . . . to save us when giving up is an option on the menu before us, and much like the fruit in the garden that day, there are days it sounds pretty darn tasty. *Right.* But not today, Beloved. Nope. Not today. Today you're gonna grab that word "will" and you're gonna eat it 'til you believe it. You sure are. And it's gonna do something in you much like good food does—it's gonna nourish you and strengthen you, and heck, maybe even give your skin a nice rosy glow. That's right.

Beloved, fill your *well* with every *will. Cling* to every *promise* to *climb* out of every *pit. Keep* every *truth* to *overcome* every *trial.* And *remember* every *have* to lead you out of every *hell.* That's right. For lest we forget, a God Who reminds us . . . I *have* worked all things together for good . . . I *have* written your story, your plans, and I *know* them, and I *declare* they are good. Sufficient to meet My purpose. *And* sweet child of Mine, because I know you won't always understand/like them, stay close and listen to My Word as I continually remind you I Am near. *Yes.* Amen. Absolutely. No doubt.

Beloved, God will strengthen you to the end. Because God is faithful, and you are worthy of strength. Don't forget.

{1 Corinthians 1:8–9}

THE REMNANT IS ENOUGH

So too, Beloved, even now, there is a remnant. And it is enough.

Yes. Enough to hold on to, enough to feed, enough to cover yourself and shelter yourself until the storm passes. There is a remnant, Beloved, and *today*, we name that remnant Enough. *Yes.*

A sip of water at the well about noon. One small boy's sack lunch. A wafer of bread sent from Heaven above for us to scoop down and pick up. A handful of flour. A shot glass of oil. The hem of His robe as she made her way through that rude dusty crowd, leaving drops of blood behind her, marking her trail like some sort of walk of shame. The small, still voice that whispered to another, "Keep going, you're almost there," as she made her way to the front of the temple that packed-house Sabbath day, crippled and hunched over as she heard the whispering and snarky remarks from the pews with every slow, painful step that she took.

Yes. But there was a remnant. A remnant that was enough. Enough to keep knocking and asking and seeking. Enough to keep dreaming and hoping and going. Enough to keep believing, and that believing is what saves us, Beloved, from abandoning that remnant, amen. It sure is.

Beloved, I don't know your storm or your season. I don't know your trial or trouble or tribulation. I don't know your struggle, and I would never dare to say that I do. What I *do* know today is this, and so I give it to you. Words I read that lit something within, and I so hope they do the same for you . . . "So too, at the present time, there is a remnant, chosen by grace." Yes. Hold on, Beloved. Grasp with both hands because this hope is *yours*. A sure and steady anchor. That's right. Even now . . . where you are . . . there is a remnant. There sure is.

{Romans 11:5}

WEEPING AND BELIEVING

No one had more faith than Jesus, and yet . . . Jesus still suffered, got upset, and wept. Beloved—you will too. This does not mean that you lack faith.

And I apologize right now for anyone who has ever, *ever* made you feel that it does. Beloved, no one had more faith on Earth than Jesus Himself. *No one.* I think of the time when, right before getting His hands dirty by washing some feet, the story tells us—He knew where He came from, and He knew where He was returning to . . . Dang, that's *power*. Seriously. So, while Jesus was here, Jesus knew Who God was, and Jesus believed God. That's faith. One with God, Jesus knew. Having *always* been with God and *knowing* He would *always* be one with God, Jesus knew. So, therefore, in turn, whatever prepositional phrase you wanna insert here, folks—no one—*no one*—had or has since had—more faith than Jesus on Earth.

And. Yet. Jesus suffered. Jesus got mad. Jesus wept. Yes. Jesus got worn out from His journey, according to John 4, and Beloved, I believe it was to show us that *we . . . will too . . . amen*. We *too* will get worn out from our journey. And we *too* will suffer and struggle at times. And we *too* will get upset. And tired. And bawl our eyes out. Amen. A God Who came down to show us that faith doesn't *cancel* our humanness . . . it *covers* it.

Beloved, your suffering, your struggling, your upsetness and weariness and weepiness, aren't signs of a lack of faith; they are signs of your humanness. And your *faith*, despite size or strength, is seeing you through . . . cuz word on the street is that a mustard-seed size will do. Indeed. Ya know, Beloved, I've been thinking a lot about this lately, and I'm beginning to believe that what it means to be free . . . is to no longer hide who you are. Fully human. God within. Holy Breath as guarantee, lest you forget. Amen. I love you, and you are loved.

GOD, GIVE ME YOU

God, give me . . .

Yes, God. Give me. Give me strength for the journey, peace for the moment, joy in the morning, and beauty from all of these ashes. Give me refuge and be my fortress and build up my faith. But please, Lord, please don't let it come via wait-training, because I know You really like that way, but I gotta tell Ya, I'm not a big fan. Just sayin'. Right.

God, give me. Give me wisdom and guidance, give me boldness and power, give me fearlessness and fortitude to do all the things. And while You're at it, Holy One, give me a thousand new reasons to get up and sing. Yes, please. God, give me. Give me patience and perseverance, a drive like no other, give me contentment, but I beg of You, please don't let it turn into complacency, cuz I seriously don't think I could take it. Right. Give me laughter to lighten the load I am carrying, give me springs in the land where You take me. Give me tears to cleanse my overwhelmed soul when the burden is too much to bear. Yes. God, give me. Give me daily bread and living water, replenish me so fully that my dry and weary bones can't help but get up and dance. And then, Lord, play an '80s tune, will You? Awesome. You're the best. Thanks.

God, give me. Give me shelter from the storm, a light at the end of this really dark tunnel, the courage to believe again, hope again, trust again, and love again and again. Oh, and Lord, remind me to extend that love to myself, cuz You know me, and I often forget. Yes, God, give me. A sign, a wink, a nod from Heaven. Give me, and I'm gonna be honest here, Lord, a break. Yes. God, give me a break. A break in the clouds, a tearing open of heaven, a few minutes to meet You for lunch at the well would really, really be swell. Yes. And amen. Just sayin'.

God, give me *You.*

WHAT GOD HAS ORDAINED FOR YOU

No one can take from you what God has ordained for you.

And not only is this unarguably-one-hundred-percent-I-am-so-not-kidding true . . . *today*, Beloved, you're gonna believe it. You sure are. You're gonna one-hundred-percent unarguably believe that what God has ordained for you cannot be taken from you. Cuz it's the truth. And you're gonna draw up from that well deep within you the living water sip of truth that reminds you . . . the Lord will perfect all which concerneth me. And yes, you're actually gonna hear "concerneth" because it just makes it seemeth more legit. (I'm grinning and I hope you are too.)

Beloved, no one can take from you what God has ordained for you. And that's a fact, Jack. And see, *believing that* is what's gonna give you strength and reignite hope and stir up passion and keep jealousy at bay, because you realize if it's true for you, it's also true for every other person on Earth, amen. It's what's gonna keep your eyes looking ahead and keep your feet marching forward while issuing your soul strict instructions. . . . March on . . . my soul . . . in strength. Right. Thanks, Deb. It's what's gonna allow you to actually lie down in green pastures instead of being made to lie down in them, because you finally understand that if it's ordained for you, then it will be yours. Yes. It's what's gonna keep you trusting and keep you dreaming and keep you wondering, pondering, and asking . . . a whole bunch of my most favorite things. They sure are.

Beloved, no one can take from you what God has ordained for you. *This* is most certainly true. Big love. And rock on.

CHANGING COURSE

You may just need to change course.

Picture it. You're on a killer road trip with your besties. It is the *best* stinkin' road trip *ever*, and you've got all the gas and all the tunes and all the snacks. I know, right? Let's go! You're cruising along and feeling the wind through your fabulous locks and laughing and making all of your plans for when you arrive at your rock-star destination, when suddenly, you find yourselves at a dead end. OK, well, everybody grab your stuff and go home, I guess. Except—*Heck no. Of course* you don't end the whole trip just because of a dead-end sign . . . *Instead you find a new road to take. Hello, yes and amen.*

You find a new road. You change course. But you keep going because, *hello* . . . you're not willing to ditch your destination over one stupid dead-end sign. *Right. And* you've come to know God enough to know that *since* you came across said sign, there's a *reason* for said sign, and so you *trust* that sign and you *turn and take a new road*, but you *sure* as heck don't quit cruisin'. *Amen.* After all, "Don't Stop Believin'" is blaring through the speakers of your crappy car stereo. *Right.* So sure, you'll stop and take note of the sign, and sure you'll reassess and consult Siri (Hello . . . God people), and *then* . . . you'll keep on your Journey (get it?), and you'll keep on believing, because that's what your mouth's belting out until your heart finally catches up and believes it. Yes.

Friends, Paul changed course. Joseph changed course. Heck, even the Wise Men changed course after visiting that cute little Savior baby, and those guys were wise. *Right.* But none of them, *not one*, quit going. And neither will you. Got it? Good. *XO.*

FASTEN YOUR SEAT BELT

Fasten your seat belt and put on your sandals, because, Baby, I'm takin' you places.

If this doesn't sum up my relationship with God Almighty at this point in my life, then I don't know what the heck does. Seriously. The angel said to him, "Fasten your belt and put on your sandals." He did so. Then he said to him, "Wrap your cloak around you and follow me."

Beloved, when I read these words today, I'm not kidding when I say I felt every single ounce of power that came with them. Seriously. Like God sitting next to me on the couch, and we're just hanging out and watching a really great show that we both totally love, when suddenly, all cool-casual like, God says to me almost nonchalantly, while not even breaking gaze with the show . . . "Fasten your belt and put on your sandals, because, Baby, I'm taking you places."

Gahhhh. I know, right? I'm taking you places. I'm bustin' you out. I'm opening doors. I'm parting that sea for you, Darlin'. *Yup.* See that big, gigantic stone? Of course you don't, because I've already rolled it out of the way for you. Read that again. I Am taking you places. I led you into this wilderness, and now I'm leading you out. Psst . . . insert the word desert or storm or flood or drought or famine in place of wilderness, and you get My drift, right, Daughter? Yup. Got it. Thanks, God.

Friends, a God Who shows up in the earliest and darkest of morns to speak one-to-one with His girl is my kinda God. Big time. Fasten your belt and put on your sandals, because, Baby, I'm taking you places. And to *that* she has but a short, two-word reply . . . Let's gooooooo. Amen. Rock on and heck yes. Believe it for you, Beloved. Believe it for *you.*

{Acts 12:8 NRSV}

THE STRENGTH TO GET UP

It's OK to pray for the strength to get up.

God will stop you in order to show you that sometimes, you need to stop. God will slow you down in order to show you that sometimes, you need to slow down. God will level you flat on your back or knock you down right on your can in order to show you that there are times—lots of them, actually—when you will *need help and that's OK, amen.* We all do. Every single one of us.

God will position people to be at the right place at the right time in order to help your eyes see. And God will position you to do the same for others. God will literally blind you by the light (song break—go ahead) in order to—hello—allow you to see clearly by that very same light. God will take you, and God will make you because God is God, and God is Parent, and God knows the plans God has for you, and you don't, and therefore not everything is going to make sense to you on every single page of your story. *Whew and Amen.*

There will be times . . . when after what you've just been through . . . the battle, the war, the race, the destruction, the devastation, the storm, the loss . . . times when you will be lying in bed . . . and what you most desperately need after the rest you are due and so worthy of . . . is the strength to get back up. And it is OK, more than OK, so far beyond more than OK that I can't even adequately describe it to you, but dangit, I'm tryin . . . to ask God *for* it. Yes. For the strength you need to get up. To rise again. And live again. And to believe once again—based on Who your God *is*—Provider, Protector, All-Powerful—that someway, somehow, by positioning someone beside you or by stirring up something inside you or both, God will. Give you the strength. To get back up. Again.

GET YOURSELF A NEW VIEW

You may need to go to the other side of the boat. Things will look different, and perspective is powerful.

There was nothing wrong with the boat they were in on that ordinary-but-not-for-long night. There was nothing wrong with the nets they were using to nab the big catch and nothing wrong with the waters they found themselves casting in. Nope. What the guys needed that night as they fished in that sea wasn't new high-tech equipment or a new location to drop their net. What they *needed* was to go to the other side of the boat . . . so they could get a new view. *Yes.* For the view would be different from this vantage point, and the perspective would completely change, and *that* is what those guys needed that night. And Beloved, truly I tell you, oftentimes we do too. Whew. And *amen.*

Cuz see, although the song encourages us not to rock the boat, sometimes that's *exactly* what we need to do if we're gonna see things anew. Mmhmm. *Yes again.* We sure do. Cuz see, the water may be just fine for fishing, and the boat we are in is actually designed and built for fishing, and the nets we have with us are strong and sturdy and ready for the haul, and so what we *may* need to do . . . is simply-not-so-simply head to the other side of the boat. Where the view has changed and things look a bit different. Where impossible suddenly looks less impossible. Where the sun that was beating on our back that felt like pressure to hurry up suddenly feels like warmth on our face that whispers, "I will provide for you no matter how long it takes." *Yes.*

My husband and I recently changed our bedroom around. We didn't buy anything new; we simply moved around what we had. When we went to bed that night, I said to him, "I can't believe how different this room looks from my side of the bed now." Here ends the sermon, my Friends. *XO.*

{John 21:1–8}

GOD LEADS IN AND GOD LEADS OUT

God led you in, and God will lead you out.

And we have to believe there is purpose and value and worth in both. That just as the Spirit led Jesus into the wilderness, we too will be led to places we don't want to go in order that we may see more clearly or more fully or in a new and expanded way . . . a way we haven't seen God before. Yes. A God Who leads *in* . . . and *out*.

A God Who awakens in us what's dead when we find ourselves in the tomb that tells us, "It's too late, you're all done, you had your chance, Darlin'." But then we remember Sarah. And a host of others who thought the same until they found themselves nursing a babe while on Medicare. Right. A God Who leads us into dry and dusty deserts so we will realize just how thirsty we are. Like our friend at the well. That day about noon. A God Who gives us time to think in bellies of whales and within prison walls and in times of silence that are often the times that are hardest of all. For Be Still and Know is awesome if what you know is the magnitude of Who God is, but news flash—worry and doubt and fear are super loud and sometimes win the fight in those quiet still moments when left alone with simply yourself. They sure do.

As I said to my women's Bible study group one day, it's amazing how you can go from peace and calm and beautiful, sweet slumber to fear and panic and who died and every single worst possibility in the whole entire universe . . . when your phone rings in the middle of the night.

Beloved, let's hold on to this truth on the page here together, OK? Let's do the whole Where Two Or More Are Gathered thing because there really *is* great strength found in numbers, and believing together stirs up within us a passion to *re*-believe what we may have forgotten. Beloved, God led you *in*, and God will lead you *out*. For the God Who wrote your journey in full is also the One Who created the map. With purpose and value and worth in every *in* . . . and every *out*. And every step along the way. *Amen.*

RESTORE, RESURRECT, OR COMPLETELY REBUILD

She trusted that He would restore, resurrect, or completely rebuild.

And truly I tell you, she didn't much trouble herself anymore with which one it would be or how. Instead, she would trust and believe that God *would.* Whether it would come by restoring, resurrecting, or completely rebuilding . . . redemption would, in fact, be hers. She could hear His voice echo through the prophet Isaiah . . . "Fear not for I have redeemed you . . ." *Past tense.* Redemption would be part of her story, and the way in which that redemption would arrive didn't matter nearly as much as the fact that redemption would indeed be a part of her story.

Perhaps it would come through restoring something within her that had been taken or spent. Perhaps new life would be brought out of that grave. Perhaps the destruction wasn't simply a figment of her imagination but was, in fact, real and necessary, because what would serve her best is a complete rebuild. And maybe, just maybe, her life, her journey on Earth, would along the way include all three. In any case, she would trust . . . that God would. She'd hold on to that promise day in and day out like the anchor that it was to keep her soul grounded while the boat swayed in all sorts of directions. And that trust would also strengthen her to look ahead and dream big dreams and keep her feet moving, marching ahead one step at a time, knowing, believing that what was promised to her would one day come. Someway. Somehow. Amen. Oh, yes.

She knew that restoration may come through stretching herself like it did for that guy with the jacked-up hand. She knew that in order for new life to arise, first something must die. Laz taught her that. Thanks, Laz. She knew that the very best way to a complete rebuild was to start by completely tearing down the old. Jesus taught her all about that with His very own life here.

Beloved, I don't know how it will look for you, this redemption that is in fact yours . . . but I want you to believe today that it will, in fact, come. Perhaps through restoration, perhaps resurrection, perhaps via a complete rebuild. But it will. Believe that. And don't stop believing. *XO.*

DON'T FORGET WHO YOU ARE

Jesus to the woman—"Don't you forget who you are."

The woman who, more often than not, is referred to as the "one who got caught." Right. The one dragged out of bed by the guys who sought to condemn her while simultaneously hoping to catch Jesus tripping up, therefore killing two birds with one stone. Except. That stone didn't kill either one of them. Mmhmm. And as I read this story for the umpteenth time, I heard Jesus say as He sent this woman that day on her way . . . Don't you forget who you are.

And perhaps today, Beloved, He is saying it to *you*—too. Don't you forget you are worthy of true love, worthy of respect, worthy of honor and joy. Yes, you are worthy. Don't you forget you are seen and heard and known and loved, and though there will be times in your life when all of that doesn't seem like it's true, I want you to remember it is. Don't forget that you are a child of God, don't forget you are fearfully, wonderfully made, don't you forget that the One Who sent you did so with purpose, and although that purpose won't always make sense to you and you won't always like it, don't you forget that it's powerful.

Don't you forget who you are. A woman kept. *In God's care.* In God's arms, in God's palm of hand, and no one and no thing can pluck you from there. Don't you forget that the number of hairs on your head and everywhere else, by the way, are counted, and don't you forget that nothing—not one thing—will somehow slip outside of God's holy sovereignty. That's right. Don't you forget who you are. Made in the image of the triune God Who knit you together, wrote your story in full, declared it was good, and then breathed God's own Spirit, God's *breath—into you*—and then sent you to this Earth to *live it.*

Beloved, I'm gonna wrap this thing up by saying to you the same thing I say to my son every morning when I drop him off at school . . . Don't you forget who you are. *XO.*

{John 8:1–11}

GATHER UP THE FRAGMENTS

Beloved, this: "Gather up the fragments left over, so that nothing may be lost."

Yes, Beloved. Yes. Gather up the fragments left over from the breaking. You know the one. Or ones. The breaking(s) that broke you, and yet here you are . . . desperately wondering if where you are is a permanent state of empty.

Beloved, gather up the fragments left over. Gather up that which *does* remain and use them to fill your baskets. And yes, I said baskets—*plural*. Gather up the fragments so that nothing is lost . . . so that not one speck of what is left over . . . will go . . . to waste. For that which is left over, that which remains, is going to feed you in the coming days. It sure is. Believe today that those fragments left over are going to be multiplied within you, because you remember a story long, long ago when God took what looked like so little and yet . . . was way, way more than enough. *Yes.*

Beloved, gather up the fragments left. Gather them up, believing that every crumb of crust and butt of bread you pick up and gather is meant just for you, and so you're sure as heck not gonna waste 'em. Whew. And also—*heck* yes. Gather up the fragments. Use them to fill your basket. For every fragment counts, you know. Every fragment worthy of being picked up. Every fragment left over . . . is yours. *Yes.* Every ounce of booty left over after the war . . . is yours. Every pebble left over after the tearing down . . . the destruction . . . is yours. And if you remember correctly, a young guy named Dave, who faced a big giant, taught us that one pebble was all that was needed. *Amen.*

Gather up the fragments left over, Beloved. I love you, and you are loved.

{John 6:12}

HE HAD HER AT LIVING

He had her at living.

A woman, worn out from her journey, heads to the well. A woman, drained by her day-to-day, makes her way to the source of a drink. A woman, alone, I imagine feeling dead inside as she makes the trip to that place she knows she must go, pondering her life thus far and wondering if this is all there is, because it feels more like death than life. . . . Until. There He was. A guy, unlike the other guys who hung out at that place, spoke to her.

I can picture these two, both worn out from their journeys, sitting next to each other at a well they both ended up at, at exactly the same precise time. About noon. Hot, hangry, and simply put—over it. You've been there, Beloved. You may in fact be there right now. And this not-by-chance conversation that includes one word that this woman I'm convinced was dying to hear . . . *living*. Yes. *He had her at Living.* And He told her how to get it. Sip by sip. Day by day. And these sips, these drops in the bucket, so to speak, would continue to fill the well within her and would gush up as needed to rehydrate her and replenish her the next time she was worn out from her journey. A water that was *living*, which meant it had power—the power within her to bring her . . . back . . . to life. Resurrection power. *Yes.*

When her journey was wearing on her, when the walk to where she was going seemed endless, when she began to wonder if this was all that there was for her . . . *that* is when that living water, that water that had been taken in drink by drink, day by day, would rise up within her . . . and remind her that *she was alive*. It would rehydrate the dead within her and allow her to dance. It would replenish within her what had been drained from the day, the week, the month, or years that she'd had. Yes. *He had her at Living.*

And so for the woman today who feels much like this woman, I hope He had you there too. I hope He had you at Living. *XO.*

{John 4:1–42}

LIFE AND LIGHT

In Him was life, and that life was the light she so desperately needed to make her way through the dark.

Life. Light. Yes. Two words we love, two words we crave, two words we desperately want to be true because dead and dark suck, *amen.*

In Him was life. I read these four words and immediately found myself vigorously nodding my head in agreement while simultaneously saying the words, "Ain't it the truth." In the knowledge of Who God is, in the knowledge of Who Jesus is . . . is *life* . . . that serves as *light.* Yes. Protector. Provider. Wine-from-Water Maker. Love. Hope. Grace. Peace. Mercy. Strength. The One Who makes all things right. Bread and Water. Shelter and Refuge. The One for Whom all things are possible, and nothing—not one thing—is too hard. Gatekeeper. Flock-feeder. Mud-using, spit-slapping Healer. Sea-parter. Stone-mover. Miracle-worker. *yes.*

In that place, secure within the inner sanctuary of my soul, behind the veil where nothing is hidden, and I am free to bare it all to the One Who is with me and for me . . . I find life. The life that resurrects that which has died. The life that stands up and shouts, "I'm not dead, I'm alive!" The life that is the light that leads me out of dark moments and truly is . . . a lamp unto my feet. Yes. A lamp to provide enough light to take the next step and not one more, because just like Abraham, I'm gonna journey this life in stages. I sure am. And I'm gonna be fed every day that I'm here, and I'm gonna be cared for every day that I'm here, and I'm gonna return to that truth over and over and over again, for it is life . . . that is light . . . and I'm gonna need that . . . amen.

Beloved, I don't know that I've *ever* felt this much passion and fervor after reading these few words from John. They hit something fierce, words that will return us . . . to who we are . . . God's *own.* Yes. Always and no matter what, and don't let *anyone* in this world convince you otherwise. For you *are.* And God *is* Life and Light. *XO.*

{John 1:1–5}

SHE WHO ENDURES, OBTAINS

And so, after she had patiently endured, she obtained.

Let me ask you something, Beloved—what do you suppose would happen if you decided right now to believe this? I mean it. Would it strengthen you to endure? Or probably, more accurately put, to *keep* enduring? Would it?

If you were in my living room with me right now, I would go to the kitchen to fetch you a hot cup of coffee, and upon my return I would lean down to hand you Heaven's nectar and say to you, "Girl, after you *endure* this (and you'd know your 'this'), you're gonna *obtain* the promise." Would it help you at *all* if I said this? Because truly I tell you, aside from the unserved cup o' joe, that's *exactly* what I'm saying to you. And it's because I *believe it* for you, *deep* in my marrow. And so I hope that if *nothing* else, *my* confidence gives *you* some strength.

Ya know, I purposely posed this pic because I wanted you to see an example of how cool God is and how God speaks and cements and reminds to the point that you find yourself giving a nod to Heaven along with a wink that says, "Oh, You are *so* good." Cuz see, as I hung out in Hebrews, I read. . . . After he had patiently endured . . . he obtained . . . and dang-it-all if that wasn't enough to kickstart the heart, and then paired with the caffeine? Please. Let's just say Girl on Fire.

Right. But then after a stint there, I did what I do, which is head into my beloved DRB . . . which is where a bright pink post-it greeted me with a great big bold, "Well *howdy good mornin' darlin!*" (I love it when she does that.)

And so thus here we are, two chicks sippin' on Heaven's nectar and hangin' out with a couple handfuls of words that paired with our theme song, the one for our *journey*, the one that sings *don't stop believing* . . . who are now ready to run the race that lies before us today, cuz we know (and we've got each other to remind each other along the way, thank God), that after we patiently *endure* . . . baby, we're gonna *obtain*.

{Hebrews 6:15 KJV; Luke 21:19 NRSV}

LET YOUR MIND GO THERE

Are you scared to let your mind go there?

There to that place you don't dare go for fear of being disappointed for like the bazillionth time. To that place where Maybe-Just-Maybe and All-Things-Are-Possible thrive and live their best lives. That place you're certain is reserved for those with a much higher calling, a more glamorous following, or who have selfies that would put the very best photographers to shame. Yes. That place where you receive a compliment or a promise or even the slightest of signs in your favor, but there's no *way* that any of those could *possibly* be for you, so you laugh it off like Sarah did—not because it's funny, but in an effort to self-protect, because disappointment is a devastating blow. Mmhmm.

Beloved, the trials and tribulations of this life do a really good job of dressing up and masquerading as the enemy, despite the fact that Jesus told us, in fact, that they'd be coming. Yes. They stop us in our tracks and lure us off the path to a place called Disbelief. They shake us to the point where we can't think straight or think clearly, and in our shaken and unclear state, we begin to ask ourselves . . . "Ya know, maybe God really *doesn't* care about me at all?"

Right. It's funny, isn't it? How our minds can so easily side with doubt? Don't believe me? Here's an example for ya: Your favorite football team is playing their biggest rival. It's 56–0 at halftime, and your team is sitting with the zero. As you head down to get your popcorn, do you think to yourself, "Dang, I can't believe we're gonna lose to these pigeons." . . . *or* . . . "Well, if those pigeons can score 56 points in a half, why the heck can't *we*?" Right? Seriously.

Beloved, let your mind go there. To the city of Possible. To the village of Maybe. To the smallest of towns we'll call Mustard Seed. That place where you can Ask again and Hope again and Believe again. For truly I tell you and have told you . . . your strength comes from believing. Which is also why I continually remind you, "*don't stop believing.*" . . . Right.

Let your mind go there, Beloved. It's a pretty cool place to abide. Big love.

IT MAY BE IN THE GOING

It may be in the going that you are made well.

The Lord said to them *go* . . . and *as they went* . . . they were made clean. As they went. In their *going*, they were made well.

Beloved, it may be in the *going* that you are made *well*. Amen-yes-and-indeed. Cuz see, the group you'd like to be a part of is great, but you gotta go. The gym or the walk around your neighborhood is great too, but you gotta go. The new land set before you, despite how scary it is leaving the land where you are, despite how desperate you are for the new . . . may be exactly where you will find what you're looking for . . . but you gotta go. For it may be in the *going* that you are made *well*. Yes.

And sometimes going looks like leaving. Leaving a life that is doing you harm, or at the very least not serving you well. Leaving a relationship that is beating the crap out of you in ways that are obvious or in ways that the naked eye can't see at all. Leaving a job that is wearing you so thin you barely recognize yourself anymore, and as a result, you allow others to tell you who you are, and FYI—they're not always right. Right. And sometimes, going doesn't involve leaving at all, but instead means moving forward *from* where you are. It involves not leaving your land, but instead expanding your tent, thus enlarging your territory, amen.

Beloved, whatever the case, truly I tell you, it *may* be in the *going* that you are made *well*. P.S.: *And this must be said*—you may be *scared* to go, and doubt and fear may do their best to *stop* you from going. So *when* they do, here's what I want you to do . . . I want you to picture your God grabbing your shoulders and looking you right in the eyes while saying *these* words to *you* . . . "You listen to Me, young lady, be strong and courageous, for I Am *with* you, *wherever* you go."

{Luke 17:11–19; Joshua 1:9}

HIDDEN BUT NOT UNSEEN

Beloved, don't confuse hidden with unseen. You are seen. If you are hidden, it is only until it is time for you to rise.

Jesus still multiplies bread. Amen. OMG, and Seriously-I'm-Not-Kidding. Here's how I know—I've read these two (yes, *two*) verses at *least* a couple of dozen times before, and yet, today, they became a *feast* at the breakfast table. Mmmhmm and amen. And Beloved, *here* are those two verses: "And again he said, 'To what should I compare the kingdom of God? It is like yeast that a woman took and hid in three measures of flour until all of it was leavened.'"

That's it. Two verses. And yet. *And. Yet.* My eyes opened wide. My heart skipped a beat. My jaw hit the floor, so it's a good thing she's used to taking a beating. Talking nonstop will do that. Because what my eye saw, what the lamp of my very being saw *this* day, in those few written words upon the page, was this—*hid . . . until . . . . it was leavened.* In other words, in my words, in the words that arose from the well deep within me . . . were these . . . Hidden . . . until . . . it (she) is ready . . . to *rise. Yes.* Which then immediately sent my mind into a tailspin as my spirit regurgitated the testimonies of all who would testify to it . . .

Moses in a basket. Until. Esther in a harem. Until. Joseph in a well. Until. Noah in the ark. Until. Ruth in the field. Until. David in the sheep pen. Until. Jonah in the fish. Until. Nehemiah in the palace. Until. Paul in the cell. Until. A woman who had been bleeding for twelve long years, and therefore was tucked away so as to not make everyone around her unclean . . . Until.

Beloved, don't confuse *hidden* with *unseen.* Like the whole host above, I assure you, *you* are most certainly *seen.* If you are *hidden,* believe this—it is only *until* . . . it is time for you to *rise.* Bing Bam Boom Put That in Your Dough and Call It Breakfast. Perspective. It's powerful, my friend. It sure is.

{Luke 13:20–21}

SURVIVING THE STORM

How to survive the storm . . .

My guess is that some amongst us today just read those five words and thought . . . Dang, if there was *ever* a day that this was for me . . . it's today. Storms. They suck, amen? And honestly, I hope that made you smile even for just a second. Because if you ask me, there's power in speaking the truth. And storms suck. Amen.

So as I picked up my DRB and found my butt right here in Luke with a header that read . . . "Jesus Calms A Storm" . . . I had to ask myself and tell myself these words. . . . Maybe *today*, reminding yourself that Jesus once *calmed a storm* is enough for you to believe He will also *calm yours*. And then I thought about the *how*. And in just four verses in the same said section of Luke, we'd see it. But *first*—let's set the stage.

One day, Jesus got into a boat with His disciples and said, "Hey, let's go to the other side of the lake." Sounds good, right? *Except*, right after Jesus decided to catch a few Zzzz's, a big storm arose. Then they *remembered*—Ohhh, wait a sec, *Jesus* is in the boat. We should probably wake Him up and tell him "*Hello*—we're dyin' here!" So they did. And Jesus did what Jesus does, which is calm storms, and Jesus is the Word, my friends, not to mention the way the truth and the life, whew, amen. *Yes.*

Listen, Beloved, Jesus didn't simply "doze off" like we do on the couch after it was our idea to watch a movie in the first place (I see you). No, Jesus *purposely took a nap because He knew He wouldn't always be with them in the flesh, and they needed to learn that even when they couldn't see Him that He was still with them*, amen.

I'll tell ya what, Beloved, disciple-training is *not* for the faint of heart. Jesus indeed woke up. Calmed the storm. And then asked those twelve guys where their *faith* was. He sure did. Because He was training them, teaching them, that the way they would survive the storms that would come . . . is to remember just who their God *is*. Provider. Protector. Powerful. Storm-Calmer. Amen.

{Luke 8:22–25}

WHEN IT DOESN'T MAKE SENSE

My Child, I know it doesn't make sense to you. Trust Me.

Picture it. You beg God for years to get you out of slavery, and *finally* you're well on your way, *except*, along the way God takes you the *long* way, *and* at one point even has you go *back* a ways and *camp* for a bit, giving the bad guys who are after you a chance to catch up, because they *too* need to know God is God. I know, right? Ugh.

Or, you're a widow with nothing left in the cupboard to feed you and your kid aside from a scoop of flour in the jar and a few drops of oil in the jug, enough to make one tiny cake for the two of you to share for what *clearly* will be your last supper, and then some guy shows up and dares to tell you to make him one *first* while assuring you that there will be more than enough and then some. Yeah right, dude. P.S.: There was.

Or, you're an orphan who is being lovingly raised by your awesome cousin Mordy, who is doing his best to keep you hidden in a foreign land, going as far as to change your name, when suddenly, you find yourself in a harem of young women, not exactly sure if you want to be "chosen" and "brought into position" or not. Right.

Beloved, I've said it before, more than once, that I believe there is great power in speaking the obvious out loud. *The path you are on will not always make sense.* The twists, the turns, the detours and roadblocks, the multiple stops along the way where you find yourself screaming at the top of your lungs, "Seriously, Lord?!? What the heck?!?" Right.

So *when*, yes *when*, the path, the road, the map of your journey just doesn't make sense . . . return to the key. That's right. The key that reminds you who your God *is*. Trustworthy. All-Knowing. Author/Perfecter/Map-Creator. Beginning *and* End. And I could go on, amen. Before you . . . behind you . . . beside you . . . *within* you. For truly I tell you, Beloved, the *path* you are on will *not* always make *sense*, but the path you are on will always have *purpose*. Amen. I love you. *XO*.

KNOWING WHO YOUR GOD IS

There is nothing that can stop a girl who knows full well Who her God is.

A God Who is near, a God Who is far, a God Who rolls away big, giant stones that sometimes stand in her way. A God Who stays, a God Who remains, a God Who is helper. A God Who redeems, a God Who restores, a God Who uses crap . . . to make stuff grow. Not to mention mud to heal. A God Who will take her stubborn self into the deep . . . because what she doesn't know . . . is that what she is looking for is found there. In the deep. A God Who will call her forward despite her weaknesses and call her up despite her past and call her out because He loves her *that* stinkin' much.

Nothing can stop such a girl. A girl who knows full well that her God is Provider, her God is Protector, and if those two weren't enough, she *also* knows that her God is All-Powerful. That nothing falls outside the city limits of Possible, and since nothing is too hard for Him either . . . she can keep on believing.

A God Who knows she is human, a God Who knows she is gonna forget, a God Who is gonna take her places she doesn't want to go just so He can *remind* her . . . by *showing* her. A God Who is Potter and tells her that she is the clay . . . which she knows darn well means she won't always like the purposes for which she was sent. A God Who will use her to show others . . . that God is God . . . and there really is no other. A God Who will lead her through the journey of her life . . . through every word written for her story before she lived even page one . . . by the God Who wrote that story of hers . . . and looked at it closely before hitting Send . . . and said to the Heavens, "It is good."

Beloved, truly I tell you, there is nothing that can stop a girl who knows full well Who her God is. Amen. *XO.*

GOD IS GONNA HELP YOU

Beloved, God is gonna help you.

I don't know how, or by what means, but because of God's unfailing-never-ending-always-more-than-enough mercy . . . God is gonna help you. I don't know if you'll welcome the *way* the help comes; I don't know if you'll even recognize it. But God is gonna help you over it. Through it. Heck, it might even be around it. It might look like keeping you hidden for a bit *or* drawing you straight out of the crowd so *you* can finally see what you're made of.

God is gonna help you. It might look far from how you want it to look—just ask Joe in that pit when rescue finally arrived, only for it to look like being taken from that pit to a palace where he'd then be a servant for years, because it was all part of the plan to get him there, amen. It might look like a rock in the dry, dusty desert that suddenly spouts life-giving water. *Or* it might look like the rock at the bottom of your rock bottom because the rock is there too, amen. It might look like someone God sends your way, like Joseph and Elizabeth to young pregnant Mary. It might look like Nehemiah showing up in the midst of your ruins, ready to help you rebuild. It might look like having enough when you really thought there was no way in heck there could *possibly* be enough, and yet here you are, eating fish and loaves on the side of the sea.

Beloved, God is gonna help you. It might look like standing beside you and crying alongside you so that you know you're not alone in your grief. It might look like providing the strength to get out of bed and get dressed and do the thing because there's a thread of you that dares to believe that today will better, and a thread is more than enough . . . yes. Just ask a woman who was drained of all that she had in every way. Or ask Job—that guy could tell you a few things.

Beloved, God is gonna help you. I want you to believe it. Like really believe it. And listen, you go ahead and take those five smooth stones and stick 'em in your satchel, because you may just be facing some giants today, OK? Big love.

PROVISION COMES AS THE PLAN UNFOLDS

Provision often comes as the plan unfolds.

For Abe and his kid, it was a ram in the thicket after the altar for sacrifice was already in place. Whew. For Esther, it was one more day to plan the perfect bad-guy reveal. Love that girl. For a bunch of Israelites, it was bread falling from Heaven each day as they continued to put one foot in front of the other and complained as they did, because that's what we do. It sure is. For the thirsty-for-real-love woman, it was a tall drink of water (instead of the drips she was used to) after she let morning pass by and got her butt to the well about noon instead, because sometimes the crowd is simply too much. A to the men.

For a group of flock-keepers, it was an angel who appeared with some pretty big news as they were tucking in their sheep for the night. For Joe, it was an extra few hours to sleep on it instead of immediately dismissing young preggo Mary. For three women I read about as told by Mark, it was a giant stone already rolled away for them . . . which was good, because halfway there they realized, "Holy crap, how the heck are the three of us gonna move this thing?" Right.

Beloved, provision often comes *as* the plan unfolds. *Yes.* I reckon that's why we are strongly encouraged to walk by faith and not by sight. Right. Provision always comes . . . because Provider is Who God *is*. If you don't see it *yet*, hang tight. You *will*. Psst . . . You may or may not recognize it as provision. (Let's not forget our ancestors who called it manna, which I stinkin' love, is translated as "what the heck is *this*??" OK, not exactly, but pretty darn close.)

Beloved, provision always comes because Provider is Who your God is. And sometimes, oftentimes, it comes *as*. Yes. As . . . the plan . . . unfolds. Amen.

THE "AFTER" PLAN IS ALREADY IN PLACE

Beloved, there is an "After the flood" plan already in place for you.

There were so many, *so many* things I wanted to write about in regards to the Scripture I read this morning. Big time. But alas, my heart-soul-and-mind were still stuck on last night. Let me explain: I spent the evening with a couple dozen coming-of-age seventh grade students after they had already spent their day learning and sporting and after-school activitying, and most of them even sitting their butts in the pew for close to an hour right before class with me. Right. Thanks for "going there" with me in your mind for a minute, Friend, I appreciate it.

I talked to them about Noah. Or tried. And how God actually gave Noah a sign that everything would be OK, that there was indeed an "after" plan already in place—*all those animals that climbed aboard two-by-two with him, not to mention his fam.* Right. Did Noah recognize that sign? Maybe. Maybe not. Do we? I reckon not always, if ever at all. I mean heck, I've read the story tons of times, and I just got that light switched on yesterday. (I'm serious, folks, God never stops multiplying loaves, so dang good.)

So after an hour of these kids listening(?) to me in all my loudness and passion, as I wondered if anyone had heard anything over their banter and antics, I asked them all this—What is *one* thing you're not gonna forget from tonight? That's when two of them raised their hands. And gave the same answer . . . "God has an After plan already mapped out for me." Score-success-and-amen. *Yes.*

For just as I told them, Beloved, today I tell you . . . There *will* be floods. There *will* be storms. There *will* be things we don't want to go through in this life. *And.* There is an *after* plan already in place. For all storms end, and all floodwaters eventually recede. Amen.

ONE WORD THAT WILL GET YOU THROUGH

How you're going to get through it in one word: Believe.

That's right. That's how you're gonna get through it. And you know your *It,* I know you do. And you're gonna get through it because you *believe.* Believe that today will be better. Believe that this too shall pass. Believe that the mountain you can't seem to escape will finally be tossed into the sea, or that you will be given the strength to climb it and slam your flag into the ground at the top as you do. That you'll laugh again, even if it's mixed like a cocktail with the tears that continue to fall. That what currently is is not always what it will be. That the pit you find yourself in is nothing more than a pit stop and not your new permanent residency. That the sun will shine again; you may not know when, but you know that you know that it will. Yes.

You're gonna get through it. Because you *believe* that you will. That's right. For what we believe determines how we proceed. It sure does. And *you* believe . . . that the God Who provides your very own breath is gonna see you through whatever it is you're going through and will remain near to you as you do. That every breath you take and every move you make is seen by the One Who sings to you, "I'll be watching you". . . and then you take a minute to sing it yourself, because whether you're a really good singer or royally suck, it's really darn good for the soul. It sure is. Believe. It is the best one-word instruction/encouragement I can think of for how to get through it. Now sit with that a minute, OK? Just one solid minute with your very own soul to soak it all in.

Beloved, believe that you will get through. Believe that you are not alone. Believe that you are worthy. Believe that you are seen, you are heard, you are known, you are loved. Believe . . . and don't stop believing.

YOU WILL RISE AGAIN

Jesus rose again. You will too.

And I can't *begin* to tell you, and I am *so* not kidding, how believing this will empower you today. Strengthen you today. Allow you to look ahead today, and perhaps even actually cause you to make plans beyond today, because that's what believing folks do. Indeed, they sure do.

Beloved, I'm not the gal to hang out with if you're looking for someone to tell you that you'll never be betrayed, or handed over, or thrown to the ground, or spit on, or cursed at, or heck, even buried alive . . . nope. But I *am* the gal who will tell you . . . *you . . . will rise . . . again. I sure am.* And since I don't expect you to necessarily take my word for it, I came with backup that I'll call the cloud . . .

A woman pulled out of her bed and thrown down into the dirt . . . rose again. A woman sick in her bed with a fever who I'm sure thought it was the end . . . rose again. A woman who had spent twelve years in her bed bleeding out . . . rose again. A guy who had laid invalid for so many years he lost count . . . rose again. A boy bound and placed on an altar for sacrifice . . . rose again. A gal who got up the guts to go to church even though she was completely hunched over, and I can't imagine how long it took to get there or the pain she was in while she did . . . rose again. And . . . you may also remember a guy named Laz and one named Jesus too. Maybe. Wink, wink.

Beloved, the cloud serves as backup when our memory grows weak. So look to the cloud, and if you're looking for a mantra today, something you can get stuck in your head like a really good song, here ya go . . . Jesus rose again. You will too. You sure will. *XO.*

OPPORTUNITIES TO HEAL

Today I pray you find opportunities to heal.

Beloved, may you be given opportunities to heal. Yes. I pray for you *opportunities.* And I pray that you recognize them. Like the woman under the table knowing even the crumbs would be enough. Like the guy with the friends who carried him to the rooftop and lowered him down to where Jesus was. Like the woman at the well, may you find opportunity to take time to sit and to think and to consider your life, and as you do . . . you realize your God is there with you . . . speaking . . . to *you.* Yes. I pray for you opportunities to heal. Your body, your mind, your heart, your soul. Opportunities to forgive and let go, opportunities to go if it's time to go, opportunities to grow even if it hurts, for they are called growing pains, no? Yes.

Opportunities to heal. To find yourself in the crowd witnessing a miracle that will spark a fire within you that dares you to believe one more time that the same could happen for you. To find yourself in a boat on a dark stormy night, and just when you think, "This is it . . . ," you see Jesus walking right towards you. To find yourself, like Hagar, alone by the side of a spring, thinking, "How in the heck am I gonna do this thing??" (In her case, single-mom life, but you can fill in your own thing), when all of a sudden you hear one strong voice that says, "You don't have to, I Am right here, and I *see you.*"

Opportunities to heal. To find yourself at the back of the church like the woman who'd spent the last eighteen years doing nothing but looking down, and then realizing Jesus is preaching, and He's calling *you* to the front, yes—to make the long walk down the aisle for others to see, because by doing so, they *too* are given an opportunity to heal by what *they* will soon see . . . you. Standing up straight. For the first time in a long time. Because you were positioned to be there. Yes.

Opportunities to heal. I pray them for you. I sure do.

A TIME TO LEAVE

She left that place . . .

There are mornings I don't make it past the first four words. This day was one of those mornings. I share this in part because there may be some in this space who believe in order to be super holy and fed fully by God, you need to sit for two hours and inhale a three-cheese omelet, side of bacon, short stack of hotcakes with syrup, and a few slices of hot buttered toast. The truth is, sometimes a wafer from Heaven is enough for the day. Is *enough for the day*. Sorry, I didn't want you to miss that.

Beloved, the first four words I read this day were these . . . "He left that place," and all I could think was . . . that happens. Yep. There are times you will stay and times when you'll leave. Times when you'll remain and times when you'll realize that where you are is no longer where you should be. Times when you've done what you can do where you are, and in order to keep growing and not be held back, you'll need to seek out new land. There will be times when you leave the flat grasslands to search for a mountain to climb. And then you'll realize it's because you desperately need to know that you're still fully alive. And there will be times when you reach the top. And times when you don't, but dang, you were sure strengthened by the climb. There will be times when the place you leave has nothing to do with physical soil, but instead the state of your soul. And these times will free you.

You will leave the place of rejection, the place of confusion, the place that just doesn't feel right. You will leave the place of shame and come out of hiding, trusting that who you are need not remain hidden. Under a bushel. No. Determined and perhaps even singing . . . I'm gonna *let it shine. Man, I hope so.*

Beloved, Jesus left that place. There will be times you do too. And take it from a girl who has left lots of places; sometimes it's hard, sometimes there are tears, and sometimes . . . it feels like a chick who has finally broken free from her shell. *XO.*

{Mark 6:1a}

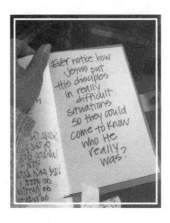

COMING TO KNOW GOD THROUGH THE HARD

Ever notice how Jesus put His disciples in really difficult situations so they could come to know Who He really was?

Me too. For truly I tell you, Beloved, if you don't know this yet, I assure you that one day you will—you will come to know Who your God is more in times of desperate need than in fruitful abundance. Yes. More in lack than in plenty. More in dark than in light. More in storms than in still, so that eventually *when* those storms come, and they will, *you*, like Jesus, will be able to be still. And know. That God. Is God. You sure will. For it is in our full humanness and fragility that we come to understand our God's holiness and strength. A strength, by the way, that we need to lean on . . . often. (Weird, it's like I can see a few hundred heads right now nodding in unison to the beat. Cool.)

A God Who loves you enough to tell you, yes, but also—*show* you. For it is in the showing that we're more likely to remember, amen? *Amen.* I always liked that Jesus taught the peeps that way. Tell and then Show. And Beloved, I say all of this to you this day, because perhaps right now, you find yourself in a really difficult situation. If so . . . believe it is because your mighty and all-knowing-all-loving God . . . is about to *show* you Who your God really is. Yes. Please believe that. A God Who remains and doesn't forsake. A God Who rules from the Heavens and yet is as close as the breath in your lungs. A God Who always provides even if you can't see it, understand it, know what to name it, or heck, even like it. That's right.

Beloved, hang in there. Difficult is difficult. There ain't no denyin' that, and your God is your God, in e-v-e-r-y difficult. Yes. Promise. *XO.*

WHEN GOD ROCKS YOUR WORLD

What if what is rocking your world right now is actually God rolling away the stone that stands in the way?

I'm not here to say of course; I'm here to present the "What if?" Yes. Because truly I tell you, Beloved, if I were in the middle of an Earthquake right now, I would *much* rather believe that it was God rolling away a stone in my life than to believe that it's my world coming to an end. I-sure-would-and-amen. So again, I'm not here to say whether or not this is true for you; I'm here to simply show you what the Word said to *me* this morn. Indeed. And *this* . . . is what . . . I read . . .

"And suddenly there was an Earthquake; for an angel of the Lord, descending from heaven, came and rolled back the stone and sat on it."

Psst . . . the "came and sat on it" part—almost as if to say "there ya go, girls"—is a *really* cool added bonus, in my opinion, by the way . . . big time. Mmmhmm. So good. And as the men who were guarding the tomb shook and played dead, the angel of the Lord spoke to those women and said to them, "Do not be afraid" . . . for clearly, he knew that they were. Hello, who wouldn't be? Exactly.

Beloved, change often feels like the Earth quaking beneath our feet; I reckon that's why it's so hard for us to remain standing when change occurs. But what if the next time that change leaves us shaking in our new boots, we think back to this story . . . and remember those two scared-out-of-their-minds women . . . and consider the possibility that what is rocking our world is actually God rolling away the stone that stands in the way? What if? Hey, it's just a thought from a girl who has watched, and lived through, God doing some shaking . . . more than once . . . no joke and amen. I bet you have too. *XO.*

{Matthew 28:1–5}

REMEMBER WHO YOU'RE TALKING TO

I'll tell ya what—prayer gets reeeally powerful when you remember Who you're talking to.

The One Who commanded light to shine out of darkness. The One Who planted the garden. The One Who made humankind from the dirt of the ground and gave them His own holy breath. The One Who once raised a dead guy out of the grave for all to see; hey wait, twice actually. The One Who once caused the sun to stand still. The One Who could do it again. The One Who once caused a woman to conceive longggg after she had quit buying tampons and pads. The One Who created a great big fish and positioned it perfectly in order to save a guy thrown overboard. The One Who took an orphan and made her Queen. The One Who took a young widow out of her homeland, led her to land she did not know, worked her there, blessed her there, and now Jesus's name is embroidered on her family tree. The One Who fed five thousand-plus with some kid's sack lunch. The One Who parted the sea. The One Who rolled away the giganto stone. The One Who set two guys free . . . not to mention everyone else. Yes.

Beloved, listen to me—prayer gets *reeeeally* powerful . . . when you remember Who you're talking to. *It sure does.* The One Who created you and vowed to never leave or forsake you. The One Whose very own holy breath you carry as guarantee. The One to Whom all things are possible, nothing is too hard, and the One to Whom no secrets—*none*—are hid. The One Who makes all things new. The One Who makes all things right. The One Who wrote your story in full, from "In the Beginning" to the final "Amen." *Yes.* The One Who has purpose *in* all things and *for* all things and doesn't waste *one single thing*. And the One Who knows . . . that we can't possibly understand the magnitude of it all . . . this life here on Earth . . . so stays near and weeps alongside us when we don't. I know, right? So good.

Beloved, one piece of guidance/advice today, OK? Remember Who you are talking to. *XO*. Big love, and amen.

GO TO THE CHALKBOARD

"My name is I Am, not I Was."—God

Even if you never lived during the time of writing things repeatedly on the chalkboard at school, my guess is you're at least partially familiar with it.

I will not throw spitwads. I will not throw spitwads. I will not throw spitwads.

You get the idea. And that method has its perks. Not only does it attempt to drill something into our heads, but after about the tenth time or so, it becomes a rhythm, allowing the mind to think about other things—indeed, allowing the mind . . . to slow down and breathe. Yes.

Beloved, go to the chalkboard. I mean it. Stand at the chalkboard and breathe as you remind yourself with every stroke of the chalk and sigh of the mind what it is about God you most need to hear. Today for me, it looks like this—

God is with me. God is for me. God is with me. God is for me. God is with me. God is for me. Over and over and over again.

Just a girl at the chalkboard with time to think about what that truly means, the magnitude of it, really—alongside her God, aptly named "I Am." Yes. The God of yesterday, *today*, and tomorrow too. A God Whose Spirit God gave you in the form of breath so you never forget. A God Who whispers in the earliest of morns and the darkest of nights . . . I Am with you. I Am for you. I Am Provider. I Am Protector. I Am All-Powerful. I Am near. I Am far. I Am beside you, and I Am within you. I Am the beginning. I Am the end. I Am all things. Yes. I Am your friend. I Am your confidant. I Am the voice cheering you on when you feel like you just can't go on, and I Am the shepherd Who sometimes makes you lie down. I Am in your storm. I Am in your war. I Am in your desert, and I Am in your pain. I Am in the manger, not in the tomb. Yes. I Am.

Beloved, go to the chalkboard. However long it takes . . . to believe it.

REJECTION PLAYS A PART

Psst . . . the rejection is part of getting you to where you belong.

And leave it to good ole' Jesus to come to Earth and go through it so we could, if nothing else, know that there's purpose for it.

Beloved, today is gonna be short and hopefully sweet-to-the-soul and right to the point. The rejection is part of getting you to where you belong. Yes.

Note. *Big* Note: You do *not* have to like it. You are not *less* of a believer if you don't like it. God *gave you* the ability to pray, with or without words, by the way, because God *knows* you won't always like the ways or understand the ways, and so you can talk to God, cry to God—heck, even scream at God. Yes. I know. You heard it here first, folks. Why? Because God *knows*. That's right. A God Who wept alongside Mary and Martha at the grave not because *He* didn't understand what was about to happen (could someone please run and get Laz a new pair of jeans) . . . but because God knew *they* didn't understand what was about to happen. *Right.* So, out of compassion for them, He wept alongside them. Yes. So good. So good.

So this isn't about *liking* the rejection; it's about *realizing* that the rejection has purpose. Yes. And what has purpose has meaning, and what has meaning has value, and what has value has worth, amen. Yes.

Beloved, rename the rejection. I mean it. Do it. Call it the Road that is getting you to where you belong. And then believe that. And don't stop believing. And OK, so maybe this wasn't so short after all. Wink, wink. I love you.

{Matthew 21:42}

EVEN YOUR LACK HAS PURPOSE

Even your lack has purpose.

Not all that long ago, a friend and I had a small home-cleaning business. We once cleaned the apartment of an elderly gentleman who lived within a large building. Upon arriving, and before departing for coffee hour with the rest of the residents, he spoke to us. And neither my friend nor I will ever forget it.

His tiny dwelling was filled from floor to ceiling with incredible paintings. My friend, who loves to paint, couldn't help but notice them, and in turn asked about them. His face lit up as he explained to us that when he and his wife moved to this country, they had nothing. Nothing aside from one farming tool in his hand with which to get started. His wife, a lover of art, wanted nothing more than to fill their humble abode with magnificent paintings, but alas, lack of money meant no such magnificent paintings. Until it didn't. For out of her desire, and because of their lack, she picked up a brush and began to paint.

Her *lack* drew *out* of her what may never have been discovered *within* her, had it not been for her lack. I know, right? Man, I love that story. And it's not even one of those "had to be there" stories because I *know* you get it. I just know it.

Beloved, even your *lack* has purpose. *Yes.* Like this woman, it may draw something out of you that you never knew was within you to provide for you in ways you never expected. It may keep you returning to God every single morning asking for the very same thing, but if so, your lack is keeping you close to Him and causing your soul to sing, "Don't Stop Believin'," which, of course, is not only satisfying you for the day but also strengthening you in ways you can't even imagine. Even your lack has purpose.

Beloved, lack is not easy. Understanding why is sometimes even harder yet. But truly I tell you, even your lack has purpose. All things do. Everything under the sun and in the Heavens above. So today I pray you look forward to the moment God shows you . . . like a house filled with your paintings . . . just what that purpose is.

GOD'S WAYS WORK

God will find ways to stoke and stir up the fire He placed within you as a mere ember. And although you will rarely like those ways, truly I tell you, they work.

And *this*, my dear friends, is most certainly true. Stoke—to poke or stir up (a fire, flames, etc.): to supply with fuel; to feed abundantly; to increase the activity, intensity, or amount of . . . wow. No doubt and amen.

Beloved, you and I can sing "(C'mon Baby) Light My Fire" all day long. . . but when it comes to having that fire *stoked* . . . well . . . not so much. And yet, God does. Yup. I know it to be true because I've lived it . . . and lived it often. I'm still living it. Maybe you are too. And I tell ya what—you will *not* understand all God's ways. You will also not *like* all God's ways because God's ways are beyond your human understanding. Fact.

So *because* both of the above statements are true, you'll do well to view your life through the lens of who you know God to *be*—yes. Provider, Protector, All-Powerful . . . Fire-Stoker. Not because God hates you, but because God refuses to let the fire He purposefully placed in you *go out. Amen.* For there is *purpose* for that fire within you. Amen again. *Huge.* So here's what I do in the heat of the stoking (pun intended), and if it helps you, awesome; if not, no problem—maybe someday it will. When I feel the heat of the fire rising up within me . . . I look to God and say with a slight head tilt . . ."Well, OK then."

I know, right? Pretty prophetic. What I mean by it is this . . . God placed that fire within me. God will find ways to stoke that fire and set it ablaze. I'm rarely, if ever, gonna like those ways. But gosh darn it, I have to admit . . . they work. They sure do. And I have a feeling that due to that look on your face, Beloved, you may just be saying that too. Or at least be willing . . . to ponder it a bit. I'll bring the s'mores supplies.

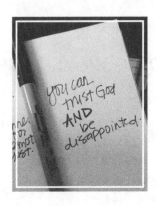

YOU CAN TRUST GOD AND BE DISAPPOINTED

You can trust God and be disappointed.

Have you ever said something similar to the following, or along the same vein . . . "I am *so* disappointed, but I trust God," or, "I am *so* sad/mad/upset, but I trust God." You have? Well then, hang with me a bit longer, cuz we're about to honor your humanness instead of dismissing it, because in case you didn't know—you're human. Yup. And . . . be advised here . . . *your humanness allows for multiple emotions to coexist.*

So let's make one simple but humungo change to our lingo, shall we? "I am *so* disappointed." Pause. Acknowledge. Honor that emotion for a hot minute or two, because hello—God gives us our emotions as a way to handle and process this life. That's my opinion anyway. For what it's worth. And then, after the pause to *feel*, we continue on, not with *but*, for Big Buts are bullies and try to act as if the emotion was ludicrous or shouldn't exist, so it bulldozes past it. Instead, we move on with *and* serve as the bridge between our humanness and God's holiness. The Judds were right by the way—love really does build a bridge.

Shall we practice? "I am *so* disappointed . . . *and* . . . I trust God." That's right. Because by acknowledging my humanness, I remember that my God is *in* my humanness *with* me, that God *knows* I don't understand and therefore weeps alongside me when my emotions cause me to weep. *Yes.*

And Beloved, God does the same for *you.* Ya know, one of the things I love best about David's Psalms are the fact that he never dismissed his reality, never tossed aside his emotion. Instead, he acknowledged it/them *and* acknowledged that God was right there with him. Beloved, your God is with you wherever you are—physically, emotionally, spiritually. You can trust God . . . *and* be disappointed. For knowing you can do both will set you free to go to God *in* it, reminding yourself God is there *with* you. And you'll have someone to lean on. Because we all need somebody to lean on, amen? (Yes, go ahead and sing if you want.) *XO.*

FAITH DOES

Faith builds. Faith plants. Faith sets the alarm. Faith does.

Yes. Faith acts, believing there is more yet to come. Faith builds the house, believing it will be occupied, and plants the tree, believing it will reap its incredible fruit. Faith sets the alarm, believing that tomorrow . . . will be better. Yes. *Better.* Faith does. Faith is not stagnant or confined; it can't be, for it is always looking ahead and stretching and growing, thus expanding its tent, enlarging its territory. Faith makes the appointment to talk to someone, believing that releasing may help in the healing. Faith joins the support group for much the same reason. Faith asks and searches and knocks and doesn't quit asking or searching or knocking until what it is that it is asking for, searching for, knocking on the door in the midnight hour for . . . is realized . . . some way. Somehow. In some form. Yes.

Faith does. Faith buys a planner for the following year. Faith fills in the empty spaces. Faith makes its bed, believing it'll be crawled into once again come nightfall. Faith applies for the job, despite feeling it probably doesn't stand a chance, but . . . maybe? Hmmm. Faith tries. Because Faith believes. It sure does. Faith does. Faith engages in the handshake. It hands over the sandal. It gives freely, knowing that God is Provider. Faith does hard things like leave bad situations, believing that although there were some treasures taken from the war . . . the heart-mind-and-soul is now ready for some much-needed peace. Yes. Faith does. It remains active to remind its soul that it has *not* perished . . . but is *alive.* Yes. Faith believes. That the sun will rise again. That the stone will be rolled again. That the mountain will be moved again, or it will be strengthened to climb it again. Yes.

Faith believes. Faith does. It sure does.

THE WORD OF GOD WILL MOVE YOU

The Word of God moved her . . . in every sense of the word.

Like Nehemiah, the Word had caused her to return to her homeland. Like Esther, it brought her to a place where she felt all alone. Like Naomi, it led her to hike up her knickers and do the hard thing, returning to the City of Bread, no matter how much the townsfolk who'd known her before would chitter-chatter about her move back. Yes.

The Word of God, written specifically and powerfully and uniquely for *her* life, *her* script, *her* playbook—the one perfectly penned by the Author and Finisher of *her* faith . . . moved her. And when it was hard, she'd remind herself that stagnant waters draw unwanted pests like mosquitoes, and she'd be OK with the waters continuing their flow.

The Word of God moved her. Like Jonah, there were times she'd try to outrun the life she was given, blind to the fact that it was a gift. And also like Jonah, it would cost her. Like Abe, it would move her to new lands that she had never seen and knew nothing about . . . all so that her God could show her . . . I Am here, and I Am Provider. Like Jesus, the Word would lead her into the wilderness, and she would face temptation after temptation to forget Who her God was . . . but she'd return to her knowing and stand firm in that place and remind herself until she was blue in the face just *exactly* Who her God was. And when, yes *when*, she emerged from that wilderness, she'd look back and realize that she was *led* to that place to *learn* in that place that the *Lord* her God would never *leave* her in that place . . . or any place for too long . . . but long enough to *give* her something *in* that place . . . and self-worth and confidence and realizing your very own strength ain't no small thing.

God's Word moved her. To believe again. To trust again. To hope again. To try again. To ask again. *Yes.* For she knew that wherever the Word moved her, wherever the Spirit of God within her led her . . . God would be there . . . just as God always had been and forever would be.

MAYBE YOU'VE FORGOTTEN

Friend, you are far more powerful than the enemy against you, for the all-powerful God is within you. Maybe you've forgotten that.

I want you to picture the enemy sitting on the shoulder opposite of your dominant hand. Now, take your dominant hand and put it into "flick" position—you know the one, where your middle finger (*how flippin' fitting, by the way*) bends down to meet your thumb pad? Right. Now, reach over and *flick away Satan like an annoying bug.* I know, right? How'd that feel? So good, so good. Now listen folks, am I simplifying here? Of *course* I am. *Because sometimes we overcomplicate things.* Also—*amen.*

Matthew. Chapter 4. Jesus is led into the wilderness (by the *Spirit, not* the devil, by the way) to *be tempted* (yup), *at His weakest* (yup), to *show us . . . we will be too.* And— to give us a way *out,* because Jesus is just super awesome like that. Yup. We will be tempted along the way, in one or more of three ways: To forget that God is *Provider.* To forget that God is *Protector.* To forget that God is *All-Powerful.* Cuz we forget . . . a *lot.* It's part of the whole human thing. Yup. And as I read this morning and listened to every one of Jesus's rebuttals to the enemy's cross-examinations, perhaps my very favorite was the last one of all, when Jesus says, "Away with you, Satan!"

Enter the whole flicking-off-the-shoulder-thing. Because today, for the first time, I heard His voice differently, in a different tone. Instead of super loud and authoritative, it was more like "Geez, dude, you're pathetic," as He flicked him off his shoulder and moved on. And I gotta tell ya, folks, I *liked* it. Can you imagine if you and I had *so* much confidence in the God Who is *in* us, that we literally scoffed and flicked off the enemy *against* us? I know, right?

Friend, maybe you've *forgotten.* That you are *far* more powerful than the enemy *against* you, for the *All-Powerful God* is *within* you. *Yes.* So the next time you're *tempted to forget* that God is Provider, Protector, All-Powerful—well, you just get your flicker finger ready. Gosh, I hope you're not only smiling, but feeling a whole lot stronger. I am too.

MAKE TRUST YOUR WALKING STICK

She'd come a long way with her God. She knew she wouldn't like all the ways God would use to speak to her and, in turn, lead, guide, direct, redirect, and reroute her. But she also knew she could trust Him. And so, she'd return to that trust and use it as a walking stick to keep moving forward.

It was a famine that caused Elimelech to pack up his wife Naomi and his two young boys and head to a land that had food. It was warning of a great flood that caused Noah to set aside his plow and his planting and get to work building an ark. It was friends from back home that visited Nehemiah in the castle and let him know that things back home really sucked, and it would be great if he could return for a bit and help them rebuild what had been torn down. For Esther, it would look like being ripped from the arms of what very well could've been her last living relative and put into a palace where she knew exactly no one. For Hagar, it would look like being used to produce and then cast aside, literally pushed out of the tent because jealousy will do that, amen. For Joe, it would be told to "Get up and go" until he and his new bride, Mary, *finally* ended up in a town called Nazareth in Galilee.

Beloved, you get my point. God has used ways that I *hated* . . . in order to lead/guide/direct/redirect and reroute me . . . to where God would next have me . . . according to God's specific and will-absolutely-be-fulfilled plan *for* me. *This* . . . is most certainly true. And Beloved, it's true for you too. It sure is.

So in those times, *and there will be times, return to Who you know God to be.* And if you feel like you *don't* feel as though you truly know Who God is, spend time with God and get to know God. For knowing God leads to trusting God . . . and trust will need to be your walking stick . . . as you move *forward* . . . into your *fulfillment.* Amen.

THE GOD OF BOTH

God will take you to the heights of Heaven and to the depths of hell so you will know He is God of both.

And you know it because you've been . . . to *both*. And there God was. But also, maybe you've forgotten. *Hey, it happens.* Storms rock the ships and threaten to completely break them apart. Fires rage the dry lands, threatening to take them out completely. Droughts can last so long that even when the rain does start to come, it's hard for the ground to receive it. And Beloved, I have *no* doubt that you've had your storms and your fires and your droughts.

The divorce. The break-up. The shake-up. The addiction that pulled you to rock bottom. The job loss. The accident. The worry that literally wrestles with you each night so intensely that it's no wonder you wake up exhausted. The fear of what is, what was, or what is to come. The anxiety that strangles your soul and quite literally feels like it's robbing you of your breath.

So, what do we do *when*, not if, the storms rock the ship, and the fire rages on, and the drought feels as though it will never end? *One thing.* Take shelter. In Who you know God to be. Return to that place deep within that says . . . God speaks from the eye of the storm (thanks, Job), which means God is *in* the storm. God saves from the fire (thanks, Dan's friends), which means I can walk through it. God send the rains in due time to the desolate ground and has even been known to make dry bones dance. (Thanks, Ezekiel.) *Right.*

We acknowledge God in *all* our ways, just like Scripture suggests, because *hello*— God is God of *all ways.* And when it comes to the heights of Heaven and the depths of hell? We return to the truth that reminds us . . . He is God of *both*. Yes. Because think about it friends, do you *really* think we'd be instructed hundreds of times to *not fear* unless it were actually *possible*? Exactly. God is God of *both*. Which means one big huge thing—no matter *where* you are . . . God is *there*. And two is better than one. Especially when one of them is Protector, Provider, and All-Powerful as in *all. Amen.*

MAYBE IT'S TIME TO REALLY LIVE

If what you've been doing hasn't been working, maybe it's time to climb the mountain, cut down/out a few things, and then return, rebuild, and really live.

The entire book of Haggai is but a page and a half, and yet the word "Consider" is in it *five* times. I guess I'll take those five times and "consider" them my five stones. Amen. Because although this book is small in size, I promise it's mighty in stature. It sure is. So as I read and "considered". . . this thought is what arose from the field called Haggai from which I was gleaning . . . God told the people to "consider how you have fared" up to now; in essence, how's that been workin for ya? Are you still tirelessly laboring and sowing yourself too thin, and yet actually harvesting very little? Are you taking in plenty, but it never feels like enough? Do you have clothes on your back, but still don't feel like you're covered? Have you been so busy taking care of the house that you've forgotten all about the temple? (Psst . . . insertion of Paul's famous question. . . . Do you not know that *you* are the temple of God?)

Beloved, when it comes to our bodies, our flesh, our tents/houses, we eventually realize that when something's not working, we need to try something *new*. May the same be true for our *souls*, our *temples eternal*. Yes. May we never forget we are *both*. Yes, *both*. We are Human. We sure are. So for the one here today desperately wanting to try something new, something they know will be hard and is wondering how in the world to do it . . . here are a few *more* words from this rock star book, OK? And bonus: God's the guest speaker.

Take courage. Take courage. Take courage. For I Am with you. My Spirit abides among you. Do not fear. The latter splendor of this house will be greater than the former, and in this place, I will give prosperity. *Believe it, Beloved.* Believe it. Hard things are often the gateway to real life. They sure are.

WHEN CHRISTMAS IS HARD

The first Christmas was hard. Yours might be too.

Yes. Maybe it's hard. Maybe it's the first Christmas you're missing someone 'round the tree, an absence felt. One that could be due to a variety of reasons . . . death, divorce, destruction, disruption, devastation, delays. Or maybe it's not the first Christmas per se, but every year still *feels* like the first Christmas because you're starting to realize that even when healing occurs, there's often a scar left behind, and scars change the landscape. Amen.

Maybe it's the first Christmas you're sitting with a new diagnosis, and you're not quite sure what to make of it. Maybe fear is sitting next to you in the waiting room. And although you're doing your best to just keep to yourself, it's not working too well, and you're starting to wonder if maybe you should just get up and go find a new seat. Next to Hope would be great. Maybe it's the first Christmas without a ton of gifts under the tree, and you're grappling with guilt about it. Maybe it's the first Christmas you're hurting in a new way or scared in a new way or starting to understand why some folks say they "just want it to be over" because you could never understand that before, and now here you are, and you realize you're nodding your head in agreement . . . quietly of course, so others don't see.

Beloved, the first Christmas was hard. Maybe this year, yours is too. The first Christmas was hard . . . *and* (not but) . . . it gave pause and time to look up at the stars. It allowed the cry of a newborn to be heard, which meant new life had arrived. It gathered the lowliest of the lowlies and the wisest of the wise all in one place to behold *one* gift that was given for *both*, and how's that for a message? Amen. It wasn't hidden in a hotel room complete with room service and a remote. No it sure wasn't. Instead, it was out in the breath of the cool night air for Mary to inhale as she practiced her breathing with labor-coach Joe at her side.

It was hard. *And.* It was still Christmas. Because hard can't stop miracles from coming in their due time. In fact, it often gives birth to them. Amen.

THE PLACE YOU DON'T WANNA GO

The place God is taking you—physically, emotionally, spiritually—that place where you don't want to go . . . could very well be . . . the place where God plans to rescue you and redeem you.

Sometimes, a girl's just gotta quote the KJV, because dang-it-all if sometimes it doesn't just hit so stinkin' sweet, amen. So here ya go, read it slow, thou(s) and shalt(s) have been known to make a girl stumble . . . let's proceed . . .

"Be in pain, (hey, hey, hey, stay with me) and labour to bring forth, O daughter of Zion, like a woman in travail: for now shalt thou go forth out of the city, and thou shalt dwell in the field, and thou shalt go even to Babylon; there shalt thou be delivered; there the Lord shall redeem thee from the hand of thine enemies. Now also many nations are gathered against thee, that say, Let her be defiled, and let our eye look upon Zion. But they know not the thoughts of the Lord, neither understand they his counsel: for he shall gather them as the sheaves into the floor. Arise and thresh, O daughter of Zion: for I will make thine horn iron, and I will make thy hoofs brass. . . ."

Yes. Amen. *Even*. *Even* to *Babylon*. For *there*, rescue and redemption will happen—yes—*there*. So, in turn, therefore; whatever dang transitional word you wanna insert here—arise and thresh, O Daughter of Zion. For I (big, bold ya-gotta-hear-it-in-God's-voice "I") . . . will strengthen you. Yes. I will strengthen you to do in this world all that I still have for you to do and experience every experience I still have for you to experience. *Yes*. And I . . . big bold I . . . will be *with* you.

Now Beloved, I implore you to read that passage above again. And if after doing so it causes you to blurt out at the end . . ."I am woman hear me roar," well then, go get 'em, Tiger. *XO*.

{Micah 4:10–13a}

PRAY WHERE YOU'RE AT

Pray where you're at.

For Jonah, it was the belly of a fish. For Paul, it was the penitentiary. For Esther, it was locked away with the rest of the harem awaiting what the king at the time would decide. And I'm not convinced she wanted the rose. Just sayin'.

Beloved, pray where you're at. Pray from the pit of your personal hell, if that's where you're at, for I promise, the flames don't frighten the God Who is *in* that fiery furnace *with* you. (Thanks, Dan's three friends, for showing us that.) Pray from your pit of despair, because why the heck *not* pray? For certainly, you've tried everything else, including but not limited to running yourself ragged trying to catch a break. Pray from your hopelessness. Pray from your worry. Pray from precisely where you're *at*, because your God *knows where you're at, hello.* That happens when the One dwells *within you*, you know. Pray from your deep, from your desert, from your dark storm, and then dare to crack the very slightest of grins as you remember that God spoke to Job *from* the eye of the storm (the eye being the place of calm, by the way), which actually reminded Job that God was *in* his storm with him. Amen and amen. Don't forget that, amen.

Friends, Jonah prayed where Jonah was at. Because Jonah knew something that would sustain him all the days of his life: Regardless of where I am, even if I am here because of my very own actions, even if I don't deserve to be heard because I haven't been a very good listener . . . *my God hears me.* The fact that I'm swimming in fish guts? Not a hindrance. The fact that Laz was in a tomb long enough to stink? Not a barrier. The fact that Dave was deep in the cave seeking refuge from his enemies? No biggie. And I could go on.

Beloved, no matter *where you are*, in *every* sense, God hears you. So pray. Not because you have to, but because not being alone in the storm, desert, wilderness, loneliness, heartache, hell, fear, worry, tornado-that-feels-like-your-life . . . helps. It really does. So pray where you're at. Knowing that you are heard, and trusting that deliverance, one way or another, always comes.

REFUSE TO STAY IN THE DARK

To pray is to refuse to stay in the dark.

It is to crack open the door and usher in light, to crack the clay pot in which you reside to let a little fresh air inside. Because it's stuffy in there, and you're over the stuffiness. Amen. To pray is to ask and to seek and to beg, if begging is where you're at . . . and to feel zero shame in doing so. That's right. It's to talk to the One Whom you cannot see, but you know that you know is there, and so you do . . . and in doing so, you realize that you're not alone because you're actually talking to Someone. And because feeling like you're going it alone royally sucks. Amen.

To pray is to fling open the gate to every Possible out there . . . to the One for Whom all things are possible. To pray is sometimes to speak and sometimes to not speak a word and instead "pour out your heart like water" (if we're gonna use Bible talk), *which* by the way, I'm convinced means to literally bawl your eyes out. *Yes.* And as you do . . . you realize that God so fearfully and wonderfully and intricately designed you . . . that your eyes were given tear ducts so you could release what is too heavy for you to carry. Wow, by the way, and amen. Yes. To pray is to ponder and dream and anticipate where God will take you next, use you next, bless you next. Yes. It's to look ahead, which is awesome, because lately you've found that your past is really tripping you up.

Beloved, to pray is to refuse to stay in the dark . . . and so you bravely . . . and boldly . . . don't. Amen. You are seen, you are heard, you are known, you are loved. Don't forget. *XO.*

YOU WILL FLOURISH AGAIN

Beloved, you will live again. You will flourish again. You will bloom again. You will.

And *man* do I wish-I-was-there-with-you-wherever-you-are-so-I-could-grab-your-shoulders-and-look-you-straight-in-the-eye-so-you-would-know-that-I-mean-these-words-to-the-tips-of-my-toes-and-I'm-not-kidding-amen.

Yes. And I'd pray that *my* confidence would give *you* strength. I sure do. But because I'm *not* with you face-to-face this morning (and if I ever am, I hope you'll make coffee), I want you to hear these words as if I were. Yes. Now, it should be noted that if you've never heard me speak, I *really* get into it and, like Horton among the Whos, I mean what I say and I say what I mean. I sure do. Oh, and I'm loud. But I digress. So, *if* in fact it should be *you* today that needs these words—*you* who needs to know that she or he will *live* again, *flourish* again, *bloom* again . . . well then, girlfriend/guyfriend—I *got you.*

Beloved, you will live again. You will flourish again. You will bloom again. Amen and amen, you sure will. After the desert, the divorce, the destruction. After the heartache, the hard, the hell you've been through. After the storm, the separation. After the sea is *finally* crossed and you find yourself on dry land again. After the flood, the famine, after the fear has subsided. After the lack, the long nights, the loneliness that can't seem to catch light.

After it all. You will live again. You will flourish again. You will bloom again. Amen and amen. I believe this for you, Beloved. I absolutely sure do. And I pray today . . . that *you do too.*

{Hosea 14:7}

NEVER STOP PRAYING

Don't you ever stop praying.

And big-time bonus if you hear me saying this in my most serious mama-voice preceded by the words, "Listen here young lady/young man . . ." because that is *exactly* how I'm saying them. And although you might buck me a little, a part of us always wants to be parented, no matter *how* old we, are because we crave a love *that* fierce. So, you're welcome. Don't you *ever* stop praying. I mean it. And should you be *tempted* to, thinking it's too late/too far gone/too impossible/why-even-bother . . . Well then, you listen here, young lady/young man—if/when you get to that point in your journey, you hit me up and I will kindly remind you of Daniel after the decree came out to not pray to his God. I mean it when I say we all need reminding, and because we're human, we kinda want a whole *bunch* of examples to kinda "prove" that it wasn't a fluke, so *here you go.*

Daniel never stopped praying, despite the decree. Paul never stopped praying in prison. Esther never stopped praying while locked away with the harem, and Jonah never stopped praying while swallowed up in that fish. Hannah never stopped praying even though she looked drunk, and Jesus never stopped praying because *hello, who doesn't want the comfort of knowing they aren't alone? Amen.* Exactly. Still with me?

Folks, here's my guess: If our guy Daniel were to have a motto, it may just be Ask Him Again—which, of course, is endearing to me, because once upon a time, way back in 2019, which in social-media land is like lost/dead/buried territory, I got up in the morn and wrote a post like I do every other day. And yet, for some reason—God's, I suppose—that little post just won't die. Could it be that it's because we desperately want to know that *it is* OK *to ask Him again?* That we want *Someone,* Who loves us like a mama, to grab our shoulders, look us in the eye, and say to us, "You listen to me, young lady/young man, don't you *ever* stop praying."

Perhaps. If so, here ya go. Don't you *ever* stop praying. Don't you *ever* stop believing. Don't you *ever* let go of the truth that you are *infinitely, unconditionally loved.* Amen.

MAYBE YOU JUST NEED SOME TIME

Beloved, maybe you just need some time.

To wonder. To ponder. To question. To think. To process. To heal. To cool down and come up with a plan so you don't rush in without one and then smack your head with regret. To sleep on it, literally, before making such a humongo decision. For as I've mentioned before, Joseph did, and aren't we glad, thus keeping young Mary from going it alone. Beloved, maybe you just need some time. To pray. Esther needed it. Jonah got it. In my reading today, Daniel just flat out asked for it. Time to lay it all out before his God. To seek mercy from God concerning this mystery. I stinkin' *love* those words, don't you? And they still speak today, ya know. And they still serve as powerful advice, and I gotta tell ya, I'm all here for it.

"Seek mercy from the God of heaven concerning this mystery."

And Beloved, *you know your mystery.* Maybe it's the mystery of should I stay or should I go now? (P.S.: You are more than welcome to pause here and sing it like ya got it. Belt it out, actually—it may help.) Maybe it's the mystery of what you should do next, where you should go, or what you should do where you're at. Maybe it's the mystery of *how* should I proceed. Lord, what should I say? Please, Lord, *please* show me what it all means.

Beloved, maybe you just need some time. To enter the sanctuary. The holiest of holies. The innermost part of you that we call Soul. Your soul, by the way, that only God knows. For there *is* a God in heaven Who gives mercy concerning our mysteries—a God Who reveals deep and hidden things, for He knows what is in the darkness, for it is not darkness to Him. That's right. God knows. Light will do that. And God is Light. Maybe you just need some time. To remind yourself Who your God is . . . and who *you* are in light of Who your God is. That's right, Mighty Warrior. That's right. *And don't you forget it, amen.*

{Daniel 2:18}

RESTORATION AFTER THE WAR

Someone today needs to know that there is restoration after the war.

Yes, " . . . restored from war. . . . " I mean it when I say that oftentimes when I'm reading, a cluster of words all but jump off the page and grab hold of me and simply won't let go. We'll call that Blessing, OK? Like today. Restored from war. *Which means* . . . restoration is possible after the war. *Yes.* And maybe today, you're feeling completely destroyed after the war you've been in. The war you are currently in. The war that is before you that you're not sure you can win. The war that feels as though it will be your end. Yes. *But alas* . . . three words. . . . Restored. From. War. *Yes.*

And Beloved, there's *more.* . . . There will be something for you to take from the war. Something gained that cannot be taken from you. Something that would not have come to you any other way than but through the war. Yes. Beloved, if you're feeling the aftereffects of the war, if you're currently in the war, if you are facing the war that you fear will completely destroy you, you listen to me, OK?

There is restoration after the war. May these words be your sword. May these words be your shield. May these words be your battle cry, amen and amen.

{Ezekiel 38:8}

THINGS WON'T REMAIN AS THEY ARE

Things shall not remain as they are.

And here's the deal, Beloved . . . those seven words? Those seven words, when apart from one another, don't mean much. But strung together, they suddenly mean quite a bit. Yeah, those seven words are *life* to the one who desperately doesn't want things to remain as they are. They sure are. It's how Scripture meets us where we are. And maybe today, it's meeting *you*. Because maybe *you* are in a place . . . of loneliness. Or pain. Or brokenness. Or fear or worry or where-is-this-light-I-keep-hearing-about-cuz-it's-dark-in-this-tunnel-amen.

Maybe you're in a season you wish would end. Maybe you've had enough of the heat, and you don't just mean physically. Maybe you're sick of being stagnant, and you're ready for the water to flow, gosh-darn-it; your dry bones could use a good dance party. Maybe you're in a place of in-between, and maybe that in-between is located smack dab between the rock and the hard place, and frankly, you're over it. Maybe you've been climbing the mountain for so long that you've stopped believing you'll ever actually reach the top, and it's time to start believing again.

If so, Beloved, it's your lucky day, because I've got seven words for you that may be just what you need to start believing again . . . Things shall not remain as they are. Amen. A God Who provides four seasons so we will know that if we hate the one we are in, that in due time another will come. A God Who is in the business of continually bringing us the new that He actually ordained long ago, but we are just now seeing it. A God Who reminds us again and again that movement is medicine, and He ain't just talking our fleshly bods, but our souls that sustain us as well. *As well.*

So, *if* you are someone who today needs to know that things shall not remain as they are, then here are seven words for you, dear Someone. . . . Things shall not remain as they are. Hold on that. Trust it. Believe it. And don't stop believing. You are loved.

{Ezekiel 21:26}

NEVER ALONE

She went where the Spirit took her. Sometimes she loved it. Sometimes she hated it. But this much she knew—she was never alone.

She knew it was true. She knew that she'd go wherever the Spirit took her because the Spirit actually filled her lungs, and therefore, she would never find herself anywhere the Spirit was not. And there would be many times along the way in which she'd need to heavily lean into that fact and simply stop and breathe. To remind herself that she was not alone. That the God Who created her indeed resided within her walls. A God Who was known to part the largest waters in order to make a path of dry land. A God Who was known to spread out a feast in the midst of the wilderness or show up walking on water in the midst of the fiercest storm. A God Who always provided—always—even if she, like her ancestors the Israelites, didn't always recognize the provision as provision.

She went where the Spirit took her. Because the Spirit led the way. Up mountains and into valleys. Across deserts where she'd wondered, "Are You *really* here?" And at times into great celebrations where she'd witness water turned into wine . . . and she would tell you that those moments were among her most favorites—perhaps right after the times where when all seemed hopeless and dark, suddenly there shone a great light. She went where the Spirit took her. A journey of discovering just how real her God is, which allowed her to be her truest self. A God Who would take her places she'd always wanted to go and places she wouldn't wish upon her greatest enemy. Yes.

But every place she would go would have holy purpose. Every stop she would make would be sacred. Every war she should fight would yield treasure, and every struggle she endured would strengthen her far beyond the hardest of workouts. Yes. This was life. And she was never alone. And Beloved, truly I tell you, and please believe me cuz I so mean it . . . Neither are you. And lest you forget, and at times you will, I want you to stop and breathe. And say to yourself through a proclamation, a whisper, or perhaps even a tear . . . "You are *here*."

GOD DON'T LOSE

What to do when it seems as though the enemy has won . . . you remind yourself God don't lose.

That's right. And you even use poor English like that because it makes you feel street-tough to do so, and you could stand to feel a little street-tough right now in the midst of the tough you are in . . . Yes.

What to do when it seems as though the enemy has won? You remind yourself . . . *God don't lose. That's right.* And you tell yourself that over and over and over again, and you make it your "how-I-got-through-it" anthem or swap out your screensaver pic or whatever the heck else you gotta do to use this sword of truth to defend and protect you and see you through, amen. (Picture yourself plowing through a mighty army with your sword outstretched to cover your . . . well, you know.) Gosh, I love when I can see you grinning.

Beloved, repeat after me: God don't lose. God is with me, for me, and seeing me through this battle, this war, this time of sorrow, this time of heartache, this time of worry and restlessness. God has written my story. It is full of purpose, and God has equipped me to fulfill it on Earth. God's love for me is not only real, but all-encompassing and will never, ever be removed from me, no matter what. Hallelujah. I will get through. God is before me and behind me. I am not alone. I am mighty.

Now . . . and please, Beloved, repeat as often as necessary . . . *believe it.* I mean it. And don't stop believing. I love you.

NOT YET

Not yet.

Oh, you didn't know that there were two teeny, tiny words that have the power to keep our friend Hope alive and living her best life? Well, Darlin', now you do. Meet my girls Not Yet. Together they make quite a powerful duo, and they've already informed me that they would absolutely *love* to come home with you, and they will *gladly* rise up to greet you each morning and serve you well whenever you need them. (I still can't get them to start the coffee though.) But I digress. And repeat. These gals can seriously serve you well when it comes to keeping hope alive, because FYI, if you didn't already know . . . sometimes it's a struggle to keep hope alive.

Not . . . *yet*. Two words that when spoken aloud spark and smolder something within. The good stuff. *Hope*. The answer to questions like: Are you all healed up? Not . . . *yet*. Are you recovered? Not . . . *yet*. Has your prayer been answered, your desire fulfilled, have you gotten the promotion, received the offer, decided on what you'll do next, met the right one, crushed the goal, made peace with it, overcome it, dealt with it, moved on? Not . . . *yet*. See what I mean? My gal pals got it goin' on. Their strong will, combined with a side-splash of sass, are the perfect combo when it comes to kicking hopelessness right to the curb. Nice job, Ladies.

Beloved, believe today that whatever it is that you're waiting for, yearning for, longing for, for you or for someone you love . . . *whatever* it is that desperately needs hope to remain alive . . . *can* be kept alive. Because you listen to me, my friend—there's a mighty big difference between No . . . and Not *yet*. That's right. Hold on. Hang on. Breathe through. Believe. And don't stop believing. Amen.

WHEN GOD GIVES YOU A HOT MINUTE

Maybe God is giving you a hot minute to think about it.

Listen, I'm not saying God is, and I'm not saying God isn't. I'm just saying *maybe God is.* Maybe you're screaming, "Why won't you say something, God??" . . . while God is over here saying, "Ummm, how about a 'You're welcome,' young lady?" Just sayin'. I mean, it's a possibility, right? A scan back in time reveals that God has actually been *known* to give folks a hot minute to think about their It. Whatever there It was. And maybe today, Beloved, whatever *yours* is. Yes. Let's take a look . . .

Young Davey out in the field while his brothers are lined up like Cinderella's stepsisters, crossing their fingers and desperately hoping to be chosen. Jonah as he sat in that giganto fish. Moses after he left his homeland after doing what he shouldn't have done, even though he felt justified doing it. Yup. Esther sequestered, giving her time to come up with that idea for a banquet to expose the bad guy. Nice thinkin', girl. Good job. Dan in the den. Paul in the prison. All of the exiles that God brought to Babylon, as told in the book Jeremiah. Mary after the big birth. A group of disciples after the big death. Shepherds as they made the trek to visit the baby King, the One the angels had told them about. Joseph, who needed a night to sleep on it because his initial thought was to immediately kick his girl to the curb after finding out she was preggo and the kid was not his. Right.

Beloved, as with nearly all of my writings, I could go on and on. But I digress. Because what I'm simply/not-simply suggesting today, as a result of what I've witnessed throughout the stories of Scripture and my own life, is this . . . Maybe God is giving you a hot minute to think about it. Yes. To ponder. To consider. To play out different scenarios in your head and think about the benefits and potential implications of both. Maybe God, in fact, *is* being silent . . . *for your benefit.* Because perhaps the famous verse rings true . . . I want you to be still . . . and *know. XO,* Beloved.

WE RIDE AT DAWN

Me: "But God, I don't wanna go."
   God: "We ride at dawn."

Beloved, if there's one thing I've learned in my years here on Earth, it's this—my resistance is no match for the God Who wrote my story in full, named it Good, and then sent me to Earth to live it out in full color. And to help make my case, let's call upon some Bible biggies who'll concur . . .

Esther. Because as far as we know, she didn't ask to be taken into a palace with a harem of other young maidens, thus being separated from the only family she had left. Right. But God brought her there because the crown that awaited her put her in prime position to free all her people, amen. Yes.

Joseph. I'm fairly certain he didn't ask his bros, "Hey! Could you please throw me into this deep well and abandon me, only to change your mind and actually sell me instead so you can make a few bucks off of me?" But Joe went, as a slave, with his new owners, to a palace where he would serve and exceed all expectations and, like Esther, be brought into position to actually save his people by providing food for them in their famine (even his bros, those scoundrels). Yup.

Jonah. The guy was given an order by God to go and deliver hard news, to which he said, "Umm, yeah, heck no!" Fine and dandy, Jonah, do as you will. God will just stick you on a ship upon stormy seas, your crewmates will toss you overboard, and there'll be a giganto fish waiting to swallow you whole, giving you a few days to think about it, and then spit you back up and send you on your way to exactly where you didn't want to go. *Right.*

Beloved, I could go on. Like for a really long time, actually. I have my own stories of not wanting to go to wherever it was, and God bypassing my excuses because they didn't hold up against God's purposeful plan for me. *Yes.* So when things don't make sense, when it seems far more like punishment than provision or protection, when you wish it were different but you know you're not God, circle back to these folks, OK? Perfect. We ride at dawn.

RELIEF COMES

Relief comes.

Two words. One pretty dang powerful truth. Amen.

Beloved, could you put these two words into your two fists today and carry them with you today, with a stubborn determination today, to not let them go, no-matter-what-amen? Could you? If these two words were the only two words that you heard today, would they be enough for you to hold on one more day, to the hope that you have (left), without completely discarding it into the trash? Would they? Beloved, relief comes. Some way. Somehow. It sure does. In ways we like—like an unexpected oasis in the midst of the desert, a surprise spring that suddenly shoots up from the land we were certain was dead. In ways we don't like—like a mighty storm that comes in due season to take down the heat and replace it with the cool air that we are so desperate to breathe.

Beloved, relief comes. It's the two-word truth that we can bury deep within and depend on when the excessive heat comes. And boy, does the heat come. No doubt. And amen. I don't know about you, Beloved, but where I live, the summer forecast is sometimes named "Oppressive," and amen to the person-who-named-it, because that is exactly, and I do mean *exactly*, what it feels like. Oppressive. So, in our lives here on Earth, the question is this: Will oppressive heat come? Yes. The next question is this: Will relief come? The answer is *also yes*.

Beloved, if you, are currently in the midst of oppressive heat . . . whatever that looks like for *you* . . . I have two words I want you to hold on to, OK? Two words for you to tell yourself over and over again until they're stuck in your heart-mind-and-soul like a really good '80s rock song . . . Relief comes. It sure does. Believe it. And don't stop believing. *XO.*

WHEN GOD GIVES YOU "WHEN"

For the one who is waiting . . . one word to hold on to . . . when.

When keeps us going. When keeps us looking ahead. When sings "Don't Stop Believin'" when we're fully ready to say "Screw it!" and stop fighting the good fight of faith 'til the end. When is the exhale of Hope. When reeks of Anticipation. When, spoken over and over again until it makes an immovable track over the land in our head, becomes the automatic response when our thoughts start to taunt us with things like, "Do you *really* think God is ever gonna do that for you??" And without even realizing it, you unknowingly smile and unknowingly answer because that's what an automatic response is—automatic. You hear yourself clear your throat and boldly interrupt with, "Excuse me, don't you mean *when*?" Yes.

When God does. When God gets me there. When I arrive. When I am better. When the fog lifts, the storm ceases, the winds are calm once again. When. When this drought is over. When this season ends. When this situation is finally resolved, or this huge assignment is finally completed. When. When sings. When rejoices. When is the voice of Faith, for we know that Faith is the assurance of things hoped for, the conviction of things not seen. (Shout-out to the amazing writers of Hebrews. Y'all rock and have helped me on my journey a *ton*.) *When.*

Beloved, Moses gave this word to the Israelites whom he'd come to love over the forty years he'd been leading them to new land—*their* new land. He gave them this word knowing that his time was drawing near and that he wouldn't be going with them into that new promised land. A word they could hold on to. A word they could return to, especially when Doubt and Fear threatened to kill/steal/destroy them. A word they could repeat in their hearts and their minds over and over and over again that would serve as strength for their souls when the journey got exhaustingly long, *amen.*

When. Take the word, Beloved. It's a really great word. And read Deuteronomy. It's a really great book. Hebrews too. *XO.* Love ya. Mean it.

ASK FOR COURAGE

Ask for courage.

To get up and believe one more day. To do the hard thing you don't want to do, but you know in your gut you must do. Ask for courage. To take the time you need to heal. To have the conversation . . . or to hold back from having said conversation until the emotion of anger has had at least a moment or two to have her time to work through it, at least a bit. Ask for courage. Courage to learn, courage to try, courage to take this leap of faith you've been hearing so much about. Courage to fly over the radar like Maverick instead of continuing to always fly under it . . . or the courage to fly under it if it's time for you to pull back.

Ask for courage. The courage to say Yes. The courage to say No. The courage to guard your ground either way. The courage to trust what it is that God planted deep within you, believing it'll come to fruition one day. Ask for courage. To make change. To be change. To help someone in this world believe that change is possible, and *you* are living proof. *Yes.* To carry yourself through this very day in a way that speaks volumes about Who your God is. Yes. Ask for courage. To stand up. To sit down. To go to the well by yourself or take that first step into the wilderness known as Unknown. Yes. Ask for courage. To be brave. To be still. To be *you* wherever you go . . . relying heavily on the fact that indeed your God is with you, and, in fact, your God will never leave you. So continually return to that tree of life, will ya? Great.

Beloved, perhaps today would be a really great day to *ask for courage.*

THE MOUNTAIN IS YOUR INHERITANCE

After all that . . . the OMG revelation . . . that mountain is my inheritance.

Sits with mouth gaping wide open. And I'm-not-kidding-amen. The mountains God moved, even the ones I didn't know about. The mountains God used to strengthen me by making me climb them, even though I didn't want to and told Him as much. The mountains I crushed. The mountains God leveled. The mountains that were made into the very roads that would take me exactly where I was to go next on my journey. . . . Yes. These Mountains . . . are *holy*. And they *are* my . . . *inheritance*. OMG. Seriously. Every one of them seeping with value and worth. Every one of them drenched with purpose (or is that just my sweat?). I digress.

Beloved, our mountains were carefully and perfectly placed by the God Who wrote our story and map to include them . . . therefore making them . . . *holy*. Yes. They are our inheritance. Our legacy. Dripping with wisdom gained. Overflowing with countless ways in which we saw God face-to-face as a result of them. Yes. We can't deny that. The nights crying into our pillow begging God to take them away. The days screaming at God, "Why? And why me? And why now? *Why?*" The mornings we didn't feel like we could get out of bed or take another step, and the evenings we collapsed in exhaustion and began questioning if it was all worth it.

Beloved, do you know how it is that I know right now that you're nodding your head in agreement, even if only internally? *Because we've all been there.* Every single one of us, despite what social-media land displays through posed pics and filters, and I mean that, amen. What if, and I mean this too, we renamed the mountains and called them our holy inheritance? Would it help? I can't say. But perhaps it can't hurt to try. Because truly I tell you, Beloved . . . Peace heals. Let that soak in, please. I love you, and you are loved.

{Isaiah 57:13}

THE GOD WHO DOES THE IMPOSSIBLE

What if the most powerful part of Mary's immaculate conception story is the fact that you don't have to do a darn thing in order for God to do the impossible?

Today, Beloved, I bring before you some super-early morning thoughts I had before cracking open the Book. Then I cracked open the Book. Cuz that's what I do. And one of my faves, King Hezekiah, shared these words he had written after he had been sick, and after he had recovered. Here's what he wrote . . . "But what can I say? For he has spoken to me, and he himself has done it." I know, right? Now he's one of your favorites too. Because did I mention the fact that H wasn't just sick with a tummy ache or a few simple sneezes? The guy was near death, *so* close in fact that the prophet Isaiah had come to him and said, "Listen, buddy, you'd better get things in order around here." So when H recovered, what he knew was this . . . I didn't do this. There's no way I could do this. God did this. And man, I'm so glad that God did.

Beloved, what if we knew *and believed* that God's ability to do the impossible doesn't hinge on whether or not you and I do and say all the "right" things? What kind of awe would it cause in our soul, and what kind of life would it bring? A pretty stinkin' awesome one, if you ask me. The fact that at *any moment* God may show up on your doorstep and tell you that you're about to bring forth something new—no matter *who* you are.

Beloved, for just *one* second, I want you to believe that *no matter who you are* or *where you've been* or *whatever the heck is going on within you* . . . it is breeding ground for what God has planned for you . . . and it's not dependent on you fitting the mold you've been led to believe is required. *Amen.* Your story's been written. It's holy, set apart. It's filled with power and purpose and all of the things, and it's perfect, as in whole and complete. *Yes.* So may you live with eyes wide open . . . believing that the next incredible OMG moment . . . will be yours.

{Isaiah 38:15}

IN A VERY LITTLE WHILE

Five words. That may be exactly the hem you need today.

To hold on to. To cling to. To refuse to let go of, cuz at this point, it's all you got. Right. Five little words that make up the hem. The hem that for today shall be enough. (A girl sits up proper and tall while speaking the word "Shall." It's just a thing that makes it more legit somehow. I encourage you to try it.)

OK, I'm back. ". . . in a very little while." In a very little while. Things will get better. The answer will come. Rest will be given, and the war will finally be over . . . and won. In a very little while. Restoration will be a part of my story. Glory will shine all around me. Healing will finally, *finally* feel like it's making some serious headway, and *finally* the battle I'm in will be over, and I'll be the victor. In a very little while. The rain will come. The rain will stop. The storm will end, and that rainbow I *know* is out there somewhere will finally be seen, and I'll snap a pic and share it online, cuz that's what us humans do.

In a very little while. Five little words that may, in fact, be just what you need today, Beloved. To hold on to and believe. Yes, *believe.* Because this is the part where I remind you that what's gonna save your spirit from diving nose-first into the pit today isn't *receiving* the answer you want today; it's *believing* you will receive the answer you want today. Amen. God in God's goodness . . . simply gives us a hem to hold on to. And *today*, I reckon that hem may look like five covered-in-yellow-so-you-and-I-don't-miss-em words—words that set aflame the hope that is wrapped in swaddling cloths and lying within the manger that is your soul. *Yes.*

Protected. Indeed. Covered. Amen. Return there. Do it. I mean it. " . . . in a very little while . . ." Believe it. For you, for someone you know, for the situation you are in that seems to be never-ending. And don't stop believin'. I mean that too. Big love.

{Isaiah 29:17}

FED AMONG THE RUINS

You will be fed among the ruins.

For the one today asking, "Now what?" After the break-up, the mix-up, the mess-up, the shake-up. After the destruction, the battle, the war, the letting-go that no one understands was far harder than simply unclenching your fist, amen. It was so much more. After whatever it was that now places you in what feels like a pile of ruins, and you're starting to wonder if you did the right thing, or if you even had a choice at all, cuz you sure never wanted to be here . . . in the ruins . . . and yet . . . here you are. Yes. So for the one asking, "Now what???" . . . Hear this. Believe this. And don't *stop* believing this or you'll leave me no choice but to grab my boom box and hike it up on my shoulder and sing to you John Cusack-style outside your bedroom window, and believe me—you really don't want that. But I do hope you're smiling now.

Beloved, you will be fed among the ruins. You *will*.

I actually read the words "shall feed among the ruins" a couple mornings ago in my daily reading, but they've stayed. And I reckon it's because they have staying power. And I've learned over the years that when certain words rise up to meet me, there's a good chance that someone in this big-yet-small world of ours may just need them. To revive them or rehydrate them or replenish them or re-strengthen them.

And maybe today, Beloved, that someone is you. If so, take and eat. This is the body given for you. Maybe it's someone you know. If so, take and feed the hungry, the sheep, the starving by the side of the sea. Maybe they're words you want to drink up and add to the well that lies deep within you—a well you can draw from when your soul is dying of thirst. *Yes.*

Beloved, you will be fed among the ruins. You sure will. Oh, and one more thing. See that first set of scenarios I mentioned? Yeah, well, then I guess you'll notice that what each have in common is one little-but-powerful word. *Up.* Bing bang boom. Believe-it-I-mean-it. Big love.

{Isaiah 5:17}

DON'T ABANDON YOURSELF

Thou shalt not be so desperate to fit in that thou abandon thy truest self.

I wrote the words. I said what I said. And then I picked up my Bible and read what I read. Amen. I read words found in Isaiah that said, "and those who forsake the Lord shall be consumed," . . . and my first thought was, "Ain't it the truth." Amen again. For if I forget the God Who is *in* me, I will, in fact, be consumed by the world *around* me and forget who I *am*. Seriously, how stinkin' good is that? If I abandon my truest self—God *in* me—then I will forget the strength that I have been given, the voice that I have been given. A voice that has changed in some ways over time, because that's how maturity works. Just ask any junior high boy.

Beloved, your truest self lies deep within. In the inner sanctuary, on sacred grounds, lodged safely and securely within the holiest of holies, darn right. Don't forget who you are. Don't abandon your truest self. Don't forsake or let go of what sets you apart—the very definition of holy, by the way. Return to yourself. For to do so, I believe, is to return to your God. The still, small voice within. The voice that may not always be recognized but still remains. The voice that may be stifled at times but continues to rise up again and again, no matter how many times you try to silence it with your self-condemnation and busyness. The voice that is . . . God *in you*. The same God Whose breath fills your lungs and serves as a moment-by-moment reminder that until that breath is returned . . . there is something right here on this Earth for you, or for you to do. Yes. For your story is complete, and your God is faithful to see you through to the very last page that won't end with "The End," but instead with "*Amen.*"

You'd better believe it. Today, Beloved, may you honor who you are. May you remember that you are worthy. May you remember that you are seen. May you remember that you are heard, even when it sure doesn't feel like it. May you not abandon your truest self but return to her instead. Big-Love-I-Mean-It-Amen. *XO.*

THE HARD STUFF

I can't say this enough—many of the flowery, feel-good verses you know were spoken in the midst of some really hard, really hard stuff.

And here's how I hope this encourages you, if that's you . . . because if you are currently in the midst of some really hard, really hard stuff, then these verses in fact are for *you.*

Yes, i.e., Jeremiah 29:11. Bible Biggie. "For I know the plans I have for you . . ." Awesome. Seriously, it's awesome. But also, keep in mind that the words were spoken to people who were someplace they did *not* want to be, and, therefore, God spoke these words to *encourage them and strengthen them to get through it. Yes.*

Here's another Biggie: Esther 4:14. "Perhaps this is the moment for which you were created." Or better translated, in my opinion—"Perhaps you have been brought into position for such a time as this . . ." To do something no one else dared to do, like approach the King without an appointment, despite the risk of having your head chopped off, because you realize that *you* are the one who has been brought into position to do so. You were brought there to *do a hard thing*—to disrupt the way things had always been done, to risk your life for the sake of *all* your people, because your cousin who raised you actually *spoke* these Bible Biggie words to our girl Esther as he framed it with, in so many words . . . "Listen, either way, God's gonna save God's people, I'm just sayin', have you stopped to consider, Esther, that perhaps *you* have been brought into position to do it? That your place in the palace isn't just fluff and plush but actually a place you've been brought to in order to bring *change?*"

Beloved, the words of Scripture, including all the Biggies, are not limited to those whose life is going swimmingly well. They're *also* for the one who feels as though he/she is drowning. They're not only for the one who is well-fed, but also for the one starving to death. They're not only for the one who feels life couldn't get any better, but also for the one who's not sure it could get any worse. Press on. Lean in. Amen.

{Jeremiah 29:11; Esther 4:14}

THE HARDEST WORKOUTS

The hardest workouts you will endure will have nothing to do with your flesh.

They may *affect* your flesh. As a matter of fact, there's a good chance that they will, but your most massive struggles/workouts/whatever you want to call them will take place deep within. Between you. And your God. The workout that screams out, "Why???" Cuz I reckon that one's the biggest. The hardest. The most painful. Amen. Every workout within that puts you right in Jacob's wrestling shoes. And when they do . . . you remember what Jacob did . . . and what Jacob said . . . I ain't letting go 'til You bless me. Amen. *That's* gonna be the end result of this workout, You hear me, God? *That's* gonna be the gain for this pain. *That's* what's gonna get me through this agony . . . the knowing that it is a part of my story . . . the one filled with glory . . . the one clothed in holiness and covering me in my humanness like fig leaves in the garden or swaddling clothes in the manger.

Beloved, the hardest workouts we endure while we're here take place within us. I know you agree. *Because you've had those workouts.* Maybe you're in the middle of one right now, and maybe it's your most grueling yet. Maybe blood-sweat-and-tears are a pretty accurate description of what the workout is bringing forth out of you. Beloved, the workouts within are the most intimate encounters you will have with your God. Just ask any wrestler if their sport is not, in fact, the most intimate. Right.

Don't let go. Endure. Your strength is increasing, and your knowing of Who your God is to you is multiplying in a way that rivals those fish and loaves on the side of the sea. Your God is with you. Within you. Drawing every ounce of purpose you have been given right out of you, for it is truly *that* mighty. Believe it. Because believing it is gonna save your butt from drowning and your heart from kissing all hope goodbye. It's gonna strengthen you to not only endure it, but to trust that in the end, it'll be worth it, and you will emerge even stronger than you were before you got called into the ring.

PRAY ABOUT ABSOLUTELY EVERYTHING

Wanna see God more? Pray about absolutely everything.

Yes. Now keep in mind that God is both light *and* shield. God will reveal, *and* God will conceal, and we *thank* God for that, because our humanness was not fashioned to fully comprehend our holiness. Read-that-again-please-amen. Yes.

To pray is to pry open our eyes. To resurrect hope. To light our own fire within through the power that we have been given—*oneness* with the Triune—God, Jesus, the Holy Spirit. Indeed. Pray about *everything*. The conversation you don't want to have. The fact that the fridge is nearing depletion and payday isn't 'til Friday. Pray about the coworker that's rubbing you every which way but right, or the workload you can't seem to balance. Ask God to show you what you need to do for your health, ahem, your *whole* health—mind, body, spirit. Ask God to give you a sign in the decision you have to make that's kicking your butt and leaving you torn. Ask God to protect him/her from the heat of the sun, or ask God to show you how He intends to provide, because you *know* God is Provider . . . and then watch for the paper clip on the sidewalk. Pray about absolutely everything. Because you *can*. Because prayer isn't limited to church pews, and it sure as heck can't be taken from you, because prayer is intimate and within and between you and your God, thank God and amen.

Beloved, I am telling you a surefire way to see God *more*. . . . Pray about absolutely *everything*. That's it. Now, there *is* something else that must be said: You will not always like the answer God gives, and *that*, my friends, is an understatement. So in those times, return to the truth that everything has value, everything has worth, everything has purpose, including you/her/him/them . . . and that *purpose* was woven into the story and into our souls before the foundation of the world, and it *will*, not "it might," it *will* be fulfilled. By the One Who is Alpha, Omega, Beginning and End, Author and Finisher and Ultimate Completer. Amen.

WHEN YOU NEED TO TAKE IT EASY

If your soul is torn by trouble, you're gonna need to take it easy.

Torn tendon. That's what the MRI revealed. Not me, but someone I know, and now that she knows, the next right steps can be taken. Steps that include . . . taking it easy. Not bearing weight upon it. Being careful not to injure it further. Knowing that it will take time to heal. Yes.

Beloved, I am *convinced* (geesh, I sound like Paul) that God gave us our *flesh* in order to teach us about our *soul.* I sure am. Cuz see, when it comes to our bodies, we seem to "get it." Cuz see, if I told this girl I know with the torn tendon to get up and run some laps around the building today, someone watching would (and should) say, "Are you crazy? Why would you make this girl with a torn tendon run laps when she can barely walk??" *Exactly.*

Our tendons tear. Our muscles tear. Our skin tears, and in turn gushes blood. Our *souls* tear too. They sure do. They *all* do from time to time. So may we learn from our flesh as to what to do when they do. . . . Take it easy. Be careful not to bear additional weight on it, which may cause it to injure further. Know that it will take time to heal. Yes. And listen, if it is not your *own* soul at this time that is torn, but the soul of someone you know, do what you'd do if he/she had a torn tendon. . . . Can I bring you something? Can I help carry that for you? Is there anything I can do that would help make your life a bit easier as you heal? Right.

Beloved, if your soul is torn by trouble, you're gonna need to take it easy. Doctor's orders. I mean it. *XO.*

{Proverbs 27:9}

GOD'S WAY OF SETTING YOU FREE

God setting you free . . . may look like people driving you out. Just remember that.

Read that again and check in with Exodus for further confirmation of this pos-sibility. And although we can't make sense of "why in the world" God would choose *this* way to set us free . . . God's Spirit within us rises up to remind us . . . My ways are not your ways. *No doubt.*

Cuz see, *we* would choose a farewell party—every time. And sometimes that's the case, and it's fabulous/amazing/all-things-awesome, and *sometimes*, that's not the case. And yet, in *every* case, I have to return to the God Who *rescues* and *sets free*. The God Who sees the oppression and hearkens unto all of the cries. The God Who frees us from what's holding us back, from who or what is keeping us in captivity. The God Who breaks chains of bondage, tears down walls, flings open prison cells, calls out slavery, turns over tables, and powerfully proclaims . . . *enough*! She is *Mine*. And it is *time*.

Beloved, the words you see on the page are words that I have lived to tell. And I tell them here, for the one who needs a new way to see through the pain. To catch light in the pit of the darkness. To give meaning, value, and worth to what felt like/feels like such severe punishment from God that you spend sleepless nights wrestling with what you could've possibly done wrong. For truly I tell you, again hear me say, that God setting you *free* . . . may look like people driving you *out*. And for those on the other side of this driving out—you didn't leave empty-handed, even if that's how it feels. And for those in the midst of it, you will *not* leave empty-handed; you will leave with something more valuable than rubies and more precious than diamonds . . .

The truth that a God Who once set His people free . . . *still does*. In ways we under-stand and in ways we don't. In ways we like and in ways we don't. In ways that taste like Heaven and in ways that reek like hell. And that very same God—the God Who sets free—will see you through to the end. *Amen.*

THE PLACE YOU DON'T WANT TO BE

Normalize this—the first place you will most likely dwell for a spell after being set free, driven out, let go . . . is the desert, the wilderness, or some other place you do not want to be.

If I do one thing here, I hope it's to take the hard and call it holy, so that if even *one* person needs to know in the midst of their hard that it is *in* the hard that new life is conceived and eventually delivered . . . then they get to *hear* that. It's to normalize our human realities so no one believes they're somehow *excluded* from God's master plan. Beloved, I can't count how many times I think to myself . . . Is part of my purpose here on Earth to say hard things so people will know that hard is actually necessary for producing new life? And by the way, Lord, if that's the case, I guess it explains a lot about me and my journey from unknowing to knowing, to copiously brave to confidently bold.

But Beloved, here's the thing—I think *normalizing* the hard *unites* us in our shared humanity, and *unity* leads to peace, and looking out for one another instead of seeking to destroy one another. So today, let's normalize *this*: The first place you will most likely dwell for a spell after being set free, driven out, let go . . . is the desert, the wilderness, or some other place you do *not* want to be. And I *guarantee* that anyone who's already experienced this is nodding their head and whispering amen. So for the one who is *currently* there . . . receive their nods and amens as proof that they *survived* that time, and you will too. Yes.

Cuz see, the thing about time in the desert, the wilderness . . . is that it's quiet, void of outside voices. The only opposition you face is the plaguing thoughts that are seeking to kill/steal/destroy you. But you won't let 'em. Cuz see, you know darn well, whether you liked it or not . . . God set you free, drove you out, freed you by letting you go . . . so now *you're* gonna take those thoughts captive . . . as you expectantly wait . . . for what's *next*.

RIGHT THROUGH THE STORM

The birds kept singing . . . right through the storm . . . and that taught her something . . . huge.

I awoke to thunder that rumbled and lightning that crashed through the darkness of morn. I could hear the sound of spring rains falling from Heaven above and the sound of it dancing upon the Earth as it arrived . . . and I could almost hear the Earth giving thanks for it. And through it all . . . the birds kept singing. And yet again, I am reminded that not *only* does God speak through God's Word, but God *also* speaks through God's World.

The birds kept singing . . . right through the storm. Perhaps as a form of communication between kindred, a battle cry to keep on singing, keep on praising, keep on trusting and believing right through the storm. Perhaps as a way to remind herself that despite all that was going on *around* her, no one could take from her the song from *within* her, the song her God had *given* her. Perhaps as a way to protect her heart-mind-and-soul from thoughts that could arise in situations like these, in these kinds of storms—thoughts like . . . "You're doomed" or "You'll never survive this." Perhaps the songs that she sang, the words that she tweeted, the lyrics she chirped off-key, sounded instead like . . . "I will survive" and "Nothin's gonna stop us now." Either way, that beautiful bird would keep on singing. For she knew that she'd be provided for and protected no matter *what* situation or storm she found herself in.

Beloved, after I wrote the words you see in the pic, I read from the Word my readings today. And if you for *one* second think that they all spoke of either songs to sing, or the clapping of hands that sounds to me much like thunder, or the very birds of the air that God made . . . well then, you're absolutely right. Cuz God is super cool like that, and confirming is His gift to us. Dang, what a great morning. Right in the midst of the storm.

{Deuteronomy 31–32; Psalm 47; Luke 12}

WHAT THE HECK IS THIS?

Umm . . . Lord . . . what the heck is this?

True or False: God rained down manna from Heaven for the Israelites when they were complaining to Moses about how hungry they were. *False.* And yes, you read that right, and yes, I'll fight ya on it if you don't believe me. Cuz truly I tell you, Beloved, this revelation will likely remain in my Top 5 forever because it is *that* freaking good *and*, I believe, absolutely life-transforming. So as the young kids say, "Let's goooo."

After the Israelites watched God part the sea that stood before them by using strong winds, and after they composed and sang their sure-to-win-a-Grammy song of praise to their God for doing the impossible . . . sure enough, after three days in the desert, they were back to complaining because FYI, *that's what we do*. We rock at it. Anywho, they complained to Moses and Aaron, cuz that's who is there (which is *also* what we do), so Moses talked to God about it, and God told him He'd rain down *bread* from Heaven. *Which God did.* But when the Israelites saw it, and it didn't look like a killer loaf of rye or fab pretzel roll, they *named it manna*, which translates (and I *so* love this): "*Ummm . . . what the heck is this?*" Which, of course, is *also* what we do.

When the provision doesn't align with our expectation. When we beg for bread, and God gives us flakes. When we ask for new mountains to climb, and God gives us twenty-seven seventh graders to teach and to guide while you're over here packin' your bags for the Alps. *Yup.* Beloved, God is Provider, so Providing is what God does. Will it always look like something we recognize as provision? History today tells us No. Will it always come in the form that we want? Also no. It may be flakes to gather to make enough for a meal, instead of a big fat cinnamon roll lathered in icing. Just sayin'.

So today, consider asking yourself . . . Is God, in fact, providing for me, but because I don't recognize it, I'm calling it manna? Cool food for thought. No pun intended. Well, kinda. *XO.*

{Exodus 16}

WATCH FOR IT

The God Who hears you . . . will send help to you. Watch for it.

Ahhh, the story of Moses, and his enormous task of leading all of God's people out . . . and there were a *lot*, and if you've ever been around a *lot*, then you *too* know, that at times—it's a *lot*. Amen. So it's proving to *be* a lot for our guy Moses, and so Moses cries out to God. Good call, M. And Beloved, I bet it's a prayer you've prayed a time or two, and I don't even have to know you to know that. Here it goes—"Ugh!! What am I supposed to *do* with these people??"

Beloved, God heard Moses. God hears *you*. God sent help to Moses. God will send help to *you*. *Watch* for it . . . and *name* it . . . God Helps. *Yes.* When Moses realized it was time to choose someone else to head into war while he prayed for the one he would send . . . there was Joshua. And when M's arms were tired and worn out, and he couldn't lift them anymore to pray through the war because the weight of what he was carrying was *so* dang heavy . . . here come Aaron and Hur, and they slide a big stone under M's butt and say, "Have a seat. The two of *us* are gonna lift your arms to heaven for a while." I know, right?

But wait . . . there's more. For Moses would need *more* than help carrying his burdens; he would *also* need guidance as to how to move forward leading these people in order to avoid total burnout. Along comes Jethro. M's father-in-law. Yup. Just like that, Jethro shows up, and not only *that*, but he brings with him his daughter, M's wife, and M's kids. Can you *imagine* how much that meant to M? Now you know why I heart Jethro, and why he made it into today's daily doodle. And J's counsel . . . to his son-in-law Moses . . . is loving, kind, and straightforward . . . "Moses, you can't do this all by yourself. It's too much for one person."

Get yourself some help. God will be with you. I know, right? So. dang. good.

{Exodus 17–18}

FUELED BY FAITH

With a faith that refused to stop believing, she would use her voice to move mountains.

A faith that refuses to stop believing can tear down walls and part seas and survive stints in blazing hot furnaces, the fires they are thrown into, and the fires they stumble and fall into all on their own. A faith that refuses to stop believing can break prison chains and call forth life from the grave, and even look forward with great expectation to the day her dry bones will dance once again, her ashes will once again give birth to beauty, her heart will fully love and *be* fully loved again . . . and her current situation and season will change. And she *knows* that it's true, so she keeps on believing and looking ahead . . . believing there's more for her. *Yes.*

A faith that refuses to stop believing knows that what may *appear* impossible is not impossible at all, as long it keeps on *believing* that all things *are*, in fact, possible for the One for Whom all things are possible, *yes and amen*. She who *believes it.* A faith that refuses to stop believing can take captive the thoughts that seek to steal/kill/destroy her as they boldly approach the threshold of her mind and *dare* to set themselves up against the knowledge of Who her God is.

A faith that refuses to stop believing knows that one drop of oil is enough, one kid's sack lunch is enough, one fist-sized cloud after years of drought-induced famine is enough . . . to spark the flame known as hope. And hope is all we need. To move forward. To keep going. It's the answer to the question, "How do you do it?" Yes. A faith that refuses to stop believing also knows that one single prayer prayed . . . spoken *or* unspoken . . . is enough to hearken the ear of the God Who *always* hears her, *no matter what* and where she is. Amen.

Beloved, the Spirit within you is God's breath. The breath of your soul while you're here on this Earth. A holy guarantee of where you were conceived and where you will one day return. It's powerful. And it can move mountains. Believe it. Love ya, mean it. Amen.

CALM ME AS YOU CALL ME

Lord, calm me . . . as You call me . . . to walk on water.

Face giants. Tear down walls. Overturn tables that need overturning. Use the voice You have given me to move mountains and set people free. Yes. Calm me as You call me. To pick up my mat and walk, because at some point, lyin' around doin' nothin' while simultaneously complaining about how "good" others have it, is enough. Calm me as You call me. To pray continuously, even when it's the same ask on repeat. To approach Your throne not *only* with my desperate needs, but also with my deepest desires, because as Your kid, I *can*. To trust You even when what I'm going through doesn't make sense, and as You know, Lord, that's a tough one.

Calm me . . . as You *call* me. To the edge of the sea or to endure the time in the wilderness, reminding me that You prepare *feasts* in the wilderness—feasts that can *only* be found there. Yes. To persevere through the war, reminding me that I won't leave empty-handed. To breathe through the pains of labor, reminding me that You *refuse* to allow pain without causing *something new* to be born. Calm me as You call me. To walk on water. To do what right now seems impossible. To keep my eyes fixed on You so I don't drown.

Calm me as You call me, Lord . . . to keep on going, keep on trusting, keep on hoping, and keep on believing that *wherever* You call me is a part of the story *you* wrote for me, which means even if I don't/can't understand it . . . I know *full well* there is purpose *for* it, cuz You *sure* as heck didn't waste the ink of Your pen, not to *mention* the blood-ink of Your Son, on what isn't purposeful. Calm me as You call me. To do the thing or not do the thing. To stand up or sit down. To get to work or take a break. To live fully in the land You have given me, knowing there's a *really* good possibility according to Your track history that there is still new land that awaits me. Yes. Calm me as You call me. Cuz a girl who walks on water . . . needs herself some steady feet.

FOR THE ONE WHO IS SCARED, ANXIOUS, OR OVERWHELMED

Maybe it's you. Maybe it's someone you know. Maybe it's both.

Beloved, today may your stopping be your starting. Yes. May you start with what steadies you before your day shakes you. May you begin your day with a renewing, a refreshing, a rehydrating and refueling, allowing you to reset to a place of resurrection hope . . . *refusing* to walk back into that grave. *Not today*, Satan. Here are a few of the lyrics I penned today . . . as a way to stop . . . be still . . . remind myself what I know to be true because the truth is a great place to start, amen.

Lord, this much I *know* . . . my life is in Your hands and in Your book. I know every page of my story's been written, and I know every word holds value and worth. I know I won't always like/appreciate/understand every word, and I *know it's* OK *if I don't*. I know You fearfully and wonderfully created me as a vessel for Your Spirit, and I know the same goes for everyone else. I know that You formed my innermost being, supplying it with all I would need as I live out my days, and because You know Your kids love a good hunt-for-treasure, You mapped out our journeys in such a way that we would continually be discovering and uncovering more and more of who You are and who we are, *amen*.

I know there won't be even *one* day in which You will not be sovereign and not *one* day when Your grace and mercy and compassions aren't new. And I'm all here for all of those Lord. Just sayin'. I know there's not *one* day that You will forget to spin the world, wake up the sun, or provide and protect as Heavenly Parent. I know that my journey is under Your watchful eye, Lord, and *because* it is . . . I can *start* this day from this place of *still* . . . this place of *rest* . . . this place of *peace* . . . which is sooo much better than starting from anxious, amen. It sure is.

CATCHING YOUR BREATH

Today may you catch your breath . . . and realize it's the God Who is with you.

The God Who has always been with you and will forever and always be with you. The God Who sees you, hears you, knows you—your name, your plight, the number of hairs on your head, the inner fight. The outer fight. Every fight. Amen. The God Who captures every tear that never sees the light of day. The God Who collects every one of 'em in a bottle and labels it, "Water for her new land, the place where her redemption will be realized and where some things will finally make sense to her as to her question of Why." The God Who sees the bite marks, the knife in your back, the hurt you're convinced will be the death of you, the pain that feels like it just won't end. The God Who whispers into your darkness . . . I promise you there is purpose for all of this, and there will be something for you to take from this war you are in. And it may just be . . . *you.*

Yes. A discovery of *you.* Of who you are. A new realization of the strength you possess, a new understanding of what lies within, a new courage and strength to persevere through whatever lies ahead because you've *done* it before, and so you *know* you can do it again. *Amen.* You are on sacred ground. You are being refined. You are being prepared. For all that lies ahead for you. A journey you can't see, mapped out by the God Who wrote your story in full before you lived day one and Who gives you your breath as holy guarantee that you're never alone, and lest you forget . . . whew . . . all you need do . . . is stop . . . and . . . *breathe.*

That's *God.* With you and within you. Always and in all ways. And *this* you shall rely on. *This* shall be your rock. *This* will will be your way to weather any storm and survive any stints in the places you don't want to be. Beloved, today may you catch your breath and know it's God. I love you. Amen.

Day 295

GOD HEARS YOUR REAL VOICE

God hears your prayer. Awesome, right? But wait—level up. God hears your voice in your prayer. I know, right?

The thing about hanging out with me at *all*, is that you must know that there will be times when bits of mind go flying all over the place and land upon you *as my mind is continually blown*. And by the way, Lord, thanks—You *know* that's my fave. Which is *exactly* what happened while I was reading Psalm 64 in the KJV—Mind. Blown.

"Hear my voice, O God, in my prayer . . ."

Yes. Hear my *voice* in my prayer. Hear my tone, my trembling. Hear my excitement, my fear, my worry, my doubt. Hear every inflection caused by my current affliction—*yes*, Lord, hear my *voice* in my prayer. Hear my voice as it shakes . . . and steady it, Lord. Hear my voice as it weeps . . . and comfort it. Hear my voice as it bravely whispers to self, "I can *do* this," . . . and confirm or dispel it. Hear my voice as it raises an octave. Hear it when it never quite catches breath. Hear my voice as it desperately tries to make sense of what the heck is going on. Hear it as it struggles to know what to do. As it tries figure out what next steps it should take . . . while resting in the truth that *You* direct every one.

Hear my voice in my prayer. As it quivers, explodes, breathes fire. And since *You* know the cause of the fire, Lord, either extinguish it . . . or fan the flames. Lord, hear my voice in my prayer. My desperation, appreciation, sorrow, lament, gratitude, joy, jealousy, hopefulness—all the stuff I got goin' on in this soul of mine, Lord, that *You* hold forever. And seriously, a *huge* thank you for that.

Beloved, God does more than *hear* your prayer. God hears your *voice* in your prayer. I know, right? How awesome is that?? *Especially* when you keep in mind that the One Who hears your voice *in* it, is the same One Who leads and guides, protects and provides—the One for Whom all things are possible and nothing is too hard. The One Who *is* your Ride *and* Die. Rock on.

THE GIFT OF GRAVE REMINDERS

Could grave reminders be among the greatest gifts we receive?

Truly I tell you, I think so. Based on Who I know God to be, I can't think of any other way to chalk up Grave Reminders, except for under the heading, "The Greatest Gifts Given This Side of Heaven."

Grave Reminders. Two words on my heart every Ash Wednesday as I look at the ashes that will soon be placed on my head as a reminder that I came from dust, and to dust I shall return. Huh. Looks to me like those ashes have purpose. Grave Reminders. The birthday cake that adds another candle and still secretly worries she hasn't yet done whatever she was sent here to do. The appointment that results in hearing words you're not ready to hear. The loss fully realized. The pain fully felt. Grave reminders. Reminders that our lives here on this Earth are fleeting for our flesh. *and yet* . . . eternal for our *souls*. Yes. For see, Grave Reminders also bring us face-to-face with the God Who goes before us and prepares a place for us, the God Who lends us His *exhale* while here in the flesh and will one day *inhale* and bring us back home.

Grave Reminders remind us that the dead don't stay dead. The tomb is temporary. Beauty arises from ashes, and new life is called out of that grave, and *that* is among the many reasons why I believe that Grave Reminders this side of heaven aren't "punishments" from God but are among the greatest gifts that God gives. Reminders to live. Reminders to rest. Reminders to hope as you peer into that empty tomb. Reminders that we are human. And human is *holy*. And holy is *hard*. Yes. Filled with blood, sweat, and tears, and worth every drop, for every *one* of our stories not only has *purpose*, but will also not go unfulfilled, and that's how we know that every story, *every* story, has power and purpose regardless of how many pages, *amen*.

Grave Reminders. Reminders that time here may be fleeting, but there's more yet to come. Beloved, today may you know you are loved. Always and in all ways. Amen.

THE "YES" YOU DON'T EVEN KNOW ABOUT

Beloved, keep in mind that every "no" you receive may be because the "yes" you don't even know about yet is gonna need that space.

Yes, indeed, it sure might. So here we are. With words I was given, and so I'm writing them out loud, here in this place, trusting that someone out there in this communal-quite-beautiful space of ours might need to hear 'em. Yes. The someone who got the No that hurled them into the drowning sea of self-deprecation. The someone who got the No they were *sure* they'd get a Yes for. The someone who heard the words, "It's not me it's you," "I'm sorry, you're just not what we're looking for," "It's gonna have to be a No this time," or any of the other hundreds of ways to deliver a No that in the end is just that—No.

And see, the thing about our humanness is that whenever we hear a No, we often fall right into the fire of fear that convinces us that we are the *only* one in this No Space—when, in fact, if we look around, we're actually joined by a multitude. We just can't see them, because nothing isolates us like rejection, or the fear of rejection. Fact-Yes-Amen.

Beloved, if you're the someone, or it's someone you know, and you/they could use a good strong shot of Brand New Perspective, then Baby, I hope today I can be your dealer. I mean it. If you got a No, a No that you never wanted, you're gonna *take* that No, and you're gonna Reframe it and Rename it, and in *doing* so you're gonna feel the effects of the shot that you got—the one I hope makes you feel better. Yes.

Beloved, please keep in mind that every No you receive, *may be* because the Yes you don't even *know about yet* is gonna need that space. In your heart. In your life. In your schedule. In your list of what matters. *Just sayin '*. Oh, and before you go, one question: Why *not* believe it?

IT'S OK TO BE HUMAN

Jesus cried out, "Why, God? Why??" . . . We will too.

One of the things I love best about Jesus, God-in-the-flesh-come-down, is the overwhelming assurance that it's OK *to be human*. Here's just a sampling of what we find—needing a minute after receiving really hard news, praying alone (just Him and God), napping on the regular (a crowd favorite), and, of course (and probably my personal fave), crying out, "*Why, God, why ?*" when things are nowhere *near* where I want them to be or *how* I want them to be. When they are so far beyond my comprehension that I'm tempted to think . . . Have I been wrong about You this whole time, Lord, because seriously, *why*? Why does my friend battle cancer so hard, why is her journey so painful? Why was my friend's son returned to You long before she was ready to release him? Why has a child not yet old enough to write her name already endured more trauma in her four years on Earth than others have endured their whole life? Why, God? Why?

Jesus cried those words out loud on the cross. And I believe . . . it was to show us that there will be times *we will too*. Yes. We too will at times cry out, *Why, God? Why?* Beloved, Jesus knew where He came from, knew where He was returning to, and knew the power He had while He was here, and yet . . . *still* cried out these very words . . . to show us that there will be times we will too. And it's not because we don't love God. Or trust God. It's because our God-given *humanness* can't *possibly* grasp our God-given *holiness*.

Beloved, our time here is holy, precious, packed with more purpose and worth than we can possibly imagine, regardless of how long our stay. And it is *more* than OK . . . to be human, to feel the pain, to not understand, to wonder why, to cry. The God Who remains *with us* wrote our stories, *all* the stories, and declared them to be good (sufficient to meet His purpose). And you, like Jesus, will accomplish all you were sent here to do. And you, like Jesus, will be *loved* through every word *lived*, and never, *ever* be forsaken. *XO.*

SEEKING LEADS TO SEEING

She who seeks God sees God.

How do I know? We use our stubbornness and put it to work for us. I *will* see God in this if I have to seek all day, all night. I will seek God in the fire until I hear God's voice. I will seek God among these ashes, no matter how much soot I get on me, until I see the beauty of God arise. I will *seek* God until I *see* God. Because I *know* . . . God is there. *There*, wherever *there* is, because when you've got a God Who is omnipresent, you can rest in the fact that wherever your *there*, *there* your God is. In the midst of the storm that is shaking you. The wilderness that's scaring you. The separation from the crowd that you're not quite sure if you should appreciate or not because you also desperately long to belong.

She would seek God in every dark moment and in every moment when it felt as though God parted the clouds just to talk to her. Every time God rolled away the stone that stood in her way, parted the sea for her to cross over, called forth life from the grave of whatever it was that she was certain was lost forever. And . . . every time that God didn't. And that's when seeking would take a bit more. A bit more grit. A bit more grace each time she fumbled in her trying.

She would seek God's face in every "No" she received, every stone left unrolled, sea left unparted, mountain left unmoved. Because she had to. Yes. If she was going to get through the good and the bad, the richer and poorer, the times of sickness and the times of health . . . her commitment was this . . . she would *seek* God until she *saw* God. And she knew she eventually would, even if it seemed impossible or God seemed a million miles off . . . because seeking *seeks* . . . *until* it *sees*.

It's not looking, "hoping" to see. It's seeking, determined to see. And see (grin), *that* kind of faith doesn't quit. It won't quit. It all-out refuses to quit. Because it knows that it knows that it knows that God *is* there . . . and so it will *seek* God . . . until it *sees* God. It sure will.

PREPARATION FOR THE NEXT PAGE

The God Who wrote your story is preparing you for the next page.

Which is why I reckon it's so hard for those of us who desperately want to know what's next to *wait* . . . and live out the words of the page we are currently on. For of *course* we don't know what's on the next page. Only the *Author* knows. Only the Author knows what the next words will say. Only the Author knows the plot twists and turns. Only the Author knows what the Author's own hand has penned from Beginning . . . all the way to The End.

So of *course* the waiting is oftentimes *hard for us*. Because what *we* don't often realize (if ever) is that the God Who *wrote* the next page of our Scripture story also *knows* the next page of our Scripture story, and is therefore *preparing* us for the next page of our Scripture story on the *current page we are on*. Yes. A God Who knows the next place you'll go. Storm you'll be in. Mountain you'll climb or watch as God moves it for you. A God Who *knows the plans* that He wrote for you . . . is *preparing* you for them . . . right here on the page you are on. *Yes.*

I started the book of Mark today. And after all these years, what I never fully realized 'til now was all the ways that God *prepared* Jesus . . . By the ministry of John B. who went before him. By His baptism in the Jordan where He heard the words that would secure His identity—You are *My Son*, My *Beloved*, with Whom . . . I Am . . . *well pleased*. And by His temptation—in the desert. A place that the Spirit of *God* (not Satan) drove Him to, by the way . . . . to *prepare* Him . . . for all that God had ahead for Him.

Yes. And truly I tell you, Beloved, the same is true for me and for you. We want to turn the page. We don't want to wait. We call it punishment instead of provision. The provision of preparation. For the next page in our story. The page that only God knows. Amen. Love ya, mean it. *XO.*

TENDETH TO LIFE

Tendeth to life.

The life within you. The life around you. Your flesh and your heart-mind-and-soul.

Tend to it. Take care of it. The journey is long. Feed your flesh with foods that give life. Feed your mind the same way. Remember that you are human, which means you are both body *and* spirit, so *both* must be cared for, amen. Remember that overthinking about everything won't add one single inch to your stature and, in fact, will cause you to shrink and retreat.

So instead, stretch yourself—your body, your faith, your thoughts that are trying to convince you *right now* that there's no way at your age you can. *Bull.* You most certainly can. And at the least you can *try*, for trying will stretch you and keep you from shrinking, and I don't want you hunched over, sweet friend of mine. I want your tent pitched towards the sunrise so it's the first thing you see every morning. And as you do, I want it to sing to you, "My mercies, My graces, My compassions, are brand new for you this day, My Girl." I want you to remember that you are a palace, and deep within you is the God of your refuge. The God Who fearfully and wonderfully formed you, knit you together, and placed you, designed and equipped you according to the plans and the purposes He has for you, and delivered you into this world for such a time as this, *amen.*

Tendeth to life. Pay attention to what your body is saying to you. Listen to the words that you speak so you'll know what your heart is full of, and then talk about that with your God. Engage with others. Ditch the "Sorry I'm late, I didn't wanna come" shirt, and instead realize that God's provision *is* God's people, and *you*, young lady, were not meant to do life alone. Seek the welfare of the land you are in, for when where you *are* is doing well, *you*, as a resident there, will do far better too. *Yes.* Reap and sow. Stir up the soil. Shine your light, despite what others may say. Use your current state of lack to reveal the gifts and the talents that lie deep within and then, for God's sake, *use* them and don't bury them, please.

Tendeth to Life.

Keep in mind—God's plan to RESTORE you, may include an active role FOR you.

Cherryan

x

Day 302

YOUR ROLE IN RESTORATION

Keep in mind—God's plan to restore you may include an active role for you.

Like asking God for a mountain to climb after years of begging Him to move every one. Like pulling yourself out of the pit you are in by using the strength that lies within. Like stretching yourself in a way you've never stretched yourself before. Just ask that dude who was in the synagogue that Sabbath morn. A guy longing for restoration. Perhaps looking for one magic touch from the Rabbi's hand, when instead he hears the words, "Stretch out yours." Yep. "Stretch out your hand."

Beloved, restoration may come as a result of your stretching. Read it again, cuz it sure might. Stretching beyond what is holding you captive—the thoughts that are keeping you bound. Fear, worry, and doubt mixed with a splash of anxiety, a shot of so-overwhelmed-you-do-nothing-at-all, and shaken with a measure of it's-too-late . . . makes for one really strong drink. One that may just knock you on your can. And convince you that you can't. Go ahead, read it again.

Beloved, God's plan for you includes restoration. Heck, it might be a whole chapter in your story, who knows? And see, the super cool thing about the dude in the synagogue that day is that it offers up for consideration the *possibility* that the restoration plan God has *for* you may just (gulp) *include* you. *Yup.*

And see, *again*, this is why I freaking love Scripture. Cuz it's filled with so much awesome good stuff to chew on. One may even call it . . . daily bread . . . for the soul. Grin. Amen. Love ya, mean it. Have a really great day, Beloved.

{Mark 3:1–12}

YOU WON'T ALWAYS BLOOM WHERE YOU'RE PLANTED

You will bloom where the conditions are right for you.

Towards the top of "Phrases I Hate" is "Bloom Where You're Planted." And before you attack, hear my Why.

I once received a beautiful orchid from coworkers after leaving a job to take hold of a new one. I'd never had an orchid before (it made me feel fancy!), so because I hadn't, I needed to take note of what my beautiful new fancy girl needed. She needed hot and humid. In order to thrive. And my first thought was . . . well, she's nothing like me, her new mama. Cuz I *sure as heck* don't thrive in hot and humid.

After a little over a year at a really great university, our daughter came to us and told us that although her desire to become a nurse was *still* her desire, she had determined that what was right for *her* (not what'd been right for her brother, who'd bloomed at this school) was to *move to new ground*. To soil that was right . . . for *her*. She knew she couldn't bloom where she was planted, and so she sought out new ground, to be *replanted.* In soil that was right for her. In air that was meant for her. In an atmosphere conducive to her ability to bear fruit based on her unique design. And that is *precisely* what happened. She bloomed where she was *re*planted.

Beloved, sometimes we need to be replanted in order to bloom; perhaps the soil we're in isn't right for us. Sometimes we need to be repotted in order to bloom. We outgrow the pot we're in, and see, when that happens to *plants*, no one blames the plant. In fact, we cheer the plant on, applauding its growth. We sure do. So how about this—instead of telling peeps (of all ages!) to bloom where they're planted, we start caring for the soil. We ask questions and give safe space for answers.

Are you blooming where you're planted? Are the conditions right for you? Is the air/atmosphere what you need in order for you to thrive? Are you feeling stuck in a pot that initially worked well, but now you're thinking maybe you've outgrown it? Blooming. It occurs when the timing is right and the conditions are favorable.

SOMETHING TO SHOW YOU

Heads up, Beloved—if God sends you into a storm, God's got something to show you in the midst of that storm.

And yes, I said *sends* you. Cuz listen, I need to believe, my *soul* needs to believe, that if I'm *in* a storm, then there is a purpose *for* the storm—even if I *despise* the storm and, like the original disciples, *freak out* in the midst of the storm—then for *one second* believe that somehow during the whole writing-of-my-story process, God handed over the pen to the enemy and said, "Here, go ahead. You can finish the rest." Yeah . . . *no*.

As part of their disciple-training, Jesus sends the guys into waters He knows will turn stormy. And He goes with them. And I picture Jesus, giving a nod to His Pops above, as if to say . . . Yup, ready when You are. And then *intentionally*, as in *on purpose*, goes to take a nap. So *why*? *Why* would Jesus intentionally nap when He *knew* His Father was about to stir up the sea? Because disciple-training ain't for the faint of heart, that's why. Because He knew He wouldn't always be with them in the *flesh* . . . so He would need to *show* them that He would be with them, *within* them, even after He'd physically *left* them. And *that*, of course, could *not* be taken from them. No matter the weather, location, or circumstances.

Or how 'bout the time He sent the guys into waters that *again* He knew would turn stormy, this time *without* Him, and then *appeared* to them, walking *upon* them, as Pete yells out to Him, "Hey! If it's really You, tell *me* to walk on water too." He did. And Pete did. At least for a while. So could it be that the storm was part of Pete's story, so that *Pete* could see that he could do what he originally thought looked impossible? Maybe. After all, with a name like Pete-the-rock-on-which-the-church-will-be-built, a guy's gotta know that what may *look* impossible . . . *isn't*.

In a storm, Beloved? Trust God has something to *show* you.

{Matthew 8:23–27; 14:22–23}

SURVIVING THROUGH BELIEVING

She wouldn't have made it through . . . had she not believed.

That's right. It's how a woman once upon a time found the strength to push through the crowd, despite all social norms that told her she couldn't, or shouldn't, or any other word used in an attempt to hold women bound by their issues. She *believed*. And *that* . . . is how she got *through*. Yes.

It's how we survive storms that arise on the waters we're on—Earthquakes in our circumstances that shake things completely out of place. It's how we survive walks in this life, unavoidable roads that take us right through the valleys of the shadows of death. We *survive*, because we *believe*. We *believe* that we will once again *see* . . . the *goodness* of God . . . in the land of the *living*. Yes. We *believe* that. And be*cuz* we believe it, we survive. Breath for our soul that whispers, "Keep going, there's more for you," in stark contrast to the words that desperately try to choke us to death—words like, "It's too late for you."

Yes, Beloved, of course I know you know those words. But how about instead of giving them airtime, we cast them into the pit of gnashing teeth and give hell something to chew on. *Yes. I love* that the God *within* me, through God's Spirit given *to* me, rises up to defend me . . . and stir me . . . and remind me . . . . Oh, Baby Girl, I got *so* much goodness left for you. Beloved, you will be tempted to believe that things will never get better. But see, *when that happens*, I'm gonna toss you a mic, and you and I are gonna belt out Howard Jones's classic, "Things Can *Only* Get Better." And you and I are gonna sing it 'til you believe it, and then we're gonna sing it again for good measure.

Amen. Thanks, Howie. Thanks, God. Thanks for stopping by for coffee this morning, Beloved. I'm gonna go get the hairspray ready now for our debut. Love ya, mean it. *XO*.

THE THING YOU WANT MOST

Beloved, the thing you want most may lie directly on the other side of what you don't want to do.

You want to stand tall, you don't want to shrink, but you also don't want to stretch yourself. You want to build up endurance for the rest of your journey but blow off the mountains when they are calling. You want peace but don't want to pursue it. You want to bring forth the new but don't want to disrupt the soil. You want complete self-awareness but don't want to be fully honest with self . . . the kind of honesty that arises through hard conversations with said-self. Yes. You want connection but fear rejection, so instead, you put up a wall of protection. You want to feel better, body and soul, but you don't want to eat better, body and soul . . . you don't want to tend to the soil.

You want real and true friendships but don't want to position yourself where potential new friendships may await you. You want to be strong but don't want to lift heavy. You want to rest but refuse to slow down. You want renewed energy but refuse to get up off the couch and start manifesting it from the storehouse within you. You want knowledge but don't want to study. You want wisdom but don't want to research. You want unity but don't want to engage in community, and, ahem, it appears those two words share a common bond, amen.

Beloved, I'm a stirrer and a shaker. Out of a great *love* for people. Cuz honestly, sometimes we all need someone to just say the darn thing that'll cause us to stop for a second and think and ask ourselves stuff. (Because believe you me, every question I present to you I have already discussed *at length* with myself.) What if what I want *most* lies directly on the other side of what I *don't* want to do? Cuz see, if you're like me, I love the deep questions, I love the hard questions, I love the questions that challenge my heart-mind-and-soul, because every challenge holds the potential for change.

Beloved, my words today are not to *shame* you, but to *stir* you. To *inspire* you, *motivate* you, and *encourage* you. Because I *believe in you*. And I *so* want full and abundant for you. *XO.*

GOD PROVIDES IN THE DURING

The bread of life that fell from Heaven each day . . . reminds us that God's provision is not solely reserved for the after but is also in the during.

I arose out of bed and wrote out these words before doing anything else because I just couldn't shake the feeling that someone in this beautiful, sacred, shared land of ours needs to hear that God's *provision* for them is not solely reserved for their *after*; it is *also* present in their *during*. *Yes.*

Now listen, we *love* the After. Every Hallmark movie concurs that Happily Ever After is the way to go, the viewer's fave. Why wouldn't it be? And we *need* the After. It's a good focal point on the wall as we labor through this thing called *life*, and we do it, of course, believing that every push exerted and every pain endured will eventually bring forth *new*. *Amen.* Yes. After the flood. After the storm. After this wandering in the wilderness *finally* ends. So yes, we *need* the After. The oasis. The land of milk. The land of honey. But see, if we're consumed only by the After, we will undoubtedly miss all the incredible provisions afforded us in the *during*.

Like a God Who dropped bread from heaven each day as the Israelites made their way to their After. As Ruth reached down into the dirt of the fields she was gleaning, scooping up more than grain to eat, but also, handfuls of purpose. A God Who prepares feasts in deserts and sends giant fish to swallow whole the one trying to run. A God Who saw fit to make sure the pit Joe was tossed into by his bros would be waterless so as not to get his fancy coat wet.

Yes. I could go on. And on and on, but in typical-Tera-fashion-as-of-late, I'll run out of room here, so for now, in *this* space, I hope the one out there who needed to hear the truth of God's provision in the *during* . . . did. Cuz see, now you've got something to watch for, and if you wanna hang with me, I'll be over here on the edge . . . of expectation. With my eyes wide open. Singin' "Don't Stop Believin.'" *XO.*

SEEKING OVER CHASING

Seek God.

I'm not a fan of the phrase "Chase God" for a number of reasons, actually. One, I think most of us are worn out enough already by all the chasing we do in this world. *Word.* Two, the word "chasing" reminds me of being the little kindergarten girl who chased a fellow little kindergarten boy around on the playground, all while the poor kid tried desperately to escape me. (And if I could remember his name, I swear I'd apologize.) And finally, because I'm not exactly sure why we are instructing and encouraging people, including kiddos and teens, to "chase God" when God is seated, *and*, as my reading today confirms, so is Jesus, right there in the right-hand throne.

Yup. After Jesus came and completed His Father's Will on this Earth, He returned home and sat down. And if you don't believe me, Hebrews 1:3. So I guess the phrase I like far better—is this: *seek* God. Yes. Seek God wherever God has you. Seek God in the circumstances you're in, regardless of how fabulous or crappy they are. Seek God like you're playing hide-and-seek as a kid who's determined to win.

Yes. Seek God the way a widow once did for her last coin left in her house . . . or the way you seek for your phone when you ughhh-I-can't-find-it-*anywhere*. Yes, Beloved, seek God like *that*, like it *matters*. Be *so* determined to *see* God that you *refuse to give up 'til you do*. Yes. Cuz see, *that* kind of determination . . . will lead to revelation. You will begin to see the God Who is near through the people God sends . . . through the moments when you catch a glimpse of His glory, mercy, compassion . . . through the flickers of light that appear in the darkness, giving you hope to believe once again.

Yes. Seek God where you are, Beloved, no matter where that is. For truly I tell you, He's there. I love you. I sure do. Amen.

{Hebrews 1:3}

Day 309

SOUL REST

For the one today whose soul could use a good Sabbath rest . . .

Go ahead. Cuz see, I *see* you in the midst of the chaos, the running, the sickness all over, when you're not even sure you're ready for the day set before you, let alone any day past. I see you in your worry, your fear, your desperation to not only handle it all and execute it all. Your worn-out flesh, yes—but *also* your worn-out *soul*. Worry will do that, you know. Fear and doubt will too. And perhaps the biggest playground bully of all is Assuming the Worst instead of Expecting the Best. Yes.

If it's you, Beloved, in any way, shape, or form, again, here's your pillow, your blankie, your couch for just a few secs. To rest. In the unchanging truth and blessed assurance of the One Who sent you to this live this crazy life anyway. Beloved, God's works were finished before the foundation of the world. Your story's been written by the Author and Perfecter of your faith, and you are living out that story right now. The purposeful plan for your life was prepared for you by the One Who is not only Provider and Protector, but also the One for Whom *all* things are possible, which is why we *don't stop believing*. We sure don't. Because Believing is our backstage pass to the sanctuary of our soul, where we can boldly approach the throne of grace *anytime* to ask for what it is that we need. Indeed.

We have a hope that is *real*. It's sure and secure. It's an anchor for our soul to cling to when the storms of life seem certain to take us right out. And we *have* this hope all the way to the end—which, of course, will be our brand-new beginning. There will be mysteries and plot twists in our earthly story, and they'll take us by great surprise. Some we will love and some we'll despise, but of course, that's cuz we're human and therefore can't possibly fully grasp our God-given holiness. So instead, to find rest for our soul, we grab hold of that anchor. That which is sure and secure. And snooze in the boat for a while. We sure do.

{Hebrews 4–6}

LORD, AS YOU KNOW

Lord, as You know . . .

It's how I start nearly all of the prayers that flow through my pen. There's just something so reassuring to me about knowing that God already knows. Like whatever it is I'm about to say, whatever situation I'm in, whatever I'm struggling with, isn't some sort of colossal shock to God as we sit and we talk. Of course it's not. For obviously, the Beginning and End knows the beginning and end. *Amen.*

So I start my beseeching, my pleading, my asking, my begging, my overwhelming-gratitude-praising with this—"As You know, Lord" . . . and then I proceed. And lay it all out and hold nothing back and talk without fear of saying the "right" words in the "right" way. I talk to God the way that I talk, and I get it all out, and ask/beg God for what it is that I need *and* what it is that I want (because FYI, you can do that, you know), and after I do . . . I usually proceed with something like this: I *know*, Lord . . .

That You are near. That You hear me. That You know the plans You have for me, and You assure me they are good. That You are with the person I'm worried about. That You are with me in this storm/trial/crap-show that's goin' down. That You already know the results of the test, the procedure, or whatever else it is that I or _____ has today. That You are faithful. That Your purpose for my life will be fulfilled, because You are a God Who completes stuff. That You are Provider, Protector, All-Powerful, and no devil in hell or on Earth can stop You, *amen.* And seriously, Lord, since You gave me Your breath as a constant reminder while here on this Earth that I'm *never* without You, I know You're gonna see me through all the stuff we just talked about.

Beloved, today I encourage you to talk to the God Who already knows. Oh, and make sure you tell God what *you* know too. *XO.*

GOD KNOWS HOW TO RESCUE

In case you forgot . . . God knows how to rescue.

"I think it right, as long as I am in this body, to refresh your memory . . ." —Pete to the Peeps in the letter we call his second. Good plan, Pete. Because as humans, forgetting stuff seems to be at the top of our to-do list—especially when that list is long, and we're overwhelmed, worn, trying to fight with worry and panic, doubt and fear, bitterness and resentment, and when the going gets tough and the tough gets going . . . right out of our mind . . . and if we're honest, we're right there with it. *Yup.* Sooooo, Pete says, let me *refresh your memory*. The Lord knows how to rescue. In case you forgot. Which you may have. So here we are, me and Pete, to refresh your memory.

Noah. His family. Rahab. The spies she protected. David when Saul was pursuing him. Daniel in the throes of the lions' den. Jonah in the belly of that massive whale (or great big fish—whatever). The widow and her kid with one drop of oil. The guys in the furnace who not only walked out of the fire, but didn't even smell like smoke (well-played, Lord). The Jewish people, through their girl Esther, with encouragement and support from cousin and adopted-Daddy Mordy (*love* that guy). Joseph from the pit, and that guy actually went on from there to the palace. (Talk about a plan Joe couldn't have imagined!) Naomi and fam from the famine. Gideon and his peeps from the Midians. Abraham from settling, like his father did, especially when he realized that his dad had died where he settled. (Ahem, folks—there are *no* words for the year *that* lightbulb went on, and the fact that his Pop's name was Terah?? Seriously, don't get me started . . . today anyway—wink, wink.)

Beloved, my point is this—the Lord knows how to rescue. Because when You are a *rescuer . . . you know how to rescue.* Exactly. Rest in that for a few minutes today, OK? Let your soul find refuge there, especially if you're in a season of waiting for that rescue to take place. Know that you are seen, heard, known, *and* loved unfailingly, wherever you are *right now*.

{2 Peter 2:9}

THE GIFT OF THE HARD

Sometimes the gift of the hard . . . is the new life that arises up out of it.

I've witnessed it. Experienced it. Lived it. Been a bearer of it. And admittedly, a giver of it. The hard. And yet . . . I've watched as new life arose from the hard. I've seen resurrection on Earth. I've seen healing and restoration arise out of death. I've seen desires of the heart come to light and arise from the darkness. I've seen joy arise from mourning and beauty arise from ashes, and I've seen these things, Beloved, because . . . *there are gifts that arise from the hard.* It could be a renewed energy, a refocus, a reignited flame within that over time has blown out. I'm here to testify to it. *And so have you.* I've seen determination arise from the hard, I've seen confirmation of purpose arise from the hard. I've seen holy anger arise from the hard that led to much-needed change, and *that* is because . . . *there are gifts that arise from the hard.*

I've seen destruction that led to complete rebuilding, and that complete rebuilding, all the way from the dust on up, is *exactly* what was needed, amen. I've seen pain put to work. I've seen tears water land. I've seen time spent *down* used to gain a whole new appreciation to when you're finally *up*, and I'm *still* convinced that's why Pete's mom-in-law hopped up outta bed and *immediately* started whipping up supper for the guys the moment she was healed, amen. I've seen a desire to know God more arise from the hard. I've seen unity arise from the hard. I've seen laughter arise from the hard, and when I do, I always think about the verse that talks about laughter being good medicine.

Beloved, *there are gifts that arise from the hard.* It's what gives the hard *purpose* and *value* and *worth*, because as you and I know, God wastes *nothing*. So as you endure your own hard, may you know God is with you. May you know that the hard is not for naught. And after you have endured for a while—for yes, there will be an after—may you witness and experience the gift, or gifts, that arise from the hard. For the hard's not for naught. It's sure not. Amen. *XO.*

ONCE YOU'VE WATCHED GOD MOVE A MOUNTAIN

Once you've watched God move a mountain . . .

. . . a part of you will be strengthened to believe that God will do it again. Amen.

Now please keep in mind, the mountain may not be Everest. You don't need it to be. It could be the call you've been waiting for. The break in your schedule that allows you to breathe. It could be the paper clip on the sidewalk that opens your eyes to seeing paper clips in all sorts of places from that moment on. Yes. Once you've watched God move a mountain . . . Something inside you will hold on to that sentence in your story, even if your brain appears to have forgotten it . . . and it will grow like that mustard seed you've heard so much about. Yes.

Once you've watched God move a mountain. Not asked you to climb it (this time), but instead shoved it right out of the way, as if to say, "Well . . . there ya go, Kiddo . . . now what are you going to do in this cleared space I have given you?" Once you've watched God move a mountain . . . a part of you will continue to trust and hang on, even when you're so mad at God that you scream and yell and swear 'til you're blue in the face and vow to never, *ever* pray again because-what's-the-point . . . but you will. Because you can't escape the knowing that God can move mountains. And you know, because you've watched God do it. Yes.

Beloved, please hear me on this—the mountain doesn't have to be Everest . . . in order for you to know . . ."God moved that mountain for me." Yes. Today may God move a mountain for you. Either Everest on the horizon or the anthill on your front sidewalk. Remember that both are powerful moves. From the One Who moves mountains. Yes. Believe it. And don't stop believin'.

TODAY'S THE DAY

Today's the day!

Thanks be to God for the exclamation point. Seriously. Today's the day!! Oh *good*, you can hear me saying it. And so now you ask, the day for what? I have no idea. Nope. But truly I tell you, Beloved, *nothing* is gonna strengthen you quite as much as arising each day and believing with all that ya got that this, in fact, is true, amen.

Yes. Today's the day!! Today's the day the answer will come. Today's the day it will finally make sense. Today's the day I'll finally feel better. Today's the day I'll turn that corner. Today's the day I will *not* be overpowered, I will *not* throw in the towel, I will *not* give in to what's trying to destroy me, amen. Yes. Today's the day someone is gonna reach out totally unexpectedly and change the course I'm on in a way that is so stinkin' awesome and unbelievable that I can't stop looking up and proclaiming, "OMG!" . . . accompanied by a squeal, of course. Today's the day a prayer I've been praying for what seems like a bazillion years suddenly seems like it's answered. Today's the day that a tiny glimmer of light appears at the end of this long dark tunnel, just enough to keep me moving towards it. Today's the day I get good news, smile and laugh out loud, hear from someone I haven't heard from in a really long time, learn something new and unlearn a few things too. Today's the day that hope is stirred-relit-sparked in a way that makes you feel like Alicia Keys as you belt out, "This girl is on fiiiiire!"

Yes. Today's the day!! Because here's the deal, Beloved, as I've said before, whether or not any of this happens today is actually secondary to *believing* it will. That's right. *believing* today is the day. *Believing* that the Author of your story, the one you're living out right now, is gonna surprise you in a way that you never saw coming yet secretly yearned for, and today is that day, hallelujah, amen. Cuz see, that's what's gonna wake up your soul the way caffeine wakes up your flesh. *It sure is.*

WHEN ALL SEEMS HOPELESS

The next time all seems hopeless, the next time all seems lost, the next time you think there's just no way . . . remember.

How Sarah felt when she got the news that despite her age, some new would be coming. How Ruth felt when Boaz took notice. How Gideon felt when he turned around and realized that angel was actually talking to *him*. How Moses felt when that great sea parted so he and his peeps could cross over. How they felt when they looked back and realized their enemies didn't. How Esther felt when the King said Yes. How Noah felt when it started to rain. How Daniel felt when he made some new animal friends in the den instead of being devoured by them. How Abraham felt when he saw that ram. How the women felt when that massive boulder had already been rolled away for them. How the shepherds felt when they realized, "Holy crap, I can't believe *we* are the first ones to hear the good news, and not all the religious uppity-ups around here." How Jonah felt as he wiped off the fish guts and shook the sand out of his shorts. How Mary and Martha felt when their dead brother Lazarus walked out of that tomb. How Jesus's disciples felt when although they were locked away tight out of fear, Jesus Himself came right in and stood there amongst them, amen.

Yes. Beloved, you and I both know I could go on and on and on, but I'm convinced at this point that you get my point. With God, all things are possible. And because that is true, we don't stop believing. That's right. We don't stop believing that our name, in fact, will be added to that list. And *so many* are already on there. Yes. For it is your nonstop believing . . . that is gonna see you through. It sure is. It's the hope that arises and sounds something like this . . .

"Well maybe . . ." "Perhaps it could . . ." "I guess it's possible . . ." "Why *not* me?"

Right. Beloved, the next time all seems hopeless, the next time all seems lost, the next time you think there's just no way . . . Remember. Amen. *XO.*

PERFECT, NOT DESTROY

What your enemies think will destroy you is actually gonna perfect you.

I know, right? Put that in your pipe and smoke it. Amen. Remember when Joe's bros tossed him into a well (which, by the way, God made sure was void of water so he wouldn't drown—hello), and then decided instead to make a few bucks and sell him off into slavery, and then go home and tell dad that he had been killed by some animal, and then Joe ended up winning the favor of the King that he served, and then ended up being put in charge of the food supply, and then Joe's bros were like literally starving to death and ended up having to go to their bro, although they didn't know it was him, and beg for food?

Whew. Take a breath, Tera. But seriously, remember that? If no, go read it. I mean it. And don't miss the end. The part where Joe reveals who he is to his bros and how he holds the loaves and includes the words—in so many words—"Yeah, and by the way, the thing you did that you thought would destroy me? Yeah, that thing got me *here*, which is a really good thing, cuz now I'm able to save your sorry butts. So hey, it's all good. Let's thank God, shall we? Amen."

OK, call it author interpretation (which it obviously is), but I *know* you hear me, Beloved. Joe realized in that moment, while looking at his bros' hungry faces, that God, in fact, had used what they had planned *against* him . . . to *perfect* him. *Amen.* I know, right? I can't even with this.

Beloved, believe it for *you.* I mean it. And don't *stop* believing it for you. I mean that too. Perhaps that's why the words "and she will rejoice in time to come" (FYI—some translations read, "laughs without fear of the future"; either way, good stuff) makes me smile so darn much. Seriously. Cuz in the midst of the ploy, she can laugh, shake her head and the dust off her feet, as she preaches some really good stuff to herself, "Oh enemy, you have no idea that you're being used by our God . . . to perfect me." Amen.

{Genesis 37; Proverbs 31}

THE STRUGGLE THAT STRENGTHENS

The struggle to decide what to do . . . is strengthening you to do what you decide.

If it feels like I'm talking directly to *you*, then I reckon perhaps I am. Cuz maybe I *am* here today, to tell *you*, that as much as the struggle to decide what you need to decide totally sucks . . . that same struggle is also strengthening you to then do what it is you decide. I told you God's ways are intricate. And often not how we would do it. Beyond our understanding, not to mention at times our liking. Right.

And here's the thing. I've said it before, and I may just say it a bazillion more times—it's about *believing* that this is true. *Yes. That* is what is gonna give this baby some *worth*. Make it count for *something*, for God's sake. Allow us to name it what we want to name it—in this case, strength-training, please. Or preparation. Or wisdom-gainer. Or something that is *good*, because we know *God is good*, which means, come hell-or-high-water, there *has* to be *good* in this thing.

I've shared with a few folks that one of the gifts of now being this age, and here it is—I have moved beyond having something to *prove* . . . to having something to *say*. Something I've learned as I've lived. Something I've learned as I've read. Something I've learned as I've stopped and looked back. And I'm *still* learning—daily—how awesome it is that you and I never stop. No doubt. Something I hope guides/provides or brings life and hope or extends compassion and mercy and grace (since we call it amazing) and echoes in the ears of whoever is listening (albeit slightly off-key) . . . don't stop believin'.

Beloved, life is a journey (no pun intended, but kinda). And *you*, Beloved, are a fully loved, worthy, and accepted human, created uniquely, fearfully, and wonderfully by your God, to do what you do on this Earth. To bear witness to the creativity of God. You sure are. Believe it and don't stop believin', Beloved, cuz believing is what saves us from the pit, and ain't *none* of us want to be there. Amen.

SOMETHING YOU'LL NEVER FORGET

Keep in mind that if God has you at a standstill, it may be to show you something you'll never forget.

God told Josh to tell those who were carrying the ark of the covenant . . . when you get to the brink of the Jordan, stand still in it. Stand still in the very waters you're so anxious to get to the other side of in order to *finally* reach the land I Am giving you, the land I have promised you. For *yes*, you're gonna cross through it, but *first*, you're gonna *stand still* in it, because I've got something to *show* you, something you'll *never* forget.

Amen. And they did. They stood still. And as they stood still, Josh reminded them that the *living* God was not only *among* them, but would also, without fail, drive out their enemies *before* them. And *knowing* this, *trusting* this, *believing* this no matter *what* . . . would in fact equip them and enable them to be strong and courageous, *just* as the Lord had commanded them. *Yes*. Look, Josh tells 'em, "The ark of the covenant, the ark of the Lord *your* God; all the truths and the promises that the Lord *your* God has *given* to *you*, is gonna go *before you* in this." And it did. And they all watched. For as *soon* as the feet of those carrying the ark *rested* in the Jordan—a river, by the way, that was at *flood* stage—as *soon* as their toes touched the *brink* of it, those flood-stage waters stood up in a heap, almost as if at attention, and those Israelites who watched it all happen walked their weary butts right through it, realizing God had done it *for them*.

Yes. With every step their feet took on that firm dry ground, they realized Who their true foundation was. Did they understand at first why they had to stand still? Why they had to rest in the water? Why they had to pay careful attention to what was going *before* them? Probably not. You might not either. But there was a good reason. Beloved, today may these words encourage you, if it feels as though God has you standing still, or resting in the very waters you so desperately want to cross over. *XO*.

{Joshua 1–3 KJV}

GOD DOESN'T NEED YOUR YES

For anyone wondering what will happen if you don't "give God your yes"...
   God will use you anyway.
   Esther didn't give God her "yes" to being orphaned, and then subsequently taken from the family member who raised her, only to be sequestered away in a palace, hoping she'd be "chosen" as queen. God used her anyway. And drew her yes out of her. Moses not only didn't give God his "yes," but he gave him a flat-out "*ummm . . . no,*" when God told him he'd be leading out thousands of Hebrews from slavery, and oh, by the way, you're gonna have to ask the king for permission, *and* he's gonna tell you no a whole buncha times, *and* yes, Moses, I realize you have a speech issue, I created you. *Right.* God used him anyway. Mary was told she'd be carrying, laboring, and ultimately delivering the Son of God for God's sake (literally). Gideon, the smallest of the least, tucked away in a winepress out of fear, was told he was gonna defeat the enemies. And there were a *lot. And oh, by the way, Gid, I'm gonna reduce your army to a pretty small crew so y'all will know it's all Me.* Psst.
   Beloved, I used to believe that we had to "give God our yes" in order to be used by God. Until the day I realized—*God is God and doesn't need my permission to do a new thing or use me to touch His world or impact one life or multiple lives, no matter how that looks, including whether or not I like or understand it.*
   Now friends, I will say *this* . . . Blessed is he/she who *does* say yes, and here's why. . . . Because then you *see* it, you *look* for it. Your eyes are wide open, and your humanness embraces it . . . and treats it as it ought to be treated . . . *holy.* Beloved, God knows what you don't. It's the advantage to being both Alpha *and* Omega, Beginning *and* End, Author *and* Finisher. So yes to giving God your "yes." It's cool to then watch your story unfold. But know this—even if you don't, God will use you.

RESTING IN THE TRUTH

Resting in the truth will help you win the war.

Resting in the truth that the Lord your God goes before you, is with you, and will never leave or forsake you. Resting in the truth that God weeps alongside you as you bawl your eyes out, because God knows you can't *possibly* understand the Why of it all. Resting in the truth that no weapon formed against you will prosper and that nothing, and I do mean *nothing*, will *ever* be able to snatch you out of God's hand. Resting in the truth that you are seen, heard, and known. Resting in the truth that God is *with* you, Mighty Warrior, and that what your *soul* has been *given* is *enough* to defeat your Satan, for the *only* place he can attack is your *thoughts*, and *you*, my friend, have been given *the power to take those thoughts captive and show 'em the door, amen.*

Resting in the truth that seasons change, and so do all things, except your unchanging God. The One, by the way, Who penned your story and knows *precisely* the plans that He has for you *from* your beginning *all the way* to your final *amen*. Resting in the truth that all storms eventually end. *Thank God.* Resting in the truth that your time here on Earth is a journey, and so, like any big road trip, you can *expect* there to be dead-ends and detours and stall-outs on the side of the road when things get over-heated, and *hey* . . . maybe, just maybe, they're a *gift* so you can cool down.

Resting in the truth that the land you've been given is holy. That the soles of your feet tread *upon* the serpent. That's right, he's *under* your feet. *Don't forget that.* Resting in the truth that nothing will ever *ever* be able to separate you from the love of God. So Sis, nestle in when you just need a hug or some time to talk it all out. A place to be heard and to shed those tears. You'll feel much better, cuz in case you haven't noticed, you were actually fearfully and wonderfully *made* . . . with *openings* for you to *release* what needs to come out. *Hello.* Beloved, resting in the truth will help you win the war. *XO.*

WHEREVER YOU ARE

You will never find yourself anywhere that God is not.

Fact. Our friend David needed to remind himself often, and he did it up big in his Psalm numbered 139, and maybe, Beloved, just maybe, you need to remind yourself too.

Beloved, you will never find yourself anywhere that God is not. *Ever.* The storm? There. The wilderness? There. The prison cell? There. The dry and dusty and oh-so-lonely desert-with-no-oasis-in-sight? Also there. The mountaintop? There. The pit? There. Rock bottom? Oh, this one's a fave—a God Who is not only there, but gives you a half-grin as He grabs your hand and says, "Where else would I be? I *Am* the Rock." I know, right? So good. But Tera . . . what about the depths of hell, the ones I feel like I'm in? Good news, my friend. Even there, God is there. I'm not kidding. Verse eight. Don't you know it.

Beloved, let me say this again in case the words aren't big enough . . . *you will never find yourself anywhere that God is not, because God vowed to never leave or forsake you, and you can take that baby straight to the bank.* You sure can. And so, *since* God is there, *wherever* you are, you . . . are not . . . alone. That's right. You may not understand *why* you are where you are, or *why* you were brought to that place, but you can sure as heck trust that you're not there alone. God is with you. *Yes.*

The same God Who strengthens your soul. The same God Who gives you His breath. The same God Who redeems and restores and refreshes and revives and renews and rehydrates and relights and repairs and rebuilds and . . . . whew . . . may just be doing a *new thing* that you simply haven't perceived yet. Beloved, wherever you are, hold on to Who you know God to be. And don't let go. *XO.*

REDEMPTION IS A PART OF YOUR STORY

Redemption is a part of your story, Beloved—you may just not be to that part yet.

Amen, amen. If I was with you, I'd grab you by the shoulders and look you square in the eye and with all that I've got in me speak these words to you, and you'd know how much I mean it. Whew and amen.

Beloved, God wrote your story. In full. "Perfect" as defined in the Word as *whole and complete*. And sometimes, I think we forget that definition, don't you? Beloved, redemption is a part of your story. Written from the beginning. By the God Who Paul was convinced (and I concur) is faithful to complete the good work He began in you. *Yes.* Redemption is a part of your story. *You may just not be to that part yet.* Yes. But what's going to keep your soul alive and refusing to roll over and not just play dead but be dead, is *believing that this, in fact, is true.*

For Beloved, that's what *faith is.* The author of Hebrews spelled it out for us, actually . . . "Now faith is the assurance of things hoped for, the conviction of things not seen." Exactly. Believing *before* seeing. Knowing *before* seeing. Assurance. Good word. Indeed. *Assurance.* You know that you know that you know—that the Author of your story didn't leave out the good parts—so you know that you know that it includes—*redemption.* Yes. In due time. At just the right part of your story.

Beloved, believe that. And don't stop believin'. For *that* is faith. And that faith is what your soul is using as fuel. To keep going. To keep enduring. To keep journeying over every hill and every mountain and through every wilderness and every desert, amen. And along the way, there are rest areas. *Yes.* There are beautiful, magnificent things for you to take in. There are gifts meant specifically for you. There sure are. As you go. Day by day and night by night. Believing and knowing and trusting that your God didn't leave anything out of your story. *Including redemption.* Amen.

{Hebrews 11:1}

Day 323

THE REALEST OF PRAYERS

The most powerful, real, raw, true, authentic, realize-you're-human prayers will most likely be three words or less.

And also mostly likely end with an exclamation point. Indeed.

Save me! Give me life! Teach me! Heal me! Don't forget me! Uphold me! Protect me! Rescue me now! Don't leave me! Be near me! Deliver me! Give me understanding! *Please*! Redeem me! Make it right! Direct my steps! Shine Your Face! Increase my faith! Give me life! *(And yes, I know I said that one twice. It's a big one.)* Turn to me! Steady my steps! Let me live! Let her live! Let him live! Let them live! Preserve my life! Light my path! Give me wisdom! Guide me! Help me! Send help! Be my help! *(Help is a big one, amen.)* Shower me! Shield me! Hide me! Protect me! Provide for me! Plead my cause! Give me courage! Use me!

Yes. Seek me out . . . so I know . . . You are near . . . and far. Close enough to hear the words within me that never catch breath . . . and far enough away to see the whole picture, amen. Beloved, your most powerful, real, raw, true, authentic, realize-you're-human prayers . . . will most likely be three words or less. And now, here's a few more three-word lines for you to keep close and safely tucked in . . . You are seen. You are heard. You are known. You are loved. You are treasured. You are valuable. You are worthy. You absolutely belong. You are God's. You sure are. Don't forget. *XO.*

WHEN YOU FIND YOURSELF
SEEKING MOUNTAINS

She found herself continually seeking mountains to climb instead of treading upon flat, even ground. And then one day, she realized why . . . it was so she could remain fully alive.

Friends, be advised—when you ask, perhaps even beg God to give you life, to revive you and strengthen you and stir something in you that you've forgotten was there or perhaps never even knew existed . . . it may come in the form of a mountain to climb.

Friends, I find myself continually seeking mountains to climb instead of treading upon the flat, even ground. And then one day, I realized why. It is so . . . I can remain . . . *fully alive.* So I can remind myself with every step that I can still climb mountains. And, lest I get discouraged, I call upon my friends Moses and Abe, who are quick to remind me that they were *far* older than I am when they made their infamous climbs. Touché guys. Touché. And well played, by the way.

Remember when I shared with y'all back on Day 311 about how the story of Terah in the big book blew my mind (of course it did—*Tera*h??) and stirred me up right out of the rut known as complacency? If not, here's a short one-sentence recap: Terah was on his way to where he wanted to go, but he stopped and settled along the way and then died where he settled. I know, right?!? Whew. But also—*hellooo.* Lord-willing, I pray I never, *ever* forget that story. Because it pulled me up right out of the rut . . . out of the pit of apathy . . . out of the dried-up well of death . . . and brought me into a wide-open space . . . a space, by the way . . . filled with mountains to climb.

Beloved, God loves you enough to give you mountains to climb. Hurdles to jump and seas to swim. Storms to endure and, yes, sleepless nights when the only name you can think to call upon is the Name that is deeply embedded within you. So here's some advice, although I realize you didn't ask. . . . Stuck in a rut? Look for a mountain to climb. I'll be cheering you on. I sure will.

{Genesis 11:31–32}

WHEN YOU DARE TO BELIEVE

Every time you dare to believe, you strengthen your soul just a little bit more.

Yes and amen, every time. Every time you dare to believe that . . . today is the day. The answer will come. Redemption will be part of your story. Yes. Every time you dare to believe that . . . you were made for more. There's purpose for the pain. A whole lotta beauty is gonna be comin' outta all of these ashes. Every time you dare to believe that . . . things will get better. The seas will part. The water will turn into wine, and you'll finally hear God calling your name in the dark. Every time you dare to believe that . . . your dreams will catch flight. Your desires will come to fruition. Your days will not only be extended but filled to the brim with full life. Every time you dare to believe, Beloved, you strengthen your soul just a little bit more. To believe again after.

Yes. *After.* After the fire. After the hurt. After all seems hopeless and lost. After the storm. After the quake. After the thing that happened that you can't seem to shake and that keeps you awake. Yes.

Beloved, every time you dare to believe, you strengthen your soul just a little bit more . . . to believe again . . . and again and again. Dare to believe, Beloved. And then don't stop believin'. Amen.

USING THE GUIDANCE GOD GIVES YOU

Why would we pray and ask God for guidance if we aren't going to do anything with it?

Why would we ask God for strength and then not use the strength we are given? Why would we ask God to open our eyes and then not use those open eyes to see? Why would we cry out with the passion of Isaiah, "Here am I! Send me!" and then not actually go?

Esther prayed. Heck, she even called upon her people to pray. And then she took the courage and the strength and the guidance she was given by her God to bravely go before the king and boldly ask for the release of her people. I'm glad she didn't pray and then sit. Jesus stood next to a woman dragged out of bed, "caught in the act," if you will. He stooped down beside her, drug his finger through the dirt, giving the folks who surrounded her with their rocks something to see and some time to think, as He asked His Father in Heaven for what He needed . . . and then rose up and did His thing and defended and protected that woman, amen.

Friends, I remember years ago telling the women I was leading about a morning that I sat and prayed . . . and prayed . . . and because God knows us, *really* knows us and our human heart, He knew I was using it as religious time-filler to avoid doing what I knew I needed to do that day. And I'll never forget what I heard Him say, despite it being so many years ago . . . "I didn't strengthen you to sit." Yikes. I know, right? Pretty bold God, amen? Also—it worked. I got up. And actually used what I had asked God for.

Which leads me to my words today . . . *why would we ask God for guidance if we aren't going to do anything with it?* Right. Do we pray? *Of course we pray.* But since praying includes asking and begging and seeking . . . we *also* take what we are given . . . and use it. Cuz seriously, who asks for something and then doesn't use it? Right. So may we ask God. And then may we use what God gives us.

Day 327

TURN THE "WHAT IF" ON ITS EAR

Take the "what if" and turn it on its ear.

The "what if" intended to take you down, the one laced with the drug of doubt. Yes. You're familiar with it; I know you are. The "what if" that is often followed by . . . You fail? You look stupid? Something happens you don't want to happen? That's why you haven't heard from her/him/them? You're too old to possibly do that? You're too young to have any sort of impact, so why bother? You fail instead of succeed, and you're inundated with "I told you so's"? God never brings the "right" one? This is all that there is?

OK. *Stop right there. (FYI: I just about broke into a Meatloaf classic there, feel free to do so.)* Cuz we've heard enough, have we not? We sure have. Time to turn the beat around.

Beloved, take the "what if" and turn it on its ear. Use it as fuel to fly, not fear. Take the "what if" intended to slow you down and use it to *spur you on*. Take the "what if" meant to deliver you worry and capture that sucker right at the gate. *Yes*. Take it captive and set it up right there at the gate against the knowledge of Who your God is . . . and we'll just *see who wins, amen*. Yikes, Tera, time for decaf. But also—I *mean it*. Take the "what if"—and *give it new life*.

What if God is positioning me for more than I could ever ask for or imagine? What if God is strengthening me by making me climb this mountain? What if, like Mary and Martha on that day they'll never forget, I'm about to witness a miracle? What if? What if all that I have been through has prepared me for all that God still has planned for me? What if the wait is *worth* it? What if what lies *within* me really *is* greater than all that is against me? Mmhmm. Indeed. Amen-my-friend-amen.

Beloved, take the "what if" and turn it on its ear, would ya? Awesome. I love ya.

WHEN GOD STIRS THE WATERS

Keep in mind that God may be stirring the waters for your benefit.

I want you to be able to see the stirred waters anew, rename them as waters that refuse to stand still, and all for your benefit—waters that continue to flow as a result of their stirring. I want you to stop and recall a story about a man long ago who couldn't seem to get up and walk and move fully and freely through his life . . . because he couldn't seem to get to those stirred waters, the stirred waters that healed—yes, *healed.*

Beloved, the phrase "stirring the waters" gets a bad rap, and I reckon it's because of its closely related "stirring the pot" cousin. (Which also is not always a bad thing by the way, but I digress.) So, my friend, if God is in fact stirring the waters that surround you, and perhaps even within you, right now at this time in your life . . . I want you to see them and name them based on Who your God is. A God Who is with you and for you and knit you and formed you and knew you long before the foundation of the world and vowed to never leave or forsake you. Yes.

I want you to remember the same three P's I drilled into my confirmation students' heads one year . . . Provider. Protector. (All)-Powerful. Yes. For when the waters are stirred, and the storms carry on, and the winds of life gust to the point where we feel as though we can no longer stand . . . we will be tempted to forget Who God is.

And when it does—yes, *when—that* is when it really helps to return. *Yes.* Return to all those things in the Book that were written way back when to remind us and encourage us and spur us on, indeed and amen. Words like . . . Be still and know. Stand firm. Be bold. Be strong and courageous (followed by "For I Am with you wherever you go" . . . whew). Words like . . . God is faithful. God's covenant is everlasting. And both extend from generation to generation. Thank God. Beloved, keep in mind that God may be stirring the waters for your benefit. For we all know what stagnant waters bring.

A GREAT DAY TO BELIEVE THAT GOD WILL

What a great day to believe that God will . . .

Part the sea you've named "Impossible." Lead you beside a still one. Open the desperate eyes of the blind, keeping in mind they may just be yours. Give you an answer. Bring some relief. Calm the waves that continue to rage. Break the cycle. Fix what is broken. Redeem what you're beginning to believe will never *ever* be redeemed. Show you a sign. Hit you over the head. Make it as clear as He did for Gideon when He made that one cloth alone drenched with dew.

Beloved, what a great day to believe that God will . . . make a way where there currently isn't one. Provide a feast in the midst of your wilderness. Work a wonder so obvious that there's no way in heck you could possibly miss it. Yes. What a great day to believe that God will . . . make it rain. Make it stop. Break open the rock. Roll it out of the way. Move the mountain. Strengthen you to climb it. Give you some much-needed peace in your storm that (seriously, God) seems to have no end. Yes. Mend what is broken. Restore what's been lost. Renew and rehydrate your dead. Yes. What a great day to believe that God will . . . cause your name to be the talk of the table in your favor. Lift you up out of the pit. Shower you with so many blessings that you'll adopt "Singin' in the Rain" as your theme song.

What a great day to believe that God will . . . Send what you need and hold back what you don't. Bring the words you've been longing to hear. Surprise you in a way that is so beyond what you could have ever asked for or imagined that you know that you know . . . OMG, God . . . it's You. What a great day to believe that God will. What a great day to sing yourself a little ditty as you're cruising along on your journey on Earth . . . here's one I'd suggest . . . "Don't Stop Believin'." Indeed. And amen. This is my story. This is my song. Don't stop believin'. What a great day indeed. To believe that God will.

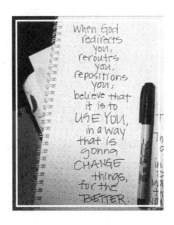

REDIRECTING, REROUTING, REPOSITIONING

When God redirects you, reroutes you, repositions you, believe that it is to use you in a way that is gonna change things for the better.

Let's see . . . Abraham. Moses. Noah and Fam. Jonah. Nehemiah. Naomi and Ruth. David. Esther. A gal by a well. Another facedown in the dirt. Saul-turned-Paul. Pete jumping ship. Joe one-day-pit, next-day-palace. Mary and Joe. Big time.

Beloved, you get my point. You catch my drift. Feel free to ride the wave. Cuz here's the thing, dear reader, right here—God has a thorough and complete perfect plan for your life. He assures you it's good, and this would be a mighty fine time to remind yourself that good is defined as meeting the expectation, the purpose . . . and we all know Whose purpose, amen. Right. So when God redirects you, reroutes you, and repositions you, I encourage you to return here to this partial list, to take a step back in history and based on all the aforementioned and all those not listed . . . believe that it is to *use you* . . . in a way that is gonna change some things . . . for the *better*. Amen.

Cuz truly I tell you, Beloved, I reckon that if we do, it's gonna allow us to move from fear to excitement. And excitement is a far better place to be. It sure is. Amen and amen, you-know-I'm-not-kidding-amen.

REVIVING WHAT HAS DIED WITHIN YOU

If what is inside you has died, speak to it. Revive it. Call it out of its grave.

Too much? Maybe. But here's the thing, folks—I am thoroughly convinced that God used my forties to make me brave so my next decade could be spent being bold. (Lord only knows what the decade after this one will bring.)

Beloved, I sometimes think that the best way to describe my writings, is a space that serves as a faith gym, which I guess makes me the personal trainer. Cool. So should you come to me and tell me that your Get-Up-and-Go has Got-Up-and-Went by way of what feels like death, well, then be forewarned that what I may just ask you to do is . . . Speak to it. Revive it. Call it out of its grave. I'm serious. And then I'd remind you—*that's what Jesus did when His friend Lazarus died.* Sweet, you caught that. Hmmm . . . was Jesus not only showing us that resurrection is real, but also that when what is inside of us dies . . . we've been given our very own breath—*God's breath,* ahem—to *revive and resurrect* it? Pause to catch that breath. Seriously. And also—I *mean it.*

Beloved, I am beyond passionate about refusing to live a life that simply goes through the motions—because robots can do that—not us. We've been given a body. We've been given a soul. And I'm convinced that for *both*—movement is medicine. Yes. One of the super cool things about David, the guy who wrote a big chunk of those Psalms you love, is that he spoke to his very own soul in order to strengthen it, comfort it, encourage it, cheer it on, remind it exactly Who God is . . . while never *once* denying or downplaying his reality. Rock on, Dave. We love you for that.

Beloved, today consider me both your personal trainer and cheerleader all wrapped into one. If what is inside of you has died, speak to it. Revive it. Call it out of its grave. For what lies within you is needed here. *Yes.* Believe that, believe that, believe that, amen. It's not too late. It's *not.* And man, I hope you hear me over here fiercely believing in you. I sure do.

THE PLACES YOU DON'T WANT TO BE

Paul in the prison and Dave in the cave taught her this: Incredible things often come . . . from the places we don't want to be.

It's true. Out of the cave, Dave wrote psalms that you and I can relate to today . . . and find comfort in knowing we aren't the only ones who struggle with all of the Whens and the Whys. Out of the prison, Paul penned letters that we now call a big chunk of the New Testament . . . words that have stood the test of time and taught much. And how about Esther sequestered? Do we remember what came out of that? Or how about the damsel in the dirt, or the one at the well about noon, or the one hunched over at the back of the temple, who Jesus called forth in front of *everyone* (how embarrassing, Lord), or the one who had bled for twelve years and everyone knew it, and then Jesus called her out right there in front of the whole dang crowd?

Now, Beloved, you don't suppose there's a chance . . . that God may be *using* the place you *don't* want to *be* in . . . to *make a difference* . . . do you?? Signs point to Yes here, folks. So the question is this—should we do some reframin' and renamin', cuz that's what we love to do here? We may feel as though God is squeezing the life right out of us, but maybe, just maybe, it's not the life God is squeezing out of us . . . but the *oil*. And seriously, isn't that a whole heckuva lot better way to look at it?? Agreed. And Indeed.

Beloved, the world needs what you've got, and although we don't always like or understand the ways God uses, we are, and will be, used for the incredible purposes for which we were sent. And the God Who created us, even gives us His own breath, as a reminder and personal guarantee while we're here . . . that we . . . are never . . . alone. Through it all. Every step and every situation. Every trouble and every trial. Every cave and every crowd. Every prison and every problem. Yes. Even in *those* places . . . the places we don't want to be. Amen.

OUR JOURNEYS DON'T TAKE PLACE ON TREADMILLS

Friends, our journeys don't take place on treadmills. And despite it all, deep down in the depths of who we are, in the innermost holy of holies encapsulated secure in our souls, lies a gratitude that in fact this is true. That as much as we cry for no hills to climb and no mountains to move and no wildernesses or deserts or storms to endure . . . our spirit/God's own breath rises up and reminds us . . . this is what we were created for. A human being placed on this Earth to reveal to the world, whether we know it or not, that God is, in fact, God. A God Who gives us hills to climb and mountains to move and wildernesses and deserts and storms to endure . . . so that we and the world will know . . . that God is Provider, and God is Protector, and God is all-Powerful, amen and amen. Our journeys don't take place on treadmills. They are not easy like that. How could they be? They're *taking us places*. Yes. Unlike the treadmill that simply stands still.

Beloved, I am convinced that part of our makeup includes a longing for home, for I can't imagine a God Who would toss us on Earth without it. And that longing, again, whether or not we are even aware of it, keeps us going. Keeps us believing. Yes. And thank God. We may say that we wish there weren't hills. We may say that we wish there weren't mountains. We may say that we wish there weren't hurdles to jump, and obstacles to overcome, and detours and roadblocks and all of the things that make our journey on Earth so dang hard . . . but also, makes it *whole and complete*.

Yes. A God Who loves us *far* too much . . . to allow our journey to take place on a treadmill. Indeed. You are never alone. Don't ever forget. Reframe the way that you see your journey. God loves you. I do too.

BELIEVE YOU WILL PRAISE GOD AGAIN

Even if you can't right now, believe you'll praise God once again.

And if you can't right now, permission to not. I mean it. You won't find me telling you to praise Him in the hallway, the one that is dark and lonely and filled with pain and grief and heartache and loss, while you wait for God to open the door. Nope. You *can* however rest assured that I'll go ahead and park my butt right next to you there. Yup. Giving you space without instruction of what you "should" do per the good Christian handbook. I may even grab your hand while joining you in your own personal hell, because it's really nice to know we're not alone there, amen? And while you're there in that pit, and I mean this, permission to set me straight if I should tell you that you must praise there in that place.

Beloved, as of late, I've felt a fire within when it comes to honoring our humanity. Because as far as I'm concerned, what could be *more* honoring to God than attributing value and worth and meaning and purpose to our humanness, seeing as though *God made us humans*? So no, you won't find me telling you what to do in the midst of your hell, but what I will do is this—I will believe alongside you that you will one day praise once again. And then, I may even break out in song, and gosh, Steve Perry will be so proud. Cuz see—that *believing*—is what keeps our soul alive as we wait for what's bound to be better. Yes. As a matter of fact, we may want to add "Stayin' Alive" to our mixtape. Sweet.

Beloved, if you can't praise right now, then you can't praise right now. God assures us false praise gets us nowhere, cuz He already knows what's real and what's not and opens His arms wide to receive authenticity as our offering. Yes. So if you can't right now, don't. But—do me this one thing, OK? *Believe* that you *will* . . . *once again.* Yes.

YOU CAN BE MAD AT GOD

Blessed is she who knows . . . that she can be mad at her God.

And frankly, if you ask me, it is a sign not of weak faith . . . but the polar opposite . . . the fiercest faith on Earth. Amen. A faith so confident in the strength of the bond between Parent and Child, Potter and Clay, Creator and Creation . . . that it holds nothing back . . . but instead brings it all. And knows . . . that *that's* . . . OK. A faith that doesn't turn *away* from God when she's mad, but instead, takes her mad *to* God. A faith that refuses to abandon her humanness in the name of what the world has deemed "religiously right," and instead brings every ounce of it, including every emotion she was equipped with in order to live fully her life right here on this Earth.

It seems we live in a world that shames us, not outwardly of course, because that wouldn't look good now, would it? But instead through the subtlety of sayings like . . . "Be so confident in God's plan for you that you don't get upset." Huh? How about be so confident in God's unfailing love for you that you actually acknowledge your upset, instead of shoving it into the recesses of your soul where it lingers and repeatedly nags as it whispers, "I'm still here, so you must not trust God."

I desperately want you to know that being mad at God is not a lack of faith. That not liking the plan does not mean you don't love your God. That tears of sadness don't equal lack of trust, and tantrums don't translate as heresy. Far from it. Instead, you are free. *And you know it.* Free to live fully in your humanness, not having to hide it, acknowledging every emotion you've been given, granted permission to not understand and still know that you are wholly and forever loved by the God Who created you and is right now providing your breath.

For truly I tell you, Beloved, anyone can have small talk, amen? But when the convo goes beyond how's-the-weather? . . . *That's* when it gets real. Amen. I love you. God loves you. In and through it all, and all means all, amen.

THE INTIMACY OF WAITING

Nothing will keep you closer to God than waiting to get what you so desperately want.

Read it again. And perhaps slow down as you do. And hey, as always, you don't have to take my word for it. You're welcome to ask the Israelites after they finally reached the promised land, or Noah after he and his crew finally got some relief from the flood, or Hannah as she prays so much folks think she's drunk, or Sarah as she's rocking Isaac to sleep, hoping to God Medicare is gonna cover some of this cost. Wink, wink again.

Friends, the waiting keeps you close. It keeps you asking until you lose your voice and keeps you knocking til your knuckles are bloody. Every day that passes, you are strengthening your faith, and you probably don't even know it. Yes. The waiting . . . is serving you. The waiting . . . is strengthening you. The waiting . . . is steering you right into the presence of God, where you can rest assured that you are seen, heard, and loved in every ask, every plead, every beg, every please-God-please. The waiting is drawing you near. It's keeping you close. It's moving you into the very front row so that you don't miss a thing.

Beloved, waiting is hard. Understatement? Are you kidding? I don't even have to answer that. It sucks. The waiting sucks. It's one of the ways of God we don't like, but then again, remember the whole "God's ways are higher than ours" thing? Right. Higher, as in beyond our human understanding. Like wayyyy beyond.

Beloved, God shows us stuff in the wait. Gives us glimpses. Draws us close. Remember Martha and Mare as they waited for their bff Jesus to come and heal their bro, but Jesus *didn't* come, and instead waited til their bro died because His plan was *bigger* than healing—it was actually resurrection, and it was gathering a crowd to show them a miracle? *Right.* Lean into that. Keep asking, keep seeking, keep believing, amen. For nothing will keep you closer to God than waiting to get what you so desperately want. Every amen. And big love.

IT IS WRITTEN

It is written.

Every word of your story. Every part of the plan. Every piece of the puzzle that yes, in the end, all work together for good. Perfectly, actually. Perfect as in whole and complete. That's right. It is written. Every moment that you will not understand. Every wonder and doubt you will have. The wonders and doubts, by the way, that will no doubt draw you closer to Him. It's true. It is written. Every bit of brokenness that will be used to feed others, every ounce of suffering that will lead you straight to the cross, every tear that you will ever shed that will be scooped up into a bottle held securely by your God and used to nourish the land you are in, or being brought to. Amen. *Whew.*

It is written. Every question you cry out in the night, wondering if God is listening. Every plea, every beg, every Why-God-Why that never escapes from your lips but is there . . . and stifled by fear. It is written. In blood, actually, if we're gonna take it that far. It is written. *Your story.* Packed with purpose, even if you can't see it. Flooded with worth of immeasurable value, even if you can't believe that that's true. Soaked with the Spirit of God Who is with you and for you and, in fact, before you . . . and beside you . . . and behind you . . . and within you, giving you your breath as a reminder and guarantee of to Whom you belong.

Beloved, I woke up in the night to these three words: It is written. It was all I could hear at first, and then all the rest began to rise up and spill out. So I tucked it away and asked God to please help me retain it 'til morning, because frankly, I didn't think that starting the coffee at 2:17 a.m. was such a wise idea. So do with these words what you will. Take them or leave them along the road. For me, they are peace. A place to rest my overwhelmed head. Words whispered to my soul from the Author and Finisher and Perfecter of my faith . . . until I hear the next three words someday . . . *It is finished.* Amen.

GOD WILL PROVIDE

One way or another, God will provide.

A ram in the thicket. A rolled away stone. A field just ready for harvest. An abundance of oil that doesn't quit flowing. Water into wine at a wedding. A fully stocked ark. A well without H2O. Another with Jesus sitting beside it to show us that we *all* get tired out from the journey at times. Yes. OMG, so much yes. A rainbow after a forty-day/month/year flood. A sunrise to greet you Good Morning. A sea that is stilled and another stirred up so that *you* can watch as He calms it. A slingshot and rock. A full suit of armor. An angel inside the cell known as prison and another in the den where all the *really* hungry lions are kept. A compassionate boss. An encouraging spouse. A friend who will fast from the world and listen. Darkness for you to get some rest. Light for you to work. Green pastures for you to lie down in even-when-you-don't-want-to-and-seriously-fight-it-amen.

Yes. The thorn in your side that keeps you abiding. Ugh. Ugh-ugh-ugh. But also—it works—so, yes. The bread sent from Heaven not only to feed you, but broken and multiplied and given for a great massive feast. The mud used to open your eyes. The beauty in exchange for the ashes. Someone to draw you up out of the water and another to remind you that you were made to walk on it. *Yes.* A cloud of witnesses. A communion of saints. The new you never thought you'd bring forth and the old and the dead brought back to life. *OMG, yes.*

Beloved, truly I tell you, I could go on and on and on, but my point today is simply this: One way or another, God will provide.

THERE'S HEALING IN SPEAKING

Maybe God hasn't answered you yet because God knows there's healing in speaking.

There is healing found in talking it out. There is healing found in being heard. And my guess is that if there's a counselor among us here today, she/he would concur, amen. *Yes.* And also, how cool is it that our God goes by the name Wonderful Counselor? I know, right? I think we forget that.

Beloved, I don't know what you're going through, what you're enduring, or how many times a day you're crying out to God and getting crickets in return. I'm simply here to offer up a new way to see it. The silence, that is. Yes. Based on Who our God is. . . . What if God's silence isn't punishment . . . but provision? What if God's silence is giving you the time and the space you need to release every "Why??" . . . Think pressure valve slowly turning to allow for escape. Yes. What if? Cuz here's the thing—I'd rather view the silence of God as *for* me—rather than against me. I sure would. For when I do . . . I can endure the silence. Note: I didn't say *like* it. I said *endure* it. My friend Job taught me that it's more-than-OK to own my humanness, and I'll always love him for that. Thanks, Job.

So today, Beloved, here's a Maybe, maybe (see what I did there?) a new way to see the silence, giving it a new name. Maybe God hasn't answered you yet . . . because God's letting you speak . . . releasing what is within . . . because God knows there's healing in that. Maybe. There is healing in being heard, Beloved. *You* are heard. Without interruption. Every word, every sigh, every tear, every cry, every why, God, why, why, why. . . . You are heard. By the One Who created you, formed you, knit you, placed you, and delivered you into our world with power and purpose, amen. Yes. Don't forget. And own your humanness. Big love.

GOD HOLDS IT ALL

If you take nothing else from the Book of Job, take this: Satan answers to God. Amen.

And I'll say it again—amen. The sovereignty of God is not up for grabs. This ain't no free-for-all. Fact. God holds the good, the bad, and the ugly, and raises up hard and calls it holy. *Yes.* Holy. Set apart. For a purpose. Amen. God gives us the Word, the body and blood, which feeds and spills out story upon story upon story that reiterate the message that says . . . Hard is Holy. And I hold the hard. Amen.

Job's life was hard—and holy. Moses too. Noah too. Abe too. Joe too. Dave too. Naomi too. Ruth too. Esther too. A bleeding woman too. A Samaritan at a well too. A guy lying inches from healing but just couldn't seem to get there too. . . . And you. Yes, Beloved, *you too.* How do I know? Because all humans endure some level of hard, and all hard is holy, for all hard is held by our God Who is holy, amen.

Do we understand it all? No. Do we, like Job, wonder why it has to be? Yes. Do we, like Mary and Martha did in their time, struggle with why God doesn't swoop in and save the day, seeing as we know darn well that He could? We sure do. And of *course* we're going to struggle, because we can't possibly understand the ways of God. That's called being human, by the way. Don't forget that.

So what do we do? How do we endure while we simultaneously fully, abundantly live? We read Job. And remember. That Satan answers to God, not the other way around. Hashtag Bing Bam Boom. We remember that God holds it all—even the hard—and calls it—holy. We remember that we are not alone in the pit or in the well or in the furnace or in the den of lions or stranded out at sea without a savior. We remember God sees, and God hears, and God knows, and God's near, and God is *still* in control. No matter what our circumstances look like, amen. We sure do. And we remind one another along the way, because we're bound to forget. And because that's what loving one another looks like. It sure is. Big love, Beloved.

BELIEVING GOD FOR REALLY BIG THINGS

Start believing God for some really big things.

As a girl who loves the Bible, loves to read the Bible, study the Bible, gobble up and devour the Bible, and dig deeper and deeper all the time into the Bible, I have also realized lately that I think that there is something to be said about overthinking the Bible. Cuz see, here's the thing folks, the Bible? The Bible is a great big collection of impossible-made-possible stories, situations, testimonies, and trials that all put together boom from the Heavens above *this* song . . . "*with God, all things really are possible.*"

Yes. The Bible as a whole is the songbook that sings, "Don't Stop Believin'." It contains all the lyrics, and you bring to the stage your very own voice. And I'll tell you what, when you sing the way your choir teacher taught you to, from way down deep instead of simply the surface, well, that's when it becomes real, don't ya know. Yup. The Bible as a whole is a compilation of people who are human just like us (hallelujah), therefore allowing and strengthening us to believe, even with just the tiniest seed or speck or very last thread . . . that it may just be true for us too.

After all, if Sarah can give birth to something new at dang near one hundred, why can't we bring something new into this world despite our gray hair? If Esther can start out her life as an orphan and end up queen, why can't we rise up and be bought into position despite where our life began? If a woman who had been hemorrhaging for twelve long years and kept in complete isolation can muster up the courage to go find Jesus and reach out and touch Him, why can't we find the courage to do what we're dying to do, despite fear of what the crowd will think?

Right. I could go on, Beloved. And if you've been here a while, you know I could. But I'm gonna run outta room here, so I'm just gonna leave you with you this: *Start believing God for some really big things.* And don't stop believin'. For believing is what keeps your heart/mind/soul alive and on fire, and, Eric Church is right, there ain't nothing like a heart on fire. Amen.

BRAVE ENOUGH TO PRAY

She was brave enough to pray.

She didn't know the plan. But she did know the promise. She didn't know how it would all work out. But she did know that it would, for He works all things together for good. She didn't know which way to go, whether to turn to the right or the left. But she did know that whether she turned to the right or the left, He would be there, leading and guiding her. She didn't know what He was doing all the time or understand it or always like it. But she did know that His ways are higher, and His thoughts are higher, and she best not lean on her own human understanding, and instead acknowledge just who He is. So she was brave enough to pray to Him.

She didn't know what tomorrow would bring. But she did know that He did, and He created it, and He said it was good, and she also knew that He had told her not to worry about it. She didn't know why there had to be a time for *everything* under the sun. But she did know He told her there was, and that He makes all things beautiful in time. She didn't know why. But she did know Who. So she was brave enough . . . to pray to Him. Yes. Brave enough to behold the One Who makes all things right, the One Who redeems and restores. The One Who is good and is with her and for her and Whose faithful love endures forever and extends to all generations. To ask the God Whom she's come to know and truly love for exactly what she needs. Each day. Each hour. Each moment. For the peace and the rest and the hope and the strength and the courage and the faith and all that her heart and mind truly need. . . . Yes. For all of those things, and a million more, are exactly in fact Who He is.

So she was brave enough to pray to Him. Yes. Brave enough to pray. Words that rocked my world a few years ago, and still do, in the very best possible way.

{2 Samuel 7:27; 1 Chronicles 17:25}

STRETCH YOURSELF

The restoration you're longing for . . . may come as a result of stretching yourself like never before. (Read it again.)

One man. One shriveled up hand. Jesus says to the man . . . S T R E T C H yourself. *Yes.* Stretch out that hand. Stretch yourself in a way you've never stretched yourself before . . . in order to restore the part of you that feels withered up, shriveled up, dried up. *Amen. Yes.*

Beloved, one of the coolest (and simultaneously hardest) things about God's ways is that they are *so* often *not* the ways we'd expect, and (more often than not) certainly *not* the ways we would *choose.* Right.

Mud in our eyes to see. (John 9:6)

Asses in our path to get us where we need to be. (1 Samuel 9:3–18)

Stretching ourselves in order to bring about recovery and restoration. *See what I mean?* God's ways. Effective, that's for sure.

Beloved, what if *today* . . . you asked yourself *this* . . . Could stretching myself . . . like never before . . . bring with it the restoration . . . the new life . . . that I'm desperately longing for? I know, right? Whew. Good Stuff. And *amen.*

{Matthew 12:9–13}

PRAY TO PUT THINGS IN PERSPECTIVE

Pray to put things in perspective. Because talking it out really helps. Prayer is not some rigid process. Prayer is a way to process your every emotion. Amen.

I know, it looks like a lot. Stay with me. Beloved, pray so you can put things in perspective. Pray because talking it out really does help. Prayer is not some rigid process; prayer is a *way to process* your every emotion, amen. Yes. And because I love you, let me give you an example based on what I personally poured out as prayer in the form of words scratched out in my journal this very morn, a good twenty minutes before I read from God's Word, cuz that's how I do it, amen. Here's what I wrote:

Lord, You know. You know what today has in store. You know what this week has in store. You know what this month and next month have in store, for they are *all* from *your* storehouse. A storehouse *full* of glory and riches and treasures of immeasurable worth; a storehouse that never runs out.

Yup. That's what I wrote. Prayed. To put. Things in. Perspective. Yes. Now, what I *didn't* necessarily expect was to then be totally blown away by the words that I would then read, but good golly, I love when God does that. Seriously. Words like . . . "We don't know what to do, but our eyes are on You." Words like . . . "Thus says the Lord to you: 'Do not fear or be dismayed at this great multitude; for the battle is not yours but God's.'" Words like . . . "Take your position, stand still, and see the victory on your behalf." And words like . . . "Believe in the Lord your God and you will be established."

I know, right?? Talk about some kick-butt words that will kick-start a girl right into her day, amen? *Amen.* OK, Beloved, I'm gonna sign off now, because *you may just want to read that all again.* Amen.

{2 Chronicles 20}

MOVIN' ON

The enemy whispers, "She doesn't like you." God whispers back, "Movin' on."

Now listen, before you send hate mail informing me that this doesn't sound super kind and loving, hear me out, OK? This is *not* about refusing to love your neighbor. That's right, it sure isn't. It's about recognizing that perhaps you are letting how someone else feels about you, or your perception of how someone else feels about you . . . trip you up or slow you down or plunge-into-the-pit-of-despair-obsessing-over-why-he-or-she-doesn't-like-you-all-the-while-missing-out-on-all-that-is-before-you-*whew*.

Listen, I have no doubt you've read a hundred posts/memes/whatever about not caring what others think. Those are not my words to you today. It's not about not caring; it's about *recognizing what may be consuming you*. Now, how do we know if something's consuming us? We answer these questions honestly: How much am I thinking about it? Dwelling on it? Is it interfering in any way with my life? Right. So see, this isn't about not loving your neighbor. Loving your neighbor is hands down the very best thing we can do while we're here on this Earth. Jesus said so, amen. My words to you today are about recognizing the thoughts that tempt you to forget Who God is. Tempt you to forget the holy journey you're on. Thoughts intended to kill/steal/destroy. Yes.

Beloved, the enemy may want you to be stuck, but *you*, my friend, can take those thoughts captive and respond to those thoughts like our good friend Nehemiah once did . . . "I am doing a great work, and I cannot come down." He sure did. For he recognized the stumbling block of distraction. And refused to give into it. And so can we. Amen. And we can do so while continuing to love our neighbor. For we know that in the end, love wins every time.

MAYBE IT'S TIME TO BEGIN THE WORK

Maybe it's time to begin the work.

I'm not saying it is, and I'm not saying it isn't; I'm saying *maybe* it is. Maybe it's time to begin the work. The work of rebuilding. The work of repairing. The work of bringing forth something new. The work of forgiving and moving beyond through resting in Who your God is. The work of moving your being. Moving your body. Heck, moving your bedroom around. Whatever. Maybe. Maybe it's time to begin the work of rearranging according to priority. The work of believing you can. The work of recognizing the cause of your tired, for that will help in determining the solution, amen.

Here's what I mean, and I warn you, this takes being uber-gut-honest with yourself, but you may as well be, because that's when real changes occur. Right. So, back to the source of your tired. Picture it. You've run a marathon. Jumped hurdles. Spent all day moving your body. You're tired. Makes sense. Yep. Now picture this. You've traveled all day in a car. You've sat, and you've sat, and you've sat some more (aside from those occasional "I gotta get out and stretch my legs" stops). You reach your destination. And you're tired. *Huh?* But also . . . it's true, amen? Right. Tired, from *not* moving at all. It's a thing. Yep. And I'm convinced it's also a thing when it comes to our heart/mind/and soul.

Friends, I don't know where you're at. I don't know what you're doing or not doing or what stage or season or where-in-the-heck-you-are in the script your Author God wrote for you. I'm simply here, on this day that God made, to offer these words in response to the words that I read and devoured this morning, cuz that's what you do with good bread . . . maybe it's time to begin the work. (Psst . . . if these words hit you "just so" . . . I'm willing to bet that it is.) Oh, now listen, before you go, there's something else that *must* be said, words Dave told his son Sol after telling him that it was indeed time to begin the work . . . *the Lord your God is with you.* That's right. Big love and amen.

{1 Chronicles 22:16–19}

SEEK GOD LIKE YOUR LOST CELL

The remote is missing. You misplaced your cell. Seek God's presence like that.

Once during a phone interview, I told the woman, "There's more than one way to be salt, for there's more than one purpose for salt. What I hope I do, as salt on this Earth, is to help make it stick, help people retain it—by connecting God's Word to their everyday real."

Fact. So, that being said, my friends . . . picture it. The remote is missing, and your favorite TV show in all the world is starting in exactly two minutes. You can't find your cell, and it's time to leave the house and oh-crap-what-am-I-going-to-do-all-my-stuff-and-everything-I-need-for-today-is-in-that-stupid-thing. (Because note: I don't know if you've noticed, Beloved, but we get mad at stuff when we can't find it.) *Right.* Here's another—I tell my kid to go upstairs to his room and find his socks. He walks in, turns around, and yells downstairs, "I can't find 'em." Then I tell him I've shoved a hundred-dollar bill in each one of those socks, and he can use that dough for *whatever* he wants. *Right.* Commence operation "Seek with All Ya Got."

Beloved, seek God's presence like *that.* Be so determined to see God in your situation, your circumstance, your sadness, your fill-in-the-blank . . . that you actually *seek* until you *find* it. God's Presence. *Yes.* And *as* you seek, remind yourself Who your God *is,* for truly I tell you, it will give you the perseverance you need . . . to keep. on. seeking. *Yes.* Because see, you know Who your God is. You know your God is Provider. You know your God is Protector. You know your God is All-Powerful. You know your God vowed to never leave you or forsake you, so you *know* that your God is *in* it. *Yes.* *Whatever* your *it.* Including all that rhymes with your *it.* Mmhmm. So you listen to me, Beloved—you *seek* until you *see.* You seek until you can rename. You seek until your perspective shifts . . . giving . . . you . . . some peace. Cuz even a drop of it matters. Amen.

Day 348

THE WARRIOR IS YOU

Your story will include great battles. Don't you forget the Warrior Who is for you, and the warrior who is you.

I mean it. Don't you forget that although David was a mighty king and a man after God's own heart, he still experienced war after war and grew weary just like we do, amen. And don't forget that springtime is often the time when the fiercest battles are fought. (P.S.: You don't have to take my word for that. 2 Samuel 11:1. You're welcome.) Perhaps it's being so close to the cusp of the new that does it. The pain before the something new that's about to burst forth. (P.S.: again. Let's hang on to the "new that's about to burst forth" part as we endure the pain of the battle, shall we? Awesome.) Don't forget that in every one of your wars, you have a Warrior who is with you and for you. For *if* you know this mighty truth, you'd call upon Him, correct? I mean, who wouldn't? Right. Don't forget the Warrior Who is for you. Don't forget the warrior who *is* you either.

Gideon forgot, remember? As the youngest kid of the weakest tribe, he forgot who he was in God's eyes—read that again, amen. Yes. Good thing God reminded him. That he was a mighty warrior. And maybe today, Beloved, He's reminding *you*. Man, I hope so. Reminding you that you are strong and courageous, because your God All-Powerful is always with you, and all means all, amen. That despite your weariness, you need only be brave enough to pray. That despite the famine, you can inquire of the Lord again and again, just like David did—even through the one that lasted three years. Right.

Don't forget that your story will include great battles, Beloved. Battles you don't want to face, yet you don't face alone. Beloved, your story will include great battles. I'm not going to add yeast to that unleavened bread. I'm sure not. What I want you to remember *in* the battles, is the Warrior Who is *for* you, and the warrior who *is* you. I sure do. Cuz you're loved. Huge. Far more than you know, and I mean that, amen.

359

WHEN YOU CAN'T MAKE SENSE OF THE PLAN

List of those in the Bible who at some point in their lives couldn't make sense of the plan God had for them: Every human in the Bible I can think of. Amen.

Sarah—Why am I old, married, and without child? Mary—Why am I young, unmarried, and with child? Noah—Why am I building this ark? Moses—Why am I charged with leading these people? These People—Why are we going the long way? Right.

Mary and Martha—Why isn't Jesus coming when he knows our brother is dying? The Woman with "the issue"—Why won't I stop bleeding? The Disciples—Why would He send us out in this storm? Isaac—Why are we climbing this mountain without a sacrifice to bring with us? Right.

Jonah—Why am I literally inside this big fish? Esther—Why was I orphaned and raised by my cousin only to be taken from him? Daniel—Why am I surrounded by all these hungry lions? Job—Why is God doing all of this to me? Seriously?? Right.

Beloved, I could go on and on and on, but I reckon you've got somewhere to be, and you're thinking you best get ready. Me too. The point is this—you won't always be able to make sense of the plans God has for you. Many of them will make at least some sense in hindsight. (No wonder the cliché says what it does.) And some will never make sense at all. But the next time you find yourself wondering . . . "What the heck, Lord? Where are You? Why? Why? *Why*???" . . . I want you to remember you're in good company. It's a piece of your story. A holy fragment. A vital part of the plans God has for you. And who knows . . . He may be positioning you to witness a miracle. Think about that. Big love and amen.

SUSTAINED, NOT SATISFIED

My Daughter, I sustained you in the wilderness, but I didn't satisfy you there . . . for I wanted you to keep going.

Friends, I remember the first time I had this revelation; it was years ago, and I remember writing something of the sort way back then too. I remember hearing these words from the One I'd come to know as All-Knowing, All-Loving, Almighty Creator and Parent. And it made sense to me. Perhaps one of the few things back then that did.

My Daughter, I sustained you in the wilderness, but I didn't satisfy you there . . . for I wanted you . . . to *keep going. Yes.*

This wasn't about discontentment; it was about drive. It was about a faith that whispered, sometimes screamed, "You are made for more" . . . and a heart-mind-and-soul that chose to believe it. And make peace with the manna. Understanding that its purpose was to sustain her, not satisfy her, in order that she would keep going. Keep going while holding on to the promise, believing and trusting that whatever it was God had next for her . . . was right over the bend . . . right on the other side of that mighty Red Sea . . . right there just beyond the Jordan. Yes. It was the *unknowing* . . . that kept her *going.* It is *still* the *unknowing* of exactly what's next, coupled with the *knowing* of Who her God is—Provider, Protector, All-Powerful—that keeps her going *today. Yes.* It's the theme song that plays in her head, "Don't Stop Believin'." And as I've said before, the fact that it's sung by a band named Journey, well that's just a bonus. Amen.

Beloved, this morning I read these words, words I've seen and continue to see come to life . . . "The manna ceased on the day they ate the produce of the land, and the Israelites no longer had manna; they ate the crops of the land of Canaan that year." They sure did. Friends, if your faith is whispering, "You are made for more," why not listen and believe that it's true? For perhaps that mystery of what is to come, paired with the knowledge of Who your God is, will keep you going, asking, seeking, amen.

{Joshua 5:12}

YOU ARE WORTH FIGHTING FOR

If God never brought you to battle, how would you know that you are worth fighting for?

Here's what I've learned, what I've witnessed in my journey thus far . . . God will bring me to battles so that I can know I'm worth fighting for. *Yes.* God will bring me to wars so I can watch as God wins. God will position me in places I don't want to be simply so I can taste and see that God really *is* Protector, Provider, All-Powerful (don't *ever* forget those three Ps)—even if it does come in the form of manna, a.k.a., *what the heck is this, Lord?* This is *not* what I meant. *Right.* So what if, based on Who we know God to be—the Author *and* Perfecter-Finisher of our stories, the One Who will be with us even unto death *and* resurrection—what if *because* we *know* all that is true, we *also* then learn to see our battles not as punishment from a God Who is "over us," but instead as a way to show us . . . God is *over* us. Yes. Over and above us as well as within us. Sovereign over *all* things. *in* it with us, whatever the *it.*

Once upon a time, God brought a man named Josh to a battle. Sensing his fear, his angst, and his woe, God said unto Joshua, "Fear them not: for I have" (please notice *past* tense here folks, cuz that's *huge*) "delivered them into thine hand; there shall not a man of them stand before thee." And with *that* kind of encouragement and *that* kind of reassurance; Josh, despite marching all night, uphill by the way, was ready for battle. He sure was. Physically after that all-night-uphill climb, and spiritually after the talk with his God . . . knowing that God was bringing him to it . . . so he could watch God be victorious. To show Josh that he and his people were worth fighting for.

Beloved, when God brings you to a battle, one that doesn't seem fair, one you so wish could be avoided, keep in mind that it *may* just be so *you* will know you're worth fighting for.

{Joshua 10:8 KJV}

HEALING BY GOING

Your healing may come as a result of your going.

This morning, I got up and read a familiar story. A group of lepers. Longing for healing. Quite literally everything falling apart for them. Quite literally losing more and more of themselves each day. (Ahem, if this feels personal, ask yourself if it is.) They stood far from Jesus, as of course good lepers would do. But they raised their *voices*, for that they *could* do, for voices carry you know (pause for '80s song break). And when Jesus *saw* them, He *said* to them, "Go show yourselves unto the priests." . . . Wait for it . . . *and it came to pass* . . . that *as they went* . . . they were cleansed.

Wait a sec—you mean they received the healing their hearts-minds-and-souls had been desperately longing for through their *going*? *Hmmmm.* One of them realized the depth of what had just happened. He stopped on the road home and turned back, and with a loud voice glorified God right there before his Lord. And do you wanna know what Jesus said to him? "Arise, go thy way, your *faith*, hath *made*, you *whole*." Yes. The one who realized that for God all things are possible, and realized that *he*, as one lone leper, was *worthy* of that healing . . . he was made *whole*. Body restored. Heart restored. Mind restored. Soul restored. His story forever to tell.

Beloved, your healing may come as a result of your going. Your going *to* and/or your walking away *from*. Your going despite hesitation, fear, or excuse . . . may just bring . . . the healing you are longing for. And you may not even fully realize it . . . until you do . . . and you find yourself praising God while belting out the best '80s songs . . . all the way home. *XO.*

{Luke 17:11–19}

CALL IT FERTILIZER

Rename the crap and call it fertilizer.

I know, right? And a howdy good morning to you too, Tera. Geesh. But also, I'm dead serious. Yep. Beloved, rename the crap and call it fertilizer. I mean it. Because all of the crap you have been through, and/or all of the crap you are currently going through, is in some way—helping you. Yes. Even if it stinks. (Wink, wink, wink, wink.)

Ya know, recently on my way home for lunch, a gal on the radio was giving some kind of Ag update. (Yes, as in agriculture; in the Midwest we have such reports, you know.) Anyway, she was talking about manure. Yes. Manure. The importance of it, the placement of it, the cost of it, *and* . . . the incredible *benefit* of it. Mmhmm. Beloved, rename the crap. I mean it. It won't magically make the crap disappear; on the contrary, it may just help you see the crap as something that is actually benefiting you, serving you, *preparing you* . . . for all of the fruit you're gonna be bearing. Boom-chicka-yes-please-ain't-no-weapon-formed-against-you-gonna-prosper-amen. *Yes.* And please also keep in mind that your God has been known to heal and open eyes with mud, and that ain't exactly something we usually want on us either . . . so there's that. Amen.

Beloved, rename the crap. Do it. Give it purpose. Give it value. Give it worth, cuz Lord knows it's costing you something. Look back at the crap you have been through, and name all of the ways it benefitted you, served you, prepared you. And rename the crap you are *currently* going through . . . and call it what it is . . . *fertilizer*. And from what I hear, it's the best. Yep. The crap. Renamed. Fertilizer. Preparing you to prosper, amen and amen and read it again. Mmmhmm.

THE OPPOSITION YOU FACE

Yes, even the opposition you face is a part of your story on Earth.

And it won't make sense. You won't understand why God would *bring* you someplace only for you then to face *opposition* in that place. You'll find yourself wondering if you made the wrong decision, or if it's some kind of punishment, or if you've done something wrong, or if maybe your time is just done, and it will never once dawn on you . . . that the opposition you are facing is a part of your story on Earth. And you won't like it. And you likely won't understand it. And since it doesn't line up with the picture of God you have in your head, you won't for one second stop to consider that perhaps it is *training you for all that still lies ahead*. Right. But see, you won't see that in the midst of it. You won't see it until after you've crossed that sea. You won't understand why God would finally lead you out from where you were . . . only to then have you face opposition.

So, what do we do? I've got an idea. (One I learned by living through it, by the way, and finally now . . . years later . . . yes, *years* . . . am able to look back and see it anew—hallelujah.) Here it goes: The next time you face opposition, take a deep breath, remind yourself that it's a part of your story on Earth . . . and then remind yourself *Who wrote your story*. That's right. The *same One* that's perfecting your faith *through* it. Provider. Protector. All-Powerful. God. Which means—it's a story that *holy*. A story that's set apart and filled with purpose and power, even when you can't see it. A story that's fulfilling God's purpose on Earth. A story specifically written for you—by the One Who knows the plans He has for you.

And if you will, allow me to say to you what Moses said to those Israelites way back then as they faced opposition in the place where God brought them . . . "Do not be afraid, stand firm, and see the deliverance that the Lord will accomplish . . ." Yes.

{Exodus 14}

THE LORD YOUR GOD GOES BEFORE YOU

Joseph's brothers threw him into a well. The well had no water in it. Friend—the Lord Himself goes before you. Don't forget.

I mean it. Don't forget. Joe's bros threw him into a well in order to get rid of him. *There was no water in the well.* They saw some Ishmaelites heading their way and thought . . . Hey! We might as well get a little something for him. So they sold him. And he was taken. *To a palace. Where he would go on to be a top dog.* Right. Friends—the Lord Himself goes before us. Jonah decided his calling wasn't for him. So he boarded a ship. But when the sea began to rage and Jonah revealed that he knew it was all his fault, they threw him overboard into that angry sea. *And God made sure there was a great big fish there to swallow him up, thus protecting him from certain death.* Friends—the Lord Himself goes before us. Esther was orphaned. Being raised by her cousin Mordecai, she was taken. Taken because she was a single fair maiden. And like our guy Joe, brought into a palace. *Where she would go to save her people from genocide.* Friends—the Lord Himself goes before us. Yes.

Beloved, I don't know what you are facing, what you are enduring, or what you have just survived . . . but I encourage you with all the love that I've got to look for all the ways, even if you see *one* . . . that the Lord Himself has gone before you. Yes. For He has. This is most certainly true. Deuteronomy 31:8 always and always and always, amen. Big love. So much love.

IN THOSE HARD PLACES

Whether you know it or not, God is with you in your hard places. And those places may be exactly where God intends to abundantly provide.

Friends, today I opened my DRB and found myself reading in Genesis 28. Here's the summary: Jacob left Beer-Sheba and headed for Haran. He wouldn't make it there in a day, so as night drew near, he grabbed a stone for a pillow and decided to call it a night. Hard place to rest your head, amen? *Right.* Jacob dreamed. (Anything to escape the reality, right?) He dreamed of a way to reach Heaven—maybe a ladder or stairway or ramp. Whatever would lift him out of this really hard place he was in. And we've all been there. And that's when the Lord appeared to our friend Jacob, *in that hard place.* And in that hard place, Jacob heard these words . . . I Am the Lord, the God of Abraham your father, and the God of Isaac; (here it comes folks) . . . *the land on which you lie I will give to you and to your offspring . . . and all the families of the Earth shall be blessed in you and your offspring.*

I know, right? *Hello.* Had Jacob heard right? Was God going to provide for him abundantly *in this hard place*? Absolutely. And as if those words alone weren't enough for our friend Jake, they were followed by *these* . . . "Know that I Am with you and will keep you wherever you go, and I will bring you back to this land; for I will not leave you until I have done what I promised you." Wowza. I can't even, folks. It's just too stinkin' good. Amen. Jake then woke up and spoke these words, "Surely the Lord is *in this place*, and I didn't know it!" No doubt.

So today, Beloved, I offer you this to ponder/consider/heed. . . . Could it be . . . that it is *in* your hard place . . . that God intends . . . to abundantly provide? Hmmm. Ask Jake . . . from Scripture, not State Farm. (Sorry, I had to.) Big love to you in your hard place, Beloved. Hold on to the promise of the God Who is with you and gives you His breath so you never forget.

WHAT IF GOD IS ANSWERING YOU?

What if? What if God is answering you, but it's just arriving in ways you never wanted or expected?

Food for thought. Followed by this—a reminder that God speaks in the silence *and* in the storms. A God Who breathes purpose into the strong winds that blow, and those strong winds are sometimes used to part seas. Remember that. A God Whose ways are not *our* ways, and if that ain't the biggest understatement, I don't know what is. Amen. A God Who speaks from the eye of the storm, which teaches us two pretty big things, if you ask me—there will be storms. And I will be with you in them. Hearing you. And *answering* you. (And Job would confirm it, thanks dude.)

Beloved, the answer may lie in the turmoil. I hate to say that, but in my years on this Earth thus far, I've learned that it's true. The answer may be in the thing that causes you to finally sit up and take notice, even if that thing is something you don't like or ever expected. I know. But it's true. Friends, you know how I love to think and ponder. To see God alive and present and continuing to ask us the questions that stir us, awaken us, cause us to think and ponder and learn-stretch-and-grow, cuz He just loves us that stinkin' much.

So today I ask you to consider this: What if God *is* answering you . . . but it's just arriving by ways you never wanted or expected? For God always listens and God always answers . . . some way, somehow, in His whole, complete, and perfect time . . . for that is what Faithful does. You are loved. Forevermore. Don't forget that either.

APPLYING PRESSURE FOR YOUR BENEFIT

Maybe it's time to put some pressure on yourself.

Because here's the deal, folks—the same Bible that uses words and phrases like "rest" and "lie down" also repeatedly uses words and phrases like "go," "get up," "the time had come," amen. It's why you won't find me trying to tell you what Scripture means, but rather, what I gleaned from the Scripture I read on that day. Which, by the way, may be, and often is, different from what I gleaned from the very same words in the past. Not a replacing, but an "adding to," for truly I tell you, Jesus ain't playin' when it comes to His ability to expand tents and multiply loaves—hallelujah. So, in a world that says, "Don't put so much pressure on yourself"—all I'm offering is this: What if it's time you do? What if it's time to apply some pressure in order to gain some strength? Seriously.

I once taught a Strength-for-Seniors class, and we would often use our own body as resistance to apply the pressure we need . . . to build strength . . . strength that we'd lost and wanted to regain. *Yes.* Maybe it's *time* to put some pressure on yourself. Maybe it's time to push. Need some cool Bible examples?

Abraham. Old and led to unknown land. Pushing through as he climbed that mountain with his boy Isaac, despite knowing what waited atop. And a God Who surprised him when he got there. Thank God. Esther. Faced with a literal life-or-death situation—and the cousin who had raised her who challenged her thinking by offering up for consideration . . . "*perhaps* you were brought into position for such a time as this." That Perhaps would cause Esther to think and decide on her own what she knew she needed to do. And spoiler alert if you haven't read her story—she did.

Friend, I'm not here to tell you what God is saying to you. I'm here to encourage you to *honestly consider* what it *is* that God is saying to you. At this point in your journey. Maybe it's time to put some pressure on yourself. Believe that you can. Commit and Push . . . showing yourself that you're still Alive. Because maybe you need the reminder. Maybe.

ALL OF IT

Look for God in all of it.

All of it. I mean it. Be *so* determined to see God in all of it—every single thing—that you look for God 'til you do. Use your stubbornness for good, for God's sake. Seriously. Look for God—in *all* of it. Your work. Your worries. Your questions. Complaints. The frets spinning 'round in your mind right now that are spewing out anxious fiery arrows of . . . How am I going to do this? How can this possibly work? Where in the world is *that* going to come from? How can I figure this out . . . *now*? Right.

Beloved, as your mind undoubtedly spins, may your eyes be determined to seek. To be still for even a second . . . and look. To see . . . God . . . *in* it. *All* of it. The answers as they arrive, even if they seem like coincidence/no big deal. The playing out of this day. The moments that may seem trivial to others, but to you? Oh man . . . you just got to watch God do what God does, and you got to watch God do it for *you*. Or someone you love. Or someone you don't. Or someone in the crowd, and watching God do it for him or for her has now stirred something in you that is daring you to believe it—for you. Yes.

Friends, here's my advice in case you'd like some—Look for God in *all* of it. All of your Its. Amen.

WHAT DO YOU REALLY WANT?

What do you want? Really?

Jesus stands still. Amen. Looking right at you so that you will know there's absolutely no mistake at all as to whom He's speaking to. And He asks you . . . What do you want? And you're surprised a bit at your initial reaction. The moment you thought you'd been waiting and waiting for . . . suddenly may have you stumped. Stopped. Leery to answer. What do you want . . . really? I don't know your answer. Maybe you don't either. And maybe that's the hardest part. But I'm willing to bet ten to one that what rises up to the top is not something you can physically hold in your flesh-covered hands. How did I know? Easy. I'm human like you.

What do you want . . . really? Maybe upon looking at your life, you have all that you could possibly want . . . and yet. Something's missing. Maybe upon closer inspection, there are some missing pieces. Maybe your life is so unmanageably full already that you don't even know what you want anymore, and maybe it's high time you ask God to show you. Hey, I'm bossy cuz I love you, OK? Plus, I've asked, ahem, *begged* God myself, to show me what it is that I really want.

Friends, today's words aren't about answering the question for you. It's about challenging you to sit with the question—with the One standing still, cuz you've got His full attention—and asking yourself, perhaps even grappling for a bit with the God Who doesn't let go—the question: What do I want . . . really? For truly I tell you, Beloved, God is near and God hears. God knows what you want. Knows what you need. Knows every desire He has buried within you, and who knows? Now may be the time for it to rise up within you and show you.

Maybe. And as you sit, don't forget—God is generous. God is wisdom. God is not going to give you what doesn't belong to you, so you don't have to worry about that, amen. So go ahead. Listen to the One Who loves you, ask you . . . What do you want . . . really?

KEEP TELLING ME, LORD

"I Am."

"I know, Lord," she whispered. "Keep telling me."

"I Am." God told her. And she begged Him to keep on telling her. Yes. I Am. God would tell her . . . "I Am." A sentence complete in itself. Remember that. I Am. I Am your Provider. I Am your Shepherd. I Am your Protector and Friend. I Am going to see you through this thing and bring you back safely to shore. I Am. I Am your Portion. I Am your Enough. I Am your Guide and your Confidant, so go ahead, Girly, and gimme all that you got. I Am. I Am the Author of your story; so believe Me, I know how it ends. I Am perfecting in you, making whole and complete the faith that I have given you. I Am. Before you. Behind you. Beside you. Within you. In other words—*I've got you.* You're covered. Amen.

I Am. The calm in the eye of the storm that won't end. The voice in the wilderness as you wander. The light in the darkness. The manna in the famine. The help when you need it, amen. I Am. I Am the One Who's been known to trouble the water in order to bring healing and wholeness. I Am Bread and Water, Sunlight and Shade; I Am also the dark cloud that brings rain. To end the drought. Because all droughts end, My Daughter . . . don't forget that. I Am in every season. Every. Single. One. I Am the same yesterday, today, tomorrow, and always . . . so no matter how bad you screw up, you can't change that. (Whew.) I Am. The beginning and the end. The Alpha and the Omega. I Am sovereign . . . over . . . *all* things. I sure Am. The good, the bad, the ugly, and every "I don't understand, Lord" in between.

I Am. And truly I tell you, sweet child of Mine . . . I Am holding you right now as you read this, secure in the palm of My hand, and *nothing* will snatch you out of it. Nothing. Ever. Amen. I Am. Now I have told you these things that you may have peace. Now go. Knowing wayyyy deep down in that gut of yours . . . I Am.

STRENGTHENED IN WAYS THAT YOU HATE

Your faith will be strengthened in ways you frickin' hate.

Job. Naomi. Esther. Ruth. Noah. Moses. Lazarus. Jonah. And whew, those last two still stink. Anyone know how to get fish guts/tomb stench out of your robe? Seriously. Ugh. A woman who bled for twelve long years; another hunched thirty-eight. A woman dragged out of her bed in the act . . . ummm . . . what were those guys who "caught" her doing there anyway? Mmmhmm. Exactly. Best get that log outta your eye, fellas. Movin' on. Hannah. Hagar. A woman by a well. Another the whole town called Whore. Parent upon parent who fell at His feet begging for help/healing/mercy/anything for the child they called Son or Daughter.

Beloved, this list could go on and on. And if it did, I have *no doubt* your name would be on it. Mine too. A list of those whose faith has been STRENGTHENED (I'm cappin' that baby, cuz I don't want us to lose sight of the end result here) in ways we frickin' hate. (I'm nothing if not a straight shooter, amen?) *Yup.* But because we have a whole cloud of witnesses that went before us, and are still here to remind us and cheer us on, we can look at those ways and rename them. We sure can. Faith training. Faith building. Faith strengthening workout just-think-of-your-bod-at-the-gym, amen. Yes.

Beloved, we may not like all the ways; we may even find ourselves whispering (OK, let's be real—shouting), "This sucks!" . . . and yes, it probably does. It *also* . . . is strengthening what is *in* you . . . for all that is yet to come *for* you. For God knows the rest of the plan, like Paul Harvey used to say, "the rest of the story" . . . and God is *providing* for you . . . by *preparing* you for it. Faithful and Provisional, for He knows the plans He has for you, amen. Yes. Trust the Trainer. *And know*—that *you*—can ask, beg, or plead—*anytime*—day, night, or from the depth of your hell—for exactly what you need—to endure, remain, and survive it. You sure can. You sure can. You sure can. Amen. I pray you can hear me cheering you on, Beloved. Big love from one of your fans. *XO.*

TAKE GOD WITH YOU

Take God with you.

    I mean it. Take God with you. Yes. *Take the knowledge of Who God is . . . with you.* Into this day. For God already knows what it holds. Amen. Take God with you— so *you* don't forget—that *God holds you as this day unfolds.* Yes. It's a page in your book, Beloved. The Author knows. And then, when this day draws to an end, tuck it into bed, and then awaken it in the morn—and take it—with you—*again.* Yes. Take God with you. Take the truth that—God *provides,* God *protects,* God is *bigger* than *any obstacle* before you—*with you.* Yes. Take *with* you the fact that—God still *moves mountains, rolls away stones, feeds the hungry, raises the dead, opens the eyes of the blind, and parts big gigantic seas, hello.*

    Yes. Take God *with* you. Don't forget the knowledge of Who God is on the kitchen counter next to your grocery list, cuz hot dang I hate when that happens, don't you? *Cuz then I don't have it when I need it.* Amen. Take God with you. Into the interview, into the meeting, into the conversation you don't want to have. Take God with you into the dark and lonely desolate places, and while you're there—pull out the knowledge that God is *Light.* Right. Take God with you, Beloved. Into the storm, into the deep, into every single thing you wish wasn't. *Yes.* Take God with you. Knowing God is Beginning and End and the One Who makes *all* things right and is *faithful in every season. Amen.* Yes. For the knowledge of Who your God *is,* Beloved . . . will *be . . .* your *. . . peace.* It sure will.

SIGNS IN THE STORM

She believed that thunder in the storm . . . and lightning in the storm . . . were God's way of letting her know that He speaks through the storm and is Light through the storm . . . because He is in her storm.

Boom. Literally. Amen. Beloved, perhaps it's time to relook at the thunder and lightning. Time to re-examine it and rename it. Time to sit with it a minute and ask yourself what you see, what you hear. Yes. And as you do, remind yourself of this, the same truth I taught a room full of seventh-graders recently . . . all storms eventually end. They do.

Thunder and lightning. God near. God with. God speaking from the eye of the storm you are in. The place . . . the presence . . . the pulpit of peace and calm in the trenches of chaos and fear. Yes. God is light. Light. *Light.* In the dark. In the dark. In the dark. Yes. Nothing hidden. Nothing unknown. Nothing that was slipped or been missed. God knows. God in. Your storm. Yes. Showing you through the thunder that thunders and the lightning that lights, for He's just that creative, amen. Always has been and always will be, world without end.

In your storm. *With* you in your storm. *Providing* for you in your storm. Yes. Don't forget. Big love.

ASK HIM AGAIN . . . AGAIN!

Ask Him again.

Here we are—back where we began.

I know, I know—you've already asked Him a million times. I see those eyes rolling. But today, ask Him a million and one. Yes. Ask Him *again*. Ask Him again for that child to come home. That marriage to be healed. That mountain to move. Ask Him again for that friendship to mend. That work to begin. That end-of-tunnel light to appear. Ask Him again for the one who needs rescue, the one who needs healing, the one who needs new direction, new guidance, new focus. Yes. Even if that "one" is you. Ask Him again for what you need. For what you want. For joy in the sorrow. Help in the struggle. A sip of living water in the heat of your schedule . . . and the time to just sit at the well, amen? Ask Him again. Ask Him again to provide springs in your land; and while you're at it, give thanks for that land, no matter how dry it is now, knowing He's given it to you with good purpose.

Yes. Ask Him again. Ask Him again to dig up the soil and plant the seeds. Ask Him again to stir up and settle, make and remake, pour out His peace that passes all understanding, because frankly, you could use a hefty dose about now. Yes. And amen. Ask Him again for all that seems lost and all that seems nowhere even near the vicinity of possible . . . and ask Him, believing He can. Yes.

Ask Him again. Not because you don't think He heard you the first million times, but because you are realizing the longer you (truly) live, that persistence is a pretty strong faith-builder—not to mention how close it keeps you to Him, for whom all things are possible and nothing is too hard, and because faith-based strength to persevere and closeness with your Creator is what you *really* need. Whew. Yes. Absolutely.

Ask Him again. With fresh eyes and a renewed spirit and a passionate resolve that He can, and if it's His Will . . . He will. And if it's not, you will keep on asking. You will keep on seeking. You will keep on believing, just like Steve Perry says. Because persistent faith is where it's at. It fastens its gaze on hope. The hope that is always three steps (Father, Son, Holy Spirit) ahead, providing the perfect focal point. Yes. And it never disappoints. Amen.

So today—bow low, look up, and ask Him *again*.

ACKNOWLEDGMENTS

I feel like this section could be a book all in itself. There simply aren't enough pages to properly acknowledge all who made this book possible, but I'll give it a shot.

Thank you to my Nana for giving me her faith while also giving me the time and space to grow into my own without judgment. Thank you to my Grandpa Cory for teaching me how to be a writer without even realizing it through countless pen-pal letters exchanged throughout my childhood. A yellow legal pad will always hold a piece of my heart because of you. I wish you were both here to read these words, and yet somehow, I trust that you hear them.

Thank you to the high school English teacher who told me I was a writer when I was sixteen. Thank you to the church elder who stood at the back of the chapel during my first message given, waiting for me to walk down that aisle following worship, grabbing my hands and telling me, "Young lady, you were made to do this."

Thank you to the pastor who told me I was a teacher and preacher with much to offer this world, and to the pastor who told me I wasn't enough. You both fueled my fire in ways that I desperately needed.

Thank you to my awesome agent, Mary, my incredible editor, Kathryn, and my coach and mentor and cheerleader, Jill. Your patience with me, the new kid on the block, encouraged me more than you know. It still does.

Thank you to Julie and Jen who split the sea for this book to go through, knowing they may not go with it. Your confidence in me still leaves me speechless.

Thank you to every Bible study girl who I was ever blessed to sit amongst, lead, and learn from. From age ten to one hundred, you brought me more than I could've ever—*ever*—brought you. I'm so grateful for you. Thank you to Sonja for being the best *yes* girl and assistant a girl could ask for.

Thank you to those who saw things in me that I never would have seen in myself and believed in those things and called out those things and gave those things value and worth. You opened my eyes to the possible and helped me believe in myself.

Thank you to my online community at Facebook and Instagram and even Visco (thanks to the teen girls in my life) and for encouraging and supporting and rallying for my words to go beyond the screen and into your hands. You really are the best.

Thank you to soooo many friends-turned-family and family-turned-friends—far too many to name without missing one—who have always been there for me, no matter what, whether this book would have become a reality or not, for it's not the basis of their love and loyalty. You all mean so very much to me.

Thank you to my Mom and Dad who not only gave me life but also took me to places I never would've chosen to go, for it was in those places that I was shaped and formed and prepared for all God had planned for me. Thank you for never telling me what I had to believe but instead allowing me to discover it on my own. I love you both more than you know.

Thank you to my kids and their people—Thomas and Haley, my light-bearing grandson Arlo, Abby and Wyatt, and our teen Jack Henry. I have learned *so* much from you, and I continue to learn so much from you year by year. I love you all *way up high*.

Thank you to my husband, Kent, and his non-surprised (yes, you read that right) face when an email arrived followed by a Zoom meeting followed by countless more Zoom meetings that resulted in a contract for me to sign. "I always knew this day would come," he told me. "I was just waiting for the world to catch up." Kent, your selfless, sacrificial, and abiding love not only brought me here but sustains me in this unknown land. I love you.

Thank you to the women of Scripture who over the years have shared their stories of bravery and courage, heartbreak and ruin, courage and boldness and strength. You have inspired me more than you will ever know, and I can't wait to have coffee in heaven with you.

And finally, God. As it was in the beginning, is now, and forever shall be, *God*. Thank you to the God Whose Spirit dwells in me, making its home deep within me, safe and secure in the sanctuary of my very soul, reminding me that I am never alone . . . and that all things really are . . . possible. I love You with all my heart, mind, and soul. Thank you.

XO.